Ma[...]
2144 Cathedral Ave
Washington, D.C. 20008
483-2339

Research Methods in the Social Sciences

Research Methods in the Social Sciences

DAVID NACHMIAS
CHAVA NACHMIAS

St. Martin's Press
New York

Library of Congress Catalog Card Number: 75-29933
Copyright © 1976 by St. Martin's Press, Inc.
All Rights Reserved.
Manufactured in the United States of America.
0987
FEDC

For information, write: St. Martin's Press, Inc.,
175 Fifth Avenue, New York, N.Y. 10010

Typography by Barbara Bert.
Cover design by James Wall.

Preface

The purpose of this book is to present a comprehensive exposition of the scientific approach in the social sciences. To this aim, we view scientific research as a process involving seven interrelated themes: generating researchable problems, constructing hypotheses, formulating a research design, measuring, collecting data, analyzing the data, and generalizing.

The book begins by examining the aims of science in the social sciences and the epistemological foundations of the scientific approach. These are the beliefs and values that scientists qua scientists share. A high measure of consensus regarding the epistemological foundations of the scientific approach is essential for the progress of the social sciences. We do not advocate, however, an uncritical acceptance of the epistemological foundations. On the contrary, rational criticism of these and other aspects of the scientific approach is the sine qua non of science.

In Chapters 2 and 3 the basic elements of empirical research and the various research designs for evaluating hypotheses are introduced. A research design is a model of proof that allows us to draw inferences concerning causality and generalizability. It is thus imperative to formulate an adequate research design well in advance and prior to the execution of other research operations. Chapter 4 discusses the significance of measurement and the various ways through which quantification is attained. Issues of validity and reliability are inseparable from measurement theory; validation techniques and methods for assessing the reliability of measurements in the social sciences are also presented in Chapter 4.

Chapters 5 through 7 present the various methods of data collection available to social scientists. In Chapter 5 controlled and noncontrolled observational methods are discussed and exemplified. Chapter 6 focuses on survey research and attitude measurement, and in Chapter 7 we explicate the intent of unobtrusive methods and discuss their various forms and uses.

The next four chapters are concerned with data processing and analysis. In Chapter 8 the concern is with constructing coding schemes and preparing the data for computer processing. Chapter 9 introduces the univariate distribution, measures of central tendency and dispersion, and various types of frequency distributions. In Chapter 10 the concept of relationship is elaborated, and measures of nominal, ordinal, and interval relationship are examined. The focus of Chapter 11 is multivariate analysis. Statistical methods of control and interpretation are analyzed, and measures of multiple relationship are discussed. Methods of causal inferences in nonexperimental research are also presented in this chapter.

The last two chapters examine methods of statistical inference. In Chapter 12 sampling and sample designs are discussed, and in Chapter 13 we analyze the strategy of hypotheses testing and introduce some commonly used parametric and nonparametric tests. The significance-test controversy, also discussed in this chapter, serves as a vivid illustration of the evolving nature of methodology in the social sciences.

This book represents the work of a political scientist and a sociologist, who have both accumulated experience in social science methodology through teaching and research efforts. The authors have collaborated closely, and except for Chapter 12, written entirely by David Nachmias, the book is a product of their joint effort.

Our literary debts are testified to in the bibliography. Our personal debts are numerous, especially to Jerry F. Medler at the University of Oregon. Several colleagues have read one or more chapters of this book; for their observations we thank Alan Mazur, Joel Migdal, David H. Rosenbloom, and Michael A. Baer. We are also indebted to Bruce S. Bowen, D. E. Pilant, Lawrence Rosen, and George V. Zito for reading the manuscript. Barry Rossinoff and Nancy Barton of St. Martin's Press have been encouraging and most helpful in bringing the manuscript to its present shape.

Contents

Preface   v

PART 1 FOUNDATIONS OF EMPIRICAL RESEARCH   1

Chapter 1. The Scientific Method   3
  Aims of Science   3
  Approaches to Knowledge   6
  The Scientific Approach   7
  The Research Process   10
  Summary   13
  References   13

Chapter 2. Basic Elements of Research   15
  Concepts   15
  Definitions   17
  Variables   20
  Hypotheses   23
  Summary   27
  References   27

Chapter 3. The Research Design   29
  The Structure of a Research Design   29
  The Components of a Research Design   31
  Experimental Designs   38
  Quasi-Experimental Designs   40
  A Comparison of Designs   46
  Summary   47
  References   48
  Study Suggestions   49

Chapter 4. Measurement   50
  The Nature of Measurement   50
  Levels of Measurement   53
  Validity   59
  Reliability   64

viii CONTENTS

    Summary   68
    References   69
    Study Suggestions   69

PART 2   DATA COLLECTION   71

Chapter 5. Observational Methods   73
    Roles of Observation   73
    Characteristics of Observations   75
    Controlled Observations   79
    Simulation   86
    Participant Observation   90
    Summary   95
    References   95
    Study Suggestions   98

Chapter 6. Survey Research   100
    Personal Interview   100
    Impersonal Survey Methods   107
    Attitude Measurement   109
    Summary   116
    References   117
    Study Suggestions   118

Chapter 7. Unobtrusive Measures   119
    Intent of Unobtrusive Measures   119
    Physical Traces   120
    Simple Observation   121
    Archival Records   123
    Content Analysis   132
    Summary   138
    References   138
    Study Suggestions   140

PART 3   DATA PROCESSING AND ANALYSIS   141

Chapter 8. Data Processing   143
    Constructing Coding Schemes   143
    The Coding and Punching Process   151
    Automatic Data Processing   156
    Special Programs   158
    Summary   160

References   161
Study Suggestions   162

Chapter 9. The Univariate Distribution   163
Frequency Distributions   164
Measures of Central Tendency   167
Measures of Dispersion   173
Types of Frequency Distributions   181
Summary   185
References   186
Study Suggestions   186

Chapter 10. The Bivariate Distribution   188
The Concept of Relationship   188
The Measurement of Relationship   193
Nominal Measures of Relationship   195
Ordinal Measures of Relationship   200
Interval Measures of Relationship   208
Summary   216
References   217
Study Suggestions   217

Chapter 11. Multivariate Analysis   219
The Concept of Control   220
Methods of Control   221
Interpretation   227
Multiple Relationships   233
Causal Models   237
Summary   245
References   246
Study Suggestions   247

PART 4   INFERENTIAL METHODS   249

Chapter 12. Sampling and Sample Designs   251
Aims of Sampling   251
The Population   252
Sample Size   253
Sample Designs   259
Nonsampling Error   265
Summary   267
References   268
Study Suggestions   269

Chapter 13. Hypothesis-Testing — 270

    The Strategy of Testing Hypotheses   271
    The Sampling Distribution   273
    Parametric and Nonparametric Tests   279
    The Test of Significance Controversy   291
    Summary   *294*
    References   *295*
    Study Suggestions   *296*

APPENDIX — 299

    Table 1. Random numbers   301
    Table 2. Areas under the normal curve   305
    Table 3. Distribution of t 307
    Table 4. Values of z for given values of r 308
    Table 5. Critical values of U in the Mann-Whitney test   311
    Table 6. Distribution of χ^2 314

Author Index   317
Subject Index   323

PART 1
Foundations of Empirical Research

CHAPTER 1
The Scientific Method

AIMS OF SCIENCE

What does science have to offer to those who take an interest in the problems of society? Why is common sense alone insufficient to explain those parts of overall human behavior that are considered "social," "psychological," "political," or "economic"? How can the scientific approach be of value in understanding undesirable phenomena such as violence? Or, more specifically, why is violence more widespread in the United States than in Denmark?

That last question could be answered with a simple common-sense explanation: Americans are more aggressive than Danes, so violence is more widespread in the United States. However, whereas such an explanation might satisfy the layperson, it would not satisfy the social scientist, for its applicability does not extend to similar phenomena. The reader is probably aware that post–World War II Mexico is less prone to internal violence than the United States, even though Mexicans are said to be more aggressive than Americans.

Social scientists are critical of explanations that do not extend to a wide range of similar phenomena. Science aims at general explanations. A general explanation of violence might take the following form: relative deprivation leads to violent behavior. Thus, if Americans feel more deprived than do the Danes, they engage more frequently in violent behavior. By the same token, violence is less widespread in Mexico because Mexicans may feel less deprived than do Americans. When scientists ask for an explanation of why a given phenomenon has taken place, they usually ask for an analysis of those antecedent factors in the situation that are responsible for the occurrence of the phenomenon (Scheffler, 1963).

Ever since Hume, such an application of the term "explanation" has been considered to be a matter of relating the phenomena to be explained with other phenomena by means of general laws. General laws, as Braithwaite (1960:1) and other philosophers of science have argued, are the ultimate goal of science:

> The function of science . . . is to establish general laws covering the behavior of empirical events or objects with which the science in question is concerned, and thereby to enable us to connect together our knowledge of the separately known events, and to make reliable predictions of events as yet unknown. . . . If science is in a highly developed state . . . the laws which have been established will form a hierarchy in which special laws appear as logical consequences of a small number of highly general laws . . . if the science is in an early stage of development . . . the laws may be merely the generalizations involved in classifying things into various classes.

As a science makes progress, its forms of explanation change. Hempel (1966) has made a distinction between two basic types of explanations: deductive and probabilistic. This classification is based upon the kinds of generalizations that the explanation employs. A deductive explanation calls for a universal generalization, a statement of the conditions under which the generalization holds true, an event to be explained (explicandum), and the rules of logic. In a deductive explanation, a phenomenon is explained by demonstrating that it can be deduced from an established universal generalization. For example, a physicist's explanation for the return to earth of a stone thrown into the air would be based on the law of gravitation. The physicist will point out that if all objects exercise a mutual attraction on one another, then the stone is expected to behave in the same way with reference to earth. The essential feature of a universal generalization is that it purports to encompass all cases that fall within the class to which it applies—past, present, and future.

Only a well-developed science can produce deductive explanations. In the natural sciences, such explanations are made possible through manipulation and control via experimentation (Lewinsohn, 1961). That is, natural scientists can deliberately produce a change in the phenomenon (manipulation) and determine with some degree of certainty its effects on another phenomenon, thus establishing and testing universal generalizations. The degree of certainty depends on the extent to which the scientist can demonstrate that phenomena other than those being investigated do not account for the produced change (control). The notions of manipulation, control, and experimentation will be extensively dealt with in subsequent chapters. Suffice it to note here that they enable the scientist in a developed science to formulate and test universal generalizations.

Few of the phenomena that interest social scientists are amenable to manipulation and control. How, for example, does one manipulate relative deprivation and observe its differential impacts on violence? Furthermore, even if a certain phenomenon can be manipulated, does the social scientist have the right to manipulate it? Is it ethical, for example, to deprive children of parental affection in order to determine the relationship of parental affection to emotional development? Most human phenomena do not lend themselves to being researched with the classic and most powerful designs of the natural sciences. Nevertheless, in their attempts to produce explanations, social scientists have been inventing alternative designs and methods through which general explanations can be verified. These, however, are usually probabilistic explanations.

A probabilistic explanation makes use of generalizations that express an arithmetical class ratio between the phenomena or generalizations that express tendencies (Meehan, 1965). That is, the generalization provides evidence for the phenomenon; the explanation cannot be deduced from the generalization. Unlike a universal generalization, such as "All X is Y," a probabilistic generalization takes the form "n percent of X is Y" or "X tends to be Y." The chief limitation of a probabilistic generalization is that no explanation can be deduced about an individual member of a class from properties of the whole class. If, for instance, one knows that 70 percent of the members of an ethnic group voted for the Democratic party for the past twenty years, one still cannot conclude with confidence that the probability that a particular member of the group voted Democratic is 7/10. Other factors, besides membership in the given class of which the generalization is true, may influence the behavior in question. The particular person may also be a member of a primary group with a long tradition of Republican political leaning, and this, in turn, may outweigh the influence of his or her ethnic identification (Meehan, 1965).

Probabilistic explanations are substantially weaker than deductive explanations, essentially because of their limited predictive capacity. With universal generalizations a scientist can deduce explanations and predictions, and in fact equate the two. Probabilistic explanations, on the other hand, pose a paradox: one can either "achieve powerful understanding of social behavior without being able to predict its character in specific situations" or "achieve precision in prediction without any knowledge of how the predicted outcome was produced" (Dubin, 1969:14).

Ultimately, social scientists aim to resolve this paradox. At present, however, two paradigms have emerged: *verstehen*, or understanding, and prediction. Social scientists of the *verstehen* tradition reject the notion of predicting human behavior in strictly mechanistic terms. It is argued that the major goal of the social sciences is to promote understanding; that understanding is the adequate criterion of explanation;

and that social scientists must attempt to construct explanations that cohere with the ideology and social structure of a society (Sjoberg and Nett, 1968). On the other hand, social scientists of the "prediction school" contend that prediction is the primary criterion for adequate explanations since it provides the most effective basis for the evaluation of explanations. Without predictive power, the adequacy of an explanation becomes a matter of consensus; that is, the extent to which scientists accept a particular explanation testifies to its adequacy (Gibbs, 1972).

APPROACHES TO KNOWLEDGE

Science is by no means the only method by which people have attempted to explain human phenomena. There are at least three other modes that have served the purpose of acquiring knowledge: the authoritarian mode, the mystical mode, and the rationalistic mode (Wallace, 1971). Cardinal distinctions among these modes are the manner in which each vests confidence in the producer of knowledge, the procedure by which an item of knowledge is produced, and the effect of items of knowledge. A description of these modes provides a comparative perspective for the assessment of the scientific method.

In the authoritarian mode, knowledge is sought by referring to those who are socially or politically defined as qualified producers of knowledge. These may be oracles in tribal societies, archbishops in theocratic societies, kings in monarchical societies, and scientists in technocratic societies. Within a given social system, different authorities may produce knowledge for different phenomena. For devout Catholics, the Pope possesses undisputed authority on matters defined as religious. Undisputed authority is also possessed by the Soviet Academy of Sciences, which in 1950 decreed that statistical theories based on probability are nonscientific; this decision was an abortive attempt to resolve the contradiction between the determinism of dialectical materialism and the theory of probability. In the authoritarian mode, the knowledge-seeker attributes the ability to produce knowledge to the social or political authority of the knowledge-producer. The procedure whereby the seeker solicits this authority affects the nature of the authority's response, but not the seeker's confidence in that response. Furthermore, although the effects of an item of knowledge obtained by this mode can lead to the eventual replacement of authority, a large number of refutations is required before this happens.

In the mystical mode, knowledge is solicited from prophets, divines, gods, mediums, and other supernaturally knowledgeable authorities. In this sense, the mystical mode is similar to the authoritarian mode. However, it differs from the latter in its dependence on manifestations of supernatural signs and on the psychophysical state of the knowledge-consumer. For example, the rites surrounding the process of astrological prophecy are aimed at persuading the consumer of the astrologer's supernatural powers. The mystical mode depends, to a large extent, on applying ritualistic and ceremonial procedures to the consumer. Moreover, under conditions of depression, helplessness, and intoxication, the knowledge-consumer is most willing to accept items of knowledge produced by the mystical mode. The confidence in the knowledge produced in this manner decreases as the number of disconfirmations increases.

The rationalistic mode focuses on the procedure by which explanations are produced. Insofar as the procedure complies with the rules of formal logic, items of knowledge are accepted. A typical example of formal logical procedures is a syllogism, such as

All A are B
All B are C
Therefore all A are C

The first two assertions of the syllogism are called "premises," and the last is called the "conclusion." The conclusion "All A are C" is logically acceptable with respect to the premises. Not all explanations are in principle verifiable by this and other syllogisms. They are accepted, however, by consumers of the rationalistic mode if they were derived in accordance with the logical procedure imposed by a particular syllogism.

THE SCIENTIFIC APPROACH

Social scientists are critical of knowledge obtained by any of the above three modes. The scientific approach relies on observations and on the methods employed to generate observations. The primary reliance on observations stems from the scientist's conception of knowledge. Scientists assume that a communication tie between human beings and the external universe is maintained through sense impressions, and that knowledge is ". . . a product of one's experiences as facets of the physical, biological and social world play upon the senses" (Sjoberg and Nett, 1968:26).

This conception of knowledge avoids the metaphysical question of whether the world exists independently of one's experiences. On the contrary, the scientific approach is based on the assumption that the world can be known only as experience is processed through the human intelligence. People's experiences, or the empirical evidence of their senses, serve scientists as data when attempting to explain psychological, political, and social phenomena. These explanations impose order on the vast collection of sense reports and, at the same time, define the boundaries of the scientific body of knowledge.

Experiences find their expression in language. People are able to speak the same language to the extent that they share certain areas of common experience. In other words, language and argumentation are the ways of organizing and objectivizing experience. A fundamental feature of the scientific approach is its ideal of objectivity, an ideal that subjects scientific knowledge to the test of independent and impartial criteria. The function of methods in science is to institutionalize the demand for objectivity in the most explicit and systematic manner. For this reason, we argue that the scientific approach relies not only on observations (experiences) but also on the methods employed to communicate and systematize observations.

It was pointed out above that scientific explanations, be they deductive or probabilistic, explicate those antecedent factors in a situation that are responsible for the occurrence of a particular phenomenon. In practice, this involves four distinct operations: (1) demonstrating covariation, (2) eliminating spurious relations, (3) establishing the time order of the occurrences, and (4) theorizing. These operations, as we argue in subsequent chapters, are also considered necessary conditions to draw causal inferences (Labovitz and Hagedorn, 1971).

Covariation simply means that two or more phenomena vary together. For example, if a change in the level of education is accompanied by a change in the level of income, one can say that education covaries with income. That is, that individuals with high levels of education have higher incomes than do individuals with lower levels of education. On the other hand, if a change in the level of education is not accompanied by a change in the level of income, education does not covary with income. In scientific research, the notion of covariation is expressed through measures of relations commonly referred to as correlations or associations. Thus, a correlation between phenomena is necessary evidence for a causal interpretation. For example, if relative deprivation is not correlated (does not covary) with violence, it cannot be a cause of violence.

The second operation requires the scientist to demonstrate that the observed covariation is nonspurious. A nonspurious relation is defined as a correlation between two phenomena that cannot be explained by a third factor. In other words, if the effects of all relevant factors are eliminated and the relation between the investigated phenomena is maintained, then the relation is nonspurious. A nonspurious relation implies that there is an inherent link between the phenomena, and that the observed covariation is not based on an accidental connection with some associated phenomena (Rosenberg, 1968). Suppose one observes that the number of firemen at a fire covaries with the amount of fire damage.

Obviously, firemen are not the cause of the damage. Thus, the amount of fire damage cannot be explained by the number of firemen at a fire, but by another factor, namely, the size of the fire. Large fires call forth more firemen and also cause more damage. The observed covariation between the number of firemen at a fire and the amount of fire damage is spurious because a third factor—the size of the fire—explains it.

The third operation, time order, requires the researcher to demonstrate that one phenomenon occurs first or changes prior to another phenomenon. For example, in a number of studies it has been shown that the correlation between urbanization and democratic political development is nonspurious (Flanigan and Fogelman, 1971). To establish that urbanization is causally related to democratic development, it must also be demonstrated that the former precedes the latter. The implicit assumption here is that phenomena in the future cannot determine phenomena in the present or past. In many cases, there is little difficulty in determining the time order of phenomena. Thus, the status of parents influences the educational expectations of their children, and not vice versa; an interest in politics precedes political participation; and depression precedes suicide. In other cases, the time order is harder to determine. Does urbanization precede political development, or does political development occur prior to urbanization? Does achievement follow motivation, or does a change in the level of motivation follow achievement? In the following chapters, the methods employed to determine the time order of events will be discussed. At this point, we merely want to stress the significance of the time-order criterion when formulating explanations.

The fourth operation involves theorizing. However, this operation poses considerable difficulties in application because of the lack of consensus among social scientists on what is meant by a theory. To some social scientists, theory simply means a thought process—a conceptualization, as opposed to an empirical observation. Other social scientists define theory in more rigorous terms. Zetterberg (1965) views theory as a formal logico-deductive system involving a set of assumptions from which verifiable explanations and predictions can be derived. In the next section, we will provide a more comprehensive discussion of the various meanings of theory and their respective functions in the research process. In the present context, theory is viewed as an interpretation of, or conceptual justification for, an observed covariation. For example, several studies report that status disintegration (persons occupying positions that make conflicting demands and expectations) covaries with suicide rates. It has also been shown that the observed covariation is nonspurious, and one can hardly dispute the argument that status disintegration precedes suicide. The role of theory in this case is to interpret the covariation. An established interpretation is that conflicting demands and expectations lead to emotional stress, which in turn leads to suicide. An interpretation specifies the causal nature of a covariation by explicating the mechanism that connects the phenomena under investigation.

THE RESEARCH PROCESS

The research process is the overall scheme of scientific activities in which social scientists engage. These activities are assumed to enhance the goals of science, since they relate to the four operations involved in establishing explanations. Seven principal types of activities may be distinguished, each of which can be regarded as a stage in the research process: problems, hypotheses, research designs, measurement, data collection, data analysis, and empirical generalizations. In the following chapters, we will discuss extensively each stage and the transitions between stages. For the moment, we will limit ourselves to a general overview of the research process.

Scientists are problem-solvers. A problem is an intellectual stimulus calling for a response in the form of a scientific answer. Not every problem, however, can be answered scientifically. Questions such as "Do I exist?" and "What does the distant future hold in store for us?" are stimulating in themselves but cannot be answered scientifically since they do not relate to empirical experiences. Other kinds of problems that do not undergo scientific research are connected with personal preferences. Problems such as "Is blue nicer than red?" cannot be answered scientifically.

Stimuli that are too general or too abstract present difficulties in the investigation and therefore are usually concretized. Problems such as "Who rules America?" or "What brings youth to universities?" can be dealt with scientifically but must be concretized. Concretization is attained by hypotheses. Hypotheses are tentative answers to researchable problems. The researcher breaks down a general problem into a set of concrete hypotheses and investigates each one separately. For example, the problem "What brings youth to universities?" involves considerations such as the motivation to study, the individual's financial state, the social background of one's family, encouragement by peers, and one's academic achievements in high school. These five considerations generate five hypotheses: (1) the inclination to enroll at university increases with the motivation to study; (2) an individual's financial state covaries with his or her propensity to study at the university; (3) youth from relatively well-to-do families tend to enroll at universities; (4) the greater the encouragement to study at university given by peers, the stronger the tendency to do so; and (5) academic achievement in high school covaries with the tendency to study at university. Each of these five hypotheses can be evaluated by observation on the basis of which it will be either rejected or accepted. The rejection option is the characteristic feature of hypotheses and the reason for viewing them as tentative answers (see Chapter 2).

The third stage of the research process involves a decision about a research design. A research design is the structure, program, and strategy upon which hypotheses are evaluated. Suppose researchers are about to evaluate the hypothesis that relative deprivation covaries with violence. How should they carry out their research to obtain an adequate explanation? How are they to establish covariation and to demonstrate that it is nonspurious? How are they to determine the time order of the phenomena? These are but a few of the queries facing researchers before conducting a study. In Chapter 3, we will discuss the various research designs available to social scientists. It will also be argued that each design defines the grounds upon which hypotheses can be evaluated.

The fourth stage of the research process involves measurement. In general, measurement may be defined as any procedure whereby observations are systematically assigned symbols. These symbols are amenable to logical, mathematical, and statistical manipulations that reveal information that otherwise could not have been revealed. Symbols can be added, subtracted, percentaged, introduced as subjects or objects in sentences, or employed as elements in graphs or diagrams (see Chapter 4).

Data collection is the stage at which researchers make their observations and record them. Data (observations) can be collected by different methods. Thus, both field observations (see Chapter 5) and survey research (see Chapter 6) can serve the purpose of collecting data for the evaluation of a given hypothesis. Any given data-collection method can also be employed to gather information concerning different hypotheses. For example, with simple observation (see Chapter 7) it is possible to collect data on different hypotheses, such as: intense interactions between members of a task group covary with the satisfaction of the members; persons addressed most often by members of a group are the leaders; or in small groups, men behave more aggressively than do women.

In the next two stages of the research process, the concern is with data analysis and empirical generalizations. An empirical generalization is a statement asserting a universal connection between phenomena. The logic whereby observations are transformed into empirical generalizations is usually referred to as induction. Braithwaite makes a distinction between two types of inductive principles. One is the principle of enumeration, ". . . according to which an inductive hypothesis is to be treated as being well established if it has not been refuted by experience and has been confirmed by not fewer than n positive instances (1960:

260). Chapters 9, 10, and 11 focus on techniques of analysis through which the principle of enumeration is applied. The other inductive principle is that of elimination, according to which ". . . an inductive hypothesis is taken to be well established if, while it has not been refuted by experience, alternative hypotheses have been so refuted" (Braithwaite, 1960:260). In Chapters 12 and 13, we will discuss the inferential methods relating to the principle of elimination.

In the previous section, it was pointed out that theorizing is an agreed-upon research operation even though its meaning is controversial. We suggested that theory be viewed as a conceptual interpretation specifying the causal nature of an empirical generalization. The place of theory in the research process is also a source of controversy. Two major conflicting schools of thought can be identified: the research-then-theory program and the theory-then-research program. The theory-then-research program has been articulated most explicitly by Popper, who suggests that scientific knowledge would advance most rapidly by the development of theories, which is then followed by attempts to falsify them through empirical research. Popper denies the systematic bearing of empirical generalizations on theorizing by taking the position that "stands directly opposed to all attempts to operate with the ideas of inductive logic" (1961:30). According to Popper, there is no logic for constructing theories. "There is no such thing as a logical method of having new ideas, or a logical reconstruction of this process. . . . Every discovery contains 'an irrational element,' or a creative intuition" (1961:32). The function of the research process is to test rather than invent theories: "whenever we try to propose a solution to a problem, we ought to try as hard as we can to overthrow our solution rather than defend it" (1961:16).

In marked contrast to those who articulate the theory-then-research program, Merton (1957:103), a proponent of the research-then-theory program, argues:

> It is my central thesis that empirical research goes far beyond the passive role of verifying and testing theory; it does more than confirm or refute hypotheses. Research plays an active role: it performs at least four major functions which help shape the development of theory. It initiates, it reformulates, it deflects, and it clarifies theory.

The research process, according to Merton, is conducive both to testing theories and to constructing them.

Clearly, the two programs aim at theories and regard them as manifestations of scientific progress. The controversy is over the place of theory in the research process. It is our position that a firm commitment to either of the two programs is not essential in the conduct of research. Science has progressed in spite of this controversy, and scientific research is being pursued under both programs. The aims of science do not preclude either the research-then-theory program or the theory-then-research program. Moreover, as Nagel (1961:86) has pointed out, the controversy is more apparent than real:

> Distinguished scientists have repeatedly claimed that theories are "free creations of the mind." Such claims obviously do not mean that theories may not be suggested by observational materials or that theories do not require support from observational evidence. What such claims do rightly assert is that the basic terms of a theory need not possess meanings which are fixed by definite experimental procedures, and that a theory may be adequate and fruitful despite the fact that the evidence for it is necessarily indirect.

Thus, empirical generalizations may generate theories, and theories may generate researchable problems to be tested as hypotheses.

SUMMARY

The ultimate aim of social scientists is the establishment of general laws covering empirical events. To this end, the scientific approach, which relies chiefly on observations and the methods employed to make and analyze observations, is employed. The function of methods is to institutionalize the demand for objectivity, which is a fundamental norm in the scientific community. Four distinct operations are performed when formulating either deductive or probabilistic explanations: (1) demonstrating covariation, (2) eliminating spurious relations, (3) establishing the time order of events, and (4) theorizing. The research process is the overall program of activities conducive to the systematic execution of these operations.

REFERENCES

Braithwaite, Richard B. *Scientific Explanation.* New York: Harper & Brothers, 1960.

Dubin, Robert. *Theory Building.* New York: Free Press, 1969.

Flanigan, William, and Fogelman, Edwin. "Patterns of Democratic Development: An Historical Comparative Analysis." In John V. Gillespie and Betty A. Nesvold (eds.), *Macro-Quantitative Analysis: Conflict, Development and Democratization.* Beverly Hills, Calif.: Sage, 1971.

Gibbs, Jack P. *Sociological Theory Construction.* Hinsdale, Ill.: Dryden Press, 1972.

Hempel, Carl G. *Philosophy of Natural Science.* Englewood Cliffs, N.J.: Prentice-Hall, 1966.

Labovitz, Sanford, and Hagedorn, Robert. *Introduction to Social Research.* New York: McGraw-Hill, 1971.

Lewinsohn, Richard. *Science, Prophecy and Prediction.* Translated by Arnold J. Pomerans. New York: Harper & Row, 1961.

Meehan, Eugene J. *The Theory and Method of Political Analysis.* Homewood, Ill.: Dorsey Press, 1965.

Merton, Robert K. *Social Theory and Social Structure.* Rev. ed. New York: Free Press, 1957.

Nagel, Ernest. *The Structure of Science.* New York: Harcourt, Brace & World, 1961.

Popper, Karl R. *The Logic of Scientific Discovery.* New York: Science Editions, 1961.

Rosenberg, Morris. *The Logic of Survey Analysis.* New York: Basic Books, 1968.

Scheffler, Israel. *The Anatomy of Inquiry.* New York: Knopf, 1963.

Sjoberg, Gideon, and Nett, Roger. *A Methodology for Social Research.* New York: Harper & Row, 1968.

Wallace, Walter L. *The Logic of Science in Sociology.* Chicago: Aldine-Atherton, 1971.

Zetterberg, Hans L. *On Theory and Verification in Sociology.* Totowa, N.J.: Bedminster Press, 1965.

CHAPTER 2
Basic Elements of Research

The research process and its various stages have been presented in a condensed manner in Chapter 1 in order to familiarize the reader with the subject. In fact, however, the process rests upon an additional set of elements. This chapter discusses four basic research elements and their relations to the construction of hypotheses. The four elements are concepts, assumptions, definitions, and variables. We will first examine the role of concepts in empirical research.

CONCEPTS

Thinking involves the use of language, which is a system of communication composed of symbols and a set of rules permitting various combinations of those symbols. One of the most significant symbols in language, especially as it relates to research, is the concept. A concept is an abstract symbol representing an object, a property of an object, or a certain phenomenon. For example, "status," "role," "power," and "relative deprivation" are common concepts in political science and sociology. Concepts such as "intelligence quotient," "perception," and "learning" are common among psychologists. Every scientific discipline develops its peculiar set of concepts that permit communication and research. The significance of concepts stems from their ability to transfer information in the form of images about experiences in the empirical world. By means of concepts, researchers can transmit to their colleagues and to the public a whole system of experiences acquired through research.

Various concepts are formed to represent different (or, at times, identical) phenomena. Let us suppose that two investigators observed that the demands of a certain group are always fulfilled by a city's mayor.

One of the investigators proposed the symbol "A" for this observation, while the other proposed the symbol "power." Essentially, there is no substantive difference between the two symbols, since both represent an identical observation. However, the symbol "power" has been accepted by scientists, whereas "A" has been eliminated. Insofar as both symbols represent the same phenomena, the choice of "power" over "A" has no scientific justification. Factors such as history (when the symbols were proposed), aesthetics, and the stature of the investigator could have influenced the choice of "power."

In general, the choice is not between two alternative concepts representing an identical observation, but between those concepts which are useful and those which are not. Useful concepts represent generalized abstractions regarding empirical phenomena. For example, "weight" is a useful concept since it implies that numerous observations of various physical objects have been found to share a similar trait: all objects are either light or heavy (i.e., they vary); and the concept "weight" represents this trait. "Income" is another example of a useful concept since it represents a trait that is common to different people: most people receive a return, greater or smaller, for their work or capital. The usefulness of a concept is evaluated by the extent to which it permits a meaningful classification of objects or traits. For example, one may ignore the ways in which spruce, pine, fir, palm, and apple differ from each other and grasp their generic resemblance via the concept "tree" (McKinney, 1966). Concepts, then, are means not only of communication but also of generalizations.

As generalizations, concepts serve to construct assumptions. A concept such as "social class" may be connected to other concepts. The linking of two or more concepts leads to the generation of assumptions, such as "if concept A, then concept B," or "the greater A, the smaller B." The combination of a number of assumptions into a system permitting deductive propositions leads to the construction of formal theories. For example, "social class" is a concept representing a common characteristic of individuals: people can be classified as belonging to the lower, middle, or upper class. An assumption may be constructed by linking "social class" to "political participation" (another concept). Thus, "political participation" covaries with "social class." The addition of a number of further assumptions will bring about the construction of a system of interrelated assumptions or a formal theory from which researchers may deduce propositions.

Concepts are abstracted from sense impressions, or percepts. In this sense, the process of conceptualization in the social sciences is one of abstracting and generalizing sense impressions. In this way, it is possible to research, organize, and isolate objects and properties of objects and subsequently to look for explanations and predictions. Basic requirements in the process of conceptualization are clarity and precision of the concepts employed. These are achieved by definitions, the characteristics of which are discussed in the next section.

DEFINITIONS

Research is based on two types of definitions: conceptual and operational. Definitions that describe concepts using other concepts are conceptual definitions. For example, a conceptual definition for "political violence" might be "aggressive behavior toward political institutions and persons occupying political roles," and another might be "the use of arms to achieve political aims." One conceptual definition of "intelligence" might be "the ability to think in an abstract manner," and another might be "the ability to solve problems." All these definitions, whether of "intelligence" or of "political violence," define a concept by means of other and usually simpler concepts. Hence, various combinations of concepts might be used to define other concepts.

The significance of this observation is that a conceptual definition is neither true nor false. If an investigator conceptually defines "power" as "a deviation from equality," one cannot reject this definition as untrue. This is so because "power" and "deviation from equality" are symbols, and symbols as such have no basis in the empirical world. One can reject the definition if the researcher does not use it consistently, or if it constitutes an extreme departure from definitions on which researchers have already reached consensus. Conceptual definitions will be rejected if they encumber communication instead of facilitating it.

Conceptual definitions that facilitate communication have two traits. First, the concept to be defined is described by other concepts, not by itself. For example, the definitions of "power" as "the ability to use power" or of "intelligence" as "an intelligent answer" are faulty conceptual definitions since they do not go any further in describing the concept to be defined. The second trait is that positive conceptual definitions are preferable to negative ones (Goode and Hatt, 1952). It is preferable to define a concept by the properties presumed to belong to it, and not by those not belonging to it. For example, defining "intelligence" as "a property that lacks form, color, weight, and character" contributes little to communication since there are many other things that lack precisely what intelligence lacks. If conceptual definitions are not empirically observable, how is the transition to the empirical level made?

Operational definitions bridge the gap between the theoretical-conceptual level and the empirical-observational level. An operational definition is a series of instructions describing the operations that the researcher must carry out in order to demonstrate the existence, or the degree of existence, of an empirical occurrence represented by a concept. In other words, the meaning of every scientific concept must be specifiable by indicating a definite testing operation that provides a criterion for its application. Such criteria are referred to as operational definitions.

A simple example of an operational definition is the one for "solubility": the chemist might say that a substance such as salt is water soluble if, when placed in water, it dissolves. In a similar way, an operational definition of "intelligence" obliges the researcher to enumerate the operations undertaken to reveal the existence, or the degree of existence, of the property represented by the concept. For example, a group of children are given a chapter to read and told to summarize it; those who fulfill the assignment are endowed with "intelligence," whereas those who fail to do so are "not intelligent."

The structure of operational definitions is quite simple. If a given stimulus (S) is applied to an object, producing a certain reaction (R), the object has a property (C), this property being an operational definition (Isaak, 1969). The structure of an operational definition is especially important in those cases where the application of stimuli or the manipulation of objects is not feasible. For example, in a certain interaction, if state A made state B to act in a manner that state B had not intended, then state A is more powerful than state B. This description may be an operational definition of the concept "power." In this case, the researcher cannot apply stimuli to the objects (states); however, a specific reaction (R) observed in a specific situation (state B gave in to state A) permits the attribution of a property (C)—"power"—to state A. The structure of this definition is identical with the structure of the definition of "solubility." Any competent observer can apply the definition, and the result can be objectively ascertained.

Many concepts in the social sciences are given operational definitions solely on the strength of reactions to specific situations, since the manipulation of the property to be defined is impossible. Thus, a researcher will argue that a certain individual is "conservative" if he or she answers a series of questions in a certain manner. The assumption here is that certain answers to specific questions (stimuli) represent particular personality patterns, one of which is "conservatism."

Two important problems arise with the transition from the conceptual-theoretical level to the empirical-observational level. The first is connected with the degree of congruence between conceptual definitions and operational definitions. If "intelligence" is defined conceptually as "the ability to think abstractly" and operationally by an intelligence test, what is the degree of congruence between the two definitions? Does the score achieved by a certain individual in an intelligence test represent everything that the concept "intelligence" is supposed to convey? The second problem arises when concepts cannot be defined operationally. For instance, "beauty," "ego," "Oedipus complex," "dialectical materialism," and "subconscious" are concepts for which no valid operational definitions have yet been constructed.

The degree of congruence between a conceptual definition and an operational definition can be evaluated with the aid of validity tests discussed in Chapter 4. At this stage, it should be pointed out that there is no absolute criterion for checking congruence, and there can indeed be situations in which an operational definition does not exhaust all the ramifications contained in a conceptual definition. Improving operational definitions and extending the degree of congruence between them and conceptual definitions constitute important challenges to social scientists (Blalock, 1968).

Concepts that cannot be given operational definitions are usually termed "hypothetical concepts" (Simon, 1969:16). Their place in the scientific method provides an unfailing source of controversy, especially among philosophers of science. Bridgman (1961), a founder of the operational approach, claimed that concepts which cannot be operationally defined (at least in principle) prevent scientific progress, and that scientists should avoid using them. According to the operational approach, the sole meaning of concepts is related to the actions that a researcher must perform:

> The concept of length is therefore fixed when the operations by which length is measured are fixed: that is, the concept of length involves as much as and nothing more than the set of operations by which length is determined. In general, we mean by any concept nothing more than a set of operations; the concept is synonymous with the corresponding set of operations. (Bridgman, 1961:5)

The orthodox operational approach did not stand the test of time, since it was recognized that hypothetical concepts had an important role in the stage of theorizing. A hypothetical concept such as "subconscious," for instance, has served in developing theories of personality and behavior, although it has not been operationally defined.

More recently, Hempel has introduced the notion "systematic import" when transformations between the theoretical and the observational levels are made. Hempel (1966:94) maintains:

> Scientific systematization requires the establishment of diverse connections, by law or theoretical principles, between different aspects of the empirical world, which are characterized by scientific concepts. Thus, the concepts of science are the knots in a network of systematic interrelationships in which laws and theoretical principles form the threads. . . . The more threads converge upon, or issue from, a conceptual knot, the stronger will be its systematizing role, or its systematic import.

Considerations of systematic import, however, are contrary to orthodox operationalism, which states that different operational criteria determine different concepts. Hempel's (1966:96) conclusion, accepted by most social scientists (cf. Gibbs, 1972), is that scientific concepts are to be evaluated with reference to their empirical applicability and systematic import:

> Empirical import as reflected in clear criteria of application, on which operationalism rightly puts much emphasis, is not the only desideration for scientific concepts: systematic import is another indispensable requirement—so much so that the empirical interpretation of theoretical concepts may be changed in the interest of enhancing the systematic power of the theoretical network. In scientific inquiry, concept formation and theory formation must go hand in hand.

VARIABLES

A variable is an empirically applicable concept that takes on two or more values. Such empirically applicable concepts as "social class," "expectations," "tolerance," "political participation," "sex," and "membership in organizations" are treated as variables. For example, social status may be symbolized by the letter "y" and differentiated by at least five values: lower, lower middle, middle, upper middle, upper. Income may be symbolized by the letter "z" and graded with three values: low, medium, high. Income can also be graded by a series of numerals, for example, 500, 1,500, and 3,000.

Some variables have only two values. For example, if the empirically applicable concept is "sex," then its values are female and male. Other examples of two-valued variables are: Republican-Democrat, middle class–working class, student-nonstudent. Variables of this type are usually called dichotomous variables. Most variables investigated in the social sciences, however, are not dichotomous; they are, instead, characterized by a large number of values.

Three types of variables, whether dichotomous or multivalued, are common in scientific research: independent variables, dependent variables, and control variables.* The variable that the researcher wishes to explain is referred to as the dependent variable, whereas the explanatory variables are termed independent variables. An independent variable is the hypothesized cause of a dependent variable, and the dependent variable is the expected outcome of the independent variable.

The distinction between the types of variables is analytic and relates to the purpose of research. An independent variable in one study may be a dependent variable in another. The decision to treat a variable

---

* Independent variables are also known as predictor variables; dependent variables, as criterion variables; and control variables, as test variables.

in terms of the above types depends on the research objective. However, after making a decision, the researcher must be consistent in his or her classification throughout the research process. This point is particularly important in the light of the criterion concerning the time order of events. For example, if in a given research it is decided to regard "relative deprivation" as an independent variable and "political violence" as a dependent variable, the hypothesis is that "relative deprivation leads to political violence." Changing the classification rule will engender the hypothesis that "political violence leads to relative deprivation."

The complexity of the phenomena investigated in social sciences results in the investigation of two or more independent variables expected to covary with a single dependent variable. For example, "political participation" is investigated in numerous studies as a dependent variable. Independent variables such as "interest in politics," "involvement," "political information," "expected utility," and "party identification" are suggested to covary with "political participation" (Milbrath, 1965).

The relation between an independent variable and a dependent variable can be illustrated with the aid of orthogonal axes. Following mathematical custom, x, the independent variable, is represented by the horizontal axis, and y, the dependent variable, by the vertical axis; x values are laid out on the x axis, and y values on the y axis. A very common way to observe and interpret a relation is to plot the pairs of xy values, using the x and y axes as a frame of reference. Let us suppose that in a study of academic achievement we have two sets of measures: x measures the number of hours a student devotes to studying each day, and y measures the number of excellent grades attained by a student in a given semester. Hypothetical data of nine students on the two measures are presented in Table 2.1, and the measures are plotted in Figure 2.1.

TABLE 2.1. Number of Hours of Study per Day and Number of Excellent Grades (Hypothetical Data)

Number of Hours of Study per Day (x)	Number of Excellent Grades (y)
8	5
7	5
6	4
5	3
4	2
4	1
3	1
2	0
1	2

FIGURE 2.1.

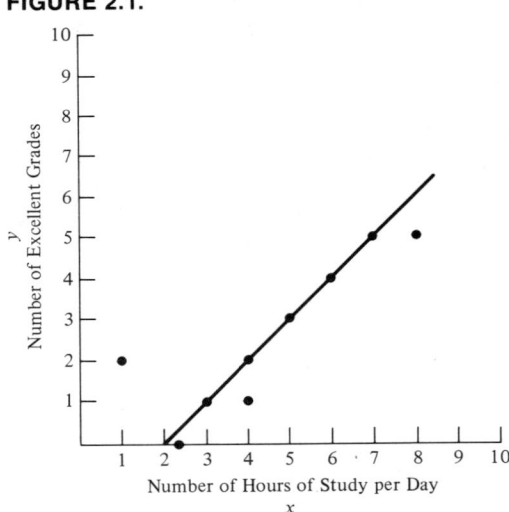

The relation between the number of daily hours of study (independent variable) and the number of excellent grades (dependent variable) can now be made tangible: high values on the x axis are related to high values on the y axis; medium values on the x axis are related to medium values on the y axis; and low values on the x axis are related to low values on the y axis. The relation between the independent variable (x) and the dependent variable (y) is depicted by the joint distribution of values. The straight line passing through the points representing pairs of values indicates the direction of the relation. Furthermore, with the aid of information about the characteristics of the straight line (its slope and intercept*), the researcher can predict the values of the dependent variable according to the values of the independent variable. Thus, for example, if the slope of the straight line is known, as well as the value of the point at which it intersects the y axis, it will be possible to predict how many daily hours of study will produce how many excellent grades.

In Chapter 1, where the notion of spuriousness was introduced, it was pointed out that a nonspurious relation between two phenomena is one that cannot be explained by a third factor. A control variable is one by which the relation between independent variables and dependent variables is tested to see whether it is spurious. In the example about firemen and fires used in Chapter 1, we saw that the control variable, "size of the fire," explained the relation between the number of firemen

* For methods of calculating the slope and the intercept, see Chapter 10.

and the amount of fire damage. Without the influence of the control variable (size of the fire), no relation would have been observed between the number of firemen and the amount of fire damage.

Another example illustrating the significance of control variables is the relation observed between political participation and government expenditure. Is the size of government expenditure (dependent variable) influenced by the extent of political participation (independent variable)? Or is the relation to be explained by a control variable? Alker (1965) examined economic development as a control variable and found that the relation between political participation and government expenditure vanished; the level of economic development influences both government expenditure and political participation. Without variability in the level of economic development, no relation would have been observed between political participation and the government expenditure. Control variables thus serve the purpose of testing the observed relation between independent and dependent variables (see Chapter 11).

HYPOTHESES

Hypotheses are tentative answers to research problems and are expressed in the form of a relationship between independent and dependent variables. Hypotheses are tentative, since their veracity can be evaluated only after they have been tested empirically. When researchers propose a hypothesis, they lack assurance that it will be verified. They construct a hypothesis, and if it is rejected, they put forward another.

Hypotheses can be derived deductively from theories, directly from observations, intuitively, or from a combination of these (Reynolds, 1971). The source from which researchers derive their hypothesis is of little significance in comparison with the way in which they reject or fail to reject it. Thus, for example, there are those who believe that it was the apple falling from the tree that brought Newton to suggest the hypothesis about gravitation. However, it was not this episode that induced scientists to accept the hypothesis, but the proof and the research methods used.

Despite the element of creativity in the choice of hypotheses, it is possible to point to a number of common sources on which social scientists draw. These sources are by no means exhaustive; rather, they are indicative of the wide array of options.

An important source of hypothesis construction is the state of knowledge in any particular science: where formal theories exist, hypotheses can be deduced. If the hypotheses are rejected, this would call for the modification of the theory. On the other hand, the failure to reject hypotheses increases the credibility of theories. Where formal theories are scarce, hypotheses are generated from conceptual frameworks. In such cases, the failure to reject a hypothesis may lead to the construction of a more systematic and rigorous theory. In either case, the hypotheses are related to the conceptual-theoretical level.

Another source of hypothesis construction is the culture on which the researcher was nurtured. Western culture has induced the emergence of sociology as an academic discipline. Problems common to France, Germany, England, and the United States found their expression in Max Weber's famous hypothesis about Protestant ethics. Not only do common features of various cultures serve as a source of hypotheses, peculiarities do as well. The peculiarity of a certain culture could cause researchers to focus on hypotheses connected with that culture and not on those characterizing other cultures. Evidence of this is the professional literature that both grows on a specific culture and feeds back into it. Over the past decade, a large part of the hypotheses on American society examined by researchers were connected with violence (Gurr, 1970). This interest is to a great extent related to the considerable increase in the level of violence in this country. In Finland, on the other hand, only a few hypotheses relating to violence have been examined.

The subculture of researchers in the various disciplines and schools of thought constitutes another source of hypotheses. Anthropologists, for example, tend to explore hypotheses about variables embodied in the world view of the anthropologist. This view is influenced not only by the general culture in which the researchers live, but also by their professional socialization in their subculture. It is not accidental, therefore, that researchers who acquired their professional skills in a certain subculture bring up hypotheses for testing that are of little interest in other subcultures. Hypotheses about political behavior are generally put forward by social scientists who received their training in the United States, whereas hypotheses concerning political institutions are of more interest to European political scientists. Fortunately, some investigators construct hypotheses that link the hypotheses being studied in the various subcultures, so that the generalizing character of the social sciences remains unimpaired.

The continuity of the research process itself constitutes an important source of hypotheses. The rejection of some hypotheses engenders the construction of new ones capable of explaining certain dependent variables. On the other hand, the failure to reject hypotheses leads to additional problems being brought up and tested. An example of the continuity of this process can be found in the research carried out regarding electoral behavior. In the forties, hypotheses concerned the political information and behavior of voters. A central assumption in these investigations was that the common citizen had up-to-date information concerning the political system, its institutions, and the salient political issues. This information was hypothesized to find its expression in voting patterns. The findings, however, were in complete contradiction to expectations. It was found that the common citizen had limited political information, and that voting patterns were not correlated with the accumulation of information. These findings brought about hypotheses concerning sociopsychological variables. Consequently, hypotheses were tested concerning the relations between primary groups and voting patterns, family background and voting patterns, party identification and voting patterns, and personality structure and voting patterns. In the sixties, a set of nonrejected hypotheses was built up that served as fertile ground for constructing causal models of voting behavior (Goldberg, 1966).

The wide array of sources need not affect the characteristics that distinguish researchable hypotheses. For hypotheses to be researchable, no matter what their source, they must meet the following requirements:

1. Hypotheses must be clear. Clarity is obtained by means of definitions. The researcher has to supply valid operational definitions for all the concepts in the research hypothesis. The professional literature and experts' opinions can be of great help in the defining process. For example, if the independent variable is "political participation," an examination of the professional literature will help to accumulate a large number of definitions that have served various researchers in their work. Among these definitions, the researcher is likely to find one suitable to his or her research hypothesis. If the definitions to be found do not satisfy the researcher, he or she can always build on others' experience while defining the variables in a way that expresses his or her own understanding. In any case, the operational definition must be specific and precise so that observation and replication are made possible.

2. Scientific hypotheses are not value-bearing. In principle, the researcher's system of values has no place within the scientific method. However, given that research in the social sciences is to a certain extent a social activity whose problems and methods are affected by the milieu in which it takes place, the researcher must be aware of his or her values and make them as explicit as possible. Indeed, as Myrdal (1944:1043) more than thirty years ago realized:

> The attempt to eradicate biases by trying to keep out the valuations themselves is a hopeless and misdirected venture. . . . There is no other device for excluding biases in social sciences than to face the valuations and to introduce them as explicitly stated, specific, and sufficiently concretized value premises.

3. Hypotheses must be specific. The researcher has to explicate the expected relations between the variables and the conditions under

which these relations will hold. A hypothesis stating that "x is related to y" is overgeneral and will not permit concrete predictions. The relation between x and y can be positive or negative. Relations between variables may be even more complex, as is illustrated in Figure 2.2. In this case, changes in the lower values of x do not bring about any changes in the values of y; changes in the medium values of x engender increasing changes in the values of y; and changes in the higher values of x bring about descending changes in the values of y (negative relation).

Relations between variables in the social sciences are not independent of time, space, or the unit of analysis. Intergroup violence involves a different perspective from that of interstate violence. The units of analysis are different; hence, the dependent variables might be different. Violence will not generally break out between states if the football team of one lost to that of the other; on the other hand, the fans of a losing team may initiate a fight. Likewise, political violence will not break out in a social system in which most of the citizens are satisfied and a deprived minority believes that care is being taken of its demands. "Satisfaction" and "care" are well-defined conditions that must find their expression in the research hypothesis. The research hypothesis will express the expected relations between the variables and the concrete conditions for the relationship. For example, it may express a positive relation between deprivation and violence and state that when there is dissatisfaction and no care is taken, deprivation will engender violence.

4. For hypotheses to be researchable, the researcher must make sure that there are methods available for testing them. Researchers can arrive at clear hypotheses, value-free and specific, and find that they lack the means to test them. How, for example, are we to test the hypothesis that "object A is longer than object B" without a ruler? Or, how are we to test the hypothesis that "the excretions of microbe C have a positive relation to disease D" without a microscope to permit the microbe

FIGURE 2.2. Possible Relations Between Variables

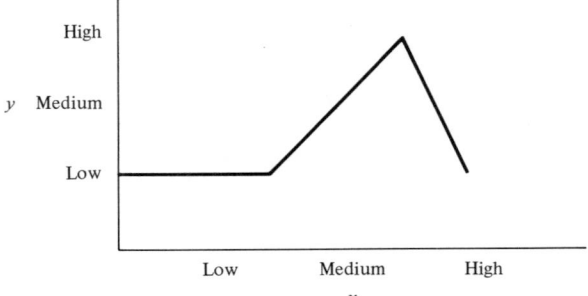

to be identified? The simplicity of these examples stresses the claim that the evaluation of hypotheses depends, to a large extent, on the existence of methods for testing them. Some social scientists attach little value to methods, for fear of being enslaved by them. It is, of course, possible to become enslaved by some method of research, if the researcher regards it as an end unto itself and not as a means. However, even hypotheses that lack methods of testing have a place in the scientific process if they are innovative. At the same time, their evaluation depends on the ability to test them, which in turn depends on the existence of techniques of research.

SUMMARY

Concepts are generalized abstractions representing empirical phenomena and serve the scientist in the process of communication and research. Assumptions and formal theories are constructed with concepts. Operational definitions link the theoretical level with the empirical-observational level. Concepts that have been operationally defined are termed variables. Within the framework of the research process, independent, dependent, and control variables are distinguishable. Independent variables are the hypothesized causes of dependent variables, and dependent variables are the presumed outcomes of independent variables. Control variables are employed to test causality between independent and dependent variables. Scientific research focuses on testing hypotheses. Hypotheses are tentative and concrete answers to intellectual stimuli, and their peculiarity consists of the possibility of rejecting them.

REFERENCES

Alker, Hayward R. *Mathematics and Politics*. New York: Macmillan, 1965.

Blalock, Hubert M. "The Measurement Problem: A Gap Between the Language of Theory and Research." In Hubert M. Blalock and Ann B. Blalock (eds.), *Methodology in Social Research*. New York: McGraw-Hill, 1968:7–27.

Bridgman, Percy W. *The Logic of Modern Physics*. New York: Macmillan, 1961.

Gibbs, Jack P. *Sociological Theory Construction*. Hinsdale, Ill.: Dryden Press, 1972.

Goldberg, Arthur S. "Discerning a Causal Pattern among Data on Voting Behavior." *American Political Science Review* 60 (1966):913–922.

Goode, William J., and Hatt, Paul K. *Methods in Social Research*. New York: McGraw-Hill, 1952.

Gurr, Ted R. *Why Men Rebel*. Princeton, N.J.: Princeton University Press, 1970.

Hempel, Carl G. *Philosophy of Natural Science*. Englewood Cliffs, N.J.: Prentice-Hall, 1966.

Isaak, Alan C. *Scope and Methods of Political Science*. Homewood, Ill.: Dorsey Press, 1969.

McKinney, John C. *Constructive Typology and Social Theory*. New York: Appleton-Century-Crofts, 1966.

Milbrath, Lester W. *Political Participation*. Chicago: Rand McNally, 1965.

Myrdal, Gunnar. *An American Dilemma*. New York: Harper & Brothers, 1944.

Reynolds, Paul D. *A Primer in Theory Construction*. Indianapolis: Bobbs-Merrill, 1971.

Simon, Julian L. *Basic Research Methods in Social Science*. New York: Random House, 1969.

CHAPTER 3
The Research Design

Once the research objectives have been determined, the hypotheses explicated, and the variables defined, the researcher confronts the problem of constructing a research design that will enable the testing of the hypotheses. A research design is the program that guides the investigator in the process of collecting, analyzing, and interpreting observations. It is a model of proof that allows the researcher to draw inferences concerning causal relations among the variables under investigation. Such inferences indicate the extent to which the researcher has met three criteria: demonstrating covariation of variables, eliminating spurious relations, and establishing the time order of events. Furthermore, the research design defines the domain of generalizability; that is, whether the obtained interpretations can be generalized to a larger population or to different situations.

In this chapter, we discuss the research design as a method of proof; we also distinguish between several research designs according to how they allow the drawing of inferences concerning causality and generalizability. In the first section, the structure of the research design is delineated. The second section deals with the four components of designs. In the third section, we differentiate between experimental and quasi-experimental designs; the last section focuses on the evaluation of these two types of designs.

THE STRUCTURE OF A RESEARCH DESIGN

The classic research design consists of two comparable groups: an experimental group and a control group. These two groups are equivalent, except that the experimental group is exposed to the independent variable (also termed the experimental stimulus) and the control group is not. To assess the effect of the experimental stimulus, measurements on the dependent variable, designated as scores, are taken twice from each group. One measurement, the pretest, is taken prior to the introduction of the experimental stimulus in the experimental group; a second, the posttest, is taken after exposure has taken place. The difference in measurements between the posttest and pretest is compared in each of the two groups. If the difference in the experimental group is significantly larger than in the control group, it is inferred that the independent variable is causally related to the dependent variable.

The classic design is often diagramed as in Table 3.1, where X designates the independent variable; O_i the measurements on the dependent variable, and d_e and d_c, the difference between the posttest and pretest in each group.

To illustrate the application of an experimental design in a social setting, let us examine a study designed to assess the effect of teachers' expectations on intellectual growth. The study, conducted by Rosenthal and Jacobson (1968), is based on the idea that one person's expectation for another's behavior can often serve as a self-fulfilling prophecy. The authors hypothesized that schoolchildren whom their teachers believed were brighter would actually become brighter because of their teachers' beliefs. A public elementary school in a lower-class community was the laboratory in which this hypothesis was tested. All the children participating in the experiment were pretested with a standard nonverbal test of intelligence. The test was represented to the teachers as one that predicted intellectual blooming. Following the pretest, each of the participating teachers was given the names of children expected to show intellectual growth. The predictions were allegedly made on the basis of the pretest; actually, however, the names of the "bloomers" were randomly chosen. The experimental group thus consisted of the expected bloomers, and all other children were in the control group. The expectation of the teachers was defined as the independent variable; the intellectual growth of the pupils was the dependent variable.

All the children in the two groups were retested with the same intelligence test after one year, and gains in intelligence were computed. A significant difference between the pretest and the posttest was found only among the children of the experimental group. This finding led the

TABLE 3.1. The Classic Experimental Design

	Pretest		*Posttest*	*Difference*
Experimental group	O_1	X	O_2	$O_2 - O_1 = d_e$
Control group	O_3		O_4	$O_4 - O_3 = d_c$

investigators to conclude that the expectation of teachers is causally related to intellectual growth.

The classic experimental design was approximated in this study because the experimental and the control groups were similar to each other, both were pretested and posttested, and the experimental stimulus (positive teacher expectation) was withheld from the control group.

THE COMPONENTS OF A RESEARCH DESIGN

The classic research design consists of four components: comparison, manipulation, control, and generalization. These components allow the investigator to draw inferences concerning the criteria of causality and the criterion of generalizability. In this section, we shall discuss each of these components as a distinct research operation.

Comparison

The process of comparison underlies the concept of covariation and association between two or more variables. Suppose a relationship exists between teaching method X and the achievement of students; one would then expect to find a joint occurrence of both the teaching method and a certain degree of achievement. That is, students will achieve more after being exposed to the teaching method than before. Similarly, those students who are studying under method X will have higher achievement than those students who are not. Thus, to assess the joint occurrence of the teaching method and achievement, a comparison is made of a group of students exposed to method X with one that is not, or of the group's achievement before and after the introduction of method X. In other words, to measure covariation, the subjects' scores on the dependent variable are evaluated before and after the introduction of the independent variable, or a group that is exposed to the independent variable is compared with one that is not. In the former case, a group is compared with itself; in the latter case, an experimental group is compared with a control group.

Manipulation

The notion of causality implies that if Y is caused by X, then an induced change in X will be followed by a change in Y. It is assumed that the relations are asymmetrical: that one variable is the determining force, and the other is a determined response. For this to be established, the induced change in X would have to be prior to the change in Y, since what follows cannot be the determining variable. If teaching method X is to influence achievement, then it has to be demonstrated that improvement in achievement takes place only after exposure to the method. This can be accomplished by some form of control over the introduction of the method, so that the investigator can measure achievement before and after the introduction. In experimental settings, especially in laboratory experiments (see Chapter 5), researchers can introduce the experimental stimulus themselves; in natural settings, on the other hand, this is not always possible. In both cases, the major evidence required to determine the time sequence is that a change occurred only after the activation of the independent variable.

Control

The third criterion of causality requires that other factors be ruled out as rival explanations of the observed association between the variables under investigation. Such factors could invalidate the inference that the variables are causally related. Campbell and Stanley (1963) have formulated this as the problem of internal validity, which is the *sine qua non* of research; it addresses itself to the question of whether the independent variable did in fact cause the observed response. The factors that may jeopardize internal validity can be classified into those which are extrinsic to the research operation and those which are intrinsic and impinge upon the results during the study period.

Extrinsic factors. Extrinsic factors refer to the possible biases resulting from the differential recruitment of subjects to the experimental and control groups. Campbell and Stanley (1963) have designated these as selection factors that produce differences in the two comparison groups prior to the research operation. As an illustration, consider Chapin's study (cf. Riley, 1963) on the social effects of public housing. This investigation was an attempt to examine the changes occurring in the social life of slum families as a result of their rehousing in public housing projects. Chapin compared an experimental group of families who had been rehoused with a control group of families who were still living under slum conditions. The main findings of the study showed a marked improvement in the social life of the experimental group, leading to the conclusion that public housing projects change the life style of their inhabitants. However, a rival explanation of the observed change in the rehoused families is that the people in new housing projects were initially different from the families serving as a control group. Perhaps the groups differed in type of employment, level of education, size of family, or attitudes. These factors could account for the observed differences between the two groups. Selection factors such as these must be controlled before the investigator can rule them out as rival explanations. Later in this section, we shall discuss methods for controlling extrinsic factors.

Intrinsic factors. Intrinsic factors refer to changes in the subjects or their background occurring during the study period, changes in the measuring instrument, or the reactive effect of the observation itself. The following five factors are the major intrinsic factors that might invalidate the interpretation given to the research findings.

1. *History.* History refers to all events occurring during the time of the study that might affect the subjects and provide a rival explanation for the change in the dependent variable. For example, in a study attempting to assess the effect of an election campaign on voting behavior, the hypothesis might be that propaganda to which voters are exposed during the campaign is likely to influence their voting. The voting intentions of the subjects are compared before and after exposure to propaganda. Differences in voting intentions of the two groups—one that has been exposed to propaganda, and another that has not—could result from differential exposure to the material or, alternatively, from events that occurred during this period; for example, additional taxes levied, governmental conflicts, war, or rapid inflation. The longer the time lapse between the pretest and the posttest, the higher the probability that historical events will become potential rival hypotheses.

2. *Maturation.* A second group of factors that may become plausible rival hypotheses is designated as maturation and includes biological and psychological processes that produce changes in the subjects with the passage of time. These changes could possibly influence the dependent variable and confound the results. Suppose one wants to evaluate the effect of a specific teaching method on student achievement and records the students' achievement before and after the method has been introduced. Between the pretest and the posttest, students have gotten older and perhaps wiser; this change, unrelated to the teaching method, could possibly explain the difference between the two tests. Maturation, like history, is a serious threat to the validity of causal inferences.

3. *Experimental mortality.* Experimental mortality refers to dropout problems that prevent the researcher from obtaining complete information on all cases. When subjects drop out selectively from the experimental or control group, the final sample on which complete information is available may be biased. In a study on the effect of the media on prejudice, for instance, if most dropouts were prejudiced individuals, the impression rendered could be that exposure to media reduced prejudice, whereas, in fact, it was the effect of experimental mortality that produced the observed shift in opinion.

4. *Instrumentation.* Instrumentation designates changes in the measuring instruments between the pretest and the posttest. To associate the difference between posttest and pretest scores with the independent variable, one needs to assume that repeated measurements with the same measurement instrument under constant conditions will

yield the same result. If such an assumption cannot be made, observed differences could be attributed to the change in the measurement instrument and not necessarily to the independent variable. The stability of measurement is also referred to as reliability, and its absence can be a threat to the validity of experiments (see Chapter 4). In the previous example, grades were used to determine achievement before and after the teaching method was introduced. A shift in grading standards between the two periods could invalidate the comparison between the test scores.

5. Testing. The possible reactivity of measurement is a major problem in social science research. The process of testing may change the phenomena being measured. The effect of being pretested might sensitize the subjects and improve their scoring on the posttest. A difference between posttest and pretest scores could thus be attributed not necessarily to the experimental stimulus but rather to the experience gained by the subjects while taking the pretest. It is well known, for example, that individuals may improve their scores on intelligence tests by taking them often. Similarly, through a pretest, subjects may learn the socially accepted responses, either through the wording of the questions or through discussing the results with friends. They might then answer in the acceptable direction on the posttest.

The extrinsic and intrinsic factors that can threaten the internal validity of a design may be controlled by several operations. Control of intrinsic factors is facilitated by the employment of a control group from which the experimental stimulus is withheld. Ideally, the control and experimental groups are under identical conditions during the study, except for their differential exposure to the independent variable. Thus, features of the experimental situation or external events that occur during the experiment are likely to influence the two groups equally and will not be confounded with the effect of the independent variable.

We will discuss briefly the way in which each of the intrinsic factors is controlled by the utilization of a comparison group. First, history cannot remain a rival hypothesis, since the control and experimental groups are both exposed to the same events occurring during the experiment. Similarly, maturation is neutralized, since the two groups undergo the same changes. Although the inclusion of a control group does not necessarily avoid the mortality problem, since the loss of cases might be differential and bias the results, the acceptable procedure is to include in the final sample only cases for which complete information is available. The influence of instrument change can be avoided by a comparison group; if the change between posttest and pretest scores is a result of the instrument's unreliability, this will be reflected in both groups. Yet, only when the groups are exposed to identical testing conditions does this method of control provide a solution to the instrumentation problem. Using a control group is also an answer to the matter of testing. The reactive effect of measurement, if present, is reflected in both groups and leaves no ground for misinterpretation.

Two methods of control are employed to counteract the effect of extrinsic factors. The first, matching, controls for variables that are known to the investigator prior to the research operation. The second, randomization, helps to offset the effect of unforeseen factors.

Matching. Matching is a way of equating the experimental and control groups on extrinsic variables that are presumed to be related to the research hypothesis. There are two ways to match the groups: by precision matching and by frequency distribution. With the first method (also known as pairwise matching), for each subject in the experimental group, another one with the same characteristics is selected for the control group. To control the effect of age, for example, for every individual in a specific age category in one group, there should be one in the same category in the second group. Having matched on the extrinsic variables, the investigator is assured that any difference found between the experimental and control groups cannot be due to the matched variables.

The main drawback in this technique is the difficulty in matching a large number of variables. When there are many relevant characteristics that need to be controlled, it is difficult to find matching pairs. Precision matching often causes a loss of about 90 percent of the cases, which have no comparable twins (Goode and Hatt, 1952).

An alternative and more efficient method is matching by frequency distribution. With this method, the experimental and control groups are equated for each of the relevant variables separately rather than in combination. Thus, instead of a one-to-one matching, the two groups are matched on central characteristics. For example, when matching for age, the average age of one group should be equivalent to that of the second. If sex is controlled, care should be taken that the two groups have the same proportion of males and females. Thus, the two groups are matched separately for each extrinsic variable. Although somewhat less precise, frequency matching is much easier to execute than precision matching and enables the investigator to control for several variables without having to discard a large number of cases.

Randomization. Matching is a method of controlling for a limited number of predefined extrinsic variables. However, there is a great number of variables that may confound the relationship between the independent and dependent variables. Even if it is possible to eliminate the effect of all relevant characteristics, one can never be sure that all factors that may be associated with the variables under investigation have been identified. There may be various factors the investigator is unaware of that may disturb the relationship and lead to invalid interpretations. This problem can be avoided by resorting to randomization, a process through which subjects are assigned to the experimental and control groups. This can be accomplished either by flipping a coin to decide which subjects will be included in the experimental group; by using a table of random digits; or by any other method which assures that any of the subjects has an equal probability of being assigned to either the experimental group or the control group (see Chapter 11).

Suppose a researcher is examining the hypothesis that the participation of workers in the decision-making process of their place of work is conducive to production. The workers are divided into control and experimental groups; the experimental group is allowed to participate in decisions concerning the work schedule and its organization. The production level of both groups is tested at the beginning and at the end of the experiment. The objective is to see whether workers who took part in the decisions are significantly more productive than workers in the control group. However, a difference in the production level can be accounted for by numerous factors other than the independent variable whose effect is directly examined. Obviously, there are a number of personality factors such as age, intelligence, and motivation that could account for the difference. The highly motivated, the more intelligent, and the younger workers could be more productive. Without a controlled assignment of the subjects to the groups, perhaps the most motivated and intelligent and the younger participants would volunteer for the experimental group, a fact that might account for the improved production level.

One way to counteract the effect of these variables is by pairwise matching. Another is to randomize the groups by flipping a coin to decide which workers are assigned to each group. The latter process assures similar distributions on all prior characteristics of the workers in both groups. It is expected that motivation, intelligence, and average age will be about the same in the two groups. Consequently, any difference in production between the groups can be interpreted as the effect of the experimental variable.

Randomization cancels out the effect of any systematic error due to extrinsic variables that may be related to the dependent or independent variables. The advantage of this method is that it controls for numerous factors simultaneously even without the researcher's awareness of what they are. With randomization, the investigator can equalize the experimental and control groups on all initial differences between them.

Generalization

Although internal validity is a crucial aspect of research, an additional significant question concerns the generalization of the findings. Surely, most research is concerned not with the effect of one variable upon another under the particular setting studied, but rather with its effect in a natural setting and on a larger population. This aspect is termed by Campbell and Stanley (1963) as the external validity of research designs, and it refers to the ability to generalize the results. Two sources of external validity that can limit the generalization of research findings are the representativeness of the sample and the reactive arrangements in the research procedure.

Representativeness of the sample. The random assignment of subjects to experimental and control groups does assure equality between the groups and thus contributes to the internal validity of the study. However, it does not necessarily assure representativeness of the population of interest. Results that prove to be internally valid might be specific to the sample selected for the particular study. This possibility becomes likely in situations where the recruitment of subjects is difficult. Consider an experiment on college students that is carefully planned yet is based on volunteers. This sample cannot be assumed to be representative of the student body, let alone the general population. To enable generalizations beyond the limited scope of the specific study, care should be taken to select the sample using a sampling method that assures representation. Probability methods such as random sampling would make generalizations to larger and clearly defined populations possible (see Chapter 12). In theory, the experimental and control groups should each constitute a probability sample of the population. The difference between them could then be generalized to the population. In practice, however, drawing a probability sample for an experiment often involves problems such as high cost and a high rate of refusal to cooperate.

Reactive arrangements. The results of a study are to be generalized not only to a larger population but also to a real-life setting. This cannot always be accomplished, especially when a study is carried out in a highly artificial and contrived situation. Consider, for example, Sherif's famous study (1937) on group influences upon the formation of norms. The study was designed to assess the influence of the group on individuals placed in an unstable situation in which all external bases of comparison were absent. Sherif created an unstable situation experimentally by using the autokinetic effect, which can be produced in complete darkness. In such a situation, a single ray of light introduced to the room cannot be localized; it seems to move erratically in all directions and to appear at different places in the room each time. The investigator examined the norms as to the movement of the light that were evolving in this context of uncertainty. The results of the study were then generalized to situations of uncertainty in real life. However, it can be claimed that an experimental situation in which subjects are placed in a dark room and are required to respond to a moving ray of light does not represent ordinary social situations, and that the observed results might very well be specific to an artificial situation alone.

In addition to the possible artificiality of the experimental setting, various features in the setting might be reactive and affect the external validity of the study. For example, the pretest may influence the responsiveness of the subjects to the experimental stimulus; its observed effect would thus be specific to a population that has been pretested.

The reactive effect of testing on the subjects can be avoided by making do with a posttest only, and the generalizability of the results can be improved by avoiding highly artificial situations (see Chapter 5).

EXPERIMENTAL DESIGNS

The various research designs can be characterized by the extent to which they adhere to all or some of the methodological criteria discussed thus far. Some designs may allow for the manipulation of the independent variable but fail to employ any method of control or an adequate sampling plan; others may include a control group but have no control over the introduction of the independent variable.

It is common to classify research designs into two major groups: experimental and quasi-experimental designs. In experimental designs, subjects are randomly assigned to the control and experimental groups, and the independent variable can be manipulated. Such designs allow for all the operations that make causal inferences possible: comparison, manipulation, and control. Quasi-experimental designs may include combinations of these elements but not all of them. Typically, these designs lack the ability to manipulate the independent variable and to randomize subjects.

The classic experimental design presented at the beginning of this chapter is one of the strongest models of proof. It allows for pretest, posttest, and control-group–experimental-group comparisons; it permits the manipulation of the independent variable and thus the determination of the time sequence; and finally, by including randomized groups, it controls for most sources of internal validity. However, this design is weak on external validity and does not allow for generalizations to be made to nontested populations. There are two variations of this design that are stronger in this respect: the Solomon Four-Group design and the Posttest-Only Control Group design.

The Solomon Four-Group Design

The pretest in an experimental setting has advantages as well as disadvantages. Although it provides an assessment of the time sequence

TABLE 3.2. The Solomon Four-Group Design

	Before		After
R	O_1	X	O_2
R	O_3		O_4
R		X	O_5
R			O_6

as well as a basis of comparison, it can have severe reactive effects. Moreover, there are circumstances under which a premeasurement period is not practical. In educational research, for instance, entirely new methods for which pretests are impossible are often experimented with. The Solomon Four-Group design, presented in Table 3.2, contains the same features as the classic design, plus an additional set of control and experimental groups that are not pretested. Therefore, the reactive effect of testing can be directly measured by comparing the two experimental groups ($O_2 - O_5$) and the two control groups ($O_4 - O_6$). These comparisons will indicate whether X has an independent effect on groups that were not sensitized by a pretest. If it can be shown that the experimental stimulus had an effect even with the absence of the pretest, the results can be generalized to populations that were not measured prior to exposure to X, and the strength of the causal inference will be greatly enhanced.

The Posttest-Only Control-Group Design

The Solomon Four-Group design is perhaps the strongest of all experimental designs. However, using such an elaborate design is often impractical and costly. The Posttest-Only Control-Group design is a variation on both the classic design and the Solomon design; it omits the pretested groups altogether. The design is diagramed in Table 3.3.

This design is identical to the two last groups of the Solomon Four-Group design, which are not pretested. Subjects are randomly assigned to either the experimental or the control group and are measured with respect to the dependent variable during or after the introduction of the independent variable. As an illustration, suppose a researcher examining the effects of a racist film on racial prejudice selects a sample that is

TABLE 3.3. The Posttest-Only Control-Group Design

R	X	O_1
R		O_2

randomly assigned to two groups. One group is shown the film, and later the two groups are interviewed. To assess the effect of the film on racial prejudice, the response to the interview in the two groups is compared. A significant difference between the groups will indicate that the film had an effect on prejudice.

The association between the independent and dependent variables is evaluated by a comparison of the control and experimental groups. Thus, the occurrence of prejudice in the experimental group is compared with its occurrence in the control group. The time order between the variables under investigation can be inferred from the randomization process used to assign the subjects to the different groups. This procedure removes any initial difference between the groups; therefore, it can be assumed that the observed difference was produced by the independent variable.

The Posttest-Only Control-Group design controls for all intrinsic sources of invalidity. With the omission of a pretest, testing and instrumentation are no longer relevant. It can also be assumed that the remaining intrinsic factors are controlled, since both groups are exposed to the same external events and undergo the same maturational processes. Additionally, the extrinsic factor of selection is controlled by the random assignment of the subjects, which removes an initial bias of either group.

QUASI-EXPERIMENTAL DESIGNS

The experimental design, as the strongest model of proof, is the reference for all other designs. However, it cannot be employed as a research plan in situations where manipulation and random allocation of respondents is impossible. These limitations very often derive from the nature of relationships studied by social scientists. Rosenberg (1968) has made a distinction between two kinds of relationships. The first is a stimulus-response relationship, characterized by an independent variable that is external, specific, and well defined, with a dependent variable being a particular response to it. For instance, relationships between reward and satisfaction, or between advertisement and consumption patterns, are of the stimulus-response kind. The second type that is predominant in social science research is between a property (usually some background characteristic) and dispositions such as attitudes, values, and orientations. Examples are the relationships between social class and political behavior or between race and prejudice.

Whereas stimulus-response relationships are well suited for experimental investigation, property-disposition relationships are not. The reason lies in the inherent differences between them on four issues. The first difference relates to the time interval between the effect of the independent variable and the response to it. In a stimulus-response relationship, the time interval is relatively short, whereas with the property-disposition type it can extend over a long period. For example, the response to a drug or to an advertising campaign can be observed within a short period, but the effects of properties such as sex, race, and social class are not of such an immediate nature.

The second difference is the degree of specificity of the independent variable. A stimulus is usually easy to isolate and identify, and its effect can be concretely delineated. However, a property (say, social class) is more ambiguous and incorporates various factors, such as prestige, occupation, and education, each exerting its relative influence. Therefore, it is often difficult with this type of variable to define the relevant causes and to manipulate them experimentally.

The nature of the comparison groups is the third difference between the stimulus-response and the property-disposition relationships. In the first, comparisons can be made of two similar groups: one that has been exposed to the stimulus and one that has not; and of a group before and after its exposure to the stimulus. In the second kind of relationship, a before-after comparison is all but impossible, especially with properties that are unalterable, such as sex and race. Similarly, it is difficult to assume that two groups having different properties are comparable in any other respect. A lower-class group and an upper-class group differ in various aspects other than class, such as value orientations, intelligence, and child-rearing practices.

Finally, the time sequence of events is the fourth difference between the two kinds of relationships. With the stimulus-response kind, the direction of causation is relatively clear, especially when the design allows for a before-after comparison. But the time sequence cannot be established with all properties. With fixed properties such as sex, race, or age, there are no difficulties, since these can be only the determining factors but never the determined effects of other factors. However, this is not the case with properties that are acquired by the individual, such as intelligence, political orientations, or education; these properties can both determine and be determined by other factors. Since it is frequently difficult to manipulate them experimentally and to allow for a before-after comparison, the time order cannot easily be established.

Due to these difficulties, the components of research designs—comparison, manipulation, and control—cannot be applied to property-disposition relationships in the pure experimental sense. Many of the factors that are of interest to social scientists can seldom be manipulated by them; moreover, human subjects cannot very often be randomly assigned to treatment groups, and most of the social processes can be studied only after a long period of time. However, social scientists have been trying to approximate the experimental model by employing data-analysis techniques that compensate for the limitations imposed at the data-collection phase. In the next section, we shall consider several quasi-experimental designs, some of which incorporate data-analysis techniques that help to deal with the problems just discussed.

The One-Shot Case Study

The One-Shot Case Study involves an observation of a single group at one point in time, usually subsequent to some event that allegedly produced change. For example, the study might be an observation of a community after an urban renewal program, a political system after general elections, or a school after it has been exposed to an innovative teaching method.

This design is an observation only of what exists at the time of the study; as such, it has no control over extrinsic and intrinsic factors. In addition, it does not allow for manipulation of the independent variable or for before-after or control-group–experimental-group comparison. Furthermore, since case studies analyze single unsampled systems, they are weak on generalization as well. Studies that employ the One-Shot Case-Study design have no checks on internal validity and thus are of little use in testing causal relations. Indeed, this design has been denoted by some methodologists as preexperimental. However, the One-Shot Case Study is useful in exploratory research. Selltiz et al. (1959) designate it as a "stimulating insight," maintaining that the intensive case-study approach is particularly useful in unformulated areas, where it might suggest hypotheses for further research.

Correlational Designs

The correlational design, often referred to as the cross-sectional study, is perhaps the most predominant design employed in survey research. It is an attempt to approximate the Posttest-Only Control-Group design by utilizing various data-analysis techniques. This design is diagramed in Figure 3.1. The dotted cell indicates information obtained during the data-analysis stage. The basic comparison between the control and

FIGURE 3.1. The Correlational Design

After

O_1

O_2

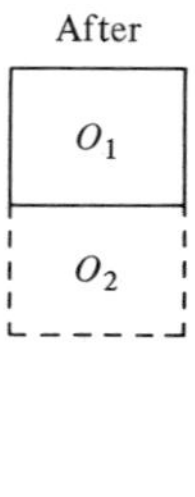

TABLE 3.4. Respondents' Marital History by Stability of Parental Home

	Percentage Ever Divorced or Currently Separated
Broken home	39.2%
Unbroken home	31.2

SOURCE: Jerold Heiss. "On the Transmission of Marital Instability in Black Families." *American Sociological Review* 37 (February 1972):82–92.

the experimental group is statistical and is based on various cross tabulations and correlational techniques.

The typical correlational study starts with a sample of individuals who are questioned about their properties and dispositions. For example, in a recent study, Heiss (1972) has attempted to examine the hypothesis that marital instability among blacks is related to a family history of instability. Data from a sample of northern urban blacks were collected on variables such as stability of parental home, marital history, sex, parental socioeconomic status, and age at the point at which the parental home broke up. To measure the effect of the hypothesized cause (stability of parental home) on the marital history of the respondents, the sample was subdivided into experimental and control groups of respondents with histories of broken and unbroken homes. The percentages of separated and divorced couples in each group were calculated.* The findings are presented in Table 3.4.

Heiss has concluded that those individuals from unstable parental backgrounds are somewhat more likely to experience divorce or separation in their own marriages. This, however, is questionable evidence for accepting the suggested hypothesis. With no before-after comparison or a random assignment of respondents to broken and unbroken homes, there is no assurance that respondents from broken homes are comparable in all relevant respects to those from unbroken homes. Numerous extrinsic factors could possibly account for the findings. For example, respondents from lower socioeconomic backgrounds might be concentrated in the broken-home group and account for the slightly higher rate of marital instability.

The most common alternative to experimental methods of control is multivariate analysis (see Chapter 11). By examining the original relationship in subcategories of the controlled variables, the researcher performs an operation similar to matching. However, as with matching, the drawback of such a method is that only known and predetermined factors can be controlled. The correlational design offers no alternative to

---

* For an extensive discussion on percentage analysis, see Chapters 9 and 10.

randomization, the only technique that disrupts any systematic relationship between the characteristics of the subjects and their exposure to the independent variable.

In most correlational designs, the limitations in the manipulation of the independent variable prevent the determination of the time sequence. In some studies, this problem can be resolved on the basis of logical considerations—as in our example, where the stability of the parental home is prior to the offspring's divorce or separation. In other studies, however, the direction of influence remains ambiguous.

A variation of the correlational design, providing a partial solution to the time-order problem, is the Ex-Post-Facto design. This design commonly reconstructs the past by asking respondents retrospective questions regarding an earlier period. For example, an investigator attempting to assess the effect of combat duty in Vietnam on the political views of soldiers could ask them about their present political views as well as about their views before their combat duty.

The drawback of retrospective questions is that the memory of respondents may be selective or distorted. Hyman (1955) has noted that reports on events that are remote in time may be distorted by subsequent experiences. A partial solution is to introduce checks in order to detect gross inaccuracies in the memory of subjects (see Chapter 6).

The Panel

A more rigorous solution to the time dilemma is the panel design, in which the same sample is examined at two or more time intervals. Panel studies offer a closer approximation to the before-after condition of experimental designs, by studying a group at two or more points in time before and after exposure to the independent variable. It is more rigorous than the Ex-Post-Facto design, as it does not rely on the respondents' memory; rather, it provides direct measurements, extended in time.

An illustration of the panel design is the classic study by Lazarsfeld, Berelson, and Gaudet (1944) on the formation of voting patterns during a presidential campaign. A sample of voters was interviewed once each month in a period from May to November, up to Election Day. The investigators attempted to determine the factors that produce changes in voting intentions during an election campaign. The main advantage of such a study plan was that it enabled the determination of the direction of causation. It was assumed that from time to time various stimuli in the election campaign would change, producing a related change in the voting preferences of the participants. With a comparison of the various measurements of the same respondents taken prior to and after exposure to the agent of change, the time order could be determined.

The main problem of panels is obtaining an initial representative sample of respondents who are willing to be interviewed at set intervals over an extended period. Moreover, even if a researcher succeeds in obtaining the commitment of respondents, there are subsequent dropouts, due to refusals to continue cooperating and difficulties in tracing respondents who move or change jobs. A serious consequence is that those who dropped out may change in a different way from the rest of the panel, thus affecting the findings. Another problem with repeated interviews with the same group is "panel conditioning"; that is, the risk that repeated measurements may sensitize the subjects. For example, members of a panel may try to appear consistent in the views they express on consecutive occasions. In such cases, the panel becomes untypical of the population it was selected to represent. One possible safeguard to panel conditioning is to give members of a panel only a limited panel life and then to replace them with persons taken randomly from a reserve list.*

The Trend Study

A longitudinal design of a different kind is the trend study, in which the same measurements are taken at different periods of time. Unlike the panel, however, the trend design does not use the same subjects; rather, it employs equivalent samples each testing period.

Trend studies are often used by government agencies to study change in population characteristics such as birth rates, divorce rates, and family size (Glock, 1967). Public opinion polls conducted by Gallup and Harris often make use of the trend study. This design was not frequently used in the past by social scientists mainly because of its high cost. However, with the fairly recent attempts to make use of data banks, and with the increased importance of secondary analysis, the trend study is becoming a useful tool for the study of change. For example, information on the American electorate recorded during the last decade at the Survey Research Center in Michigan has been utilized by political scientists to study trends in political attitudes and in voting (Schulman and Pomper, 1975).

Another example of trend analysis is a study by Farley and Hermalin (1971), who examined trends in family stability among blacks and whites from 1890 to 1964. The trend-study design was particularly useful for a study of this kind, since the only sources of information dating that far back were records kept by the Census Bureau. The researchers employed demographic indicators of family stability such as the proportion

---

* For this and other methods for checking panel conditioning and overcoming problems of sample mortality, see Marion G. Sobol, "Panel Mortality and Panel Bias," *Journal of the American Statistical Association* 54 (1959):52–68; and Leslie Kish, *Sampling Survey* (New York: Wiley, 1965).

of illegitimate births and the current marital status of adults. By comparing illegitimate fertility rates and the proportion of single adults in a period extending over almost eighty years, the investigators could plot trends in family stability and observe change over time. For example, rates of childbearing by unmarried women are higher now than they were thirty years ago, suggesting a trend away from family stability. This trend is similar for both races.

The trend-study design can be used to study changes of a gradual nature such as changes in attitudes and values. It is particularly useful in studies extending over a long period of time, since, unlike the panel, this design is not sensitive to the problem of mortality. There are, however, two major threats to the internal validity of trend studies: history and instrumentation. History is a plausible rival hypothesis, since observed change can be attributed to simultaneous events occurring during the period covered by the study. Trend studies using census data are vulnerable to the problem of instrumentation, since changes may often be a function of the quality in the data-gathering methods (Leege and Francis, 1974).

A COMPARISON OF DESIGNS

This discussion on research designs has focused on two basic problems of scientific research: inferring causation and generalizing the findings. These problems pose a basic dilemma: to secure unambiguous evidence about causation, one frequently sacrifices generalizability. Campbell and Stanley (1963) have narrowed this down to the problematic relation between internal and external validity. Most designs that are strong on internal validity are weak on external validity, and vice versa.

Perhaps the most serious threat to the internal validity of research designs is adequate control of extrinsic and intrinsic factors. In generalizability, the main issues are the representation of the researched population and of a real social situation. External validity is increased by increasing the heterogeneity of the sample and of the experimental situation (Aronson and Carlsmith, 1968). These issues are juxtaposed; as one increases realism and heterogeneity, one may frequently sacrifice control.

This is the point where the weaknesses and advantages of experimental and quasi-experimental designs can be compared. Whereas experiments are strong on control and weak on representation, quasi-experiments (especially surveys) are strong on representation but weak on control (Kish, 1959). Experiments have several advantages. First and foremost, they enable valid causal inferences to be made by exerting a great deal of control, particularly through randomization, over extrinsic and intrinsic variables. The second advantage is their control over the introduction of the independent variable, thus permitting the direction of causation to be determined. These advantages of experiments are the shortcomings of quasi-experiments. Lack of adequate control over rival explanations and difficulties in manipulating the independent variable prevent the researcher from drawing unambiguous inferences.

However, although the experiment is accepted as the scientific method *par excellence*, it has several shortcomings. The most frequent criticism lodged at experiments, especially laboratory experiments, is that they are artificial and removed from real-life situations. It is maintained (Draber and Haas, 1967) that social life cannot be replicated in experimental settings and, thus, that important issues cannot be analyzed there. A second problem concerns the sample design. In experimental designs, it is difficult to represent a specified population, since most experiments include volunteers or have an incidental sample at best. Nonrepresentative samples prevent the investigator from generalizing to populations of interest and limit the scope of the findings. On the other hand, most correlational designs are carried out in natural settings and permit the employment of probability samples. This allows statistical inferences to be made to broader populations and permits generalizations to real-life situations.

Given that no design can solve simultaneously the problems of control and representation, the investigator is faced with a difficult choice. Although in practice the nature of the study dictates this choice, it is generally accepted that the attainment of internal validity is more crucial than the attainment of external validity. Still, both experimental and quasi-experimental designs can be improved. Experiments can increase external validity by clearly defining the population to be studied and by drawing sampling units from this population following a scientific sample design. Correlational studies can greatly improve their internal validity by including auxiliary information as a control against rival hypotheses. Moreover, with recent statistical techniques such as path or causal analysis (see Chapter 11), for example, time sequences can be more clearly specified, and the quality of causal inferences can be greatly improved.

SUMMARY

A research design is the program that guides the investigator in the process of collecting, analyzing, and interpreting observations. It allows inferences concerning causal relations and defines the domain of generalizability. The classic research design consists of four components: comparison, manipulation, control, and generalization. These components allow the investigator to measure the covariation of the independent and dependent variables, to establish that the relationship between them is nonspurious, to specify the time order, and to allow the generalization of the results to a larger population or to different situations.

Research designs are classified into two major groups: experimental and quasi-experimental. Experimental designs allow for comparison, manipulation, and control and thus make causal inferences possible. Quasi-experimental designs, which are predominant in the social sciences, typically lack the ability to establish the time order between the variables or to exert sufficient control over extrinsic factors. Multivariate analysis is the most common alternative to experimental methods of control and is usually employed with the correlational design. The panel and the trend-study designs provide an alternative to the manipulation of experimental stimuli. Although these designs are weak on control, they usually allow the generalization of the results to larger populations and to different situations.

REFERENCES

Aronson, Elliot, and Carlsmith, James. "Experimentation in Social Psychology." In Gardner Lindzey and Elliot Aronson (eds.), *The Handbook of Social Psychology*. Reading, Mass.: Addison-Wesley, 1968.

Campbell, Donald T., and Stanley, Julian C. *Experimental and Quasi-Experimental Designs for Research*. Chicago: Rand McNally, 1963.

Drabek, Thomas E., and Haas, Eugene J. "Realism in Laboratory Simulation: Myth or Method?" *Social Forces* 45 (1967):337–346.

Farley, Reynolds, and Hermalin, Albert I. "Family Stability: A Comparison of Trends Between Blacks and Whites." *American Sociological Review* 36 (1971):1–17.

Glock, Charles Y. *Survey Research in the Social Sciences*. New York: Russell Sage Foundation, 1967.

Goode, William J., and Hatt, Paul K. *Methods in Social Research*. New York: McGraw-Hill, 1952.

Heiss, Jerold. "On the Transmission of Marital Instability in Black Families." *American Sociological Review* 37 (February 1972):82–92.

Hyman, Herbert. *Survey Design and Analysis*. New York: Free Press, 1955.

Kish, Leslie. "Some Statistical Problems in Research Design." *American Sociological Review* 24 (1959):328–338.

Lazarsfeld, Paul F., Berelson, Bernard, and Gaudet, Hazel. *The People's Choice*. New York: Duell, Sloan & Pearce, 1944.

Leege, David C., and Francis, Wayne L. *Political Research*. New York: Basic Books, 1974.

Moser, C. A., and Kalton, G. *Survey Methods in Social Investigation*. London: Heinemann Educational Books, 1971.

Riley, Matilda W. *Sociological Research I: A Case Approach.* New York: Harcourt, Brace & World, 1963.

Rosenberg, Morris. *The Logic of Survey Analysis.* New York: Basic Books, 1968.

Rosenthal, Robert, and Jacobson, Lenore. *Pygmalion in the Classroom.* New York: Holt, Rinehart & Winston, 1968.

Schulman, Mark A., and Pomper, Gerald M. "Variability in Electoral Behavior: Longitudinal Perspectives from Causal Modeling." *American Journal of Political Science* 21 (1975):1–18.

Selltiz, Claire, et al. *Research Methods in Social Relations.* New York: Holt, Rinehart & Winston, 1959.

Sherif, Muzafer. "An Experimental Approach to the Study of Attitudes." *Sociometry* 1 (1937):90–98.

STUDY SUGGESTIONS

1. You are to evaluate the hypothesis that flexible work schedule increases productivity of assembly line workers. Test this hypothesis by setting up alternative research designs as follows: (a) an experimental design; (b) a correlational design. Outline the structure of each design, indicating how the study is to be executed. How do these designs compare in allowing you to infer that flexible work schedule is causally related to productivity? How do the two designs compare in their generalizability power? Which design is most suited for this type of problem? Why?

2. Give examples of hypotheses from your field of specialization for which the following designs are best suited: (a) the Solomon Four-Group design; (b) the One-Shot Case Study; (c) a panel; and (d) a trend study.

3. In a study of the effect of early retirement on morale it was found that workers who retired early were generally less satisfied and of lower spirits than those who retired on time. What are the alternative explanations for these differences? List the variables that could provide these alternative explanations. How can these variables be controlled in an experimental design? In a correlational design?

4. Select three research studies that have appeared recently in major journals in your field. Consider these studies and state the research problem under investigation. Indicate which research design has been used by the investigators. How did the investigators examine covariation among the variables under study, control for spurious relations, and handle the problem of their time sequence? In each case list the relevant research operation. Examine these studies critically, indicating whether the conclusions reached were warranted by the specific research design employed. Could the research problem be examined with a better design? Which one?

CHAPTER 4
Measurement

In previous chapters, we considered operationalism and the various research designs through which the relations between variables are evaluated. Variables were defined as observational properties possessing two or more values. Identification of and differentiation between values are attained through measurement and quantification.

THE NATURE OF MEASUREMENT

Measurement may be viewed simply as a procedure in which a researcher assigns numerals to properties, objects, or events according to rules (Stevens, 1951). Let us suppose that someone intends to purchase a new car. Having found that the difference in price among the various small cars is minute, this individual has decided to make the purchase on the basis of which model best meets the following requirements: design, economical operation, and service. These three features vary. For example, one model may be well designed and economical to operate, but the service supplied by the manufacturer may be unsatisfactory. Accordingly, the buyer has decided to rank each of the three features by five numbers: 10, 11, 12, 13, and 14. Number 10 indicates total dissatisfaction, and number 14 stands for the highest degree of satisfaction. Numbers 11, 12, and 13 indicate increasing degrees of satisfaction with the feature being examined. The buyer examines five models. Table 4.1 summarizes the evaluation of each model according to the three criteria that were set. After examining the scores, the buyer decides to purchase car *C* because it received the highest score on all three counts, indicating the highest degree of satisfaction.

This is an extremely simplified instance of measurement, but it con-

TABLE 4.1.

	Design	Economy	Service
Car A	10	11	10
Car B	13	14	12
Car C	14	14	14
Car D	14	12	13
Car E	10	12	14

veys the idea expressed in the definition. The buyer assigned numerals to objects according to rules. The objects, the numerals, and the rules for assignment were contained in the instructions imposed by the buyer. The numerals, which are the end product of measurement, might be used for comparison, evaluation, and the assessment of relations between the various properties, or variables. For example, the buyer might compute measures of relation between design and economy or between design and service.

Further clarification of the three basic concepts used to define measurement—numerals, assignments, and rules—is called for. A numeral is a symbol of the form I, II, III, ..., or 1, 2, 3, ... A numeral has no quantitative meaning unless one imputes to it such a meaning. Numerals can be used to label objects such as football players, driving licenses, individuals drawn in a sample from a population, or events. Numerals that are given quantitative meaning become numbers; these enable the use of mathematical and statistical techniques for purposes of description, explanation, and prediction. In other words, numbers are amenable to statistical analyses and mathematical manipulations, which in turn reveal new information about the objects or events being measured.

In the definition of measurement, the term "assignment" means mapping. Numerals or numbers are mapped onto objects or events. To illustrate the mapping idea in measurement, consider Figure 4.1,

FIGURE 4.1.

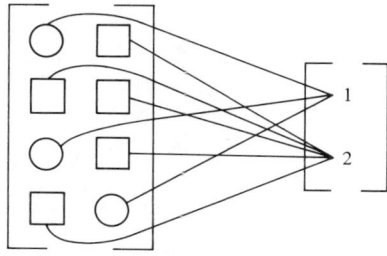

which shows a number of circles and squares on the left and two numbers on the right; 1 is mapped onto the circles, and 2 onto the squares.

The third concept used to define measurement is that of rules. A rule explicates the way in which numerals or numbers are to be assigned to objects or events. A rule might say: "Assign the numerals 10 through 15 to political systems according to how democratic the systems are. If a political system is very democratic, let the number 15 be assigned to it. If a political system is not at all democratic, let the number 10 be assigned to it. To political systems between these limits, assign numbers between the limits." Or suppose that a group is composed of three Democrats and two Republicans, and that one uses the following mapping rule: "If an individual is a Democrat, assign him or her 1; if an individual is a Republican, assign her or him 2." The measurement of the variable (party affiliation) is illustrated in Figure 4.2.

Measurement, then, is the assignment of numerals or numbers to objects, events, or properties according to rules. Rules are the most significant component of the measurement procedure because they determine the quality of measurement. Poor rules make measurement meaningless. Measurement is meaningless when it is not tied to reality, and the function of rules is to tie the measurement procedure to reality. Meaningful measurement is attained only when the measurement procedure has an empirical correspondence with reality. For example, suppose someone is measuring the softness of three objects. If object A can scratch B and not vice versa, then B is softer than A. Similarly, if A can scratch B, and B can scratch C, then A can probably scratch C, and one can deduce that object C is softer than object A. These are observable propositions, and numbers indicating degrees of softness can be assigned to each of those objects after executing a few scratch tests. In this case, the measurement procedure and the number system are isomorphic to reality.

Isomorphism means similarity or identity of structure. In measurement, the crucial question to be asked is whether the numerical system is similar in structure to the structure of objects or events being measured. Are the two similar in some structural aspect? To the physical

FIGURE 4.2.

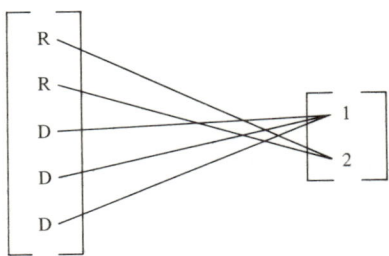

scientist, the problem of isomorphism is often of secondary concern, because the relation between the objects being observed and the numbers assigned to the observations is quite direct. The social scientist, on the other hand, must almost always be alert to the fact that "in order for him to be able to make certain operations with numbers that have been assigned to observations, the structure of his method of mapping numbers to observations must be isomorphic to some numerical structure which includes these operations" (Siegel, 1956:22). If two systems are isomorphic, their structures are the same in the relations and operations they allow for. Thus, if a researcher assigns numbers to objects and then manipulates these numbers by, say, adding them, he or she is implying that the structure of this measurement is isomorphic to the numerical structure known as arithmetic.

Most frequently, social scientists measure the properties or characteristics of objects or, more precisely, indicators of properties—not the objects themselves. Properties such as democracy, motivation, hostility, and integration cannot be directly observed; one must infer them from the observation of presumed indicators of the properties. If elections are held regularly in a political system, one may infer that this is an indicator of the system's democracy. If someone achieves a certain score in a motivation test, we may infer something about this person's level of motivation. In these examples, some identifiable behavior is an indicator of an underlying property. Although the process of measuring directly observable properties is identical to the one for measuring indicators of properties, the rules in the latter are much more difficult to formulate, and the researcher must rely on large inferential leaps. Thus, indicators are specified by operational definitions; after observation of the indicators, numerals or numbers are substituted for the values of the indicators, and statistical and mathematical operations are executed. Obviously, the numerical structure that substitutes indicators must be similar, in its relations and operations, to the structure of indicators; that is, the two must be isomorphic.

LEVELS OF MEASUREMENT*

The requirement of isomorphism between numerical systems and empirical properties (or indicators of properties) leads to a distinction among different ways of measuring, that is, to distinct levels of measurement.† The operations permissible on a given set of numbers are

---

* In the following discussion, the terms "objects," "properties of objects," "indicators," and "variables" will be used interchangeably, since the same rules apply to all of them.

† The term "scales of measurement" is sometimes used instead of "levels of measurement." A scale may be thought of as a tool for measuring; a speedometer is a scale, as is a ruler or a thermometer.

dependent on the level of measurement attained. Here we will discuss four levels of measurement—<u>nominal, ordinal, interval, and ratio</u>—and the rationale of the operations that are permitted with each level.

Nominal Level

The weakest level of measurement is the nominal level. At this level, numbers or other symbols are used to classify objects. These numbers or symbols constitute a nominal, or classificatory, scale. By means of the symbols 1 and 2, for instance, it is possible to classify a given population into males and females, with 1 representing males and 2 standing for females. The same population can be classified by religion; Christians might be represented by the numeral 6, Jews by 7, and Muslims by 8. In the first case, the population was classified into two categories; in the second, into three. As a rule, when a set of objects can be classified into categories that are exhaustive (i.e., they include all objects) and mutually exclusive (i.e., with no case in more than one category), and when each category is represented by a different symbol, a nominal level of measurement is attained.

Mathematically, the basic property of the nominal level of measurement is that the properties of objects in one category are equal to each other, but not to anything else in their identical aspect. The logical properties of equivalence are reflexivity, symmetry, and transitivity. Reflexivity means that every object in one of the categories is equal to itself. For example, $a = a$ in the "Christians" category. Symmetry is defined as the relationship when if $a = b$, then $b = a$. Transitivity is the relationship when if $a = b$, and $b = c$, then $a = c$. These three logical properties are operative among objects within the same category, but not necessarily between categories. For instance, these relations will apply to all persons classified as "Christian," but not between "Christians" and "Jews."

At the nominal level, the classification of objects may be equally well represented by any set of symbols. The symbols may also be interchanged without altering any information, if this is done consistently and completely. Accordingly, only statistics that would remain unchanged by such transformation are permissible at the nominal level. In Chapters 9 and 13, we will discuss some of these statistics.

Ordinal Level

Many properties studied by social scientists are not only classifiable but also exhibit some kind of relation. Typical relations are "higher," "greater," "more desired," "more difficult," and so on. Such relations may be designated by the symbol (>), which means "greater than." In

[handwritten note: order or rank; but not equidistant from one another]

reference to particular properties, > may be used to designate "is higher than," "is greater than," "is more desired than," and so on. For instance, it can be hypothesized that France is more democratic than the Soviet Union but less so than England, or that socialist parties are less militant than communist parties but more so than religious parties. In general, if (in addition to equivalence) the relation > holds for all pairs of objects engendering a complete rank ordering of objects, an ordinal level of measurement is attained. Consider a property such as "social acceptability." In social acceptability, all members of the upper class are higher than all members of the middle class. All members of the middle class, in turn, are higher than all members of the lower class. The equivalence relation holds among members of the same class, whereas the > relation holds between any pair of classes.

The > relation is irreflexive, asymmetrical, and transitive. Irreflexivity is a logical property wherein it is not true that for any a, $a > a$. Asymmetry means that if $c > b$, then $b \not> a$. Transitivity means that if $a > b$, and $b > c$, then $a > c$. In other words, if a variable such as "conservatism" is measured on the ordinal level, one can infer that if person a is more conservative than person b, and if b is more conservative than c, then a is more conservative than c; and that the > relation is maintained with regard to all the individuals in the group.

To exemplify measurement at the ordinal level, consider the following common practice of measuring attitudes. Attitudes are measured by means of a series of questions (a test), with the alternative answers being ranked in ascending or descending order. For instance, one of the questions used to measure political alienation is "People like me have a lot of influence on government decisions." The respondent is asked to mark the number representing his or her degree of agreement or disagreement with this statement. The correspondence between the numbers and the answers might be made as in Table 4.2. Other questions on the same attitude are presented to the respondent, who can then be ranked according to his or her responses to all the questions. Suppose a researcher employs ten statements in all, each including four alternative answers, with (1) standing for "definitely agree," (2) for "agree," (3) for "disagree," and (4) for "definitely disagree." The highest score that can be achieved in this test is 40 (i.e., a score of 4 on each of the ten questions), and the lowest is 10. To simplify matters, it is assumed that the respondents answered all questions. A respondent whose score is

TABLE 4.2.

Definitely Agree	Agree	Disagree	Definitely Disagree
(1)	(2)	(3)	(4)

TABLE 4.3. Ranking Individuals by Their Scores on a Test of Political Alienation

Respondent	Score	Rank
S_1	10	seventh
S_2	27	third
S_3	36	second
S_4	25	fourth
S_5	20	fifth
S_6	40	first
S_7	12	sixth

40 will be regarded as the most alienated and will be ranked first. Another, whose score is nearest to 40—say, 36—will be ranked second, and so on for each individual in the group. The ranking process ends when all the respondents are ranked by their scores on the political alienation questionnaire.* Table 4.3 displays hypothetical scores and rankings of seven respondents. An examination of the table reveals that respondent S_6 is the most alienated, whereas respondent S_1 is the least alienated.

The ordinal level of measurement is unique up to a monotonic transformation; that is, any order-preserving transformation does not change the information obtained. It does not matter what numbers one assigns to a pair of objects or to a category of objects, so long as one is consistent. It is a matter of convenience whether to use lower numbers for the "more preferred" states, although we do usually refer to excellent performance as "first class" and to progressively inferior performances as "second class" and "third class."

The numbers assigned to ranked objects are called rank values. Rank values are assigned to objects according to the following rule: the greatest (or the smallest) object is assigned 1; the next in size, 2; the third in size, 3; and so on to the smallest (or greatest) object, which is assigned the last number in a given series. In the last example, S_6 is assigned 1, S_3 is assigned 2, S_2 is assigned 3, S_4 is assigned 4, S_5 is assigned 5, S_7 is assigned 6, and S_1 is assigned 7. It is important to stress that ordinal numbers indicate rank order and nothing more. The numbers do not indicate that the intervals between them are equal, nor do they indicate absolute quantities. It cannot be assumed that because the numbers are equally spaced, the properties they represent are also equally spaced. If two respondents have the ranks 7 and 5, and two others are ranked 4 and 2, one cannot infer that the differences between the two pairs are equal.

* Methods of attitude measurement are discussed in Chapter 6.

It has already been argued that transformations that do not change the order of properties are permissible at the ordinal level. Accordingly, mathematical operations and statistics that do not alter the order of properties are also permissible. For example, a statistic that describes the central tendency of ordinal numbers is the median. The median is not affected by changes in any numbers that are above or below it, so long as the number of numbers above and below remains the same (Chapter 9). Other appropriate statistics will be discussed in Chapters 10 and 13.

Interval Level *order with exact distance*

If, in addition to being able to order a property of an object in terms of the > relation, one also knows the exact distance between each of the objects, and this distance is constant, then an interval level of measurement has been achieved. In addition to saying that one object is greater than another, one can also specify by how many units the former is greater than the latter. For example, with interval measurement it is possible to say not only that Mike is taller than Bob but also that Mike is four inches taller. To make these quantitative comparisons, one must have a unit of measurement; if a unit of measurement has been established, an interval level of measurement has been achieved. Variables measured at the interval level include height, temperature, time, income, and intelligence quotient. An interval level of measurement, then, is characterized by a common and constant unit of measurement that assigns a real number to all pairs of objects in the ordered set. In this kind of measurement, the ratio of any two intervals (distances) is independent of the unit of measurement.

The structure of the interval level of measurement is such that the differences between objects are isomorphic to the structure of arithmetic. Numbers may be assigned to the positions of the objects so that the operations of arithmetic may be meaningfully executed on the differences between these numbers. The following formal properties are operative at the interval level of measurement:

1. Uniqueness: if a and b stand for real numbers, then $a + b$ and $a \times b$ represent one and only one real number.
2. Symmetry: if $a = b$, then $b = a$.
3. Commutation: if a and b denote real numbers, then $a + b = b + a$, and $ab = ba$.
4. Substitution: if $a = b$ and $a + c = d$, then $b + c = d$; and if $a = b$ and $ac = d$, then $bc = d$.
5. Association: if a, b, and c stand for real numbers, then $(a + b) + c = a + (b + c)$, and $(ab)c = a(bc)$.

Any change in the numbers assigned to the objects measured must preserve not only the ordering of the objects but also the relative differences between the objects. In a more formal language, the interval level of measurement is unique up to a linear transformation. Thus, the information obtained at this level is not affected if each number is multiplied by a positive constant and then a constant is added to this product. All the common statistics are applicable to interval data. These are considered in Chapters 9, 10, 11, and 13.

Ratio Level

Properties that have natural zero points can be measured on the ratio level of measurement. Properties such as weight, time, length, and area have natural zero points and are measured at the ratio level. At this level, the ratio of any two numbers is independent of the unit of measurement. The interval and the ratio levels are similar, and the rules by which numbers are assigned are the same, with one exception. For a ratio level of measurement, we apply the operations and the numbers to the total amount measured from an absolute zero point; for an interval level, we apply the operation to differences from one arbitrary point. A ratio level of measurement, most commonly encountered in the physical sciences, is achieved only when all four of these relations are operationally possible to attain: (1) equivalence, (2) greater than, (3) known distance of any two intervals, and (4) a true zero point.

Variables that can be measured at a ratio level can also be measured at the interval, ordinal, and nominal levels. As a rule, properties that can be measured at a higher level can also be measured at lower levels, but not vice versa. A variable such as party affiliation can be measured only at a nominal level. The formal properties characterizing each level of measurement are summarized in Table 4.4. The symbol X represents the existence of a property at a certain level, and O represents its absence. For example, whereas the equivalence property exists at each of the four levels, only the ratio level is characterized by a natural zero.

TABLE 4.4. Levels of Measurement and Their Characteristic Properties

Level	Equivalence	Greater Than	Fixed Interval	Natural Zero
Nominal	X	O	O	O
Ordinal	X	X	O	O
Interval	X	X	X	O
Ratio	X	X	X	X

Earlier, we pointed out the kinds of numerical operations and statistics that are, in a strict sense, legitimate and permissible with each level. Some authors tend to deemphasize this question (Games, 1967). The problem, however, is significant enough to warrant a few additional comments.

Mathematics and statistics are contentless languages. They deal with numbers and are not concerned with whether the numbers represent the essence of the matter being investigated. Their foremost advantage is in being precise and in enabling researchers to reveal information about data that cannot otherwise be revealed. A question such as "To what extent are a series of variables related?" can be meaningfully and precisely answered by computing measures of relations. Given the numbers, any kind of statistical operation can be performed. Social scientists are concerned with empirical properties, and numbers are used chiefly to gain a better understanding of the relations between these properties. Employing numerical systems and statistics that are not isomorphic to the structure of empirical properties is of little use in advancing our knowledge. Strictly speaking, statistics that assume a certain level of measurement should not be applied to data on a lower level, although they may be used for higher levels.

VALIDITY

The problem of validity arises because measurement in the social sciences is, with very few exceptions, indirect. Under such circumstances, researchers are never completely certain that they are measuring the precise property they intend to measure. Validity is concerned with the question "Is one measuring what one thinks one is measuring?" For example, does electoral turnout measure political development? Is agreement with the statement "This world is run by a few people in power, and there is not much the little guy can do about it" an indicator of the variable "alienation"? Clearly, it is always necessary to gather some sort of evidence which provides confidence that a measuring device does in fact measure what it appears to measure.

Three basic kinds of validity can be distinguished, each of which is concerned with a different aspect of the measurement situation: content validity, empirical validity, and construct validity. Each of these three types includes several kinds of evidence and has special value under certain conditions.

Content Validity

There are two common varieties of content validity: face validity and sampling validity. Face validity rests on the investigator's subjective evaluation as to the validity of a measuring instrument. In practice, face validity does not relate to the question of whether an instrument measures that which the researcher wishes to measure; rather, it concerns the extent to which it measures that which it appears to measure according to the researcher's subjective assessment. For example, an investigator intends to measure the variable "liberalism" by a questionnaire consisting of ten statements. After making up the questionnaire, the researcher reviews each statement to assess its content as to the extent to which it is related to "liberalism." To ascertain this assessment, the researcher might consult a number of specialists (judges). If there is agreement among the judges, the researcher will presumably contend that the questionnaire does not lack face validity and that, consequently, it measures "liberalism." Disagreement among the judges would impair the face validity of a measuring instrument.

The main problem with face validity is that there are no replicable rules for evaluating the measuring instrument, and one has to rely entirely on subjective judgments. Nevertheless, face validity serves a significant function in the process of constructing and formulating measuring instruments. A researcher who constructs an instrument must rely, first and foremost, on his or her own skill and judgment; at later stages, he or she can validate the instrument by performing other validity tests.

The primary concern of sampling validity is whether a given population of situations or behavior is adequately sampled by the measuring instrument in question. That is, does the content of the instrument adequately represent the content population of the property being measured? The underlying assumption of sampling validity is that every variable has a content population consisting of an infinite number of items (statements, questions, or indicators), and that a highly valid instrument constitutes a representative sample of these items. In practice, problems arise with the definition of a content population, since this is a theoretical and not an empirical population.* These problems impair the effectiveness of sampling validity as a test of an instrument's validity. However, sampling validity has an important advantage: it requires the researcher to become acquainted with all the items that are known to belong to the content population. Sampling validity is especially common in innovative research, where investigators attempt to construct instruments and employ them for the first time. After the instrument has been used, its validity can be evaluated by other tests.

Empirical Validity

The concern of empirical validity is with the relations between the measuring instrument and the measurement results. It is assumed that if

---

* These problems are discussed in Chapter 12, in which sampling techniques are presented.

a certain instrument is valid, then there should exist certain empirical relations between the results produced by the instrument and other properties or variables. Evidence to support the existence of a relation is obtained by measures of correlation appropriate to the level of measurement. Of the various tests designed to evaluate empirical validity, predictive validity is the most widely used. For this reason, it is discussed at some length below.

Predictive validity is characterized by prediction to an external measure referred to as a criterion and by checking a measuring instrument against some outcome. In other words, predictive validity is the correlation between the results of a given measurement with an external criterion. For example, one can validate an intelligence test by first obtaining a set of test scores on a group such as college freshmen and by then obtaining the grade-point averages that these freshmen made during their first year of college. A correlation coefficient is then computed between the two sets of measurements.* The obtained correlation is usually called the validity coefficient. Should the correlation between the scores on the intelligence test and the grade-point averages be equal to or greater than 0.50,† the predictive validity of the intelligence test is established. Other criteria that might be used to validate intelligence tests are ratings of adjustment, ratings of performance, and units produced in a certain period of time.

The process by which the predictive validity of an instrument is evaluated is illustrated in Figure 4.3. A property (U) is measured by a certain measuring instrument (M), and the researcher desires to evaluate the predictive validity of the instrument. To assess its predictive validity, a criterion (Q) whose validity is undisputed is used. The measurements obtained by M are correlated with the measurements obtained by Q. The size of the validity coefficient (r_{MQ}) measures the predictive validity of the instrument.

Two general points are to be noted when using the predictive-validity test. One relates to the validity of the criterion; and the other concerns the considerations which induce an investigator to use a measuring instrument and not the criterion itself; for example, why not measure grade-point averages directly? In regard to the second point, in some cases the criterion is technically difficult or too expensive to use, and in other cases investigators have to measure a property before they can make use of the criterion. For example, the scholastic ability of a student has to be evaluated prior to his or her admission to a university.

With regard to the validity of the criterion, two common methods

---

* A correlation coefficient is an index of the degree of relation between two measures; see Chapter 10.

† There is nothing sacred about this value. It is merely a matter of convention.

FIGURE 4.3.

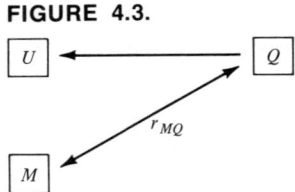

are used. One method rests on agreement among researchers that a certain criterion is valid to evaluate a measuring instrument. The agreement is subject to tests of face validity and sampling validity. A somewhat different method is to express the relationship between the instrument and the criterion in terms of the percentage of individuals (or other objects) who would be correctly classified by the instrument according to their known group membership (Helmstadter, 1970).

Suppose one desires to evaluate the validity of a measuring instrument designed to measure political conservatism. If one has theoretically sound reasons for arguing that people in the lower class are more conservative than people in the middle class, the two groups can be compared as a check of predictive validity. In this case, social class serves as an indirect criterion to the predictive validity of the instrument. If it is empirically observed that persons in the lower-class group are as conservative as persons in the middle-class group, the instrument lacks predictive validity. On the other hand, a relatively high correlation between social class and conservatism will validate the instrument. However, one should be aware that a high correlation is a necessary but not a sufficient condition to the predictive validity of an instrument, because the indirect criterion (social class) may also be related to properties other than political conservatism. Thus, the instrument might measure other properties instead of political conservatism. An indirect criterion, then, is more useful for disvalidating rather than validating a measuring instrument.

Construct Validity

Construct validity involves relating a measuring instrument to an overall theoretical framework in order to determine whether the instrument is tied to the concepts and theoretical assumptions that are employed. Cronbach, an early proponent of construct validity, has observed that "whenever a tester asks what a score means psychologically or what causes a person to get a certain test score, he is asking what concepts may properly be used to interpret the test performance" (1960:104). The theoretical notions one has about the property being measured lead the investigator to postulate various kinds and degrees of relationships between the property and other specified variables. In order to demonstrate construct validity of a measuring instrument, an investigator has to show that these relationships do in fact hold. We shall illustrate the utility of construct validity through Rokeach's (1960) research on dogmatism.

On the basis of theoretical reasoning, Rokeach constructed a dogmatism scale. This instrument consists of statements believed to tap close-mindedness, a way of thinking presumably associated with any ideology regardless of content. Rokeach argued that the ideological orientations of individuals are related to their personalities, thought processes, and behavior. One example among many that can be given is his prediction that dogmatism is related to opinionation. Rokeach undertook an extensive series of investigations aimed at testing his theory and the construct validity of his measuring instruments. In one instance he used what has been called the known-groups technique. In this method, groups of people with known characteristics are administered an instrument, and the direction of differences is predicted. Rokeach had college professors and graduate students select friends who, in their opinion, they considered to be open-minded and close-minded. The dogmatism scale clearly differentiated the two groups. When testing different religious groups, Rokeach found that Catholic students were more dogmatic than Protestant students, a finding that supported his prediction. Rokeach also found that communists obtained higher scores on the dogmatism scale than did liberals. Rokeach's findings are not clear-cut; nevertheless, they furnish evidence of the construct validity of the dogmatism measure.

Cronbach and Meehl (1955) describe the logical process of construct validity in the following way: first, a proposition that an instrument measures a certain property—say, property A—is set forth; second, the proposition is inserted into the present theory of property A; third, working through the theory, one predicts other properties that should be related to the instrument and properties that should exhibit no relation to the instrument; finally, one collects data that empirically confirm or reject the predicted relations. If the anticipated relationships are found, the instrument is considered valid. On the other hand, if the predictions do not hold up, there are three possibilities: (1) the instrument does not measure property A; (2) the theoretical framework that generated the predictions is incorrect; or (3) the research design failed to test the predictions properly. The researcher must then make a decision as to which of these three conditions has occurred. Such a decision is based on a careful reconstruction of each of the four steps constituting the validation process.

Campbell and Fiske (1959) suggested another method of construct validation involving correlation matrices. This is the convergent-discriminant conception of validity, or the multitrait-multimethod matrix technique. This method stems from the notion that different methods of measuring the same property should yield similar results, whereas different properties should yield different measurement results regardless of the measuring instrument. Operationally, this means that correlation coefficients among scores for a given property measured by different instruments should be higher than correlations among different properties measured by different instruments. Evidence of the construct validity of an instrument must therefore make use of both a convergent principle—that is, two measures of the same property should correlate highly with one another even though they represent different methods— and a discriminant principle, which implies that two measures should correlate highly with one another if they measure different properties even though a similar instrument is used. Thus, the validation process requires the computation of intercorrelations among measuring instruments that represent at least two properties, each measured by at least two different instruments.

In view of the distinction between the three types of validity, the reader is probably concerned as to which validity test to use when evaluating the validity of a given measuring instrument. Although there is no simple solution to this problem, its significance has led a team of experts from different disciplines to recommend that thorough examination of a measuring instrument must include information about the three types of validity.* Thus, in the first phase of the construction of a measuring tool, one might evaluate theories that would serve as a foundation for the instrument; next, a content population of items from which a representative sample is to be drawn might be defined; and finally, the validity of the instrument might be assessed by correlating it with an external criterion.

RELIABILITY

The subject of reliability would not occupy a central place in the methodological literature if the measuring instruments used by social scientists were fully valid. In many instances, validity evidence is almost entirely lacking; one has to evaluate the measuring instrument with respect to other characteristics and assume its validity. A frequently used method for evaluating an instrument is its degree of reliability.

Reliability is an indication of the extent to which a measure contains variable errors; that is, errors that differed from individual (or some other object) to individual during any one measuring instance, and that varied from time to time for a given individual measured twice by the

---

* See American Psychological Association Committee on Psychological Tests, "Technical Recommendations for Psychological Tests and Diagnostic Techniques," *Psychological Bulletin Supplement* 51 (1954):part 2, 1–38.

same instrument. For example, if one measures the length of a given object in two points of time with the same instrument—say, a ruler—and gets slightly different results, the instrument contains variable errors. Because of the indirect nature of measurements in the social sciences, the errors that occur when social variables are measured are likely to be much greater than those which occur when physical variables are measured. Factors such as momentary absent-mindedness, ambiguous instructions, and technical difficulties (a pencil breaks while the subject is filling in a questionnaire) may cause the introduction of variable errors. These errors are called variable errors because the amount of error varies from one individual to the next, and also because the amount of error is different for a given individual each time he or she is tested (Helmstadter, 1970).

Each measurement, then, consists of two components: a true component and an error component. Reliability is defined as the ratio of the true-score variance to the variance in the scores as measured.* Algebraically, each person's observed score can be represented as

$$x_i = t_i + e_i \qquad (4.1)$$

where x_i = score actually obtained by person i
t_i = true score for person i
e_i = amount of error that occurred for person i at the time the measurement was made

Expressed in variance terms, we get

$$\sigma_x^2 = \sigma_t^2 + \sigma_e^2$$

where σ_x^2 = variance of observed scores
σ_t^2 = variance of true scores
σ_e^2 = variance of errors

Reliability, defined as the ratio of true-score variance to observed-score variance, can be expressed as

$$\text{Reliability} = \frac{\sigma_t^2}{\sigma_x^2} = \frac{\sigma_x^2 - \sigma_e^2}{\sigma_x^2} \qquad (4.2)$$

From Equation (4.2) it can be seen that if the measurement involves nothing but error, then $\sigma_x^2 = \sigma_e^2$ and the reliability is zero. On the other hand, when there is no variable error at all, $\sigma_e^2 = 0$, and the ratio defined as reliability becomes

$$\frac{\sigma_x^2}{\sigma_x^2} = 1$$

* The variance is a measure of the spread of observations (scores); it is a description of the extent to which the observations differ from each other. See Chapter 9.

The reliability varies on a scale from zero to one, having the former value when the measurement involves nothing but error, and reaching one when there is no variable error at all in the measurement.

In practice, it is impossible to compute directly the true score independently of the amount of error that occurs in any particular measurement. Consequently, the ratio $\dfrac{\sigma_t^2}{\sigma_x^2}$ has to be estimated. There are three major ways of estimating reliability: the test-retest method, the parallel-forms technique, and the split-half method.

Test-Retest Method

This method corresponds most closely to the conceptual definition of reliability. A measuring instrument is administered to the same group of persons at two different times, and the correlation between the two sets of observations (scores) is computed. The obtained coefficient is the reliability estimate. With this method, error is defined as anything that leads a person to get a different score on one measurement from what he or she obtained on another measurement. Symbolically,

$$r_{xx'} = \frac{S_t^2}{S_x^2} \tag{4.3}$$

where x = performance on the first measurement
  x' = performance on the second measurement
  $r_{xx'}$ = correlation between x and x'
  S_t^2 = estimated variance of the true scores
  S_x^2 = calculated variance of the observed scores

The correlation $r_{xx'}$ provides an estimate of reliability defined as a ratio of the true variance to the observed variance.*

The test-retest method has two main limitations. First, the fact that an individual has been tested on one occasion may influence the measurement on subsequent tests. If the instrument is a questionnaire, the individual may remember specific questions and simply respond the same way as on the first administration, thus yielding a high but overestimated reliability estimate. Second, human properties are continually in a state of flux. It is possible that changes may have occurred in the measured property during the measurement interval, thus lowering the estimate of reliability. The test-retest method, then, may either overestimate or underestimate the true reliability of the instrument, and in many cases it is difficult to determine which has occurred.

---

* For methods of computing the correlation coefficient, see Chapter 10.

Parallel-Forms Technique

One way of overcoming the two limitations inherent in the test-retest method is through the use of the parallel-forms technique. This technique requires two forms of a measuring instrument that may be considered parallel. The two forms are then administered to a group of persons (or other objects), and the two sets of measures (scores) are correlated to obtain an estimate of reliability. With this technique, there is the problem of determining whether the two forms of an instrument are in fact parallel. Although statistical tests have been developed to determine whether the forms are parallel in terms of statistical measures, the checking with respect to the content of the forms must be made on a judgmental basis (Gulliksen, 1950).

Split-Half Method

This method estimates reliability by treating each of two or more parts of a measuring instrument as a separate scale. Suppose the measuring instrument is a questionnaire. The questionnaire is separated into two sets, using the odd-numbered questions for one set and the even-numbered questions for the other. Each of the two sets of questions is treated separately and scored accordingly. The two sets are then correlated, and this is taken as an estimate of reliability. To correct the correlation coefficient obtained between the two halves, the following formula, known as the Spearman-Brown prophecy formula, may be applied:

$$r_{xx'} = \frac{2r_{oe}}{1 + r_{oe}} \tag{4.4}$$

where $r_{xx'}$ = the reliability of the original test
r_{oe} = the reliability coefficient obtained by correlating the scores of the odd statements with the scores of the even statements

This correction assumes that an instrument that is $2n$ questions long will be more reliable than an instrument that is n questions long; and that since the length of the instrument has been halved by dividing it into odds and evens, the full instrument will have a higher reliability than would either half.

Cronbach, Rajaratnam, and Gleser (1963) introduced a revision to the traditional concept of reliability. These authors maintain that the chief concern of reliability theory is to answer the question "To what universe of potential measurements do we wish to generalize?" Thus, instead of reliability, the notion of generalizability is invoked. Generalizability implies that what one really wants to know about a set of measurements is: To what extent and with respect to what properties are they like other sets of measurements one might have taken from a given universe of potential measurements? And to what extent and with respect to what properties do they differ from other measurements one might have drawn from that universe of potential measurements? If one asks the likeness and difference questions with respect to a universe of potential measurements, one is asking about the limits of generalizability of the results of one's set of measurements. Whether we consider a particular relation among measurements to be evidence of reliability or generalizability depends on how we choose to define likeness and difference of conditions and measures. The construction of what is same and what is different in sets of measurements depends, in turn, upon the research problem.*

SUMMARY

Measurement is the assignment of numerals or numbers to variables, objects, or events according to rules. The most significant concept in this definition is "rules." The function of a rule is to tie the measurement procedure to reality; to establish isomorphism between a certain numerical structure and the structure of the variables being measured. Upon establishing isomorphism, mathematical and statistical operations with the numbers that stand for the properties can be executed. The requirement of isomorphism between numerical systems and empirical properties leads to a distinction among four levels of measurement: nominal, ordinal, interval, and ratio. In general, the mathematical operations permissible on a given set of numbers are dependent on the level of measurement obtained.

The notions of validity and reliability are inseparable from measurement theory. Validity is concerned with the question of whether one is measuring what one thinks one is measuring. Traditionally, three basic types of validity have been distinguished, each of which relates to a different aspect of the measurement situation: content validity, empirical validity, and construct validity. To validate a certain measuring instrument, information about these three types must be looked for. Reliability is an indication of the extent to which a measure contains variable errors. Operationally, it is assumed that any measure consists of a true component and an error component, and that the proportion of the amount of variation in the true component to the total variation measures reliability. This measure can be estimated by one or more of the following methods: test-retest, parallel-forms, and split-half. More

---

* For the mathematical formulation of the generalizability index see Cronbach, Rajaratnam, and Gleser (1963); and Goldine C. Gleser, Lee J. Cronbach, and Nageswars Rajaratnam, "Generalizability of Scores Influenced by Multiple Scores of Variance," *Psychometrika* 30 (1965): 395–418.

recently, the notion of generalizability has been introduced. Generalizability implies that the main concern of reliability is with the extent to which a set of measurements is like other sets of measurements that might have been drawn from a given universe of potential measurements.

REFERENCES

Campbell, Donald T., and Fiske, Donald W. "Convergent and Discriminant Validation by the Multitrait-Multimethod Matrix." *Psychological Bulletin* 56 (1959):81–105.

Cronbach, Lee J. *Essentials of Psychological Testing*. New York: Harper & Row, 1960.

Cronbach, Lee J., and Meehl, Paul E. "Construct Validity in Psychological Tests." *Psychological Bulletin* 52 (1955):281–302.

Cronbach, Lee J., Rajaratnam, Nageswars, and Gleser, Goldine C. "Theory of Generalizability: A Liberalization of Reliability Theory." *British Journal of Statistical Psychology* 16 (1963):137–163.

Games, Paul A. *Elementary Statistics*. New York: McGraw-Hill, 1967.

Gulliksen, Harold. *Theory of Mental Tests*. New York: Wiley, 1950.

Helmstadter, G. C. *Research Concepts in Human Behavior*. New York: Appleton-Century-Crofts, 1970.

Rokeach, Milton. *The Open and the Closed Mind*. New York: Basic Books, 1960.

Siegel, Sidney. *Nonparametric Statistics for Behavioral Sciences*. New York: McGraw-Hill, 1956.

Stevens, S. S. "Mathematics, Measurement and Psychophysics." In S. S. Stevens (ed.), *Handbook of Experimental Psychology*. New York: Wiley, 1951.

STUDY SUGGESTIONS

1. Historian Arthur Schlesinger, Jr., has taken the position that "the mystique of empirical social research leads its acolytes to accept significant only the questions to which the quantitative magic can provide answers. As an humanist, I am bound to reply that almost all important questions are important precisely because they are *not* susceptible to quantitative method. What he denies is that it can handle everything which the humanist must take into account; what he condemns is the assumption that things which quantitative methods can't handle don't matter. I would suggest that these are the things that matter most." Discuss.
2. Is "justice" measurable? If yes, why measure it?
3. What indicators would you suggest to select in constructing a mea-

sure for democracy? Specify the level of measurement for each indicator.
4. Is "intensity of interaction" a valid measure of group cohesiveness? How could the measure be validated?
5. Valid measures are also reliable, but reliable measures are not necessarily valid. Discuss and bring examples that support your arguments.

PART 2
Data Collection

CHAPTER 5
Observational Methods

Having decided what and how to investigate, the researcher is confronted with the problem of data collection. Social science data are obtained when investigators record observations about the phenomena being studied or have the observations recorded for them. In either case, three general forms of data collection may be distinguished: observational methods, interviewing and survey research, and nonreactive techniques. Each of these three forms refers to a number of particular methods, the most common of which are discussed in the following chapters. In the present chapter, we will consider methods of data collection that rely primarily on observation.

ROLES OF OBSERVATION

Modern social science is rooted in observation. Political scientists observe, among other things, the behavior of occupants of political roles; anthropologists observe simple societies and small communities; social psychologists observe interactions in small groups. In a sense, as the Webbs (1932:158) have pointed out, all social research begins and ends with observation:

> An indispensable part of the study of any social institution, wherever this can be obtained, is deliberate and sustained personal observation . . . from which the investigator may learn a lot. He clarifies his ideas, which gain in precision and discrimination. He revises his provisional classifications, and tests his tentative hypotheses. What is even more important, the student silently watching a town council or a trade union committee at work, or looking at the conference of politicians and educationists, picks up hints that help him to new hypotheses, to be, in their turn, tried on other manifestations of his subject matter.

The main virtue of observation is its directness; it makes it possible to study behavior as it occurs. The researcher does not have to ask people about their own behavior and the actions of others; he or she can simply watch them do and say things. This, in turn, enables the generation of firsthand data that are uncontaminated by factors standing between the investigator and the object of research. For example, when asking people to report their past behavior, distortions in recall may significantly contaminate the data, but the extent to which an individual is capable of memorizing things has little effect on data collected through observational methods.

Moreover, data collected by observation may describe the observed phenomena as they occur in their "natural" settings. All too many research techniques introduce elements of artificiality into the researched environment. An interview, for instance, is a form of face-to-face interaction, subject to peculiar problems because of the lack of consensus surrounding the roles of researcher and respondent. In such an interaction, the respondents might behave in a way that is not characteristic of their typical behavior (see Chapter 6). Artificiality can be minimized in observational studies, especially when the observed are not aware of their being observed or when they become accustomed to the observer and do not perceive of him or her as an intruder.

Some studies focus on subjects who are unable to give verbal reports or to articulate themselves meaningfully. Gellert (1955) has suggested that it is necessary to use observation in studies of children because it is difficult for children to introspect and to remain attentive to lengthy adult tasks. Riesman and Watson used observational methods because the people studied "had no language for discussing sociable encounters, no vocabulary for describing parties except to say that they were 'good' or 'bad,' no way of answering the question 'What do you do for fun?' " (1964:313).

Observational methods might also be used when persons are unwilling to express themselves verbally. Observation demands less active cooperation on the part of the individuals being studied than do verbal reports. Furthermore, verbal reports can be validated and compared with actual behavior through observation. Riley (1963) maintains that even though dispositions to act politically and socially may be best assessed by questionnaire, observational methods are required to assess the "acting out" of these dispositions. Finally, the relationship between a person and his or her environment is often best maintained in observational studies. Opportunities for analyzing the contextual background of behavior are improved by the researcher's ability to observe the environment in operation with the observed.

Observation takes many forms. It includes the most casual experiences as well as the most sophisticated laboratory devices (for example, one-way-vision screens, video cameras, and audio-introspectometers). The many forms of observation make it a suitable method for a variety of research purposes. It might be used in exploratory research to gain insights that will subsequently be tested as hypotheses. Observational methods might also be used to collect supplementary data that may interpret or qualify findings obtained by other methods; or they might be used as the primary methods of data collection in descriptive studies.

Observation may take place in "natural" settings or in the laboratory. A problem such as coalition formation may be studied as it occurs in a real-life situation or in the laboratory room. Observational procedures may range from complete flexibility, guided only by a general problem, to the use of specialized instruments prepared in advance. The researchers may themselves participate in the activities of the group they are observing; they may be viewed as members of the group but minimize their participation; they may be defined as observers who are not part of the group; or their presence might be concealed from the people being observed (Selltiz et al., 1959). Whatever the purpose of the study and the observational procedure used, three major considerations are to be dealt with if the obtained data are to be scientifically meaningful. These will be discussed in the following section.

CHARACTERISTICS OF OBSERVATIONS

The first and most significant consideration concerns a decision with respect to what should be observed. Suppose someone interested in studying the relation between frustration and aggression hypothesizes that frustration covaries with aggression. To test this hypothesis, frustration and aggression are to be observed. This, however, requires clear and precise operational definitions of the two variables. Moreover, the definitions must be subjected to checks on validity and reliability.

Observable indicants of the variables "frustration" and "aggression," and of other variables in general, might be nonverbal, spatial, extralinguistic, or linguistic (Weick, 1968). Nonverbal behavior is "the body movements of the organism . . . [and] consists of motor expressions . . . [which] may originate in various parts of the body" (Ekman, 1957:141). Nonverbal behavior has been extensively studied, and it has been repeatedly shown to be a valid indicator of social and psychological processes.* Ekman suggests that observations of nonverbal behavior generate data which can serve "to repeat, contradict, or substitute for a verbal message, as well as accent certain words, maintain the com-

---

* See, for example, Albert E. Scheflen, "Natural History Method in Psychotherapy: Communicational Research," in Louis A. Gottschalk and Arthur H. Auerbach, eds., *Methods of Research in Psychotherapy* (New York: Appleton-Century-Crofts, 1966), pp. 263–289.

municative flow, reflect changes in the relationship in association with particular verbal messages and indicate a person's feeling about his verbal statement" (1965:441).

Spatial behavior refers to the attempts of individuals to structure the space around them. For example, people move toward, move away from, maintain closeness, and maintain distance. The range, frequency, and outcomes of such movements provide significant data as is illustrated by Alger's (1966) study on the spatial behavior of the 110 delegates on the Administrative and Budgetary Committee of the United Nations General Assembly. Alger observed 69 of the 70 meetings of this committee during the fall of 1962 and recorded 3,475 private interactions (participants in private conversations, length of private conversations, the name of the initiator of the private conversation, and so on). The author observed that records of private interaction give a different view of the committee activities than do records of participation in public debate (e.g., attendance in meetings and resolution sponsorship). Furthermore, it was found that there was a higher correlation between number of interactions and number of persons in delegation, amount of United Nations support, and the wealth of a nation than there was between number of public speeches and these same measures.

Words, or linguistic content, constitute only a small portion of verbal behavior. Noncontent behaviors such as rate of speaking, loudness, tendency to interrupt, and pronunciation peculiarities constitute a fruitful source of data and are generally referred to as extralinguistic behavior. The significance of extralinguistic behavior to the study of human behavior has already been documented in numerous studies. For example, a vocal characteristic such as pitch accurately measures emotional states (Soskin and Kauffman, 1961). The average unit length of spontaneous speech increases as the size of the group increases (Soskin and John, 1963). These are but two applications of extralinguistic indicants to the study of behavior; they demonstrate the potential significance of noncontent behavior to observational studies.

The fourth class of indicants of variables is termed linguistic behavior; that is, the manifest content of talking and the structural characteristics of talk. Indices of linguistic behavior have been widely used in studies on social interaction. Bales (1950), for example, devised a system for organizing and coding the process of interaction in groups involved in problem-solving activities. Bales's system, known as "Interaction Process Analysis," or IPA, contains twelve kinds of distinctive behaviors within which the interaction of group members can be coded and analyzed. The IPA code of categories is shown in Table 5.1.

The second major consideration in observational studies concerns the timing and the recording of observations. Obviously, it is impossible to make continuous observations from the beginning to the end of time, so a decision must be made about when to observe. An acceptable approach to this problem is to follow a time-sampling schedule. Time sampling refers to the selection of observation units at different points in time. Observation units can be selected in systematic ways so as to ensure representation of a defined population of behavior. For example, one might make one's observations for a fifteen-minute period of each hour randomly selected after stratification by day of the week and hour of the day (see Chapter 12). Time samples have the advantage of assuring the researcher of representative samples of ongoing occurrences. However, they are inadequate when the purpose is to observe events or behavior that occur infrequently.

TABLE 5.1. IPA Code of Categories

Social-emotional Area: *Positive*		A	1.	Shows solidarity (raises others' status, gives help, reward)
			2.	Shows tension release (jokes, laughs, shows satisfaction)
			3.	Agrees (shows passive acceptance, understands, complies)
Task Area: *Neutral*	Answers	B	4.	Gives suggestions (direction, implying autonomy for others)
			5.	Gives opinions (evaluation, analysis, expresses feeling, wish)
			6.	Gives orientation (information, repeats, clarifies, confirms)
	Questions	C	7.	Asks for orientation (information, repetitions, confirmation)
			8.	Asks for opinions (evaluation, analysis, expression of feeling)
			9.	Asks for suggestions (direction, possible ways of action)
Social-emotional Area: *Negative*		D	10.	Disagrees (shows passive rejection, formality)
			11.	Shows tension (asks for help, withdraws out of field)
			12.	Shows antagonism (deflates others' status, defends or asserts self)

SOURCE: Robert F. Bales. "A Set of Categories for the Analysis of Small Group Interaction." *American Sociological Review* 15 (April 1950):258 (with permission).

In addition to developing a time-sampling design, a system for obtaining accurate records of the occurrences has to be devised. Such a system can be constructed by either a deductive approach or an empirical approach (see Chapter 8). A deductive approach implies that the researcher begins with a conceptual definition, then specifies indicators of the property, and then standardizes and validates the resulting instrument (Straus, 1964). The deductive approach is implemented when observations are assigned to categories at the time the record is made. On the other hand, the empirical approach requires first the selection of indicators and postpones definitions until some pattern is identified. Each approach involves some risk. With the deductive approach, it is difficult to foresee whether the conceptual definition is precise. The empirical approach, on the other hand, poses difficulties in interpreting the observations. The ideal way to reduce these risks is to combine the two approaches. Weick suggests that "in the ideal sequence, the observer would start with the empirical approach, obtain extensive records of natural events, induce some concepts from the records, and then collect a second set of records which are more specific and pointed more directly at the induced concept" (1968:402).

Regardless of whether the investigator opts for the deductive or empirical approach, or combines the two, the categories to which observations are assigned must exhibit certain characteristics. Medley and Mitzel (1963:298) suggest that a category system is to

> limit the observation to one segment or aspect of . . . behavior, and construct a finite set of categories into one and only one of which every unit observed can be classified. The record obtained purports to show, for each period of observation, the total number of units of behavior which occurred and the number classifiable in each category.

In other words, the categories must be explicit, exhaustive, and mutually exclusive. An explicit category is specified in terms of the occurrence to be observed, the situation in which the occurrence takes place, and the event that precedes or follows the observed occurrence (Beller, 1959). For instance, Borgatta (1962:278) has explicated the "shows tension increase" category in his Interaction Process Scores observational system in the following way:

> In this category are scored the periods of tenseness that grow largely out of impasses or bankruptcy of conversation. Most of the scores that fall into this category are the awkward pauses, which are usually punctuated by clearing of throats, looking around by one person or another, etc. For the whole group, however, it is sometimes noted that the level of participation grows more tense because of the general personal involvement of the group.

The third major consideration in observational studies relates to the degree of inference required of the observer. Most records in observation involve inferences. An investigator observes a certain act or behavior; he or she must process this observation and make an inference that the behavior measures a certain variable. Some observational systems require a low degree of observer inference; for example, such straightforward acts as "asks a question," "suggests a course of action," "interrupts another group member," and the like. Many acts, however, require a higher degree of inference. Suppose one observes an adult striking a child. An inference has to be made whether this act represents "aggression," "aggressive behavior," "hostility," or some other variable (see Chapter 4). The correctness of such an inference depends to a large extent on the competence of the observer. Well-trained observers are likely to make more reliable inferences, other things being equal.

To increase the reliability of inferences, training programs applicable to various observational situations were designed. Typically, a program begins with an exposition of the theory, the research hypotheses involved in a given study, and an explanation of the category-system constructed to record the observations. After the trainees have had an opportunity to raise questions, they try to use the category-system on a group that demonstrates the phenomena of the type the observers will be expected to record when the actual data collection begins (Heyns and Zander, 1954).

The extent to which decisions regarding the three major considerations are rigorously implemented is a criterion by which one can distinguish between controlled and noncontrolled observational systems. A controlled observational system is typified by clear and explicit decisions on what, how, and when to observe; a noncontrolled system posits fewer commitments on the part of the researcher and allows greater flexibility. For example, in controlled observation, a time sample is usually drawn prior to observation; in noncontrolled observation, time samples are rarely taken. The choice between controlled and noncontrolled observation depends to a large extent on the research design; that is, controlled observation is most frequently utilized with experimental research designs and seldom with quasi-experimental designs. In the next three sections, controlled and noncontrolled observational systems are discussed.

CONTROLLED OBSERVATIONS

Controlled observations are carried out either in the laboratory or in the field. These two settings share a common concern with respect to the researcher's purpose. In both, the investigator wishes to infer causality by maximizing control over extrinsic and intrinsic variables while employing one of the various experimental research designs and systematically recording observations. We shall first discuss the peculiarities of laboratory experimentation.

Laboratory Experimentation

The most controlled method of data collection in the social sciences is laboratory experimentation; it involves the introduction of conditions in a controlled environment (laboratory) that simulates certain features of a natural environment. Laboratory experimentation allows the construction of a situation with closely supervised manipulation of one or more variables at a time in order to observe the effects produced.

Classic examples of laboratory experimentation are the Asch (1958) experiments on interpersonal influence. Asch's objective was to examine the social and personal conditions that induce individuals to yield to or resist group pressures when such pressures are perceived to be contrary to fact. Asch developed a procedure for placing an individual in intense disagreement with his or her peers and for measuring the effect of this relationship upon him or her. Eight individuals were instructed to match the length of a given line with one of three unequal lines. Each member of the group was asked to announce her or his judgment publicly. In the midst of the test, one individual found himself or herself suddenly contradicted by the entire group. This contradiction was repeated a number of times during the experiment, because Asch had instructed the seven other members of the group to respond at certain points with wrong judgments. The errors of the majority were large, ranging between 0.50 inch and 1.75 inches. The eighth individual confronted a situation in which a group unanimously contradicted the evidence of her or his senses. This individual, commonly referred to as the critical subject, was the object of investigation. Asch also used a control group in which the errors introduced by the majority were not of the same order encountered under experimental conditions. One of the interesting findings was the marked movement toward the majority: "One third of all the estimates in the critical group were errors identical with or in the direction of the distorted estimates of the majority. The significance of this finding becomes clear in the light of the virtual absence of errors in the control group . . ." (1958:177).

The Asch experiment exemplifies the two major advantages of laboratory experimentation: it allows rigorous control over extrinsic and intrinsic variables, and it provides unambiguous evidence about causation. Asch eliminated the effects of many variables that might have caused critical subjects to yield to or to resist group pressure; this increased the possibility of observing existing differences due to their experimental treatment. Moreover, Asch could unambiguously specify what caused the movement of his critical subjects toward the majority, because he himself controlled and manipulated the independent variable—the seven members of the group who were told when to respond with wrong judgments. Furthermore, Asch varied the experimental treatment in a systematic way, thus allowing for the precise specification of important differences. Finally, the experiment was constructed in a way that enabled a clear detection of the effects of the experimental treatment: the critical subjects had to state their judgments publicly. They had to declare themselves and to take a definite position vis-à-vis their peers. They could not avoid the dilemma by pointing to conditions external to the experimental situation.

Laboratory experiments vary in complexity and design, depending on the research problem and the ingenuity of the experimenter. For example, Deutsch and Krauss (1960, 1962) developed the "Acme-Bolt trucking game" to study the effects of conflict and threat on bargaining and cooperation. In this experiment, each subject "operates" a trucking firm (Acme or Bolt) through a control box and a visual display panel, with lights showing the movement of trucks. A constant sum of money, minus the cost for the trip's elapsed time, is paid to each player for carrying a load from a starting point to a destination. As shown in Figure 5.1, each subject has two routes to his or her destination: a short main route and a long alternate route. The characteristics of this experiment are such that if a subject takes the alternate route, he or she loses at least ten cents on the trip; if both take the main route, they will meet on its one-lane section and be deadlocked unless one of them backs up. The

FIGURE 5.1. Subjects' Road Map in the Acme-Bolt Trucking Game

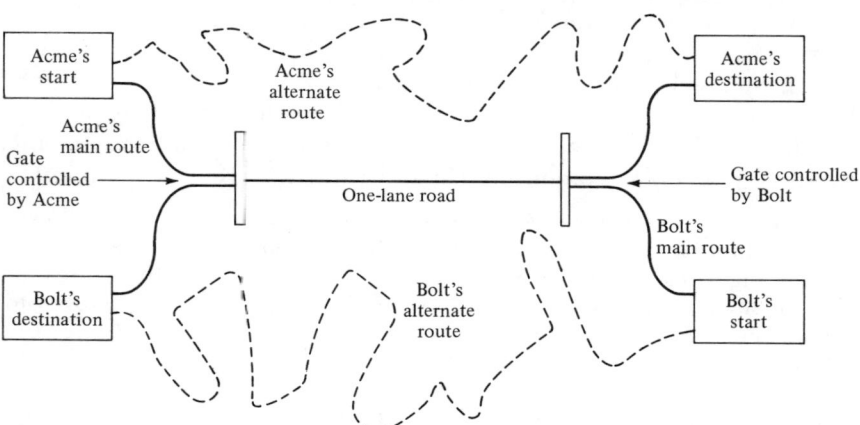

SOURCE: Morton Deutsch and Robert M. Krauss. "The Effect of Threat upon Interpersonal Bargaining." *Journal of Abnormal and Social Psychology* 61 (1960):183. Copyright © 1960 by the American Psychological Association. Reprinted by permission.

conflict lies in the consideration that it is to each subject's interest to go through the one-lane route before the other, but that some agreement on ensuring access to the main route is mutually beneficial. This problem contains both competitive and cooperative elements, thus providing a basis for the investigation of variables that affect the difficulty with which bargainers can reach an agreement. For instance, the researchers investigated the effect of a threat in the form of "gates" that a subject could close to indicate that the other subject could be prevented from completing her or his trip on the main route. The three basic conditions set in the experiment were such that a gate was possessed by both subjects, only one subject, or neither subject. Deutsch and Krauss (1960) hypothesized that the competitive interest provided by gates would introduce elements of self-esteem that would make cooperation most difficult in the two-gate situation and least difficult in the no-gate situation. The results of this experiment supported the hypothesis that the joint outcome—that is, the combined payoff of Acme plus Bolt—was highest in the no-gate case and lowest in the two-gate condition.

To examine the effects of joint or shared rewards in cooperative behavior, Azrin and Lindsley (1956) used several mechanical instruments to help with their experiment. They first asked pairs of children to play a "game" in which they were reinforced with candy when they made a cooperative response. The children faced one another across a table with a glass partition between them. Each had a metal stylus and a metal plate with three holes. The children were instructed to play the game any way they wanted to by placing the styli in the holes. Next, they were told: "While you are in that room some of these [jelly beans] will drop into this cup. You can eat them here if you want to or you can take them home with you." The children were then left alone. The apparatus used in the experiment was wired so that if the styli were placed in opposite holes within 0.04 second of each other, a red light flashed on the table and a single jelly bean fell into a cup accessible to both children. This was an indicant of cooperative response, and the candy served as reinforcement. Azrin and Lindsley (1956:101) report:

> Observation through a one-way vision screen disclosed that leader-follower relationships were developed and maintained in most cases. Almost immediately eight teams divided the candy in some manner. With two teams, one member at first took all the candy until the other member refused to co-operate. When verbal agreement was reached in these two teams, the members then co-operated and divided the candy.

These three experiments illustrate both the significance and the variability in setting the stage for the experiment. Experimenters have to construct a set of procedures that capture the meaning of their conceptualization and that enable the testing of hypotheses. This, in turn, demands the invention of a method of measuring the effect this has on the behavior of the subject and the construction of a setting within which the basic manipulations make sense and the measurements are valid.

At this point, the reader might question the meaningfulness of these laborious procedures, since none of the experiments described above represents a "real-world" situation. In the Asch experiment, critical subjects were judging a very clear physical event (the length of lines) and were contradicted by their peers. However, in everyday life, it is almost inconceivable to find oneself in a situation where the unambiguous evidence of one's senses is contradicted by the unanimous judgments of one's peers.

This seeming dilemma is resolved if a distinction is drawn between two senses in which any given experiment can be said to be realistic (Aronson and Carlsmith, 1968). In one sense, an experiment is realistic if the situation is realistic to the subject, if it involves that individual and has impact on him or her. This kind of realism is commonly termed experimental realism. Thus, in the Asch experiment, the critical subjects underwent an experience that caused them to exhibit signs of tension and anxiety. The critical subjects were reacting to a situation that was as "real" for them as any of their ordinary experiences.

The second sense of realism refers to the extent to which events occurring in a laboratory setting are likely to occur in the "real world." This type of realism is called mundane realism. An experiment that is high on mundane realism and low on experimental realism does not necessarily yield more meaningful results than one that is high on experimental realism and low on mundane realism. Were Asch to observe interpersonal influences in the "real world," he probably would not have found a situation so clearly structured for observing the effects of group pressure on individual members. Moreover, assuming that such a situation could have been found, the effects of intrinsic and extrinsic variables could not have been controlled for, and the obtained findings would have been ambiguous and inconclusive. Experimental realism enables the experimenter to increase the internal validity of the experiment by producing a significant effect within the experimental situation.

With all their advantages, laboratory experiments are not immune to systematic bias, the effects of which have only recently been demonstrated. Two types of bias may intrude into experiments: bias due to the demand characteristics of the experimental situation itself and bias due to the unintentional influence of the experimenter (see Chapter 3).

Bias due to demand characteristics results in situations where the subjects know that they are in an experimental situation and are aware of the fact that they are being observed and that certain responses are expected from them. Consequently, subjects may not respond to the experimental manipulations as such, but to their interpretation of what responses these manipulations are supposed to elicit from them. Even if the subject is "told that there are no right or wrong responses, he knows that there are answers that will enhance or diminish his value as a person in the experimenter's eyes" (Aronson and Carlsmith, 1968: 61). The subject may discover the research hypothesis and respond in a manner consistent with it in an attempt to cooperate with the experimenter. One common way to reduce this source of bias is through deception. Subjects are not told the true hypothesis of the experiment but some other credible hypothesis. Thus, if a subject modifies his or her responses so as to support or refute the incorrect hypothesis, the results relating to the true hypothesis are not affected in a systematic way.

The second kind of bias may result from the experimenters themselves. To demonstrate the experimenter bias, Rosenthal and Fode (1963) devised a person-perception experiment in which they used twenty photographs of persons that were previously judged to be neutral with respect to reflecting failure or success. Subjects were asked to rate each photo along a success-failure continuum. In running the test, several experimenters expected high ratings and several expected low ratings. Those expecting subjects to rate the pictures high obtained significantly higher ratings than those expecting low ratings. An acceptable solution that might reduce the experimenter bias is to keep the person who runs the experiment ignorant of those specific experimental conditions that subjects are in. Another technique that achieves similar results is the use of taped instructions. With taped instructions, unnecessary interactions between the experimenter and the subjects are avoided, thus minimizing the chances for the introduction of bias.*

Observations in the laboratory are recorded on the spot during the experimental session. Often, mechanical devices such as motion pictures, tape recordings, and television are used to obtain an overall view of the occurrences. Next, the units of observation are assigned to a well-structured category-system, such as the one reproduced in Table 5.1. Categorization may also take place during the experimental session if the system of recording is prepared and pretested well in advance. With a well-prepared system of recording and trained observers, the degree of inference required of the observers is minimal.

Field Experimentation

The major difference between laboratory experimentation and experiments in the field is, as the terms imply, the setting. A laboratory experiment involves the introduction in a controlled environment of condi-

---

* For a comprehensive discussion of these and other bias-reducing techniques, see Aronson and Carlsmith (1968:61–70).

tions that simulate certain features of a natural environment. A field experiment, on the other hand, is a research study in a "natural" situation in which one or more independent variables are manipulated by the experimenter under as carefully controlled conditions as the situation permits. In terms of research designs, the contrast between the laboratory experiment and the field study is not sharp. The differences are mostly matters of degree. However, the difficulties involved in controlling intrinsic and especially extrinsic variables are often greater in field experiments.

A classic example of field experimentation is the Coch and French (1948) study on resistance to change. The research objective was to find out why production workers strongly resist changes in methods and jobs, and what can be done to overcome this resistance. To this end, participation in planning was regarded as an independent variable that affects production, resignations, and aggression. It was hypothesized that resistance to change could be significantly reduced by increased participation in decisions or processes that lead to change. This hypothesis was tested in the main plant of the Harwood Manufacturing Corporation. Factory workers were divided into three groups. The members of the control group did not participate in any of the discussions and decisions about changes in the plant. Two experimental groups did participate in discussion and decision in different degrees: participation by representation and total participation. It was found that the no-participation group developed strong resistance after changes in the plant occurred; the group that participated through representation developed very little resistance; and the total-participation group did not develop any resistance. Moreover, in the total-participation group, the level of production increased after the changes in the plant occurred. The investigators could infer that the experimental treatment (i.e., the degree of participation in discussions and decisions about changes before executing them) was inversely related to resistance to change; the higher the degree of participation, the lower the resistance to change.

The Coch and French study was a field experiment in which the investigators relied mainly on systematic observation within a naturally occurring behavior system. The experimenters intruded in this system by introducing and manipulating one independent variable, the effects of which were clearly observed. This experiment illustrates the main virtue of field experiments: they are appropriate for investigating complex social interactions, processes, and changes in natural settings.

As indicated earlier, the main weakness of field experiments is that of control; the control of intrinsic and especially of extrinsic variables is rarely as tight as in laboratory experiments. To meet this problem, French (1953) has suggested the following procedures. First, whenever possible, the experiment is replicated in the same setting. For example,

French (1950) replicated the Harwood Manufacturing Corporation experiment and obtained results similar to those obtained in the original experiment. If replication is not intended, preliminary experiments are conducted in order to ensure that the experimental manipulations produce observable differences. If the experimental manipulations are not sufficiently strong to produce differences, the field conditions are simplified. It has also been recommended that experimental treatments be applied to units of small size (individuals or small groups) rather than large institutions. Smaller units permit easier manipulation and provide opportunities for preliminary experimentation and replication. Finally, the size of the experimental manipulation is reduced by confining it to a relatively short period of time; longer periods increase the chances of unforeseen events taking place.

Procedures for recording observations in field experiments are similar to those in laboratory experimentation. Records are taken on the spot during the experiment. Mechanical instruments such as tape recordings, motion pictures, and television are standard aids in field experimentation. The systematization of data is achieved through the use of observation schedules and category-systems discussed earlier in this chapter.

SIMULATION

Simulations constitute the third major form of observational method. A simulation is an operating model that represents some aspect of reality. The referent, or reality, represented by a simulation may be some present, past, or hypothetical phenomenon. The model simplifies reality, and the elements of reality incorporated in it are reduced in complexity (Hermann, 1968). Unlike other models, the elements in simulations are capable of assuming different values as a given simulation operates. That is, simulations contain rules for transforming the values of their elements in such a way that when a value of one element is changed, related properties can be adjusted accordingly. The ability to control and manipulate time and change is the distinguishing feature of simulations and the reason for terming them "operating models" (Brody, 1963).

The principal research advantage of simulations are the manipulative opportunities that they provide. These opportunities facilitate research in various ways. First, simulations enable one to investigate experimentally, phenomena that are usually studied quasi-experimentally. Consequently, the researcher may control for extrinsic and intrinsic variables and identify confounding factors that are hard to delineate even in field experiments. Zelditch and Evan point out that the common nonexperimental technique of "dealing with contamination is to hold constant the contaminating factor, c.[*] But where a and c, or b and c, are highly correlated in natural settings, obtaining a sufficient number of the necessary contrasts may be costly or even impossible. In such a case it may be necessary to create the required contrasts artificially" (1962:50). In this sense, simulations can be regarded as extensions of experimental methods.

Second, simulations enhance the generation of researchable hypotheses and the construction of heuristic models. The ability to re-create past or rare events, and to construct situations that are ordinarily inaccessible to researchers, may yield new insights into previously unexplained or partially explained phenomena. For example, the TEMPER simulation was designed to simulate Cold War conflicts. One of its major accomplishments lies in its explicit modeling, which permits the operationalization of variables previously unstudied. For example, one hypothesis in TEMPER is: "Tactical hostility between all nations is used to determine the perceived values for counterforce utility, desired land, level of military operations, and verbal threat" (Clemens, 1968:82). This proposition was transformed into the following explicit equation:†

$$\text{Tactical hostility} = \frac{\text{perceived desire for land}}{4}$$
$$\times \text{ military capacity} + 5 \text{ (tactical threat)}$$

where Military capacity = (military coercion motivation)
+ (defense spending motivation)
+ 10 (tax motivation) + 5 (tactical threat)

Third, simulations offer opportunities to predict future states of affairs. For instance, the Simulmatics Corporation has applied a simulation to the 1960 and 1964 American presidential elections. The electorate is represented by 480 types of voters. Every voter type is identified by a combination of characteristics, including geographical region, city size, race, sex, religion, and socioeconomic status. For each voter type, information is obtained on 52 political variables, such as intention to vote and opinions on various political issues. Before the simulation is applied to a particular election, the researcher decides what variables and issues are most salient. Equations are formulated to express the impact of the salient issues on the different types of voters (Pool, Abelson, and Popkin, 1965).

Three general types of simulations may be distinguished: (1) computer simulations; (2) man simulations, or games; and (3) man-computer simulations. This classification is based on the extent to which human

---

* For methods of statistical control, see Chapter 11.
† For the evaluation of the equation, see Clemens (1968:82–83).

actors are involved in the operation of a specific simulation. In computer simulations, for example, humans are not involved as elements or units of the model.

Computer simulations are operational models that have been programed for high-speed computing equipment. The computer is used to generate a sequence of interactions that constitute a process. Three basic units can be distinguished in the computer: a memory unit, an operation unit, and a control unit. The most important feature of computer simulation is a program of instructions that is stored in the memory unit at the start of the simulation (the run). The memory unit also stores data for transfer and use according to directions from the control unit. The operation unit executes those logical and arithmetical operations that it is instructed to carry out by the control unit. Since all forms of instructions are contained in the program, computer simulation is essentially a programing task.*

Benson (1959) designed a simple computer simulation program that reproduces a number of features of the international political system. The simulation describes political counteractions to specific actions in well-structured situations and the effects on situations of a given action-counteraction cycle. The model consists of action and situational variables and a program that explicates the relationship of variables to outcomes. The action variables consist of nine possible acting nations (the nine major powers); nine possible target nations (which are chosen from recent tension areas); and nine possible intensity levels of action: diplomatic protest, United Nations action, severing diplomatic relations, propaganda-subversion campaign, boycott, troop movements, full mobilization, limited war, and all-out war. The situational variables describe the state of the international system at any given moment when action is taking place. Four situational variables are included in the model: national power expressed in terms of war potential, distribution of this power, the degree of involvement of one state with another, and the propensity of each state to act or counteract.

One action cycle is described as follows: action instructions that specify the acting nation, the form of the action, and the place in which it takes place are

> entered in the machine as a "play." Following . . . [these instructions] the program automatically selects a logical counteraction for each of the other eight large states. . . . After the choice of counteractions, the program recomputes the relative strength of the nine actor states and assigns them new war potential indices. By comparing these with the original set, gain or loss from the cycle of activity is revealed. At the choice of the user of the pro-

---

* For an excellent introduction to the computer and basic programing, see Alexandra I. Forsythe et al., *Computer Science: A First Course* (New York: Wiley, 1969).

gram, the action cycle may substitute the modified indices of power distribution resulting from the previous play for the original set, and use them as the basis for the selection of counteractions. . . . Also at the choice of the user, the program will hold the results of two successive cycles and compare them for relative advantages or disadvantages to the actor state or states. (Benson, 1959:2–3)

The second type of simulation, man simulations, or games, uses people in a laboratory setting to simulate people in the real world. For example, a number of individuals are divided into groups that are placed in a laboratory room. Each group is instructed to imagine that it represents the government of some nation. Simulated international situations involving treaties, alliances, threats, wars, and the like are then played out by these groups.

Coleman (1964) constructed a simple legislative game to examine collective decision-making and bargaining. Six to eleven individuals assume the role of legislators representing hypothetical constituencies. These legislatures attempt to remain in office by passing bills that the voters in their constituencies favor and by defeating bills that the voters oppose. In the bargaining period that precedes the vote on each bill, any legislator may agree to support bills that do not affect his or her constituents in exchange for a vote from another legislator on a bill that is significant for his or her reelection. After the game's eight bills have been passed, tabled, or defeated, the legislators are able to predict whether they will be reelected for another session.*

The third type of simulation is man-computer. This type is an attempt to combine the advantages and overcome the limitations of the two other types. Typically, those parts of a theory that are developed are programed for the computer, and those aspects that are ambiguous are represented by human players. In man-computer simulations, persons might play the role of decision-makers, while the computer is responsive to the players' activities.

The Northwestern Inter-Nation Simulation (INS) is illustrative of the virtues of man-computer simulations. In the INS, as Guetzkow (1963:106) describes it:

> Actions with the inter-nation simulation originate through individuals and groups. The human beings participating in the simulation represent the decision-makers within national political systems. A group of 2 or 3 to 5 or 6

---

* Man simulations are also being used for teaching purposes. However, the findings on their pedagogical merits are inconclusive. For a positive evaluation, see Chadwick F. Alger, "Use of the Inter-Nation Simulation in Undergraduate Teaching," in Harold Guetzkow et al., eds., *Simulation in International Relations: Developments for Research and Teaching* (Englewood Cliffs, N.J.: Prentice-Hall, 1963). For a critical view, see Bernard C. Cohen, "Political Gaming in the Classroom," *Journal of Politics* 24 (1962):367–381.

decision-makers along with their resources and capabilities operate as a nation. Some or all of these nations in turn may combine to form supra-groups. . . . The simulation thus consists of components at three levels—individuals (decision-makers); groups (nations); and supra-groups (alliances or international organizations).

The simulation rests upon a series of variables that are specified mathematically before a run. For instance, the relation of outcome of revolution to a nation's internal control is explained by the formula

$$p(SR) = 1 - k'(FC_{ic}/FC) \tag{5.1}$$

where $k = 2$; $p(SR)$ is the probability of success of revolution; and (FC_{ic}/FC) designates the percentage of total national force capability allocated to the maintenance of internal control (Guetzkow, 1963). The variables describing the internal characteristics of a nation are programed, and their initial values are set by the researchers. Subsequently, the values are manipulated by fixed equations. In contrast, relations among the variables related to the international system are not programed. The players who act as internal or external decision-makers determine the relations. The players' role is to decide, among other things, how to allocate resources in order to accomplish goals that are either brought to the game or developed during its course. The players may negotiate, bargain, threaten, form coalitions, wage war, or carry out other plans that involve resource allocations.

As with other data-collection methods, the simulation method has some built-in problems, the most significant of which centers on the issue of validity. In order to incorporate simulation findings into the scientific body of knowledge, a high degree of correspondence has to be established between any given operating model and its reference system. To date, however, the most frequently applied criterion of validation has been face validity, which is based on impressionistic evaluations of researchers and players (see Chapter 4).

PARTICIPANT OBSERVATION

The least controlled method of observation is participant observation. This method refers to those "forms of research in which the investigator devotes himself to attaining some kind of membership in or close attachment to an alien or exotic group that he wishes to study" (Wax, 1968: 238). In doing so, the participant observer attempts to share the world view and to adopt the perspective of the people in the situation being observed. His or her role is that of "conscious and systematic sharing, insofar as circumstances permit, in the life activities, and on occasion, in the interests and affects of a group of persons" (Kluckhohn, 1940: 339). Direct participation on the part of the observer in the activities of those being studied often entails learning their language, their habits, their work patterns, and the like.

The rationale for wanting to share the life experiences of the persons being observed stems from the conviction that a better apprehension of reality is achieved through it. The participant observer maintains that the scientific aims are better pursued whenever it is possible to explicate the experiences of the observed as reflected in the experiences of the observer. This conception of science is deeply rooted in the idealistic notion of knowledge and finds its modern expression in the symbolic interaction approach (Manis and Meltzer, 1967).

Participant observers do not completely divorce their methodology from the canons of the scientific method. In a sense, they attempt to add another perspective to it. The prescriptions of objectivity, validity, and reliability, and the designs for causal inferences, are embodied in their research, most often implicitly. These are deliberately made unstructured and flexible so as to maximize the understanding of empirical phenomena. Geer (1964:337) exemplifies the employment of the scientific methodology in the following excerpt:

> My use of hypotheses falls roughly into three sequential types. The first operation consisted of testing the crude yes-or-no proposition. By asking informants or thinking back over volunteered information in the data . . . I stated a working hypothesis in the comments and began the second operation in the sequence: Looking for negative cases or setting out deliberately to accumulate positive ones. . . . Working with negatively expressed hypotheses gave me a specific goal. One instance that contradicts what I say is enough to force modification of the hypothesis. . . . The third stage of operating with hypotheses in the field involves two-step formulations and eventually rough models.

In its final stage of development the hypothesis is not of the "x causes y" type; rather, an all-inclusive set of propositions (a model) is developed to explain the totality of the phenomenon.

Models are constructed with the analytic induction method that represents an approximation of the before-after design. Lindesmith (1952:492) describes the method of analytic induction as follows:

> The principle which governs the selection of cases to test a theory is that the chances of discovering a decisive negative case should be maximized. The investigator who has a working hypothesis concerning his data becomes aware of certain areas of critical importance. If his theory is false or inadequate, he knows that its weaknesses will be more clearly and quickly exposed if he proceeds to the investigation of those critical areas. This involves going out of one's way to look for negative evidence.

Data to be used for analytic induction are collected while the investigator assumes either a complete participant role or a participant-as-observer role. A complete participant role means that the observer is wholly concealed, his or her research objectives are not made known, and he or she attempts to become a member of the group under observation. The complete participant interacts with the observed "as naturally as possible in whatever areas of their living interest him and are accessible to him" (Gold, 1958:219). For example, Festinger, Riecken, and Schachter (1956) studied a group of persons who predicted the destruction of the world. The nature of the group led the authors to believe that if they presented themselves as researchers, then entry to the group would be denied. Consequently, they posed as individuals interested in the activities of the group and became full-fledged members trying to be "nondirective, sympathetic listeners, passive participants who were inquisitive and eager to learn whatever others might want to tell us" (1956:237). Sullivan, Queen, and Patrick (1965) investigated motivations and attitudes of the personnel in a military training program. One of the researchers "enlisted" as a basic trainee and became a full-fledged member of the group. His identity, research objectives, and role as a researcher remained unknown to members of the group, including his own commanding officer.

Complete participation has been justified on the grounds that it makes possible the study of ordinarily inaccessible groups or accessible groups that do not reveal to outsiders certain aspects of their culture. In spite of these advantages, and perhaps because of them, the complete participation role has been severely criticized on methodological and ethical points. Erikson (1965:368) rejects all field observations that do not make the role of the researcher and the intent of his study known beforehand, because they constitute an invasion of privacy and may harm the observed:

> The sheer act of entering a human transaction on the basis of deliberate fraud may be painful to the people who are thereby misled; and even if that were not the case, there are countless ways in which a stranger who pretends to be something else can disturb others by failing to understand the conditions of intimacy that prevail in the group he has tried to invade.

The complete participation role poses several methodological problems. First, observers may either become so self-conscious about revealing their true selves that they are handicapped when attempting to perform convincingly in the pretended role; or they may "go native," incorporating the pretended role into their self-conception and losing the research perspective (Gold, 1958). Second, the problem of deciding what to observe is most delicate because the researcher cannot evoke behavior. For example, the observer must be careful not to ask questions that might raise the suspicions of the persons observed. Third, recording is not feasible on the spot; this has to be postponed until the observer is alone. But time lags in reporting introduce selective bias and distortions through memory. Sullivan, Queen, and Patrick point out that the disguised observer had serious problems of reporting, and was "never certain whether his reports were adequate or whether he was 'getting across' what he was observing" (1965:662).

In view of these methodological limitations coupled with ethical considerations, participant observers most often assume the participant-as-observer role. This type of role makes the researcher's presence as a scientist known to the group being studied, thus minimizing problems of role-pretending. The participant-as-observer attempts to establish close relationships with members of the group who subsequently serve as both informants and respondents. Janes's (1961:447) research illustrates the participant-as-observer role:

> Field work was begun by visiting town, country and school officials, and the newspaper editor to explain the purpose of the study and to ask their co-operation. . . . In time social interaction was initiated by attending church, joining a veterans' organization, returning visits to neighbors, and later spending social evenings with the families of several young business men of the community.

A participant-as-observer confronts three major problems: establishing relationships with members of the group; finding sourceful and reliable informants; and maintaining the observer-observed relationship. The ease with which relationships with members of a group are established depends, to a large extent, upon the nature of the group and the skills of the researcher. Evans-Pritchard exemplified this point: "Azande would not allow me to live as one of themselves; Nuer would not allow me to live otherwise. Among Azande I was compelled to live outside of the community; among Nuer I was compelled to be a member of it. Azande treated me as a superior; Nuer as an equal" (1964:15). Once relationships have been established, the researcher is regarded as a provisional member of the group. He or she learns how to behave in the group and teaches the observed how to act toward him or her. Next, the observer is accepted as a "categorical member" of the group. By this time rapport will have been established, areas of observation will be agreed upon, and informants will be providing information (Denzin, 1970). Whyte's (1955:283–302) experiences illustrate several phases in this process:

> I began with a vague idea that I wanted to study a slum district . . . I made my choice on very unscientific grounds: Cornerville best fitted my picture of what a slum district should look like . . . I learned early in my Cornerville period the crucial importance of having the support of key individuals in any groups or organizations I was studying. Instead of trying to explain myself to everyone, I found I was providing far more information about myself and my study to leaders such as Doc than I volunteered to the average corner boy. I always tried to give the impression that I was willing and eager to tell just as much about my study as anyone wished to know, but it was only to group leaders that I made a particular effort to provide really full informa-

tion . . . Since these leaders had a sort of position in the community that enabled them to observe much better than the followers what was going on and since they were in general more skillful observers than the followers, I found that I had much to learn from a more active collaboration with them.

Intimate relationships with informants may, however, bias the informants' reports, as Whyte (1955:301) himself has observed:

Doc found this experience of working with me interesting, and yet the relationship had its drawbacks. He once commented: "You've slowed me up plenty since you've been down here. Now, when I do something, I have to think what Bill Whyte would want to know about it and how I can explain it. Before, I used to do things by instinct."

Eventually, the researcher departs from the group being studied, and relationships with members of the group and informants are terminated. The problems arising due to termination depend on the kinds of relationships established during the study period. If the observed have come to view themselves as friends of the observer, then their demands on him or her will be great. If the investigator has come to regard the observed as friends, his or her ability to maintain objectivity might be impaired. The researcher may overidentify with the observed and start to lose the research perspective.

A participant-as-observer can evoke behavior of the individuals being studied. The strategy of evocation consists of constructing a situation that has meaning for the group studied in order to observe the behavior that occurs within that context. The behavior evoked may range from routines, such as an annual ceremony for an abundant harvest, to acts that rarely take place in the field (Claster and Schwartz, 1972). To minimize elements of artificiality in the evoked behavior, researchers tend to assume specific roles as required by the situation. For example, Schwartz and Schwartz (1955) report that institutionalized mental patients viewed the researcher as a helping person, and through this role the researcher gained some insight into what it was that patients expected from the medical staff.

The participant-as-observer can record his or her observations on the spot during the event. The documentation may take the form of a diary, or it may be a daily record of each event. These original notes are later re-analyzed and placed under the appropriate categories of a category-system. If the study is focused and the objects to be observed are well defined, recording and categorizing can be pursued during the observation period. When constant recording interferes with the quality of observation, devices for remembering things can be designed. For example, Lindgren (1935) associated the first outstanding incident that occurred during the observation with a word beginning with "a," the next incident with a word beginning with "b," and so forth. These key words guided him later when writing up a fuller account of the occurrences.

When notes are not taken on the spot but immediately after the observation, opportunities for distortion and misrepresentation increase. Strauss et al. (1964:29) made use of certain notational conventions to minimize distortions:

> Verbal material recorded within quotations signified exact recall; verbal material within apostrophes indicated a lesser degree of certainty or paraphrasing; and verbal material with no markings meant reasonable recall but not quotation . . . impressions or inferences could be separated from actual observations by the use of single or double parentheses.

Such a recording system is vulnerable to a great amount of observer inference, unlike the recording systems employed in controlled observations.

SUMMARY

Observation is considered to be the archetypical method of scientific research. If one wishes to understand, explain, and predict what exists, one can simply go and observe it. But if one's findings are to be incorporated into the scientific body of knowledge, one's observations must be carried out with reference to three crucial queries: (1) what to observe, (2) where and when to observe, and (3) how much to infer when recording observations.

Answers to these questions depend on the research problem and are confined to the research design. When the researcher's objective is to test a hypothesis experimentally, the units of observations are explicitly defined; a setting is chosen—laboratory or field; a time sample is drawn; and the observations are systematically recorded with as little observer inference as possible. These operations typify controlled observations and simulations.

The least controlled method of observation is participant observation. This method refers to those forms of research in which the researcher attempts to attain some kind of membership in or close attachment to a group that he or she wishes to study. The research objective is broadly defined; the units of observation are explicated ad hoc and in the field; neither samples of events nor time samples are drawn; and observations are recorded with a great amount of inference.

REFERENCES

Alger, Chadwick F. "Interaction in a Committee of the United Nations General Assembly." *Midwest Journal of Political Science* 10 (1966):411–447.

Aronson, Elliot, and Carlsmith, James. "Experimentation in Social Psychology." In Gardner Lindzey and Elliot Aronson (eds.), *The Handbook of Social Psychology*. Reading, Mass.: Addison-Wesley, 1968.

Asch, Solomon E. "Effects of Group Pressure upon the Modification and Distortion of Judgments." In Eleanor E. Maccoby, Theodore M. Newcomb, and Eugene L. Hartley (eds.), *Readings in Social Psychology*. New York: Holt, Rinehart & Winston, 1958.

Azrin, Nathan H., and Lindsley, Ogden R. "The Reinforcement of Cooperation Between Children." *Journal of Abnormal and Social Psychology* 52 (1956): 100–102.

Bales, Robert F. "A Set of Categories for the Analysis of Small Group Interaction." *American Sociological Review* 15 (April 1950):257–263.

Beller, Emanuel K. "Direct and Inferential Observations in the Study of Children." *American Journal of Orthopsychiatry* 29 (1959):560–573.

Benson, Oliver. "A Simple Diplomatic Game—or Putting One and One Together." Paper read at the American Political Science Association Convention, Washington, D.C., September 1959.

Borgatta, Edgar F. "A Systematic Study of Interaction Process Scores, Peer and Self-Assessments, Personality and Other Variables." *Genetic Psychological Monographs* 65 (1962):219–291.

Brody, Richard A. "Some Systemic Effects of the Spread of Nuclear Weapons Technology: A Study Through Simulation of a Multi-nuclear Future." *Journal of Conflict Resolution* 7 (1963):663–753.

Claster, Daniel S., and Schwartz, Howard. "Strategies of Participation in Participant Observation." *Sociological Methods and Research* 1 (1972):65–96.

Clemens, Walter C., Jr. "A Propositional Analysis of the International Relations Theory in Temper—A Computer Simulation of Cold War Conflict." In William D. Coplin (ed.), *Simulation in the Study of Politics*. Chicago: Markham, 1968.

Coch, Lester, and French, John R. P., Jr. "Overcoming Resistance to Change." *Human Relations* 1 (1948):512–532.

Coleman, James S. "Collective Decisions." *Sociological Inquiry* 34 (1964): 166–181.

Coplin, William D. "Simulation as an Approach to the Study of Politics." In William D. Coplin (ed.), *Simulation in the Study of Politics*. Chicago: Markham, 1968.

Denzin, Norman K. *The Research Act: A Theoretical Introduction to Sociological Methods*. Chicago: Aldine, 1970.

Deutsch, Morton, and Krauss, Robert M. "The Effect of Threat upon Interpersonal Bargaining." *Journal of Abnormal and Social Psychology* 61 (1960): 181–189.

Deutsch, Morton, and Krauss, Robert M. "Studies of Interpersonal Bargaining." *Journal of Conflict Resolution* 6 (1962):52–76.

Ekman, Paul. "A Methodological Discussion of Nonverbal Behavior." *Journal of Psychology* 43 (1957):141–149.

Ekman, Paul. "Communication through Nonverbal Behavior: A Source of Information about an Interpersonal Relationship." In Silvan S. Tomkins and Carroll E. Izard (eds.), *Affect, Cognition, and Personality*. New York: Springer, 1965.

Erikson, Kai T. "A Comment on Disguised Observation in Sociology." *Social Problems* 14 (1967):366–373.

Evans-Pritchard, Edward E. *The Nuer*. Oxford: Clarendon, 1965.

Festinger, Leon, Riecken, Henry, and Schachter, Stanley. *When Prophecy Fails*. Minneapolis: University of Minnesota Press, 1956.

French, John R. P., Jr. "Field Experiments: Changing Group Productivity." In James G. Miller (ed.), *Experiments in Social Process*. New York: McGraw-Hill, 1950.

French, John R. P., Jr. "Experiments in Field Settings." In Leon Festinger and Daniel Katz (eds.), *Research Methods in the Behavioral Sciences*. New York: Holt, Rinehart & Winston, 1954.

Geer, Blanche. "The First Days in the Field." In Phillip E. Hammond (ed.), *Sociologists at Work*. New York: Basic Books, 1964.

Gellert, Elizabeth. "Systematic Observation: A Method in Child Study." *Harvard Educational Review* 25 (1955):179–195.

Gold, Raymond L. "Roles in Sociological Field Observations." *Social Forces* 36 (1958):217–223.

Guetzkow, Harold. "Structured Programs and Their Relation to Free Activity Within the Inter-Nation Simulation." In Harold Guetzkow et al. (eds.), *Simulation in International Relations: Developments for Research and Teaching*. Englewood Cliffs, N.J.: Prentice-Hall, 1963.

Hermann, Charles F. "Simulation: Political Processes." *International Encyclopedia of the Social Sciences*. New York: Macmillan, 1968:274–281.

Heyns, Roger W., and Zander, Alvin F. "Observation of Group Behavior." In Leon Festinger and Daniel Katz (eds.), *Research Methods in the Behavioral Sciences*. New York: Holt, Rinehart & Winston, 1954.

Janes, Robert W. "A Note on the Phases of the Community Role of the Participant Observer." *American Sociological Review* 26 (1961):446–450.

Kluckhohn, Florence. "The Participant-Observer Technique in Small Communities." *American Journal of Sociology* 45 (1940):339–342.

Lindesmith, Alfred R. "Two Comments on W. S. Robinson's 'The Logical Structure of Analytic Induction.'" *American Sociological Review* 17 (1952):492–493.

Lindgren, E. J. "Field Work in Social Psychology." *British Journal of Psychology* 26 (1935):174–182.

Manis, Jerome G., and Meltzer, Bernard N., eds. *Symbolic Interaction*. Boston: Allyn and Bacon, 1967.

Medley, Donald M., and Mitzel, Harold E. "Measuring Classroom Behavior by Systematic Observation." In Nathaniel L. Gage (ed.), *Handbook of Research on Teaching*. Chicago: Rand McNally, 1963.

Pool, Ithiel de Sola, Abelson, Robert P., and Popkin, Samuel L. *Candidates, Issues, and Strategies: A Computer Simulation of the 1960 and 1964 Presidential Elections*. Cambridge, Mass.: MIT Press, 1965.

Riesman, David, and Watson, Jeanne. "The Sociability Project: A Chronicle of Frustration and Achievement." In Phillip E. Hammond (ed.), *Sociologists at Work*. New York: Basic Books, 1964.

Riley, Matilda W. *Sociological Research I: A Case Approach*. New York: Harcourt, Brace & World, 1963.

Rosenthal, Robert, and Fode, Kermit L. "Psychology of the Scientist: V. Three Experiments in Experimenter Bias." *Psychological Reports* 12/13 (1963): 491–511.

Schwartz, Morris S., and Schwartz, Charlotte G. "Problems in Participant Observation." *American Journal of Sociology* 60 (1955):343–353.

Selltiz, Claire, et. al. *Research Methods in Social Relations*. New York: Holt, Rinehart & Winston, 1959.

Soskin, William F., and John, Vera P. "The Study of Spontaneous Talk." In Roger G. Barker (ed.), *The Stream of Behavior*. New York: Appleton-Century-Crofts, 1963.

Soskin, William F., and Kauffman, Paul E. "Judgment of Emotion in Word-Free Voice-Samples." *Journal of Communication* 11 (1961):73–80.

Straus, Murray A. "Measuring Families." In Harold T. Christensen (ed.), *Handbook of Marriage and the Family*. Chicago: Rand McNally, 1964.

Strauss, Anselm, et al. *Psychiatric Ideologies and Institutions*. New York: Free Press, 1964.

Sullivan, Mortimer A., Queen, Stuart A., and Patrick, Ralph C. "Participant Observation as Employed in the Study of a Military Training Program." *American Sociological Review* 23(1958):660–667.

Wax, Rosalie H. "Participant Observation." *International Encyclopedia of the Social Sciences*. New York: Macmillan, 1968:238–240.

Webb, Sidney, and Webb, Beatrice. *Methods of Social Study*. London: Longmans Green, 1932.

Weick, Karl E. "Systematic Observational Methods." In Gardner Lindzey and Elliot Aronson (eds.), *The Handbook of Social Psychology*. Reading, Mass.: Addison-Wesley, 1968.

Whyte, William F. *Street Corner Society*. 2nd ed. Chicago: University of Chicago Press, 1955.

Zelditch, Morris, Jr., and Evan, William M. "Simulated Bureaucracies: A Methodological Analysis." In Harold Guetzkow (ed.), *Simulation in Social Science: Readings*. Englewood Cliffs, N.J.: Prentice-Hall, 1962.

STUDY SUGGESTIONS

1. The IPA system is intended to show that there are universal processes of interaction for groups involved in problem-solving activities. In this assignment you are to observe four or five of your friends in interaction as they discuss some topic of interest to them—pollution, population control, United States foreign policy, employ-

ment, or whatever. This discussion can take place either in a contrived situation (ask your friends to get together to discuss an issue) or in the field (you can listen in on strangers talking in a cafeteria, a coffee shop, or a bar). While the group is engaged in conversation, record their acts employing the IPA code of categories. Later, analyze the interactions and discuss your results.
2. Prepare a simple "man simulation" on a topic of your own.
3. For what research purposes would you recommend participant observation?

CHAPTER 6
Survey Research

Observational methods of data collection are suitable for investigating phenomena that can be observed directly by the researcher. However, not all phenomena are accessible to the investigator's direct observation; occasionally, therefore, the researcher must collect data by asking people who have experienced certain phenomena to reconstruct these phenomena for him or her. The researcher approaches a sample of individuals presumed to have undergone certain experiences and interviews them concerning these experiences. The obtained responses constitute the data upon which the research hypotheses are evaluated. Three major methods are used to elicit information from respondents: the face-to-face interview, the mail questionnaire, and the telephone survey. These methods can be subsumed under the concept "survey research." In the following sections we discuss and compare the three methods.

PERSONAL INTERVIEW

The interview can be regarded as a face-to-face interpersonal role situation, in which an interviewer asks respondents questions designed to obtain answers pertinent to the research hypotheses. The questions, their wording, and their sequence define the extent to which the interview is structured.

The most structured form of interview is the schedule-structured interview, in which the questions, their wording, and their sequence are fixed and are identical for every respondent. This is done to make sure that when variations appear between responses, they can be attributed to the actual differences between the respondents, not to the interview. The researcher attempts to reduce the risk that changes in the wording of questions, for example, might elicit differences in responses. The schedule-structured interview is based on three crucial assumptions: (1) that for any research objective "the respondents have a sufficiently common vocabulary so that it is possible to formulate questions which have the same meaning for each of them" (Richardson, Dohrenwend, and Klein, 1965:40); (2) that it is possible to phrase all questions in a form that is equally meaningful to each respondent; and (3) that if the "meaning of each question is to be identical for each respondent, its context must be identical and, since all preceding questions constitute part of the contexts, the sequence of questions must be identical" (Richardson, Dohrenwend, and Klein, 1965:43).

The second basic form is the focused, or nonschedule-structured, interview. This form has four characteristics: (1) it takes place with respondents known to have been involved in a particular experience; (2) it refers to situations that have been analyzed prior to the interview; (3) it proceeds on the basis of an interview guide specifying topics related to the research hypotheses; and (4) it is focused on the subjective experiences regarding the situations under study (Merton and Kendal, 1946). Although the encounter between the interviewer and the respondent is structured and the major aspects of the study are explicated, the respondent is given considerable liberty in expressing his or her definition of a situation that is presented to him or her. The focused interview permits the researcher to obtain details of personal reactions, specific emotions, and the like. The interviewer, having previously studied the situation, is alert and sensitive to inconsistencies and omissions of data that may be needed to clarify the problem.

The least structured form of interview is the nonstructured, or nondirective, interview. Here, no prespecified set of questions is employed, nor are the questions asked in a specified order. Furthermore, no schedule is used. With little or no direction from the interviewer, respondents are encouraged to relate their experiences, to describe whatever events seem significant to them, to provide their own definitions of their situations, and to reveal their opinions and attitudes as they see fit. The interviewer has a great deal of freedom to probe various areas and to raise specific queries during the course of the interview. For example, Becker's study of marijuana users is based on nonstructured interviews:

> The interviews focused on the history of the person's experience with the drug, seeking major changes in his attitude toward it and in his actual use of it and the reasons for these changes. Generalizations stating necessary conditions for the maintenance of use at each level were developed in initial interviews, and tested again and revised in the light of each succeeding one (1953:236).

The decision as to which form of interview to use for a particular research objective is not an easy one, given the relative advantages and limitations of each form. Using a schedule-structured interview provides more assurance that variations in responses are due to actual differences between respondents; at the same time, however, the researcher risks losing insights obtainable primarily by nonstructured interviews. It is widely accepted that the nonstructured interview and the focused interview are best suited for quasi-experimental designs, whereas the schedule-structured interview is appropriate for experimental designs (Maccoby and Maccoby, 1954). Furthermore, if the researcher is concerned with ascertaining the respondent's meanings and definitions, the less structured interviews are more suitable. If, however, the researcher desires to collect the same amount of information from all respondents, then a schedule-structured interview is necessary. Occasionally, it is possible to combine the forms so that certain standard information is obtained from all respondents in a structured manner, whereas other information is collected from only some of the respondents in a nonstructured manner.

The Question

The basis of all interviews is the question. Kahn and Cannell (1957) have suggested that the interview must serve two purposes: (1) it must translate research objectives into specific questions whose answers will provide the necessary data for hypothesis-testing; (2) it must also aid the interviewer in motivating the respondent so that the necessary information is obtained. It is to these ends that the question becomes the focus around which the interview is constructed. Four major considerations are involved: (1) wording of the question, (2) open-ended or fixed-alternative questions, (3) leading questions, and (4) sequence of questions.*

Wording of the question. The question must be worded so that it is comprehended by the respondent in the way that the researcher means it to be. For example, the researcher's vocabulary might include a word such as "charismatic," which would not be understood by the proverbial man-on-the-street. If the respondents are individuals from all walks of life, then the interviewer's vocabulary should be understandable by the average eighth-grader. Furthermore, words that are subject to a wide variety of interpretations should either be avoided or qualified by specifying their frame of reference. Asking whether one is a liberal might, according to one's interpretation of the term, refer to one's education, one's politics, one's profession, or one's sex life. On the other

---

* These considerations regarding questions are also involved in other survey methods.

hand, a question such as "Do you consider yourself liberal? Politically, I mean" instructs the respondent to use the political frame of reference in answering the question. Question wording requires that the respondent understand the question, and that it have one and the same meaning for each respondent unless the researcher desires to assess differentials in meaning.

Open-ended or fixed-alternative questions. Questions in an interview can be either open-ended or fixed-alternative. In a fixed-alternative question, respondents are offered a set of answers from which they are asked to choose the one that most closely represents their views. For example, to measure political conservatism in the United States, Campbell et al. (1960) used, among other questions, the following fixed-alternative question:

"*All groups can live in harmony in this country without changing the system in any way.*"
  ☐ Strongly agree   ☐ Disagree
  ☐ Agree   ☐ Strongly disagree

Agreement with the question indicated conservatism.

Answers to fixed-alternative questions can be more elaborate. To measure group cohesiveness, Seashore (1954) asked,

"*Do you feel that you are really part of your work group?*"
  ☐ Really a part of my work group
  ☐ Included in most ways
  ☐ Included in some ways, but not in others
  ☐ Don't feel I really belong
  ☐ Don't work with any one group of people
  ☐ Not ascertained

Fixed-alternative questions are easy to ask and quick to be answered; they require no writing by either respondent or interviewer, and their analysis is straightforward. Their major drawback is that they may introduce bias, either by forcing the respondent to choose from given alternatives or by making the respondent think of alternatives that might not have occurred to him or her.

Open-ended questions are not followed by any kind of choice, and the respondents' answers are recorded in full. For instance, the question "What do you personally feel are the most important problems the government in Washington should try to take care of?" is an open-ended question used frequently in questionnaires administered by the Survey Research Center at the University of Michigan. The virtue of the open-ended question is that it does not force the respondent to adapt to preconceived answers: having understood the intent of the question, one can express one's thoughts freely, spontaneously, and in one's own language. If the answers to open-ended questions are unclear, the interviewer may probe; that is, ask the respondent to explain further or to give his or her rationale for something stated earlier. Open-ended questions, then, are flexible; they have possibilities of depth; they enable the interviewer to clear up misunderstandings; and they encourage rapport. However, open-ended questions are difficult to answer and still more difficult to analyze. The researcher has to design a coding frame in order to classify the various answers; in this process, the details of the information provided by the respondent might get lost (see Chapter 8).

The appropriateness of either open-ended or fixed-alternative questions depends upon a number of factors. Some years ago, Lazarsfeld (1944) suggested the use of the following considerations to determine appropriateness:

1. The objectives of the interview. Fixed-alternative questions are suitable when the researcher's objective is to lead the respondent to express agreement or disagreement with an explicit point of view. When the interviewer wishes to learn about the process by which the respondent arrived at a particular point of view, an open-ended question is likely to be more appropriate.

2. The respondent's level of information about the topic in question. Open-ended questions provide opportunities for the interviewer to ascertain lack of information on the part of the respondent, whereas fixed-alternative questions do not. Obviously, it is futile to raise questions that are beyond the experiences of respondents.

3. The extent to which the topic has been thought through by the respondent, so that his or her ideas about it are well structured. The open-ended question is preferable in situations where the respondents have not yet crystallized their opinions. The use of a fixed-alternative question in such situations involves a risk that in accepting one of the alternatives offered him or her, the respondent's choice may be quite different from the opinion the respondent would express if he or she went through the process of recall and evaluation of his or her experience.

4. The ease with which the content of the answer can be communicated by the respondent or the extent to which the respondent is motivated to communicate on the topic. The fixed-alternative question requires less motivation to communicate on the part of the respondent, and the response itself is usually less revealing (and hence less threatening to the respondent) than in the case of the open-ended question. The interviewer who uses fixed-alternative questions tends to encounter less frequent refusals to respond.

Sometimes there may be good reasons for asking the same question in both open-ended and fixed-alternative form. For example, an open-ended answer to the question "Who rules America?" will provide a clear idea of the respondent's perception of the political system and the significance that the person attaches to different power groups. Although this datum is most valuable, it might impede comparison of one group of respondents with another. Furthermore, one cannot be sure that the respondent mentioned all the information of importance to him or her; factors such as the inability to articulate ideas or a momentary lapse of memory may cause omission of significant points. Therefore, the researcher can ask the same question again, later in the interview, but this time with fixed alternatives.

Leading questions. The term "leading question" refers to a question phrased in such a manner that it appears to the respondent that the interviewer expects a certain answer. A question designed to elicit general attitudes toward social protest might read: "How do you feel about student protest?" The same question phrased in a leading form might read: "You wouldn't say that you were in favor of student protest, would you?" A more subtle form of leading question might be: "Would you say that you are not in favor of student protest?" This last question makes it easier for respondents to answer "yes" than "no." In answering "yes," they are agreeing with the language of the question and are not contradicting the interviewer.

Another kind of leading question makes use of words that have become emotionally loaded, either favorably or unfavorably. Words such as "socialist," "starvation," "beautiful," and "bureaucrat" make respondents react not so much to the issue posed by the question as to the loaded phrase itself. Consider the following two questions: "The President has made several public statements advocating school integration. Do you think we should integrate our schools?" and "Socialists have always advocated school integration. Do you think we should integrate our schools?" These two questions are loaded but in different directions; more respondents will tend to agree with the first.

Leading questions are to be avoided if one is looking for undistorted responses. Under certain circumstances, however, leading questions may serve the research objective. The question "Would you favor sending food overseas to feed the starving people of India?" was used to determine the number of people who were so strongly opposed to shipping food to other countries that they rejected the idea even within the strong emotional context of "starving people" (Kahn and Cannell, 1957:129).

Sequence of questions. In an interview, a series of questions is presented to respondents. The questions may be presented at random or in a systematic manner. Two general patterns of questions have been found to be most appropriate for motivating respondents to cooperate and for eliciting fruitful information: the funnel sequence and the inverted funnel sequence.

In the funnel sequence, each successive question is related to the previous question and has a progressively narrower scope. For example, if one were interested in finding out how respondents' views of social problems are related to the newspapers they read, one might want to know what sorts of things the respondents think of as social problems; the perceived relative significance of each problem; the amount of information they have on the topic; their sources of information; and whether certain newspapers have influenced their thinking on the problem. The following questions form a funnel sequence: (1) "What do you think are some of the most important social problems facing the nation?" (2) "Of all the problems you have just mentioned, which do you think is the most important one?" (3) "Where have you obtained most of the information about this problem?" (4) "Do you read the *Washington Post*?" When the objective of the interview is to obtain detailed information, and the respondent is motivated to supply the information, the funnel approach helps the respondent recall details more efficiently. Furthermore, by asking the broadest questions first, the interviewer can avoid imposing a frame of reference before obtaining the respondent's perspective. When the objective of the interview is to discover unanticipated responses, broader questions should be pursued first (Gorden, 1969).

In the inverted funnel sequence, narrower questions are followed by broader ones. When the topic of the interview does not strongly motivate the respondents to communicate—either because the topic is not important to them or because the experiences are not recent enough to be vivid in their memory—it may be helpful to begin with the narrower questions, which are easier to answer, while reserving the broader (and more difficult) ones until later. If the purpose is to obtain a generalization in the form of a judgment regarding a concrete situation, and if the interviewer is unfamiliar with the facts but the respondent knows them, then narrower questions aimed at establishing specific facts should precede questions requiring an overall judgment (Gorden, 1969).

The personal interview, as a face-to-face interpersonal role situation, is beset with peculiar problems, especially with regard to the validity and reliability of the information obtained. Consider, for example, an attribute such as social class. Lenski and Leggett (1960) examined the effects of socioeconomic discrepancies between interviewers and respondents; they found that respondents of low status expressed deference to a middle-class interviewer by acquiescing to two agree-disagree propositions, even when the two propositions were contradictory to one another.* Such biasing effects can, to a certain extent, be minimized by proper controls and by careful observation of nonverbal behavior in the

---

* For an examination of other possible sources of invalidity, see Derek L. Phillips, *Knowledge From What?* (Chicago: Rand McNally, 1971), pp. 21–49.

interview. Gorden (1969:67) has summarized the interviewer's tasks with regard to nonverbal behavior as follows:

> (a) to observe a broad range of non-verbal activity and be alert for inconsistencies; (b) to be alert for changes in respondent's non-verbal activity . . . ; and (c) to interpret the meaning of any inconsistencies and changes in non-verbal behavior in the broader context of the verbal communication and the situation in which the interview is taking place.

IMPERSONAL SURVEY METHODS

Under certain conditions and for a number of research purposes, the interpersonal role situation may be avoided altogether, and impersonal survey methods might be found useful. We will examine two common impersonal methods: the mail questionnaire and the telephone survey.

Mail Questionnaire

When Selltiz et al. argue that "questionnaires can be sent through the mail; interviewers cannot" (1959:239), they point out one of the chief advantages of the mail questionnaire; it is cheaper than personal interviewing. The mail questionnaire does not require a trained staff of interviewers; all it needs is the cost of planning, sampling, duplicating, mailing, and providing stamped, self-addressed envelopes for the returns. The processing and analysis are usually also simpler and cheaper than those of personal interviews. The second major advantage of the mail questionnaire is that it reduces biasing errors that might result from the personal characteristics of interviewers and from variabilities in their skills. Mail questionnaires are also used when questions demand a considered (rather than an immediate) answer, or if the answer requires consultation of personal documents or other people; or when the questions are of an embarrassing nature. With such questions, a mail questionnaire may elicit a higher response rate than a personal interview.

As with personal interviews, the question is the basis of the mail questionnaire. Considerations involved with the wording of questions, with open-ended or fixed-alternative questions, with leading questions, and with the sequence of questions must be carefully dealt with, especially because of the nonpresence of an interviewer when the questionnaire is being answered. Opportunities to motivate the respondent, to clarify questions, or to probe do not exist with the impersonal mail questionnaire.

The main problem with mail questionnaires is that of obtaining an adequate response rate. For many mail surveys, the reported response rates are much lower than for personal interviews. The typical response rate for a personal interview is about 95 percent, whereas that for a mail survey is between 20 and 40 percent. The researcher who uses a mail questionnaire is almost always faced with the problem of how to estimate the effect the nonrespondents may have on his or her findings.* Four more limitations are inherent in the mail questionnaire method: (1) They can be used only when the questions are simple and straightforward enough to be comprehended with the help of the printed instructions and definitions. (2) The answers have to be accepted as final; there is no opportunity to probe beyond the given answer, to clarify ambiguous answers, or to appraise the nonverbal behavior of respondents. (3) The researcher cannot be sure that the right person completes the questionnaire; an individual other than the intended respondent may complete it. (4) The respondent can see all the questions before answering any one of them, so the various answers cannot be regarded as independent (Moser and Kalton, 1971). If these limitations are of little significance to a concrete research objective, the mail questionnaire might be used instead of the personal interview.

Telephone Surveys

The second impersonal method of collecting information is by telephone. Telephone surveys, however, have little to recommend them beyond speed and relatively low cost. Where too few households have telephones, the method is not useful for studying the general population. Furthermore, only simple, superficial questions can be posed, and there is no possibility of obtaining detailed information. A telephone survey may be applicable to specific populations, such as individual telephone subscribers or firms. They are particularly useful for obtaining information about what an individual is doing at the time of the call. Accordingly, the method has been most frequently used in radio and television research; for instance, to find out what television program the respondent is watching at the time of the call.

In deciding which survey method is best suited for one's research, one has to evaluate which criteria are most significant to the research objective. For example, if a researcher plans a long interview with a representative sample† of the general population and wishes to control for nonverbal behavior, and if sufficient funds are available, a form of personal interview is preferable, possibly the schedule-structured interview. On the other hand, if the aim is to find out which television programs are most popular, a telephone survey might be adequate. Table 6.1 presents some of the comparative advantages and limitations of the three methods of survey research.

* The response rate is of a greater significance when making generalizations; see Chapter 12.

† A sample is representative if the measurements made on its units produce results equivalent to those that would be obtained had the entire population been measured; see Chapter 12.

TABLE 6.1. Evaluation of Three Survey Methods

Criteria	Personal Interview	Mail	Telephone
Cost	High	Low	Moderate
Response rate	High	Low	Moderate
Control of interview situation	High	Low	Moderate
Applicability to geographically dispersed populations	Moderate	High	Moderate
Applicability to heterogeneous populations	High	Low	Low
Obtaining detailed information	High	Low	Low

ATTITUDE MEASUREMENT

Thus far our concern has been with the methods by which personal experiences are elicited from respondents. Not all personal experiences, however, were intensively studied by social scientists. Survey research has been utilized chiefly to obtain data on respondents' backgrounds, opinions, attitudes, and reasons for behavior. Background data include information on variables such as the sex of the respondent, his or her age, marital status, education, occupation, income, political party affiliation, and the like. Of the remaining three types of information, data on attitudes are most frequently collected. In this section, we discuss the major techniques used in survey research for measuring attitudes.*

An attitude is a tendency to act or react in a certain manner when confronted with certain stimuli. The individual's attitudes are expressed, in speech or other behavior, only when the object of the attitude is perceived. A person may have strong attitudes for or against communism, but these are aroused and conveyed only when that person encounters some issue connected with communists, or when he or she is confronted with a stimulus such as a question in an interview.

Attitudes can be described by their content (what the attitude is about), by their direction (positive, neutral, or negative feelings about the object or issue in question), and by their intensity (an attitude may be held with greater or lesser vehemence). To one person, communism may be but of passing interest; to another, it may be of great significance and lead him to join anticommunist organizations. One would expect the latter to agree or disagree more strongly than would the former to questions dealing with, say, free trade with Red China.

Attitudes are measured by attitude scales consisting of five to two dozen or more attitude statements, with which the respondent is asked

---

* For other issues involved in the study of attitudes, see Martin Fishbein, ed., *Readings in Attitude Theory and Measurement* (New York: Wiley, 1967).

to agree or disagree. An attitude cannot be measured by a single question, because this approaches an attitude from only one direction and hence might give unreliable results (Oppenheim, 1966). For example, if a respondent strongly disagrees with the statement "Trade with Red China should be encouraged," this does not imply a broad anticommunist attitude. This person's disagreement may be due to personal circumstances; for instance, the person may think that it will harm his or her business. By using several attitude statements, one can reduce the effects of one-sided responses.

An essential requirement of attitude scales is that the attitude statements composing the scale be scaled; that is, that the statements be selected and put together from a much larger number of attitude statements according to certain techniques. The various techniques of attitude-scaling can be subsumed under the following categories: (1) arbitrary scales, (2) scales in which the items are determined by judges, and (3) scales based on item analysis. In the following discussion, the Thurstone scale of equal-appearing intervals is an example of a judgment scale, whereas the Likert technique is a scale based on item analysis.

Arbitrary Scales

Arbitrary scales involve a battery of questions that are selected on an a priori basis. Numerical values are assigned arbitrarily to the item or question responses, and these values are summed to obtain scores. These scores are then interpreted as indicating the attitude of the respondent. Consider the following scale of five statements designed to measure alienation:

1. Sometimes I have the feeling that other people are using me.
   ☐ Strongly agree ☐ Disagree
   ☐ Agree ☐ Strongly disagree
   ☐ Uncertain
2. We are just so many cogs in the machinery of life.
   ☐ Strongly agree ☐ Disagree
   ☐ Agree ☐ Strongly disagree
   ☐ Uncertain
3. The future looks very dismal.
   ☐ Strongly agree ☐ Disagree
   ☐ Agree ☐ Strongly disagree
   ☐ Uncertain
4. More and more, I feel helpless in the face of what's happening in the world today.
   ☐ Strongly agree ☐ Disagree
   ☐ Agree ☐ Strongly disagree
   ☐ Uncertain

5. People like me have no influence in society.
   ☐ Strongly agree ☐ Disagree
   ☐ Agree   ☐ Strongly disagree
   ☐ Uncertain

Suppose we arbitrarily score responses in the following way: Strongly agree = 4; Agree = 3; Uncertain = 2; Disagree = 1; and Strongly disagree = 0. Thus, a respondent who answers "Strongly agree" to all five statements will have a total score of 20, indicating a high degree of alienation; a respondent who answers "Strongly disagree" to all five statements will have a total score of zero, indicating that that person is not alienated. In reality, most respondents will obtain scores between these two extremes, and the researcher has to work out a scoring system classifying respondents according to their degree of alienation. For example, respondents who score zero to 6 are not alienated; respondents who score from 7 to 13 are somewhat alienated; and those who score between 14 and 20 are most alienated.

This scale is arbitrary because there was nothing about the procedure to guarantee that any one statement or item tapped the same attitude as the other items. Is item 3 in the scale tapping the same aspect of alienation as does item 5? Does item 4 scale with the remaining items? Will another researcher who uses the scale get the same findings? That is, is the scale reliable? These central questions in attitude-scaling remain unanswered if the researcher makes use of arbitrary scales.

Thurstone Scales

Among the scales in which attitude statements (hereafter "items") are determined by judges, Thurstone's technique of equal-appearing intervals provides the most significant contribution. Earlier, it was argued that scaling involves ranking individuals according to a classificatory system. The Thurstone technique was developed to accomplish this in such a way that the intervals between the rankings assigned by the scale would approximate equal intervals.

The general procedure of the Thurstone technique is to ask judges to rank items into categories. The researcher then selects from these categories a number of items (usually fifteen to twenty) to form the scale. Items are selected from each of the ordered categories, giving preference to items on whose ranking the judges agreed. The procedure involves five steps: (1) compiling scale items; (2) having judges order the possible items; (3) computing the average value for each item; (4) selecting the specific scale items and computing the ogive values (cumulative percentage values); and (5) testing the relevancy of the items.

First, the researcher composes a large number of items concerning the attitude to be measured. The items should cover the entire range of attitudes, from extremely favorable to extremely unfavorable, including neutral items. Each item should refer to the present; express only one idea; be brief, unambiguous, and relevant; and be in a form that permits it to be endorsed or rejected in terms of a definitely expressed attitude (Schmid, 1966). Each item is written on a separate slip of paper.

The second step is to have judges rank the items into a number of categories according to how favorable or unfavorable the items are to the attitude being investigated. Judges should be selected by a probability sampling design so that their views represent the population to be scaled (see Chapter 12). Each judge ranks each item on a scale according to favorableness of the item to the attitude, usually in seven or eleven categories. Thus, a given item might be ranked in the third category by one judge and in the eleventh by another. Each judge compiles seven or eleven sets; these are combined into one master set of seven or eleven categories (all items in set 1 for each judge are placed in master set 1, etc.).

In the third step, the slips are regrouped by item. Suppose a given item had slips in sets 5, 9, 10, 11. All the slips for this item are collected and put aside. Each item thus has a set of slips whose number corresponds to the number of judges. For each item the median value is calculated (see Chapter 9); all items with a median 1 are placed in the 1 category; all those with median 2 are placed in the 2 category; and so on, up to seven or eleven.

The fourth step is to select the specific items to be used in the final scale. Two criteria are applied. First, the full range of the scale has to be represented, which is done by ensuring that at least one item is selected from each of the final seven or eleven categories. Second, items in each category are selected according to how much agreement there was among judges that the item belongs in that category; the items that are selected in this way have the least dispersion. To identify the items with the least dispersion, Thurstone used the "Q value" method. Q values are measures of dispersion based on computing graphic medians and ogive values. Hypothetical data on one item are presented in Table 6.2 and illustrated in Figure 6.1, in which the y axis stands for the cumulative percentage of judges and the x axis for category numbers (eleven categories are used). It should be noted that a graph of Q values is to be constructed for each item.

From Figure 6.1, one can see that 25 percent of the judges ranked the item in category 4 or lower; 70 percent ranked it in category 7 or lower; and 98 percent ranked it in category 9 or lower. The 0.25, 0.70, 0.98, and so on levels are the ogive levels. The graphic median can be calculated by reading the category number that corresponds to the 0.50 level; in this example, the graphic median is 5.3. The median value represents the scale value of the item.

SURVEY RESEARCH

TABLE 6.2. Hypothetical Data on the Distribution of Judges' Selections for One Item

Category Number	Number of Judges	Cumulative Percentage
1	0	0
2	10	5.5
3	20	15.5
4	35	25.0
5	60	40.0
6	80	55.0
7	49	70.0
8	30	90.0
9	15	98.0
10	1	100.0
11	0	100.0
	N = 300	

A (quartile) dispersion is the difference between the category numbers corresponding to the 0.75 level and the 0.25 level, or $Q_3 - Q_1$. This difference is known as the Q value, or coefficient of ambiguity. In our example, the coefficient of ambiguity equals $6.4 - 4.2$, or 2.2. If that is the lowest Q value for any item in that particular category, that item will be selected for the final scale because it reflects the highest degree of agreement among the judges. A low value of the coefficient of ambiguity indicates a low degree of ambiguity in regard to an item.

FIGURE 6.1. Graph of Q Values for Data in Table 6.2

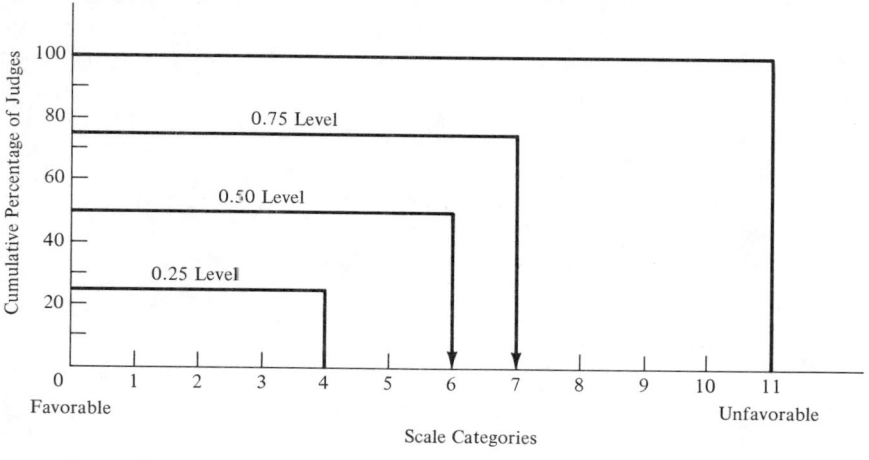

The fifth step concerns relevancy. Each item should be relevant. Relevancy is determined by plotting the responses of each item against all other items. Generally, judges tend to be consistent in their evaluations of the various items in a scale. For example, if a number of judges endorse items with scale values around 2.0, they will not usually endorse items that deviate markedly from this value, for example, items with scale values of 6.0 or 7.0. If responses to a given item are markedly inconsistent, the item is irrelevant and should be eliminated from the scale.

The final scale to be administered is made up of a battery of fifteen to twenty unambiguous, relevant items arranged randomly, representing a graded series of values from "extremely favorable" to "extremely unfavorable." The reliability and the validity of the scale can be evaluated by any of the methods discussed in Chapter 4.

Likert Scales

The second method of scale construction is generally referred to as the "technique of summated rating," or the Likert technique. The Likert technique is less tedious than the Thurstone method. It does not rely on judges' assessments and is widely used in the professional literature.

Five steps can be distinguished in the construction of a Likert scale. In the first step, the researcher compiles a series of items expressive of a wide range of attitudes from extremely positive to extremely negative. Each item calls for checking one of five fixed-alternative expressions such as "strongly agree," "agree," "undecided," "disagree," and "strongly disagree."* In this five-point continuum, weights of 1, 2, 3, 4, 5 or 5, 4, 3, 2, 1 are assigned, the direction of weighting being determined by the favorableness or unfavorableness of the item. To measure attitudes toward employment of older people, Kirchner (1957) developed a twenty-four-item scale using the Likert method. The following four items illustrate the scoring technique:

1. Most companies are unfair to older employees.
   - ☐ Strongly agree   ☐ Disagree
   - ☐ Agree   ☐ Strongly disagree
   - ☐ Undecided
2. I think that older employees make better employees.
   - ☐ Strongly agree   ☐ Disagree
   - ☐ Agree   ☐ Strongly disagree
   - ☐ Undecided

* Occasionally, three, four, six, or seven fixed-alternative expressions are used. Other expressions such as "almost always," "frequently," "occasionally," "rarely," and "almost never" are also used.

3. In a case where two people can do a job about equally well, I'd pick the older person for the job.
   ☐ Strongly agree ☐ Disagree
   ☐ Agree   ☐ Strongly disagree
   ☐ Undecided
4. I think older employees have as much ability to learn new methods as do other employees.
   ☐ Strongly agree ☐ Disagree
   ☐ Agree   ☐ Strongly disagree
   ☐ Undecided

This scale was scored by assigning weights for response alternatives to positive items (acceptance of hiring older persons). The weights were assigned as follows: Strongly agree—5; Agree—4; Undecided—3; Disagree—2; Strongly disagree—1. If negative items (i.e., items indicating rejection of employment of older persons) had been included in the scale, their weights would have been reversed.

In the second step, a large number of respondents, selected randomly from the population to be measured, are asked to check their attitudes on the list of items. Next, the third step, a total score for each respondent is calculated by summing the value of each item that is checked. Suppose a respondent checked "Strongly agree" in item 1 (score 5); "Undecided" in item 2 (score 3); "Agree" in item 3 (score 4); and "disagree" in item 4 (score 2). His or her total score is $5 + 3 + 4 + 2 = 14$.

In the fourth step, the researcher has to determine a basis for the selection of items for the final scale. This can be done either with the internal consistency method—that is, correlating each item with the total score and retaining those with the highest correlations (see Chapter 4)—or with "item analysis." Both methods yield an internally consistent scale. With either method, the problem is to find items that consistently separate those who are "high" on the attitude continuum from those who are "low." With item analysis, each item is subjected to a measurement of its ability to separate the "highs" from the "lows." This is called the discriminative power (DP) of the item. In calculating the DP, the researcher sums the scored items for each respondent and places the scores in an array, usually from the lowest to the highest scores. In the final step, the researcher compares the range above the upper quartile (Q_1) with that below the lower quartile (Q_3), and the DP is calculated as the difference between the weighted means of Q_1 and Q_3 (Table 6.3).

The DP index is computed for each of the possible scale items, and those items with the largest DP indices are selected. These are the items that best discriminate among judges expressing differing attitudes toward the measured attitude. Any of the tests of validity discussed in

TABLE 6.3 *DP* Computing Table for One Item

Group	Number in Group	Item Scores					Weighted Total*	Weighted Mean†	DP $(Q_1 - Q_3)$
		1	2	3	4	5			
High (top 25 percent)	9	0	1	2	3	3	35	3.89	2.00
Low (bottom 25 percent)	9	1	8	0	0	0	17	1.89	

SOURCE: Adapted from Gardner Murphy and Rensis Likert. *Public Opinion and the Individual.* New York: Harper, 1938, p. 289, Table 68. Copyright 1938 by Harper & Row, Publishers, Inc. By permission of the publishers.

* Weighted total = score × number checking that score

† Weighted mean = $\frac{\text{weighted total}}{\text{number cases}}$

Chapter 4 are applicable to the summated rating scales. The reliability of the scales is usually evaluated with the split-half reliability test, also discussed in Chapter 4.

SUMMARY

A survey is any procedure in which data are systematically collected through some form of solicitation, such as personal interviews, mailed questionnaires, and telephone surveys. The personal interview is a face-to-face interpersonal role situation in which the interviewer asks the respondent questions designed to obtain answers pertinent to the objective of the research. Since the personal interview is a role situation, adequate precautions must be taken to avoid biasing errors. Impersonal survey methods are less vulnerable to errors that might result from interactions between the interviewer and the respondent; however, they are beset with other problems, especially with regard to the response rate. A decision as to what survey method to use for a particular research objective depends on a number of considerations, the most significant of which are summarized in Table 6.1.

Four major problems must be dealt with when preparing a survey: (1) question wording, (2) choice of open-ended or fixed-alternative questions, (3) use of leading questions, and (4) the sequence of questions. Each of these problems calls for a careful evaluation of the research hypotheses, the research design, and the population to be surveyed.

Surveys are often used to collect background information, data on opinions, and information on attitudes and reasons for behavior. Of these, attitude measurement has undergone the greatest amount of methodological development. Attitudes are measured with attitude scales. Three techniques of scale construction are arbitrary scales, scales in which the items are determined by judges, and scales based on item analysis.

Survey research leans heavily on sampling methods. If researchers wish to generalize their findings, they have to administer the questionnaire to a representative sample of respondents drawn from a well-defined population. The various sampling methods used to obtain representative samples are discussed in Chapter 12.

REFERENCES

Becker, Howard S. "Becoming a Marihuana User." *American Journal of Sociology,* 59 (1953):235–242.

Campbell, Angus, et al. *The American Voter.* New York: Wiley, 1960.

Gorden, Raymond L. *Interviewing: Strategy, Techniques and Tactics.* Homewood, Ill.: Dorsey Press, 1969.

Kahn, Robert L., and Cannell, Charles F. *The Dynamics of Interviewing.* New York: Wiley, 1957.

Kirchner, Wayner K. "The Attitudes of Special Groups toward the Employment of Older Persons." *Journal of Gerontology* 12 (1957):216–220.

Lazarsfeld, Paul F. "The Controversy over Detailed Interviews—An Offer for Negotiation." *Public Opinion Quarterly* 8 (1944):38–60.

Lenski, Gerhard, and Leggett, John C. "Caste, Class and Deference in the Research Interview." *American Journal of Sociology* 65 (1960):463–467.

Maccoby, Eleanor E., and Maccoby, Nathan. "The Interview: A Tool of Social Science." In Gardner Lindzey (ed.), *Handbook of Social Psychology.* Reading, Mass.: Addison-Wesley, 1954.

Merton, Robert K., and Kendal, Patricia L. "The Focused Interview." *American Journal of Sociology* 51 (1946):541–557.

Moser, C. A., and Kalton, G. *Survey Methods in Social Investigation.* London: Heinemann Educational Books, 1971.

Oppenheim, N. A. *Questionnaire Design and Attitude Measurement.* New York: Basic Books, 1966.

Richardson, Stephen, Dohrenwend, Barbara S., and Klein, David. *Interviewing: Its Forms and Functions.* New York: Basic Books, 1965.

Schmid, Calvin F. "Scaling Techniques in Sociological Research." In Pauline V. Young (ed.), *Scientific Social Surveys and Research,* Englewood Cliffs, N.J.: Prentice-Hall, 1966.

Seashore, Stanley E. *Group Cohesiveness in the Industrial Work Group.* Ann Arbor: Survey Research Center, Institute of Social Research, University of Michigan, 1954.

Selltiz, Claire, et al. *Research Methods in Social Relations*. New York: Holt, Rinehart & Winston, 1959.

STUDY SUGGESTIONS

1. Prepare a focused interview on a topic of your own. Interview at least ten persons from different occupational groups. Drawing on this experience, prepare a schedule-structured interview.
2. Prepare a scaled set of five questions of increasing or decreasing intensity.
3. Compare the Thurstone technique with Likert's summated rating method. Which method would you recommend for use when constructing a "political morality" attitude scale?

CHAPTER 7
Unobtrusive Measures

INTENT OF UNOBTRUSIVE MEASURES

With the exception of the complete participation method of data collection, all methods considered so far take place in either contrived or "natural" settings in which the observed or the respondents are aware of being research subjects. This may produce errors from either the respondent or the investigator, which, in turn, impair the internal and external validity of the research findings. Some of the possible kinds of errors were pointed out in our discussions of the various research designs and the methods of data collection. We will summarize them briefly in order to illuminate the significance of unobtrusive measures in empirical research.

Four basic kinds of errors may be introduced by the respondent: (1) the guinea pig effect, (2) role selection, (3) measurement as change agent, and (4) response sets (Webb et al., 1966). The guinea pig effect refers to the observation that

> The measurement process used in the experiment may itself affect the outcome. If people feel that they are "guinea pigs" being experimented with, or if they feel that they are being "tested" and must make a good impression, or if the method of data collection suggests responses or stimulates an interest the subject did not previously feel, the measuring process may distort the experimental results (Selltiz et al., 1959:97).

Role selection designates those activities which result from the demand characteristics of experimental situations (see Chapter 5). Research subjects tend to choose specialized roles while being investigated; these, in turn, may not be the roles that typify the subjects. Changes due to measurement are considered the third kind of error and are termed "measurement as change agent." For example, the measurement instrument may induce changes in the respondent's opinions or behavior. The fourth kind of error is the response set, whose presence is most critical in survey research. For example, respondents will endorse an attitude statement more frequently than they will disagree with its opposite (see Chapter 6).

The three major kinds of errors that may be introduced by the researcher are: (1) interviewer effects, which means that the characteristics of the interviewer may influence the responses of the respondent; (2) change in the research instrument; that is, the researcher may obtain different measurements at different times due to factors such as an increase in his or her skill; and (3) population restrictions, which refer to the fact that any given data-collection method defines the boundaries of the population that can be studied; for example, illiterate persons are excluded from populations studied by mail questionnaires.*

To a large extent, errors stemming from either the researcher or the respondent can be minimized by a proper research design and sensitive measuring instruments (see Chapter 4). These, however, provide no absolute guarantee that all error has been eliminated. To cross-validate one's findings, unobtrusive measures can be used. Unobtrusive measures are also used, as will be illustrated, as a primary data-collection method for specific research purposes.

An unobtrusive measure is any method of data collection that directly removes the researcher from the set of interactions, events, or behavior being investigated. For example, public archival documents represent an unobtrusive measure because the conditions leading to their production are not influenced by an intruding researcher. Unobtrusive measures avoid the contamination that might arise when investigators and subjects confront one another in data-collection situations. With unobtrusive measures, the individual "is not aware of being tested, and there is little danger that the act of measurement will itself serve as a force for change in behavior or elicit role-playing that confounds the data" (Webb et al., 1966:175). These measures range from private and public archives to simple behavior observations of people at work or play; from physical-trace analysis to contrived observations based on mechanical equipment.

PHYSICAL TRACES

Physical traces and evidence left behind by a population are generated without the producer's knowledge of their future use by researchers. Webb et al. (1966) make a distinction between two broad classes of

---

* For a comprehensive discussion of these and other errors that may be introduced by the investigator, see Webb et al. (1966). The present section leans on this pioneering work.

physical evidence: erosion measures and accretion measures. Erosion measures are the natural remnants of some population's activity that has selectively worn certain objects. For example, the wear on library books is an index of their popularity, and the number of miles accumulated by police officers in their patrol cars measures their daily activity. Thus, one can cross-validate the verbal reports of police officers on their daily activities by checking the number of miles accumulated in their patrol cars.

Accretion measures constitute a population's deposit of materials. In this case, the researcher examines those remnants that are left by people and are suggestive of some behavior. For example, Denzin (1970) has suggested that deposits of love letters in waste containers be used as a measure of troubled interaction patterns. Wallace (1965) found that hotel clerks assess a person's relationship with legal authorities by the number of possessions that person leaves behind. Settings on the dials of car radios can be used to estimate the popularity of different radio stations by recording the position of the dials when cars are brought in for service.

Physical-trace analysis poses certain difficulties in the collection and interpretation of data: The time needed for collection, the dross rate, and the quality of the data pose restrictions. More significant, however, is the fact that in many instances the researcher lacks sufficient data on the population from which the physical traces are drawn to make generalizations (see Chapter 12).

SIMPLE OBSERVATION

Simple observations are the second basic variety of unobtrusive measures. They occur in those situations "in which the observer has no control over the behavior or sign in question, and plays an unobserved, passive and unobtrusive role in the research situation" (Webb et al., 1966:112). Although in all other respects, simple observations take on the methodology of other observational methods, including participant observation, their peculiarity derives from the fact that the researcher does not intervene in the production of the material.

There are four basic types of simple observations.* The first is the observation of exterior body and physical signs that are indicants of behavior or attitudes. Examples of such signs include tattoos, clothing styles, ornamental objects such as jewelry, and other types of possessions. Stone reports that when one of his respondents was asked if he chose to wear a greater variety or smaller variety of clothes when at work,

---

* To some extent these types correspond to the indicants of behavior discussed in Chapter 5. The basic difference, however, lies in the methods of observation and in the place of the investigator in the data-collection process.

he replied: "A smaller variety so you look the same every day. So people will identify you. They look for the same old landmark" (1962:95). Phillips (1962) has provided multiple indicators of the changes in Miami resulting from the influx of a hundred thousand Cubans. Two years following the Castro revolution, the author observed bilingual street signs, Latin-American foods on restaurant menus, radio broadcasts in Spanish, and services held in Spanish by forty Miami churches. In this study, exterior signs in public places served as indices of social change.

A second type of simple observation is the analysis of expressive movement. The focus of observation is on the various features of the body that express the self and interpretations of social interactions. For example, Schubert (1959), studying the Supreme Court, has suggested that the speech, grimaces, and gestures of the justices when hearing oral arguments are rich sources of data for students of the Court.

A major problem in the investigation of facial and body gestures is the determination of what a particular gesture conveys. For instance, a smile may mean relief or happiness, and a frown may indicate involvement in thought or disapproval. The meaning of a gesture has to be determined for both the person expressing it and the recipient. The situation in which the gesture is expressed must also be considered. A smile at a funeral probably means something quite different from a smile at a wedding (Denzin, 1970).

Physical-location analysis is the third type of simple observation. The main purpose of this mode of observation is to investigate the ways in which individuals use their bodies in a social space. In Chapter 5, we discussed some indicants of spatial behavior; these, however, are investigated in laboratory settings. Physical-location analysis focuses on behavior that occurs without the researcher's intervention in the conditions which elicit the behavior. To observers of Russian internal politics, for instance, information on who stands next to whom in Red Square reviewing the May Day parade is a clue of stability or change in the power elite. The proximity of a politician to the leader is a direct indication of his status, and his physical position is interpreted as symptomatic of other behavior that gave him the status position (Webb et al., 1966).

Seating aggregation may be used as an index of interracial relations. In their study of seating aggregation, Campbell, Kruskal, and Wallace used the clustering of blacks and whites as an index of attitude:

> Where seating in a classroom is voluntary the degree to which the Negroes and whites present sit by themselves versus mixing randomly may be taken as a presumptive index of the degree to which acquaintance, friendship and preference are strongly colored by race, as opposed to being distributed without regard to racial considerations (Webb et al., 1966:123).

Observations of language behavior represent the fourth form of simple observation. Unobtrusive language analysis focuses on samples of conversations and the interrelationship of speech patterns to locale, to categories of persons present, and to time of day. The analysis combines the study of physical locations with that of expressive movements.

Psathas and Henslin examined the rules and definitions employed by cab drivers as they located points of delivery and pickup on the basis of dispatcher messages. These messages were analyzed with regard to the information they conveyed and the action taken by the driver. Each item of information was assigned a special category that represented unique directions for the cab driver. For example, if a driver was told to "drive-up-and-get-out, he must do more than merely drive up. His instructions involve getting out of the cab and actively looking for the passenger in a place where the passenger is presumed to be" (1967:433).

Earlier, it was pointed out that the main advantage of simple observation is that the researcher has no part in structuring the observational situation and remains unobserved while observing. This eliminates errors that otherwise could have been introduced by the observed. Simple observation, however, is beset with some particular problems. First, the recorded observations might not represent a wider population, thus limiting the scope of findings. Second, error might be introduced from fallibilities of the observer. The observer may become more attentive as he or she learns the task and becomes involved with it. Third, only certain phenomena can be observed. If the observer is to remain unnoticed, then the settings most amenable to simple observation will be public; private settings are inaccessible to simple observation. Fourth, much of the data collected by simple observation do not generate explanations: "The data . . . don't offer the 'why', but simply establish a relationship" (Webb et al., 1966:127). This, in turn, is one of the reasons for using simple observation mainly to supplement data collected by obtrusive methods.

ARCHIVAL RECORDS

The third major form of unobtrusive measures is the analysis of public and private archival records. These data are collected from diverse sources such as actuarial records, political and judicial records, government documents, the mass media, and private records such as autobiographies, diaries, and letters. A large amount of data in the form of public and private archival records is readily available to social scientists. Some of these records have been compiled specifically for purposes of research, whereas others have been prepared for more general use.

Public Records

Four basic varieties of public records may be distinguished (Webb et al., 1966). First are actuarial records concerning the demographic characteristics of the population served by the record-keeping agency. These records range from birth and death statistics to records of marriages and divorces. Second are political and judicial records concerning court decisions, legislators' activities, public votes, budget decisions, and the like. Third are governmental and quasi-governmental documents such as crime statistics, records of social welfare programs, and weather reports. Fourth are the various reports, news items, editorials, and other communications produced by the mass media. Each of these four types contains information that has been used for numerous and diversified research purposes. In the following discussions, exemplars of social science research are used to illustrate the varied uses of public archival records.

Actuarial records. Most societies maintain continuing records on births, deaths, marriages, and divorces. Such data have been used by social scientists for both descriptive and explanatory purposes. For example, Webb et al. (1966) report that Winston investigated the preference for male offspring in upper-class families by examining birth records. He noted the sex of each child in the birth order of each family. A preference for males was indicated if the male-female ratio of the last child born in families estimated to be complete was greater than that ratio for all children in the same families. The information contained in birth records enabled him to segregate an upper-class sample of parents and to test his hypothesis.

Middleton (1960) examined fertility levels with two sets of data: fertility values expressed in magazine fiction and actuarial fertility levels at three different time periods. For 1916, 1936, and 1956, the author estimated fertility values by observing the size of fictional families in eight American magazines. A comparison with population data for the same years showed that shifts in the size of fictional families closely paralleled shifts in the true United States fertility level.

Death records were used in Warner's (1959) study on death and its accouterments in an American city. Warner investigated official cemetery documents to establish a history of the dead. He found the social structure of the city mirrored in the cemetery. For example, the father was most often buried in the center of the family plot, and headstones of males were larger than those of females. Moreover, a family that had raised its social status moves the graves of its relatives from less prestigious cemeteries to more prestigious ones.

Political and judicial records. Voting statistics have been used widely to study electoral behavior as well as voting patterns of legislators. Collections such as *A Review of Elections of the World* and *America at the Polls: A Handbook of American Presidential Election Statistics, 1920–1964** provide useful electoral data. *The Congressional Quarterly Almanac* has provided periodic information on the U.S. Congress since 1947, including data on the background characteristics of members of Congress, information on major items of legislation, tabulations of roll-call votes, and a survey of political developments. Taylor et al., *World Handbook of Political and Social Indicators* (1972), report cross-national data on 148 political and social measures, such as electoral participation, counts of riots by country per year, numbers of irregular government changes, and inequalities in income distribution.† To review the literature on cross-national studies of electoral behavior that have employed voting statistics would require more than a one-volume book, but Lipset and Rokkan (1967) have edited a comprehensive reader on the subject that may serve as a good starting point.

Research on the social backgrounds of legislators and on their political behavior is less voluminous. The political slant of legislators has been perhaps the most popular research topic. As early as 1949, Gage and Shimberg measured "progressivism" in the U.S. Senate. The authors sampled the senators' votes on eighteen bills evaluated to measure progressivism and found that (1) younger senators are not more progressive than older senators; (2) senators from the same state do not tend to vote the same way; and (3) regional differences are significant in explaining voting differentials.

MacRae (1954) selected a sample of critical votes by consulting the roll calls published in the *New Republic* and the *CIO News*. His assumption was that these sources would publish only reports of votes on issues germane to their presumably liberal readers. From these, MacRae obtained a "liberal index" depending upon the direction of the vote.

Roll-call votes were employed by Riker and Niemi (1962) to examine the question of congressional coalitions. The authors took votes on eighty-seven roll calls, noting whether a member of Congress (1) voted on the winning side, (2) voted on the losing side, (3) did not vote when eligible, and (4) did not vote when ineligible. The rolls were classified into subjects, and an index of coalitions was constructed.

The *Congressional Record* contains information that can be used to study the behavior not only of members of Congress but also of those outside the Congress. For example, it is a common practice for a member of Congress to insert in the *Record* newspaper columns that reflect his

---

* Institute of Electoral Research, *A Review of Elections of the World* (London: Dillon's University Bookshop, issued biennially). Richard M. Scammon, ed., *America at the Polls: A Handbook of American Presidential Election Statistics, 1920–1964* (Pittsburgh: University of Pittsburgh Press, 1965).
† For an annotated bibliography of other collections, see Gurr (1972).

or her point of view. In a study of political columnists, Webb (1963) employed these data for an estimate of conservatism-liberalism among Washington's columnists. Individual members of Congress were assigned a liberal-conservative score by evaluations of their voting record published by two opposing groups—the Conservative Americans for Constitutional Action and the Liberal Committee on Political Action of the AFL–CIO. Columnists were then ordered on the mean score of the members of Congress who placed their articles in the *Record*.

Data contained in the handbook by Taylor et al. (1972) and in similar collections have been used primarily in cross-national research. These data are commonly referred to as aggregate data and involve peculiar considerations with regard to their reliability, comparability, and inferential potentials. The reader is advised to consult Merrit and Rokkan (1966) and Gurr (1972) for the issues involved in making inferences from aggregate data. The following studies are examples of research employing aggregate data.

Rae and Taylor (1970) tested James Madison's proposition that large republics are less subject to tyrannical policies than are small ones, by using measures of size and fragmentation (e.g., fragmentation of political parties by votes) for twenty contemporary republics. The authors report that (1) tyranny decreases with size; and (2) if one controls for area, then tyranny decreases as factions become more diverse in the absence of a one-party majority. Fragmentation, however, represents only one aspect of a more complex system leading to tyrannical policies. The intensity of fragmentation, the composition of crosscutting cleavages, and the potentials for coercion are three more aspects that can be tested with aggregate data.

Wagner's law of increasing state activity was tested with aggregate data. The law is an attempt to delineate the causes of the growth of government activity. To this end, it was hypothesized that in developing societies, governmental activity increased faster than economic output. The author attributed his law to a variety of factors: increasing involvement of government in economic enterprise; increasing demands for social services such as education, welfare, and public health.* In the United States, however, the growth of governmental activity has occurred in spurts during crisis periods and not as a steady acceleration. To test this deviation, Dye (1972) computed from aggregate data the government expenditures as percentages of the gross national product over a period of seventy years. He observed that since 1900, wars and severe depressions have been related to significant increases in govern-

---

* Wagner's study is discussed at length in Alan T. Peacock and Jack Wiseman, *The Growth of Public Expenditures in the United Kingdom* (Princeton, N.J.: Princeton University Press, 1961).

mental activity. National emergencies provide the opportunity for governments to increase the scope and magnitude of their activities.

Cutright (1967) tested the theory that social stratification is concerned with the distribution of material rewards and with the socio-economic and political conditions that account for differences in the way the distributive process allocates a nation's product. The author measured the degree of intersectorial income inequality in fifty nations. This measure served as a dependent variable, which was then related to the following independent variables: level of economic development, political institutions and the distribution of power, farm rental and the propertied class, military participation ratio, dependence of a nation on foreign trade, level of gross domestic capital formation, and the size of the powerless labor force. To test these relations, aggregate data reported in Russett et al. (1964) were used.

The votes of a judicial body provide data for a number of research purposes. Schubert (1963) employed statistical analyses of past voting behavior by U.S. Supreme Court justices to predict future votes. Snyder (1959) used past voting behavior in a study of the degree of uncertainty in the whole United States judicial system. In one measure, uncertainty was operationally defined by the number of reversals of lower-court decisions by the Supreme Court. With the precedent principle of *stare decisis*, there should be few reversals if certainty is high.

Jaros and Mendelsohn (1967) examined the proposition that the sentencing behavior of judges in lower-level trial courts is the consequence of the playing of a legal-professional role. The authors studied the sentences imposed by three judges of Detroit traffic court during two one-week periods in the summer of 1966. Data were gathered on all complete cases tried during these periods. It was found that social attitudes, professional role considerations, and community values motivate judicial behavior.

Governmental documents. We have already seen the fruitfulness of analyzing governmental documents such as birth and death records. Other governmental and quasi-governmental documents may also serve as a source of data. Durkheim (1951), for example, used weather reports in his study of suicide. Lombraso used governmental documents to study the effect of weather and time of year on scientific creativity. He drew a sample of fifty-two physical, chemical, and mathematical discoveries and noted the time of their occurrence. His evidence showed that twenty-two of the major discoveries occurred in the spring, fifteen in the autumn, ten in the summer, and five in winter (Webb et al., 1966).

City budgets were the data of Angell's (1951) research on the moral integration of American cities. He constructed a "welfare effort index" by computing local per capita expenditures for welfare; he combined this with a "crime index" based on FBI data, to get an "integration index." More recently, budgets have been used as indicators of policy statements. The expenditure side of the budget shows "who gets what" in public funds, and the revenue side tells "who pays the cost." The budgetary process provides a mechanism for reviewing governmental programs, assessing their cost, relating them to financial sources, making choices among alternative expenditures, and determining the financial effort that a government will expend on these programs. Davis, Dempster, and Wildavsky (1966) examined the federal budget in consecutive periods and identified two variables that explain the greatest portion of budgetary allocations in any year:

> 1. The agency request for a certain year is a fixed mean percentage of the Congressional appropriation for that agency in the previous year plus a random variable for that year. 2. The Congressional appropriation for an agency in a certain year is a fixed mean percentage of the agency's request in that year plus a variable representing a deviation from the usual relationship between the Congress and the agency for the previous year.

The mass media. The fourth type of public record is the mass media. This is the most easily available source of social science data. Accordingly, research using data obtained from the mass media is voluminous, and only one example will be discussed in the present section.*

Grusky (1963) studied the relationship between administrative succession and subsequent change in group performance. From the sports pages, Grusky obtained data on the performance of various professional football teams, as well as the timing of changes in coaches and managers. He found that changing a manager makes a difference in the performance of a team.

The mass media record people's verbal communications; these, in turn, have been analyzed to test a variety of propositions. With the introduction of content analysis, research using the mass media as a primary source of data has rapidly accelerated. Holsti has observed that "during the first two decades of the century, an average of approximately 2.5 content-analysis studies appeared each year. During the next three decades, the annual average frequencies rose to 13.8, 22.8, and 43.3 respectively, and by 1950–1958, this figure had more than doubled again to 96.3" (1968:607).

Private Records

Unlike public records, private records are difficult to obtain. Nevertheless, they can be of great value to researchers who wish to gain insights

---

* For other studies using the mass media as a major source of unobtrusive data, see Webb et al. (1966).

by inspecting the subject's own definition of a situation or an event. Private records include autobiographies, diaries, letters, essays, and the like. Biographies are the most frequently used type of private record; they reflect the author's interpretation of his or her personal experiences. The diary is a more spontaneous account, as its author is not constrained by task-attitudes that control the production of biographies (Allport, 1942). Both biographies and diaries are initially directed to one person—the author. Letters, on the other hand, have a dual audience—the writer and the recipient—and they often reflect the interaction between them (Denzin, 1970). These three main types of private records are written documents focusing on the author's personal experiences. They are usually produced on the author's own initiative and express his or her personal reflections (Selltiz et al., 1959).

The autobiography. The uniqueness of the autobiography is that it provides a view of a person's life and experiences before they are fragmented by the process of analysis (Allport, 1942). The investigator may gain an understanding of a person's life in its natural setting, thereby avoiding contamination in the process of problem conceptualization. The autobiography provides "an 'inside picture' of the subject's life, and a side that is neither fully apparent nor fully public" (Denzin, 1970: 227).

Allport (1942) has distinguished three major types of autobiographies, each of which may serve different research objectives. The first is the comprehensive autobiography, which covers a full cycle of the subject's life from his or her earliest memory and integrates a large number of experiences. Helen Keller's accounts of her life as a blind deaf-mute exemplify the comprehensive autobiography. The second type is the topical autobiography, which focuses on a limited aspect of the subject's life. For example, Sutherland (1937:v), studied only one phase of the life of a professional thief:

> The principal part of this book is a description of the profession of theft by a person who had been engaged almost continuously for more than twenty years in this profession. This description was secured in two ways: first, the thief wrote approximately two-thirds of it on topics and questions prepared by me; second, he and I discussed for about seven hours a week for twelve weeks what he had written, and immediately after each conference I wrote in verbatim form . . . all that he had said in the discussion.

The third type is the edited autobiography, which is a monitored version of the subject's account. The investigator selects only those experiences which are relevant to the research purpose. The purpose of the editing process is to clarify and organize the material so as to illuminate the points relevant to the research hypotheses.

The diary. Diaries provide a firsthand account of the subject's life experiences. Written close to the occurrence of events, they convey immediate experiences unimpaired by distortion of memory. Diaries are not constricted by the fear of public showing; therefore, they reveal events and experiences that were considered significant at the time of their occurrence.

Allport (1942) has classified diaries into three types. The intimate journal is a continuous record of the subject's subjective perception of his or her experiences over a long period of time. The second type, the memoir, is rather impersonal and is written in a relatively short time; it resembles an objective record of the subject's affairs. The third type, the log, is also impersonal and contains a record of events, meetings, visits, and other activities of the subject during a limited period of time.

Some social scientists find the intimate journal rather useful since it contains authentic expressions of one's perceptions over a prolonged period of time. Selltiz et al. (1959) exemplify the utility of the personal journal through Bühler's study of adolescents. Bühler compared the diaries of girls in three successive generations and demonstrated that in a period of considerable cultural changes between 1837 and 1910, in which the diaries were written, some basic characteristics of youth, such as the need for intimate relationships, remained unchanged. The intimate journal not only provides a person's subjective perceptions over an extended period, but also allows the investigator to compare two or more time periods in a person's life and to observe continuities and changes.

Letters. Letters are used widely by historians but infrequently by social scientists. One of the earliest attempts to employ letters as a source of social data was the Thomas and Znaniecki (1958) study on the Polish peasant. The authors collected letters sent between Poland and the United States to research the problems that arose when the immigrants moved from the old country to the new society. The letters enabled the investigators to examine, among other things, the subjects' personalities and the kinds of interactions they had with the recipients of the letters.

In a more recent study, Dexter (1964) analyzed letters that were sent to members of Congress, thereby examining the nature of public opinion reflected in these letters. One of the interesting findings in this study is that of the hundred letters advocating support for a higher minimum wage, only seventy-five were written by persons eligible to register, and of these only thirty-five were actually registered. In some cases, the letters had been stimulated by interest groups; such letters can be identified by clues such as similarity of phrasing and time of mailing.

Suicide notes serve as an illustration of a particular kind of letter to which no reply is expected. Spiegel and Neuringer (1963) analyzed such notes to test the hypothesis that a necessary condition for suicide is the inhibition of dread that is invoked by the suicidal intention.

Authenticity. One of the main problems in using private documents is the possibility that they might not be authentic. There are two possible kinds of unauthentic records: records that have been produced by deliberate deceit and records that have been unconsciously misrepresented by the author (Selltiz et al., 1959). Records may be falsified or forged for the sole purpose of gaining prestige or material rewards. For example, writers who claim to have an intimate knowledge of the subject's life can more easily sell an alleged biography to a publishing company; such was the case with the fake biography of Howard Hughes, which was sold in 1972 to a reputable publisher under false pretenses. Several procedures can be used to check whether private records are genuine. First, the authorship should be critically examined. Second, the date of the document has to be established, and dates that are mentioned must be verified. For instance, if the author refers to a particular event, say, a riot, it can be learned whether the event had occurred at the time the document had purportedly been written.

The second kind of authenticity is much more difficult to detect. Documents may not necessarily be false, yet they can easily distort the truth for the following reasons: the authors of letters, diaries, or autobiographies may not remember the facts; or they may try to please the recipient of the document by exaggerating; or perhaps they are restricted by norms and conventions and thus forced to present a somewhat distorted picture. Chapin (1920:37) has suggested that the following critical questions be answered before a document is accepted as an authentic record:

1. What did the author mean by a particular statement? What is its real meaning as distinguished from its mere literal meaning?
2. Was the statement made in good faith?
   a. Was the author influenced by sympathy or antipathy to tell an untruth?
   b. Did vanity influence him?
   c. Was he influenced by public opinion?
3. Was the statement accurate?
   a. Was the author a poor observer because of mental defect or abnormality?
   b. Was the author badly situated in time and place to observe?
   c. Was he negligent or indifferent?

With answers to these questions, the investigator will usually be able to eliminate records that are in doubt and accept the rest as credible evidence.

CONTENT ANALYSIS

Data obtained from archival records and documents can be more systematically analyzed with the method of content analysis. One can analyze the content of letters, diaries, newspaper articles, minutes of meetings, and the like. Content analysis is a method of data analysis as well as a method of observation. Instead of observing people's behavior directly, or asking them about it, the researcher takes the communications that people have produced and asks questions of the communications. The content of communication serves as the basis of inference.

Broadly defined, content analysis is "any technique for making inferences by systematically and objectively identifying specified characteristics of messages" (Holsti, 1968:601). Objectivity refers here to an analysis that is pursued on the basis of explicit rules which enable different researchers to obtain the same results from the same messages or documents. In a systematic content analysis, the "inclusion or exclusion of content is done according to consistently applied criteria of selection; this requirement eliminates analyses in which only materials supporting the investigator's hypotheses are examined" (Holsti, 1968:598).

Applications of Content Analysis

Although content analysis is always performed on a message, it may also be used to answer questions about other elements of communication. Lasswell (1965:12) formulated the basic question that can be raised by researchers: Who says what, to whom, how, and with what effect? More explicitly, a researcher may analyze messages to test hypotheses about (1) characteristics of the text; (2) antecedents of the message; or (3) effects of the communication. These three questions differ, as Holsti (1968) points out, with respect to the questions asked of the data, the dimension of communication analyzed, and the research design.

The most frequent application of content analysis has been to describe the attributes of the message. For example, the concern of one aspect of research on Revolution and Development of International Relations (RADIR) was with the survey of political symbols. Research designs were constructed to enable the testing of hypotheses on "world revolution" by identifying trends in the usage of symbols that express major goal values of modern politics. Editorials from ten prestigious newspapers in the United States, England, France, Germany, and the Soviet Union were analyzed for the period 1890 to 1949. Editorials appearing on the first and the fifteenth day of each month were coded for the presence of 416 key symbols. These symbols included 206 geographical terms, such as names of countries and international organizations, and 210 ideological symbols, such as "equality," democracy," and "communism." When a symbol appeared it was scored as present, and the expressed attitudes toward it were recorded with reference to one of the following three categories: approval, disapproval, or neutrality. Data from 19,553 editorials were used to trace changing foci of attention and attitude. One of the many reported findings is that symbols of representative governments are used where the practice is under dispute, not where it is an accepted part of the traditions (Pool, 1952).

In a more recent study of a substantially different subject matter, Maher, McKean, and McLaughlin (1966) examined the characteristics of schizophrenic language. The explicit research purpose was to identify the systematic differences between language judged to be thought-disordered and language judged to be free from thought disorder. To this end, the authors used documents produced by patients under conditions of spontaneity. The documents ranged from long-term sets of diaries to obscenities scrawled on matchbook covers. A sample of text constituting fifty words was drawn from each document. The samples were coded in accordance with a division of the text into simple thought sequences, or simple units of thought. Each unit included a subject, verb, objects, and modifiers plus the source of the thought, the attributive subject, and the verb. The text was divided into these units, and each word was assigned to categories by its function in the text. Among other findings, the authors report that (1) documents judged to be free from thought disorder used fewer objects per subject than did those judged pathological; and (2) documents judged normal contained more qualifiers per verb than those judged pathological.

The second application of content analysis is that in which a text is analyzed in order to make inferences about the sender of the message and about the causes or antecedents of the message. A well-known attempt to determine the sender's identification is the Mosteller and Wallace (1964) study on who wrote *The Federalist Papers,* Nos. 49 to 58, 62, and 63. The authors started with four sets of papers: those known to have been written by Madison, those thought to have been written by Madison or by Hamilton, and those thought to have been written by both. Upon examining the texts of the known set of papers, the investigators were able to select words that differentiated between the two authors. For example, the word "enough" tended to be used by Hamilton but not by Madison. These key differentiating words were then used in combination to attribute authorship of the disputed papers. The data strongly supported the claim of Madison's authorship.

Shneidman (1961) inferred personality traits of speakers from logical and cognitive characteristics of their verbal communications. Texts were coded into two category sets: idiosyncrasies of reasoning, which included thirty-two categories consisting of idiosyncrasies of relevance, idiosyncrasies of meaning, and the like; and cognitive manipulations, which consisted of sixty-five styles of thought development, such as switching from normative to descriptive mode. To illustrate the method, the researcher examined the logical styles of Kennedy and Nixon in their first two television debates and that of Khrushchev in speeches delivered at the United Nations. Shneidman constructed for each idiosyncrasy of reasoning the logical conditions under which idiosyncrasy is controverted or cancelled. Inferences regarding psychological characteristics of the message's sender were then drawn. For example, Khrushchev was characterized in the following way:

> He feels that others are prone to misunderstand his position and yet he desires acceptance and will even sacrifice other needs or ends to achieve it. He is moody and needful of approval. . . . He trusts his own instincts, his "natural feel" for things. He is painstaking in certain areas, but in general is impatient and suspicious of detail or subtlety (1961:61–62).

Content analysis has also been used to infer aspects of culture and cultural change. McClelland (1958) tested his "need of achievement" theory by analyzing the content of literature in different cultures. An individual with high n-Achievement is someone who wants to succeed, who is nonconforming, and who enjoys tasks that involve elements of risk; n-Achievement is "a sum of the number of instances of achievement 'ideas' or images" (1958:520). The hypothesis that "a society with a relatively high percentage of individuals with high n-Achievement should contain a strong entrepreneurial class which will tend to be active and successful particularly in business enterprises so that the society will grow in power and influence" was tested by scoring samples of literature from different periods of Greek civilization.

The next major application of content analysis is that in which inferences are made about the effects of messages on the recipient. The researcher determines the effects of A's messages to B by content-analyzing B's messages. Alternatively, one can study the effects of communication by examining other aspects of the recipient's behavior. (Holsti, 1968). Content analysis serves to delineate the relevant independent variables that are correlated with the recipient's behavior. Berelson's study is perhaps the earliest attempt to examine the effects of messages on the recipient. During the 1940 presidential campaign, themes of political appeals were identified by content-analyzing public and private media. The public was then surveyed on its reactions to the content of the arguments. The relationship between content and recipients is summarized in the following way:

> Why do people come across arguments and why do they accept them? . . . Mainly, people come across the arguments which the mediums of communication emphasize; they also tend to see the arguments they want to see and other arguments whose statement is appealing . . . people accept the argu-

ments which support their own general position; they also tend to accept the arguments which they see in the public communications and those whose statement is persuasive (Berelson, 1942:63).

Units and Categories

The content-analysis procedure involves the interaction of two processes: specification of the content characteristics to be measured, and application of the rules for identifying and recording the characteristics when they appear in the texts to be analyzed. The categories into which content is coded vary with the nature of data and the research purpose. Before discussing general procedures for category construction, it is necessary to specify the various recording units used in research and to make a distinction between recording units and context units. The recording unit is the smallest body of content in which the appearance of a reference is counted (a reference is a single occurrence of the content element). The context unit is the largest body of content that may be examined in characterizing a recording unit (Berelson, 1952). For example, the recording unit may be a single term; but in order to note whether the term is treated favorably or unfavorably, one has to consider the entire sentence in which the term appears (the context unit). Thus, the sentence is taken into account when recording (and subsequently when coding) the term.

Five major recording units have been used frequently in content-analysis research: words or terms, themes, characters, paragraphs, and items. The word is the smallest unit generally applied in research. Its application results in a list of frequencies of selected words or terms. For example, Lasswell (1965), in a study on propaganda detection, reports that the *Moscow News* frequently used twenty-seven key political terms during 1938–1939. Eight of these terms and their frequencies are presented in Table 7.1.

TABLE 7.1. Frequency of Use of Key Political Terms

Term	*Frequency*
Bourgeois	61
Class	92
Class struggle	97
The party	172
Red Army	162
The people	1,136
Revolution	217
Exploitation	54

For many research purposes, the theme is a useful recording unit. In its simplest form a theme is a simple sentence, that is, subject and predicate. Since in most texts themes can be found in clauses, paragraphs, and illustrations, it becomes necessary to specify which of these places will be searched when using the theme as a recording unit. For example, one may consider only the primary theme in each paragraph or count every theme in the text. Themes are most frequently employed in the study of propaganda, attitudes, images, and values.

In some studies, the character is employed as the recording unit. In this case, the researcher counts the number of persons rather than the number of words or themes. This, in turn, enables the examination of traits of characters appearing in various texts.

The paragraph is the fourth recording unit. However, it is rarely used because of difficulties in classifying and coding the various and numerous things implied in a single paragraph.

The item is the whole unit employed by the producer of a message. The item may be an entire article, a book, a speech, or the like. Analysis by the entire item is appropriate whenever the variations within the item are small and insignificant. For example, news stories can often be classified by subject matter such as crime, labor, or sports.

Eventually, recording units are classified and coded into categories. The problem of category construction, as Berelson (1952:147) points out, is the most crucial aspect of content analysis:

> Content analysis stands or falls by its categories. Particular studies have been productive to the extent that the categories were clearly formulated and well adapted to the problem and to the content. Content analysis studies done on a hit or miss basis, without clearly formulated problems for investigation and with vaguely drawn or poorly articulated categories are almost certain to be of indifferent or low quality as research productions. ... Since the categories contain the substance of the investigation, a content analysis can be no better than its system of categories.

Among the types of categories employed frequently in content-analysis research are the following (Holsti, 1968):

"What is said" categories:
    SUBJECT MATTER. What is the communication about?
    DIRECTION. How is the subject matter treated (e.g., favorable-unfavorable; strong-weak)?
    STANDARD. What is the basis on which the classification by direction is made?
    VALUES. What values, goals, or desires are revealed?
    METHODS. What methods are used to achieve goals?
    TRAITS. What are the characteristics used in description of people?
    ACTOR. Who is represented as undertaking certain acts?

AUTHORITY. In whose name are statements made?
ORIGIN. Where does the communication originate?
LOCATION. Where does the action take place?
CONFLICT. What are the sources and levels of conflict?
ENDINGS. Are conflicts resolved happily, ambiguously, or tragically?
TIME. When does the action take place?

"How it is said" categories:

FORM OR TYPE OF COMMUNICATION. What is the medium of communication (radio, newspaper, speech, television, etc.)?
FORM OF STATEMENT. What is the grammatical or syntactical form of the communication?
DEVICE. What is the rhetorical or propagandistic method used?

Categories must relate to the research purpose, and they must be exhaustive and mutually exclusive. Exhaustiveness ensures that every recording unit relevant to the study can be classified. Mutual exclusivity means that no recording unit can be included more than once within any given category-system. The researcher also has to specify explicitly the indicators that determine which recording units fall into each category. This enables replication, which is an essential requirement of objective and systematic content analysis (see Chapter 8).

Most content-analysis research is quantitative in one form or another. Quantification may be performed by employing one of the following four systems of enumeration: (1) A time/space system that is based on various measures of space (for example, column inches) or units of time (for example, minutes devoted to a news item on the radio) to describe the relative emphases of different categories in the analyzed material. (2) An appearance system that calls for searching the material for appearance of a certain attribute. The size of the context unit determines the frequency with which repeated recording units occurring in close proximity to each other are counted separately. (3) A frequency system in which every occurrence of a given attribute is recorded. The use of the frequency system was exemplified in Table 7.1. (4) An intensity system. This is generally employed in studies dealing with attitudes and values. Methods of quantifying for intensity are based on the construction of attitude scales (see Chapter 6). For example, using the "paired comparison" technique developed by Thurstone, judges decide which possible pair of intensity indicators is rated higher on a scale of attitudes. The judgments are then used to construct categories into which recording units are placed.*

---

* The most recent development in content analysis is the programing of computers to process the variety of operations involved in textual analysis. It is beyond the scope of this book to survey these developments, but a good start would be Philip J. Stone et al., *The General Inquirer: A Computer Approach to Content Analysis* (Cambridge, Mass.: MIT Press, 1966).

SUMMARY

Unobtrusive measures are intended to produce data that are free from the errors that either the subject or the researcher may introduce when confronting one another in data-collection situations. An unobtrusive measure is any method of data collection that directly removes the investigator from the set of interactions, events, or behavior being studied. In this chapter we have discussed and exemplified erosion and accretion measures, simple observation, and archival records—public and private.

Data obtained from archival records and documents can be systematically and quantitatively analyzed with the method of content analysis. The method enables the making of inferences by rigorously and objectively identifying specified characteristics of messages.

REFERENCES

Allport, Gordon W. *The Use of Personal Documents in Psychological Research*. New York: Social Science Research Council, 1942.

Angell, Robert C. "The Moral Integration of American Cities." *American Journal of Sociology* 57 (1951):1–140.

Berelson, Bernard. "The Effects of Print upon Public Opinion." In Douglas Waples (ed.), *Print, Radio, and Film in Democracy*. Chicago: University of Chicago Press, 1942.

Berelson, Bernard. *Content Analysis in Communication Research*. Glencoe, Ill.: Free Press, 1952.

Chapin, Stuart F. *Field Work and Social Research*. New York: Century, 1920.

Cutright, Phillips. "Inequality: A Cross-National Analysis." *American Sociological Review* 32 (1967):562–578.

Davis, Otto A., Dempster, M. A. H., and Wildavsky, Aaron. "A Theory of the Budgetary Process." *American Political Science Review* 60 (1966):529–547.

Denzin, Norman K. *The Research Act: A Theoretical Introduction to Sociological Methods*. Chicago: Aldine, 1970.

Dexter, Lewis A. "Communications-Pressure, Influence or Education?" In Lewis A. Dexter and David M. White (eds.), *People, Society and Mass Communications*. New York: Free Press, 1964.

Durkheim, Emile. *Suicide*. Translated by J. A. Spaulding and G. Simpson. Glencoe, Ill.: Free Press, 1951.

Dye, Thomas R. *Understanding Public Policy*. Englewood Cliffs, N.J.: Prentice-Hall, 1972.

Gage, Nathaniel L., and Shimberg, Ben. "Measuring Senatorial Progressivism." *Journal of Abnormal and Social Psychology* 44 (1949):112–117.

Grusky, Oscar. "Managerial Succession and Organizational Effectiveness." *American Journal of Sociology* 69 (1963):21–31.

Gurr, Ted R. *Politimetrics*. Englewood Cliffs, N.J.: Prentice-Hall, 1972.

Holsti, Ole R. "Content Analysis." In Gardner Lindzey and Elliot Aronson (eds.), *The Handbook of Social Psychology*. Reading, Mass.: Addison-Wesley, 1968.

Jaros, Dean, and Mendelsohn, Robert I. "The Judicial Role and Sentencing Behavior." *Midwest Journal of Political Science* 11 (1967):471–488.

Krout, Maurice H. "An Experimental Attempt to Determine the Significance of Unconscious Manual Symbolic Movements." *Journal of General Psychology* 51 (1954):121–152.

Lasswell, Harold D. "Detection: Propaganda Detection and the Courts." In Harold D. Laswell et al., *The Language of Politics: Studies in Quantitative Semantics*. Cambridge, Mass.: MIT Press, 1965.

Lipset, Seymour M., and Rokkan, Stein, eds. *Party Systems and Voter Alignment*. New York: Free Press, 1967.

MacRae, Duncan, Jr. "Some Underlying Variables in Legislative Roll Call Votes." *Public Opinion Quarterly* 18 (1954):191–196.

Maher, Brendan A., McKean, Kathryn O., and McLaughlin, Barry. "Studies in Psychotic Language." In Philip J. Stone et al., *The General Inquirer: A Computer Approach to Content Analysis*. Cambridge, Mass.: MIT Press, 1966.

McClelland, David C. "The Use of Measures of Human Motivation in the Study of Society." In John W. Atkinson (ed.), *Motives in Fantasy, Action and Society*. Princeton, N.J.: Van Nostrand, 1958.

Merrit, Richard L., and Rokkan, Stein, eds. *Comparing Nations: The Use of Quantitative Data in Cross-National Research*. New Haven: Yale University Press, 1966.

Middleton, Russell. "Fertility Values in American Magazine Fiction: 1916–1956." *Public Opinion Quarterly* 24 (1960):139–143.

Mosteller, Frederick, and Wallace, David L. *Inference and Disputed Authorship: The Federalist*. Reading, Mass.: Addison-Wesley, 1964.

Phillips, R. H. "Miami Goes Latin under Cuban Tide." *New York Times*, March 18, 1962, p. 85.

Pool, Ithiel de Sola. *Symbols of Democracy*. Stanford, Calif.: Stanford University Press, 1952.

Psathas, George, and Henslin, James N. "Dispatched Orders and the Cab Driver: A Study of Locating Activities." *Social Problems* 14 (1967):424–443.

Rae, Douglas W., and Taylor, Michael. *The Analysis of Political Cleavages*. New Haven: Yale University Press, 1970.

Riker, William H., and Niemi, Donald. "The Stability of Coalitions on Roll Calls in the House of Representatives." *American Political Science Review* 56 (1962):58–65.

Russett, Bruce M., et al. *World Handbook of Political and Social Indicators*. New Haven: Yale University Press, 1964.

Schubert, Glendon. *Quantitative Analysis of Judicial Behavior*. New York: Free Press, 1959.

Schubert, Glendon. *Judicial Decision-Making*. New York: Free Press, 1963.

Selltiz, Claire, et al. *Research Methods in Social Relations*. New York: Holt, Rinehart & Winston, 1959.

Shneidman, Edwin S. "A Psychological Analysis of Political Thinking: The Kennedy-Nixon 'Great Debates' and the Kennedy-Khrushchev 'Grim Debates.'" Mimeographed. Cambridge, Mass.: Harvard University, 1961.

Snyder, Eloise C. "Uncertainty and the Supreme Court's Decisions." *American Journal of Sociology* 65 (1959):241–245.

Spiegel, Donald E., and Neuringer, Charles. "Role of Dread in Suicidal Behavior." *Journal of Abnormal and Social Psychology* 66 (1963):507–511.

Stone, Georgy P. "Appearance and the Self." In Arnold M. Rose (ed.), *Human Behavior and Social Processes*. Boston: Houghton Mifflin, 1962.

Sutherland, Edwin H. *The Professional Thief*. Chicago: University of Chicago Press, 1937.

Taylor, Charles L., et al. *World Handbook of Political and Social Indicators*. New Haven: Yale University Press, 1972.

Thomas, William I., and Znaniecki, Florian. *The Polish Peasant in Europe and America*. New York: Dover, 1958.

Wallace, Samuel E. *Skid Row as a Way of Life*. Totowa, N.J.: Bedminster Press, 1965.

Warner, W. Lloyd. *The Living and the Dead*. New Haven: Yale University Press, 1959.

Webb, Eugene J. "How to Tell a Columnist: II." *Columbia Journalism Review* 2 (1963):20.

Webb, Eugene J., et al. *Unobtrusive Measures: Nonreactive Research in the Social Sciences*. Chicago: Rand McNally, 1966.

STUDY SUGGESTIONS

1. What factors limit the extent to which unobtrusive measures can be substituted for obtrusive ones?
2. What information in Taylor et al. (1972) is of relevance to your field of interest?
3. Discuss the potential advantages and the various limitations of private records when used as the sole data in social science research.
4. What types of news are emphasized in your daily newspaper? What types of news were emphasized in it twenty years ago? Specify the content you want to describe and prepare a coding scheme for tallying the data.

PART 3
Data Processing and Analysis

CHAPTER 8
Data Processing

Data processing is the link between data collection and data analysis. It involves the transformation of the observations gathered in the field into a system of categories and the translation of these categories into codes amenable to quantitative analysis. The codes are then recorded on punchcards and processed mechanically through computers and unit record equipment. This chapter will focus on the major aspects of coding and automatic data processing.

CONSTRUCTING CODING SCHEMES

Coding is the process of classifying responses into meaningful categories. It involves combining detailed information into a limited number of categories that enable simple description of the data and allow for statistical analyses. The main purpose of coding is to simplify the handling of many individual responses* by classifying them into a smaller number of groups, each including responses that are similar in content (Lazarsfeld and Barton, 1951).

Suppose an investigator has gathered information on the occupations of several hundred individuals. The following are examples of the occupations listed:

Lawyer	Practical nurse
Barber	Migrant farm laborer
Carpenter	Executive
Broker	High school teacher
Elevator operator	Electrician
Veterinarian	Advertising agent

---

* In the following discussion, "responses," "answers," "observations," "acts," and "behavior" are used interchangeably.

These data are not amenable to analysis without a prior reduction into some system of categories. One acceptable way to classify them is according to the following categories:

1. *Professional and managerial:* lawyer, veterinarian, executive, high school teacher
2. *Technical and sales:* advertising agent, broker
3. *Service and skilled labor:* barber, elevator operator, practical nurse, electrician, carpenter
4. *Unskilled labor:* migrant farm worker

This system of categories allows for the classification of occupations according to the level of income, prestige, and education that they hold in common, permitting the researcher to handle four well-defined categories rather than several hundred specific occupations. Systems of categories such as this one, used to classify responses or acts that relate to a single item or variable, are referred to as coding schemes. The principles involved in the construction of such schemes are discussed in this section.

The previously discussed methods of data collection can be classified according to whether they utilize an inductive or a deductive system of coding. Inductive coding means recording the data as closely as possible to their original detail and postponing categorization: "The observer asks questions about what he is measuring only after he is comfortable that something stable is being measured precisely" (Weick, 1968:402). On the other hand, the deductive approach requires that data be recorded according to some preconceived scheme that is applied as the record is being made. With this method, broad categories are employed to classify observations, and original detail is largely disregarded. Most data-collection methods that use a precoded classification system implement a deductive approach.

In many surveys, categories are constructed in advance and the respondents are asked to classify themselves. For instance, the following fixed-alternative question has been precoded, and the respondents place themselves in the appropriate category:

> *With Respect to Your Own Personal Role in Seeking to Bring about Changes in Your High School and/or in Other Institutions of Our Society, Which One of the Following Statements Best Describes Your Own Position?*

1. ☐ I consider myself an activist.
2. ☐ I am in sympathy with most of the activists' objectives, but not with all of their tactics.
3. ☐ I am not emotionally involved, one way or the other.

4. ☐ I am not sure that I approve of what the activists are trying to do, but I have no strong objection to letting them try.
5. ☐ I am in total disagreement with the activists.

Similarly, in controlled observations, the coding scheme employed is prepared in advance, and the observed behavior is systematically recorded. For example, Bales's Interaction Process Analysis is based on the notion that there is a sequence of interactional events that develops within all groups regardless of their function or composition. Observed "acts" are coded into one of twelve categories, which are based on this sequence (see Table 5.1).

In exploratory research or in pilot studies, data are collected without a predesigned system of categories. Therefore, the coding scheme is constructed on the basis of raw material. With the inductive method of coding, the first step is to select a representative sample of responses and note all the answers to the particular item to be coded. When the selection is sufficiently large and varied for a pattern to emerge, the coding scheme can be constructed. This preliminary scheme is then systematically applied to the data.

The inductive method is most frequently applied to coding responses to open-ended questions or to data obtained from documents or through the method of participant observation. Consider, for example, the responses to the following question, designed to determine the effect of adolescent subculture on academic achievement (Coleman, 1959): "What does it take to get to be a member of the leading crowd?"

Some of the responses were:

Wear just the right things, nice hair, good grooming, and have a wholesome personality.

A good athlete, pretty good looking, common sense, sense of humor.

Money, cars, and the right connections and good personality.

Money, clothes, flashy appearance, date older boys, fairly good grades.

Be a sex fiend, dress real sharp, have own car and money, smoke and drink, go steady with a popular boy.

Be a good athlete, have a good personality, be in everything you can, don't drink or smoke.

Athletic ability sure helps.

Have pleasant personality, good manners, dress nicely, be clean, don't swear, be loads of fun.

A nice personality, dress nice without overdoing it.

Good in athletics, wheel type, not too intelligent.

These responses indicate some of the attributes that characterized the adolescent subculture in the late fifties. Responses that were mentioned 10 percent or more of the time were included in a coding scheme employed to analyze the data. The results of this analysis are presented in Table 8.1, in which the major categories of response and their frequencies are listed.

Categories are not always easily identified. Often, the process of constructing a comprehensive coding scheme is a long one and involves switching back and forth between the raw data and the evolving scheme until the latter is applicable and ties in with the general purpose of the study. Lazarsfeld and Barton (1951:160), examining some general principles of coding, illustrate this process by using some of the coding schemes constructed in the study, *The American Soldier* (Stouffer, 1965). In an attempt to determine which factors offset combat stress, the investigators of the American soldier drew up a preliminary list of categories on the basis of many responses:

1. Coercive formal authority.
2. Leadership practices—for example, encouragement.
3. Informal group:
   a. Affectional support.
   b. Code of behavior.
   c. Provision of realistic security and power.
4. Convictions about the war and the enemy.
5. Desire to complete the job by winning war, to go home.
6. Prayer and personal philosophies.

These preliminary coding schemes enabled the investigators in this study to classify the raw data and substantially reduce the number of

TABLE 8.1. Percentage Distribution of the Criteria for Membership in the Leading Crowd Perceived by Boys and Girls

Criterion for Membership in the Leading Crowd	*Boys*	*Girls*
Good personality, being friendly	26.6%	48.7%
Good looks, beauty	14.3	28.9
Having nice clothes	9.0	27.4
Good reputation	17.9	25.9
Having money	7.7	14.2
Good grades, being smart	11.9	11.6
Being an athlete (boys only)	16.3	—
Having a car (boys only)	10.7	—

SOURCE: James S. Coleman. "Academic Achievement and the Structure of Competition." *Harvard Educational Review* 29 (1959):333. Reprinted with permission of the publisher.

responses to be analyzed. Yet, a further modification was introduced after it was noted that formal sanctions are often more effective when channeled through informal group sanctions and internal sanctions. Conversely, the norms of the informal groups are influenced by formal sanctions as well as by individual conscience. On this basis, the responses were reanalyzed, and additional information was obtained to produce a modified coding scheme (Table 8.2).

The following responses conform to the modified categories in Table 8.2:

(a) I fight because I'll be punished if I quit.
(b) I fight because it's my duty to my country, the Army, the government; it would be wrong for me to quit.
(c) I fight because I'll lose the respect of my buddies if I quit.
(d) I fight because it would be wrong to let my buddies down.
(e) You have to look out for your buddies even if it means violating orders, or they won't look out for you.
(f) You have to look out for your buddies even if it means violating orders because it would be wrong to leave them behind.
(g) I am fighting because I believe in democracy and hate fascism.

Both the deductive and the inductive approaches have their respective shortcomings and advantages. The deductive method has been criticized for violating the continuity and complexity of behavior (Gellert, 1955). A preconstructed coding scheme is often rigid and does not allow for new insights on the part of the investigator. In addition, omission of descriptive detail may limit reanalysis at a later stage. Con-

TABLE 8.2. How Norms Bear on Individual Behavior in Combat

Underlying Source of Norms	*Channels*	
Norms of formal authorities	*Direct:*	
	(a)	Formal sanctions
	(b)	Internal sanctions
	Via group norms:	
	(c)	Informal group sanctions
	(d)	Internal sanctions
Norms of informal groups	(e)	Formal group sanctions
	(f)	Internal sanctions
Individual norms	(g)	Internal sanctions

SOURCE: Paul F. Lazarsfeld and Allen Barton. "Qualitative Measurement in the Social Sciences: Classification, Typologies, and Indices." In Daniel Lerner and Harold D. Lasswell (eds.), *The Policy Sciences*. Stanford, Calif.: Stanford University Press, 1951:161. Reprinted with permission.

ceptual definitions are sometimes imprecise, and when the data are precoded according to these definitions, it is difficult to reclassify it later according to a revised set of categories. Instead, a new set of records must be obtained (Weick, 1968). However, the deductive approach alerts observers to the dynamics of the situation by directing their attention to predefined and established concepts. Moreover, the observational process may benefit from the omission of superfluous detail.

The chief advantage of the inductive approach is its flexibility and richness, which enable the researcher to induce explanations from the findings. Moreover, it allows for a variety of coding schemes to be applied to the same observation, and it often suggests new categories as well (Weick, 1968). The shortcoming of this method is that researchers may be bogged down by the mass of details when they try to explain the data. Sometimes too little context is preserved for the coder to determine which details are trivial and can therefore be eliminated.

The preference for either coding strategy depends on the purpose of the investigation. In exploratory studies, where concepts are not well defined, the researcher will be faced by a mass of raw data for which ready-made categories do not exist. The inductive method is then well suited, for it permits concrete categories to be adapted to the data. Conversely, in studies testing formulated hypotheses, preconstructed categories are derived from the theory, and the deductive approach is applied. Alternatively, it is possible to combine both strategies, starting with the inductive approach and obtaining extensive information from which some concepts are induced, and then collecting a second set of data that is better formulated and more specific.

Whichever method of coding is employed, inductive or deductive, whether the coding scheme is taken from an existing theory or developed from the data, the requirements of a good coding scheme are the same. The first requirement is that the coding scheme be linked to the theory and the problem under study. Questions and other stimuli may elicit responses that can be classified in terms of different dimensions. Answers to a question such as "In what way are you affected by the energy crisis?" may cover a general concern about the economy, about the consequent changes in life style, or even about changes in the international system. The researchers have to decide in terms of which dimensions the coding is to be constructed (Moser and Kalton, 1971). They may concentrate solely on the political aspects, or they might decide to code in terms of economic considerations. The decision is guided by the aim of the particular study, which will determine the dimensions chosen for coding.

The second requirement of a coding system is that it be exhaustive. That is, the categories must be so constructed that each and every response on behavior can be classified. An example of lack of exhaustiveness would be the classification of marital status into three categories only: "married," "single," and "divorced." If the group had included a widower, then the requirement of exhaustiveness would be violated because this person could not be fitted into the coding scheme. Any classification can become exhaustive by including a category labeled "other" or "miscellaneous." Although this is an accepted solution, it should, if at all possible, be avoided, as it defeats the purpose of the coding process, which is designed to distinguish between cases in terms of the properties under study (Lazarsfeld and Barton, 1951).

The categories must also be mutually exclusive, so that each case is classified only once. This requirement is violated either when some of the categories overlap or when more than one dimension provides a basis for classification. An example of the first error would be the classification of religious affiliations as Christian, Muslim, Jew, and Catholic. Catholics are also Christians, and each case classified as Catholic could also be assigned to the Christian group. The solution would be to eliminate the Catholic category; or, if a more specific classification of the Christian group is desired, this broad category would have to be further subdivided into all its different denominations.

The second violation may be due to mixing different dimensions in the classification of observations. For example, a coding scheme that codes occupations according to the categories: "white collar," "blue collar," "government employee," "union worker," and "self-employed" includes two dimensions, namely, type of work and form of employment. These dimensions cannot be lumped together. The categories could be divided into two separate coding schemes: (a) 1. blue collar, 2. white collar; (b) 1. government employee, 2. union worker, 3. self-employed. Alternatively, these schemes can be combined into a two-dimensional system whose categories would be: (1) blue collar and union worker; (2) blue collar and government employee; (3) blue collar and self-employed; (4) white collar and union worker; (5) white collar and government employee; and (6) white collar and self-employed.

A further consideration in the construction of a coding scheme is how detailed it should be. In other words, how many categories will the scheme include? On the whole, it is preferable to include too many categories rather than too few, since reducing the number later is easier than splitting an already coded group of responses. However, the number of categories is limited by the number of cases as well as by the anticipated statistical analyses. Categories that include very few cases cannot be retained in the coding scheme unless they represent particularly rare responses of special interest to the researcher.

Purely technical considerations are also likely to dictate the number of categories retained for a final analysis. A very detailed coding scheme will present difficulties when the data are transferred to punchcards.

These cards, as we shall see later, consist of eighty columns, each containing twelve categories. Although more than one column could be used if necessary (i.e., if there are more than twelve categories), this complicates the analysis and slows it down.

In coding open-ended questions or other nonstructured material, coders are required to exercise their own judgment in classifying responses according to the coding scheme. However, when given rules cannot be applied automatically, different coders may arrive at different coding. In such instances, the coding process becomes unreliable, a problem that is just as serious as the unreliability of interviewers or observers. Sussman and Haug noted that "the largest component of processing error occurs in the coding phase of data analysis" (1967: 56). In an independent double coding of 2,775 cases, they found an especially high coding variability in responses to open-ended questions. Similar findings were reported by Durbin and Stuart (1954). They employed several coders who were given ten different coding operations ranging from purely mechanical tasks to the coding of answers to open-ended questions. Although the items that required automatic coding produced low variability, in the more complex items requiring judgment and interpretation, complete agreement was obtained only on an average of about half the items. To increase coding reliability, it is advisable to keep coding schemes as simple as possible, as well as to give the coders thorough training. The simplest solution is to compare the codings of two or more coders and resolve all differences by letting them reach a decision concerning problematic items.

Another problem concerning discrepancies in interpretation of responses is much less frequently discussed in the literature. It has to do with differences between the coder and the respondent in interpreting the meaning of the response. This question was formulated in a study attempting to assess whether the respondent and the coder would reach agreement as to the meaning of the response (Kammeyer and Roth, 1971). In other words, how would the subjects themselves code their answers within the set of categories provided by the researcher? If the subjects, who provide the answers, could also serve as coders, would their coding differ from that of other coders, or would the subject-coders code their own responses as they are coded by others? Sixty-four college students were asked to complete a questionnaire that included fixed-alternative as well as several open-ended questions. Later on, every subject independently coded the questionnaires of several other participants as well as his or her own. A subject's coding of her or his own response was compared with the way that response was coded by others. The comparison revealed significant differences, with a consistent pattern indicating that the coding of a response deviates from the subject's actual attitudes, the direction of this deviation being determined by the content of the item. The less structured the item, the larger the discrepancy between the respondent's interpretation and that of a coder. These findings raise some serious problems regarding the process of coding nonstructured material. It is clear that such bias might affect relationships between the variables investigated.

THE CODING AND PUNCHING PROCESS

Once the first step in data processing—the construction of a coding scheme—is completed, the data may be coded according to the specified rules and transferred to punchcards. First, however, the categories are to be translated into symbols that are amenable to automatic processing and further analysis. These symbols are usually numerical codes utilized either for coding background information (e.g., age, income) or information on perceptions, attitudes, and behavior. Information can be coded either in actual numbers or in arbitrary numerical codes representing any agreed meaning. The digit 9 standing for the quantity 9 is an example of an actual number. The same digit can also be assigned to designate properties such as "yes," "no," "U.S.A.," or $100. Researchers are free to assign a digit any meaning they wish, provided that meaning is consistent within the particular coding scheme. However, for items that frequently reappear in various studies, standard coding systems are employed. An example is the coding scheme developed by the Survey Research Center of the University of Michigan, parts of which are reproduced in Table 8.3. The system conforms to U.S. Census Bureau practice and is employed by many investigators in the social sciences.

The coding schemes with their assigned symbols, together with specific coding instructions, may now be assembled in a code book. A code book will identify a specific item of observation and the code number assigned to describe each category included in that item. If the information is to be transferred to machine punchcards, the code book will also identify the column in which it is entered. In Table 8.4, individuals are identified by their city school district, the type of school they attend and its name, and their sex. Each of these items is designated by a set of alternative codes, and the number of the column in which it is to be punched.

Not all data lend themselves to direct punching from original material, and information must sometimes be recorded on coding sheets before being punched. The common coding sheet has the same format as the punchcard, with eighty columns, corresponding to the eighty columns on the card. Usually it has twenty-five lines, each line corresponding to one punchcard. The form of recording will depend on the format of the unit records that are employed in processing the data. If it is to be keypunched, horizontal listing is preferable. In this format, the items are

TABLE 8.3. Examples of Coding Conventions

Code	Content
A	*The basic scheme*
1	Yes ("good" or most positive)
5	No ("bad" or least positive)
7	Other
8	I don't know
9	Not ascertained
0	Inapplicable (or none)
B	*Agreement*
1	Agree strongly
2	Agree, but not very strongly
3	Not sure; it depends
4	Disagree, but not very strongly
5	Disagree strongly
C	*Age*
	Code actual age
D	*Income*
	Give actual dollar amount
E	*Number of children (or adults)*
	Code actual number
F	*Sex*
1	Male
2	Female
G	*Race*
1	White
2	Negro
3	Other

listed across the top, with the case numbers down the side. Each item is assigned its own column or columns, the first columns being allocated to the case number. The characteristics of the respondents given in Table 8.5 can be listed on the coding sheet presented in Figure 8.1. The codes have been determined by the code book presented in Table 8.4.

The Punchcard

Typically, coded data are transferred from a code sheet, or from an original record, to punchcards. With computer analysis, as well as with

TABLE 8.4. A Code Book Format

Column	Item	Code	
06	City school district	1	Binghamton
		2	Johnston City
		3	Vestal
07	Public or parochial	1	Public
		2	Parochial
08	Name of school	1	C. Fred Johnson
		2	Dickinson
		3	MacArthur
		4	Vestal High
09	Sex of respondent	1	Male
		2	Female

TABLE 8.5. Background Characteristics of Five Respondents

Case number	City school district	Type of school	Name of school	Sex
00001	Binghamton	Public	Dickinson	Male
00002	Johnston City	Parochial	MacArthur	Female
00003	Vestal	Public	Vestal High	Male
00004	Vestal	Public	Vestal High	Female
00005	Johnston City	Parochial	MacArthur	Male

unit record equipment, punchcards are usually the primary means of input. An example of an ordinary punchcard is reproduced in Figure 8.2. The card has eighty columns, each containing digits from 0 to 9, together with two more unmarked positions above the 0, designated as 10 and 11 for the lower and upper positions, respectively. Ordinarily, each item is allocated one column, but one may use more columns if necessary. To record a digit in a particular column, a hole is punched in that column, in the position required. The first few columns are usually reserved for an identification code. Each case is identified by a number, and that number is punched on every card containing information about that case. If there are 1,000 cases, the first four columns would be used for identification numbers running from 0001 to 1000. If the information on a certain case exceeds one card, more cards can be used, each of which will then contain the case's identification number, as well as an additional column identifying the card number.

The principle involved in using punchcards is easily illustrated by the card reproduced in Figure 8.3. The first five columns identify the

154   DATA PROCESSING AND ANALYSIS

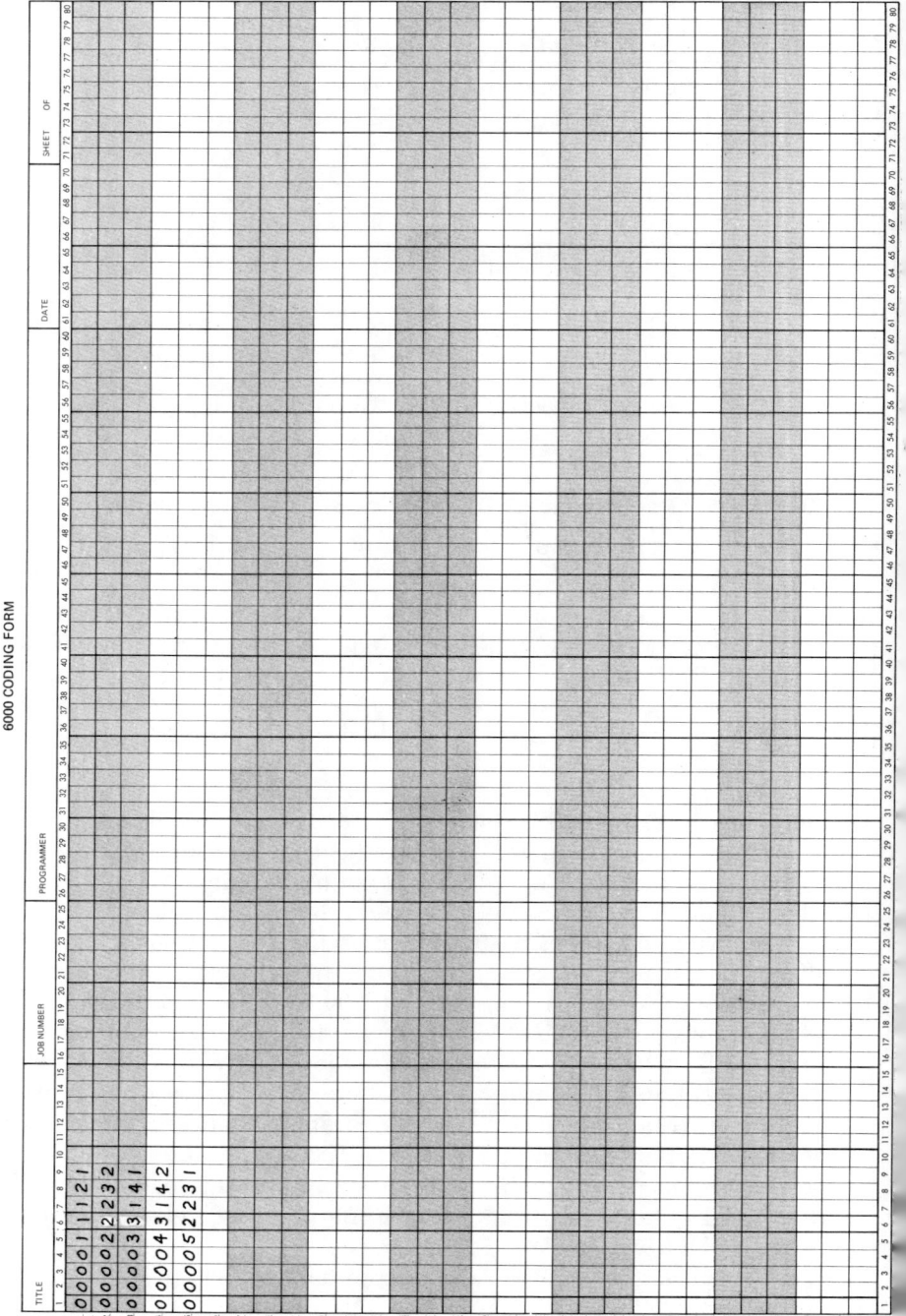

FIGURE 8.1. A Coding Sheet

FIGURE 8.2. A Punchcard

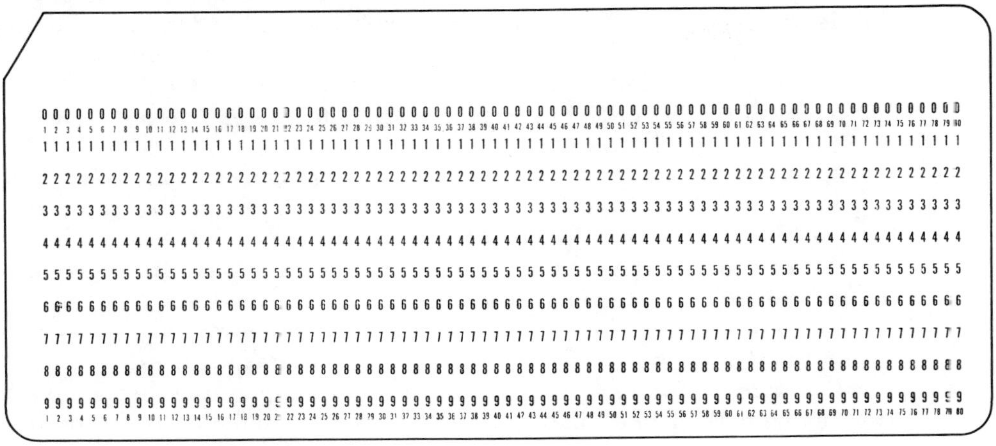

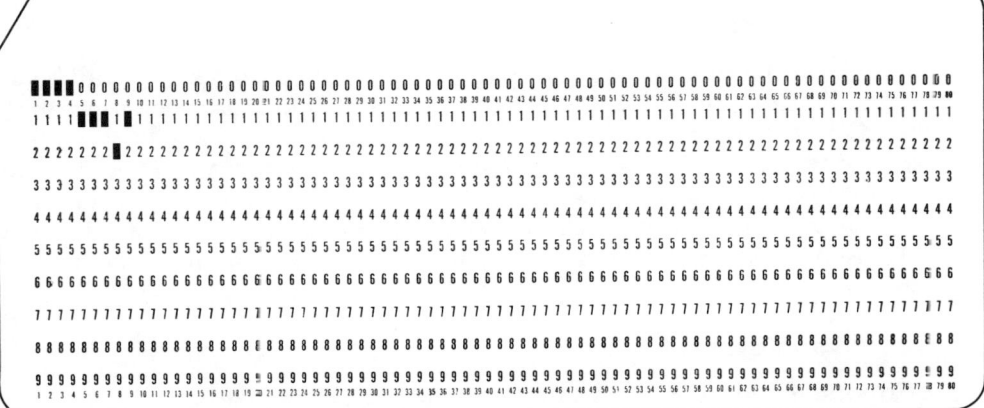

FIGURE 8.3. Recording Responses on Punchcards

case number with a "0" punched in the first four columns and a "1" punched in column 5. A "1" punched in column 6 indicates that this respondent is from the Binghamton school district; a "1" in column 7 identifies the school as a public school; and the "2" punched in column 8 identifies it as the Dickinson School. Finally, since the first respondent is male, the digit "1" is punched in column 9.

To conclude the discussion on coding and recording information on punchcards, several suggestions concerning these procedures are listed below.*

---

* These suggestions appear in most data-processing manuals. We have based our discussion on Benson (1969) and Janda (1965).

1. *Use a "natural" coding scheme.* Digits should run in some familiar ordering, with "high" responses represented by the larger numbers. Thus, responses like "never," "only once," and "more than one time" should be coded 1, 2, and 3 rather than 3, 2, and 1. With items that have no logical ordering, it is advisable to use the larger digit for the most frequent response.

2. *Avoid the use of blank space as coding category.* Many computer programs do not distinguish between blank space and zero punches. Thus a blank space would be interpreted as a zero. The zero, however, is a valid digit to use and is employed to designate "no answer," "no information," and similar categories.

3. *Do not use the "−" and "+" punches.* In computer processing, these punches are not easily interpreted as coding categories.

4. *Use one punch per column.* Sometimes, respondents are allowed to give more than one answer to a question, in which case it seems reasonable to punch all answers in one column. However, this practice complicates computer processing (Moser and Kalton, 1971).

AUTOMATIC DATA PROCESSING

Data can be processed either with unit record equipment or with computers. Unit record machines perform specific functions such as sorting, printing, or tabulating. In the last decade, computers have been widely used to perform the functions of unit record equipment. Yet a great deal of the preliminary processing required before data are ready for computer analysis can be accomplished with these machines, and for that reason we shall briefly describe some of the more important units.

The Keypunch

Information is usually recorded on a punchcard by a keypunch machine. The most common machines are the IBM 24 Card Punch and the IBM 26. The IBM 26 is identical to the 24 but has the additional ability to print the information above the column in which it is punched. The card is punched by operating a typewriterlike keyboard that punches letters, digits, and other special characters. The cards are fed into position by pressing a "feed" button and are punched one column at a time. After each card is punched, the card is automatically positioned for the next column. The card is automatically stacked when completed. Control cards can be prepared and rolled around a drum contained in the machine for punching a large number of cards with the same format. Other functions that can be automatically controlled are skipping columns, printing, ejecting, and feeding cards.

The Counter Sorter

The counter sorter is used to sort data into groups, to order it according to sequences, and to tally the cases in each group. This machine can process 650 cards per minute and is useful for large quantities of card input. The machine operates on one column at a time and distributes the cards into stacks according to the hole punched in the column for which the sorter is set. Suppose one wishes to sort out all the female voters from a file of Republican voters. Female is represented by a "2" punched, say, in column 60. To sort out all the females, the sorting mechanism would be positioned to read column 60, and the complete file would be placed in the hopper. When the start key is pressed, the cards are advanced under the sorting mechanism and all cards that have a "2" punch in column 60 will be directed to a special passage. The others will be rejected into the reject pocket. The counter sorter does no computations, but, with its sorting and tallying mechanism, it can do most of the tabulations required at the preliminary processing stage.

The Tabulator

The tabulator, which can add, subtract, and accumulate totals, is mainly used for printing contents of cards. The tabulator operates through control panel wiring. By using a standard listing control panel, the contents of cards can be printed simply by placing them in the hopper and pressing the "start" button. Complex tabulations, as well as some statistical calculations, can also be carried out by the tabulator, but these require fairly complex wiring.

Electronic Computers

The development of electronic computers, and their widespread use by social scientists, have led to a significant development in the processing and analysis of data. It is far outside our scope to discuss the revolutionary aspects of computers or to provide a general introduction to computer science. Instead, we shall limit ourselves to their function in the social sciences.

Computers can perform all the specialized functions of unit record machines, but at a much higher speed. Indeed, there is little doubt that the most important property of computers is operating speed. In less than twenty years, computing speed has vastly increased, enabling operations previously impossible owing to their size and complexity. It has been noted that "the electronic computer will prove to be the most versatile and influential scientific instrument so far invented. It will play a larger role in the scientific histories of the future than even such obvious challengers as the microscope and the telescope" (Wrigley, 1962). Yet, at present, most social scientists use the computer mainly for manipulating or compiling large masses of data. Although the computer has proved to be of tremendous help for these operations, it is not in this capacity that it provides the greatest contribution. Those who predict a glorious future for computers maintain that the main advantage "is its ability to do mathematics in a hurry" (Weeg, 1961:28). Thus, it is in the development of high-powered statistical procedures that computers can be utilized by social scientists.

SPECIAL PROGRAMS

Despite the complexity of computers, most researchers do not need to know a great deal about their operations in order to use them. Large libraries of computer programs are provided by most computer installations, and the user only has to learn how to use the appropriate programs. For that, it is not necessary to know computer languages or how to write programs. All the necessary information is described in manuals, and the user need only be familiar with those that contain programs of interest to him or her.

Most library programs are general-purpose programs, but two now in wide use meet almost all the particular needs arising in processing and analysis of social science data. These are: the Biomedical Computer Programs—BMD (Dixon, 1973) and the Statistical Package for the Social Sciences—SPSS (Nie, Bent, and Hull, 1970).

Biomedical Computer Programs (BMD)

Originally designed for medical research, BMD programs were written for problems that involve data covering many variables for a few cases or many observations on few variables. These problems characterize many of the research projects in the social sciences, and the BMD has thus been widely applied. The package has been prepared with the following goals in mind (Dixon, 1973): (1) To provide programs for the common task of data processing and statistical analysis. (2) To provide the programs in "package" form so that they can be used with simple coded instructions. (3) To provide these "packages" in a general form so that a wide variety of problems may be handled by each program.

The BMD package has six general classes of programs: (1) Description and Tabulation: various routines for simple data description and for obtaining bivariate correlations (see Chapter 10). (2) Multivariate Analysis (see Chapter 11). (3) Regression Analysis: has simple and multiple regressions, with several variations such as stepwise regression (see Chapter 11). (4) Special Programs: includes programs for Guttman scale analysis, as well as for contingency table analysis (see Chapter 10). (5) Time Series Analysis: designed to analyze change over time. (6) Variance Analysis: includes several programs for analysis of variance, such as one-way design, factorial designs, analysis of covariance, and others.

Statistical Package for the Social Sciences (SPSS)

SPSS is an integrated system of computer programs designed especially for the analysis of social science data. It is a comprehensive package that enables the user to perform different types of operations in a simple and convenient manner. SPSS contains some of the most common routines employed by social scientists in data processing and analysis. Aside from simple counting and tabulating, it has several features that enable the user to handle missing values; to recode the data; to transform the variables; and to sample, select, and weight the data. Missing data are a common occurrence in social science research, as it is frequently difficult to obtain a complete set of data for every case in the sample. The program has special features to process such missing data, even though some of the cases may not have a valid measurement. There are also provisions that enable the investigator to recode the variables, if the coding system used to record the observation is not convenient for all of the analysis. The original coding can be replaced by new symbols, and a new coding system can be applied. The process can be used to alter the values of the variables, either temporarily or permanently.

The variable-transformation programs allow for new variables to be constructed from the values of other variables. This function is useful especially when scales and indices have to be constructed. The variable "social class," for example, can be constructed from the variables "education" and "occupation." Like the recoding process, variables can be transformed permanently or on a temporary basis only.

Another routine in the SPSS package enables the researcher to obtain a random sample of the cases (see Chapter 12), to select specific cases for processing and analysis, or to weight a sample that has been oversampled or undersampled. The weighting process allows each case to be considered more or less heavily than others.

The data-analysis programs in the SPSS package are divided into four classes: (1) univariate distributions, (2) bivariate distributions, (3) multivariate distributions, and (4) special programs.* The first class contains programs designed to describe the characteristics of univariate distributions. They can produce frequency distributions, as well as various statistics such as the mean, mode, standard deviation, and range. There are three statistical procedures for that purpose: CONDESCRIP-

---

* These distributions are discussed in Chapters 9, 10, and 11, respectively.

TIVE, designed for use with interval scale variables, and CODEBOOK and MARGINALS, designed for use with ordinal and interval variables. For bivariate distributions, SPSS contains two procedures, CROSSTABS and FASTABS, which construct two-way to n-way cross tabulations of variables and allow the researcher to compute a variety of statistics. Two additional programs for computing correlations are available: PEARSON CORR produces zero-order or product-moment correlation coefficients for interval data, which is normally distributed. For other data, a procedure designated as NONPAR CORR enables the computation of either Spearman or Kendall rank-order correlation coefficients, or both.

The third class of programs includes procedures that produce partial correlation and multiple regression. First to nth-order partial correlation coefficients can be calculated with the PARTIAL CORR procedure that operates on raw data or from matrices of simple correlation coefficients.

With the procedure of REGRESSION, a variety of multiple-regression calculations can be obtained. Analysis can be performed upon a fixed number of variables; alternatively, with the use of a stepwise technique, variables are allowed to enter the regression equation sequentially, depending upon their explanatory power. As with PARTIAL CORR, this program can operate either on raw data or on a matrix of correlation coefficients.

Finally, the fourth class of programs has routines for the calculation of Guttman scales and factor analysis. The GUTTMAN SCALE procedure computes the scale as well as several statistics that help the user to determine the quality of the scale. These are the coefficient of reproducibility, the minimum marginal reproducibility, the percent improvement, and the coefficient of scalability. Factor analysis is performed by the procedure FACTOR that includes the principal components: factoring, alpha factoring, Rao's canonical factoring, and image factoring. The types of rotations that may be used are the varimax, equimax, quartimax, and some oblique rotations.*

SUMMARY

Data processing is a link between data collection and data analysis whereby observations are transformed into codes that are amenable to quantitative analysis. At the first stage of data processing, numerous individual observations are classified into a smaller number of categories so as to simplify the description and analysis of the data. Such systems of categories are referred to as coding schemes.

* For a comprehensive text on factor analysis, see Rummel (1970).

Coding schemes must be linked to the theory or the problem under study, which dictates the categories to be included in the scheme. The other requirement of a coding scheme is that it be exhaustive and mutually exclusive so that all observations can be classified and that each one can be classified only once. Coding schemes enable the translation of the data into symbols, usually numerals, that allow automatic processing. The translation is usually guided by a code book, which includes the coding schemes with their assigned symbols together with specific coding instructions.

Coded data are processed either with unit record equipment or with computers. Unit record machines, such as the keypunch or the sorter, perform specific functions such as punching or sorting, whereas computers not only perform all these functions with much greater speed but also enable the researcher to use high-powered statistical procedures for analysis. Researchers make use of library computer programs for processing and analysis. Two programs are widely used in social research: the Biomedical Computer Programs (BMD) and the Statistical Package for the Social Sciences (SPSS). These programs include numerous procedures ranging from simple descriptive techniques to the most sophisticated multivariate analyses.

REFERENCES

Benson, Oliver. *Political Science Laboratory*. Columbus, Ohio: Merrill, 1969.

Coleman, James S. "Academic Achievement and the Structure of Competition." *Harvard Educational Review* 29 (1959):330–351.

Dixon, Wilfred J. (ed.). *Biomedical Computer Programs*. Berkeley: University of California Press, 1973.

Durbin, James, and Stuart, Alan. "An Experimental Comparison between Coders." *Journal of Marketing* 19 (1954):54–66.

Gellert, Elizabeth. "Systematic Observation: A Method in Child Study." *Harvard Educational Review* 25 (1955):179–195.

Janda, Kenneth. *Data Processing*. Evanston, Ill.: Northwestern University Press, 1965.

Kammeyer, Kenneth C. W., and Roth, Julius A. "Coding Responses to Open-Ended Questions." In Herbert L. Costner (ed.), *Sociological Methodology 1971*. London: Jossey Bass, 1971.

Lazarsfeld, Paul F., and Barton, Allen. "Qualitative Measurement in the Social Sciences: Classification, Typologies, and Indices." In Daniel Lerner and Harold D. Lasswell (eds.), *The Policy Sciences*. Stanford, Calif.: Stanford University Press, 1951:155–192.

Moser, C. A., and Kalton, G. *Survey Methods in Social Investigation*. London: Heinemann Educational Books, 1971.

Nie, Norman, Bent, Dale H., and Hull, C. Hadlai. *Statistical Package for the Social Sciences*. New York: McGraw-Hill, 1970.

Rummel, R. J. *Applied Factor Analysis*. Evanston, Ill.: Northwestern University Press, 1970.

Stouffer, Samuel A. *The American Soldier*. New York: Wiley, 1965.

Sussman, Marvin B., and Haug, Marie R. "Human and Mechanical Error—An Unknown Quantity in Research." *The American Behavioral Scientist* 11 (1967):56.

Weeg, Gerald P. "The Electronic Computer." In Richard D. Duke (ed.), *Automatic Data Processing*. East Lansing: Michigan State University, 1961:23–29.

Weick, Karl E. "Systematic Observational Methods." In Gardner Lindzey and Elliot Aronson (eds.), *The Handbook of Social Psychology*. Reading, Mass.: Addison-Wesley, 1968:357–451.

Wrigley, Charles. "The University Computer Center." In Harold Borko (ed.), *Computer Applications in the Behavioral Sciences*. Englewood Cliffs, N.J.: Prentice-Hall, 1962.

STUDY SUGGESTIONS

1. Prepare a nonstructured questionnaire on a topic of interest. Interview at least ten respondents.
   a. Construct a coding scheme for all items.
   b. Construct a code book that will include the code for each item and its location on a machine punchcard.
   c. Code your information on a coding sheet.
   d. Transfer the coded data from the code sheet to punchcards.
   e. Tally the cases in each category of all items by using the counter sorter or a computer program.
2. Data are coded according to a deductive or an inductive system of coding depending on the specific method of data collection employed. What is the proper system of coding for each of the methods of data collection that is discussed in Chapters 5 through 7?
3. Give the data set and code book of Question 1 to two of your friends to be recoded by them. Compare the results obtained by the three of you and discuss the reliability of your coding scheme.

CHAPTER 9
The Univariate Distribution

The preliminary stage of analysis consists of quite ordinary methods designed to provide a straightforward description of the data. Once coded, each item is summarized in some tabular form, and measures such as averages and percentages are calculated to describe its main characteristics. It is common to begin the analysis by showing how the respondents are distributed on all the items of the investigation. A distribution might show, for instance, that twenty of the eighty respondents included in a sample are males, and the rest are females; that forty-six are Democrats, twenty are Republicans, and fourteen do not identify with any party. Such listings of the number of observations that fall into each of several categories are termed frequency distributions. Frequencies are often converted into proportions or percentages; these are helpful in assessing the weight of a single category in relation to other categories of the distribution or in relation to other distributions.

Often, it is useful to obtain some average value that is representative of the distribution. For example, one may need to answer such questions as: "What is the most typical political orientation of this group of respondents?" or "What is their average income?" These questions can be answered by using measures of central tendency. The three commonly used statistical measures of central tendency are the mode, the median, and the arithmetic mean.

Measures of central tendency can be misleading if they are not accompanied by measures of dispersion that describe the amount of dispersion in the distribution. Whereas the measures of central tendency reflect the most typical or average characteristics of the group, the measures of dispersion indicate how many members of the group deviate from it and the extent of the deviation. Whereas a small deviation denotes that most responses are clustered around the measure of central tendency, a large deviation indicates that the measure is a poor representation of the distribution.

Finally, one of the important steps in examining a distribution is the identification of its general form. Certain kinds of forms are characteristic of different empirical phenomena. For instance, many income distributions have few extremely high incomes; most incomes are concentrated in the middle or lower ranges. Such distributions are skewed toward the higher values. On the other hand, intelligence distributions are typically symmetrical; most scores are concentrated in the middle range, with very few extremely high or extremely low scores.

It is our purpose in this chapter to explicate the main characteristics of single-variable distributions. In the first section, the frequency distribution is defined and described. The second section focuses on measures of central tendency, and the third, on measures of dispersion. The last section deals with the general form of distributions, with a focus on one general theoretical distribution—the normal curve.

FREQUENCY DISTRIBUTIONS

The data that have been coded and prepared for automatic processing are now ready for analysis. The first task is to construct frequency distributions to examine the pattern of response* to each of the independent and dependent variables under investigation. A frequency distribution of a single variable, sometimes referred to as a univariate frequency distribution, is the frequency of observations in each category of a variable. For example, an examination of the pattern of response to the variable "religious affiliation" would involve a description of the number of respondents who claimed they were Protestants, Catholics, or Jews.

To construct a frequency distribution, the researcher simply lists the categories of the variable and counts the number of observations in each. Table 9.1 is an example of the standard form of a univariate frequency distribution. The table has five rows, the first four being the categories of the variable, which appear in the left-hand column, and the right-hand column shows the number of observations in each category. This number is called a frequency, and is usually denoted by the letter "f." The last row (marked "F") is the total of all frequencies appearing in the table. When the categories are mutually exclusive so that each observation is classified only once, the total number of frequencies is equal to the total number of observations (marked "N") in the sample. In the following discussion, we shall assume that $F = N$.

* In the following discussion, "responses," "answers," "observations," "cases," "acts," and "behavior" are used interchangeably.

TABLE 9.1. The General Form of a Univariate Frequency Distribution

Category	Frequency (f)
I	f_I
II	f_{II}
III	f_{III}
IV	f_{IV}
Total	F

With nominal variables, the categories may be listed in any arbitrary order. Thus, the variable "sex" may be described with the category "male" or the category "female" listed first. However, the categories of ordinal variables represent different quantities and are therefore arranged in order of magnitude. As an illustration, consider the frequency distribution (Table 9.2) from a study that examined the effect of parent-child authority patterns on educational aspirations. The variable "authority patterns" is listed according to the degree of authoritativeness in family relationship.

When interval variables are to be summarized in frequency distributions, an initial decision must be made as to the number of categories to be used and the cutting points between them. Since interval variables are ordinarily continuous, the classification into distinct categories may be quite arbitrary. For example, age may be classified into one-year, two-year, or five-year groups. Similarly, income can be classified in a number of ways. Unfortunately, there are no simple guidelines for making this decision; it depends on the purpose of the classification, on the pattern of the distribution, and on the number of observations.*

TABLE 9.2. Authority Patterns in the Family

Authority Patterns	f
Democratic	1,858
Mixed	759
Autocratic	105
Total	2,722

SOURCE: Judie Sinclair and Richard A. Rehberg. "Selected Social Influences on Adolescent Educational Goals" (unpublished).

* On construction of categories, see Chapter 8. On frequency distributions of interval scales, see Blalock (1972:41–47).

Summarizing the data by constructing frequency distributions of single variables is only the first step in data analysis. Next, the frequencies must be converted into figures that can be interpreted easily. An absolute frequency is meaningless in itself; it needs to be compared with other frequencies. For instance, the significance of 2,000 registered Democrats in one community can be assessed only in relation to the number of all registered voters, to the number of registered Republicans, or to the number of registered Democrats in other communities.

Frequencies expressed in comparable numbers are called proportions or percentages. A proportion is obtained by dividing the frequency of a category by the total number of responses in the distribution. When multiplied by 100, a proportion becomes a percentage. Proportions are usually expressed as f_i/N and percentages as $f_i/N \times 100$, with f_i denoting the frequency of category i and N denoting the total number of responses. Both proportions and percentages reflect the relative weight of a specific category in the distribution. For example, the relative weight of the category "autocratic" (Table 9.2) is expressed by the proportion $105/2.722 = 0.038$ or by the percentage $105/2,722 \times 100 = 3.8$ percent. These figures indicate that only four out of every hundred families in the group have autocratic interaction patterns with their children.

Proportions and percentages permit the comparison of two or more frequency distributions. Note, for instance, the social-class distribution of rural and urban populations displayed in Tables 9.3 and 9.4. Although in absolute numbers the middle class was more predominant in rural areas, the two populations—rural and urban—were unequal numerically; thus, a straightforward comparison of the absolute frequencies is misleading. Instead, to assess the relative weight of the classes within each distribution, the frequencies should be expressed in percentages, which reveal that the impression gained from the absolute frequencies was indeed misleading. Whereas the middle class constituted 75 percent of the rural population, it was 80 percent of the urban group. The new figures make it easier to visualize the frequency of the rural middle class relative to the frequency of the urban middle class.

TABLE 9.3. Social-Class Distribution: Rural Population (in Absolute Frequencies and Percentages)

Social Class	f	Percentage
Upper middle	60	15%
Middle	300	75
Lower	40	10
Total	400	100

TABLE 9.4. Social-Class Distribution: Urban Population (in Absolute Frequencies and Percentages)

Social Class	f	Percentage
Upper middle	20	8%
Middle	200	80
Lower	30	12
Total	250	100

MEASURES OF CENTRAL TENDENCY

When only a short summary of the data is required, the entire distribution need not be presented. To describe the educational standard of Americans by listing the schooling of all citizens of the United States would be rather impractical. Instead, it could be pointed out that most Americans are high school graduates, or that the average level of education in the United States is twelve years.

In most distributions, the observations tend to cluster around a central value. For instance, any income distribution can be characterized by the most frequent income or an average income. Similarly, attitude distributions cluster around a certain range. This property can be utilized when attempting to represent a distribution by a single value. The use of such a value not only allows for economy in describing the distribution, but also facilitates comparison of different distributions. One is able to compare the average income in the United States with the average income in England, or to contrast the average intelligence of Russian students with that of American students.

Statistical measures that reflect a "typical" or an "average" characteristic of a frequency distribution are referred to as measures of central tendency. The three most commonly used are the mode, the median, and the arithmetic mean.

The Mode

The mode is the category or the observation that appears most frequently in the distribution. It is used as a measure of central tendency mostly with distributions of nominal variables. To identify the mode, one singles out the category containing the largest number of responses. As an illustration, consider the distribution of religious groups presented in Table 9.5. The distribution includes five categories; the first, the Protestant group, is the most predominant. This category is thus the mode of the distribution.

TABLE 9.5. Frequency Distribution of Religious Groups

Religious Group	f
Protestant	62
Catholic	52
Jewish	10
Muslim	12
Buddhist	2
Total	138

Most distributions are unimodal; that is, they include only one category in which most of the cases are concentrated. At times, however, the distribution is bimodal: it includes two such maximum points. Such a pattern usually exists in distributions that combine two populations. For instance, the distribution of the heights of adults is bimodal; it comprises both men and women, and each sex is characterized by a different typical height.

Although easily calculable, the mode is a sensitive indicator. Its position might shift whenever the manner of the distribution's division into categories is altered. Therefore, it is not a very stable measure of central tendency.

The Median

The median is a positional measure that divides the distribution into two equal parts. It is defined as the observation that is located halfway between the smallest and the largest observations in the distribution. For example, in the series 1, 3, 4, 6, 7, the median is 4. The median can be calculated with observations that are ranked according to size, and as such it can be employed with variables that are at least ordinal.

The median is obtained for ungrouped data by locating the middle observation. For an odd number of cases, it is the observation $(N + 1)/2$, where N is the total number of cases. Consider, for example, the following set of nine observations:

$$6, 9, 11, 12, \underset{\underset{\text{Median}}{\uparrow}}{16}, 18, 21, 24, 30$$

The fifth observation $[(9 + 1)/2]$ divides the distribution in half; the median is therefore the value of the fifth observation, 16. With an even number of observations, the median is located halfway between the two middle observations and is calculated as an average of the observations $N/2$ and $N/2 + 1$. For example, in the following set of observations

$$1, 3, 4, 5, \underset{\underset{\text{Median}}{\uparrow}}{6}, 7, 8, 9$$

the median is the average of the fourth (8/2) and the fifth (8/2 + 1) observations: $(5 + 6)/2 = 5.5$

For grouped data, the median is located by interpolating within the interval containing the middle observation. The formula for finding the median is:

$$Md = L + \frac{N/2 - F}{f} \times i \qquad (9.1)$$

where Md = median
L = the lower limit of the interval containing the median
F = the accumulated sum of the frequencies of all intervals preceding the interval containing the median
f = the frequency of the interval containing the median
i = the width of the interval containing the median

To illustrate the computation of the median, consider the distribution in Table 9.6. The table shows the age distribution of 134 subjects, divided into eight ten-year age groups. Because there are 134 observations (N = 134), the median has the value of the sixty-seventh observation (134/2 = 67). The cumulated frequency column shows that there are sixty observations preceding the interval 41–50. The interval 41–50 contains twenty-five more observations. Hence, the sixty-seventh observation is located within the interval 41–50. It is necessary to find the exact age corresponding to the seventh case in this interval. These seven cases constitute 7/25 or 28 percent of the cases in the interval. As the width of the interval is 10 (years), we must add 28 percent of 10, namely, 2.8

TABLE 9.6. Age Distribution of 134 Subjects (Hypothetical)

Age	Frequency	Cumulated Frequency
0–10	10	10
11–20	12	22
21–30	17	39
31–40	21	60
41–50	25	85
51–60	20	105
61–70	18	123
71–80	11	134
Total	134	134

years, to the upper limit of the interval preceding the interval containing the median. The median is therefore $41 + 2.8 = 43.8$. These steps can be summarized by employing Equation (9.1) to calculate the median:

$$Md = 41 + \left(\frac{\frac{134}{2} - 60}{25} \times 10\right) = 41 + \left(\frac{7}{25} \times 10\right) = 41 + 2.8 = 43.8$$

At times, it is useful to identify values that divide the distribution into three, four, or ten groups. For example, the admissions office of a university that has decided to accept one-fourth of its applicants will be interested in finding the 25 percent with the highest scores in the entrance examinations. That is, it will locate the value of the third quartile, the point above which lie 25 percent of the observations.

Equation (9.1) can be adjusted to locate other positional values such as the first quartile (the point below which lie 25 percent of the observations), the third quartile, or the first decile (the point below which lie 10 percent of the observations). The only adjustment required is the division of the total number of cases into the required proportion. For the first quartile, the equation is:

$$Q_1 = L + \left(\frac{N/4 - F}{f} \times i\right) \qquad (9.2)$$

for the third quartile:

$$Q_3 = L + \left(\frac{3N/4 - F}{f} \times i\right) \qquad (9.3)$$

and for the first decile:

$$D_1 = L + \left(\frac{N/10 - F}{f} \times i\right) \qquad (9.4)$$

To illustrate the calculation of other positional values, the data contained in Table 9.6 are employed to find the first decile:

$$D_1 = 11 + \left(\frac{\frac{134}{10} - 10}{12} \times 10\right) = 11 + \left(\frac{3.4}{12} \times 10\right) = 11 + 2.8 = 13.8$$

An example of the use of positional measures is given in Table 9.7, which describes the education of twelve groups. The investigators compared the median education of each group. The medians reflect the educational characteristics of twelve different populations, each represented by one single value. For instance, 50 percent of the white rural males completed at least 12.3 years of education; such extended schooling was enjoyed by a smaller ratio of the equivalent black population, whose median was only 8.9 years.

TABLE 9.7. Median of Years of Schooling

	White	Black
Males		
Residents of city center	12.1	8.7
Residents of suburbs	12.1	9.7
Residents of rural areas	12.3	8.9
Females		
Residents of city center	12.1	10.5
Residents of suburbs	12.3	10.7
Residents of rural areas	11.8	8.0

The Arithmetic Mean

The arithmetic mean is the measure of central tendency most frequently used. It is suitable for representing distributions measured on an interval level and is amenable to mathematical calculations; it also serves as a basis for other statistical measures. The arithmetic mean is defined as the sum total of all observations divided by their number.

In symbolic notations, the mean is defined as:

$$\bar{X} = \frac{\sum_{i=1}^{N} X_i}{N} \tag{9.5}$$

where $\bar{X}$ = the arithmetic mean

$\sum_{i=1}^{N} X_i$ = the sum of total observations

N = the number of observations

According to this equation, the mean ($\bar{X}$) of the series 6, 7, 12, 11, 10, 3, 4, 1, is 54/8 = 6.75.

When the mean is to be computed from a frequency distribution, it is not necessary to add up all the individual observations. Instead, each category can be given its proper weight by multiplying it by its frequency. The following equation can be used:

$$\bar{X} = \frac{\sum_{i=1}^{N} f_i X_i}{N} \tag{9.6}$$

where $\sum_{i=1}^{N} f_i X_i$ = the sum total of all categories multiplied by their respective frequencies.

Table 9.8 presents data on the amount of schooling received by thirty-four individuals. The mean education of this group can be calculated by using Equation (9.6). To calculate the value of $\sum f_i X_i$ (column 3), each category (column 1) is multiplied by its frequency (column 2), and the products are added up. The mean number of years of schooling is therefore:

$$\bar{X} = \frac{278}{34} = 8.18$$

With ordinal and interval data, observations may be grouped together to form interval-like categories. For example, income can be grouped into intervals of $2,000 each (0–2,000; 2,001–4,000; 4,001–6,000, etc.). When categories are grouped in intervals, one representative value has to be chosen from each interval. It is common to select each interval's midpoint to represent it.

Unlike the mode and the median, the arithmetic mean takes into account all the values in the distribution, making it especially sensitive to extreme values. For example, if one person in a group of ten earns $60,000 annually and each of the others earns $5,000, the mean income of the group would be $10,500, a figure that is not a good representation of the distribution. The mean will thus be a misleading measure of central tendency whenever there are some observations with extremely high or low values.

The three measures of central tendency analyzed above can be used to represent univariate distributions. However, each has its own characteristics, which both prescribe and limit its use. The mode indicates the point in the distribution with the highest density, the median is the distribution's midpoint, and the arithmetic mean is an average of all the values in the distribution. Accordingly, these measures cannot be universally applied. How then does one know when it is preferable to use the mode, the median, or the mean? There is no single answer to the

TABLE 9.8. Distribution of Years of Study

(1) Years of Study	(2) f	(3) $f_i X_i$
2	3	6
3	2	6
6	5	30
8	10	80
10	8	80
12	4	48
14	2	28
Total	N = 34	$\sum f_i X_i = 278$

question; it depends on the objective of the study. For example, if the researcher is investigating the average level of income of a group so as to establish how much each person would receive if all incomes were equally divided, the mean would be most pertinent, as it reflects the highest as well as the lowest income. If, on the other hand, the information is needed to estimate the eligibility of the group to receive financial aid, the mode would be appropriate, since it shows the most typical income and is unaffected by extreme values.

The application of any measure of central tendency also depends on the level of measurement of the variable being analyzed. The mode can represent the distribution of party affiliation, which is a nominal variable. On the other hand, the median can be applied to ordinal variables such as political attitudes. The arithmetic mean is used with interval variables such as income and age. Generally, it is possible to use the measures appropriate for lower levels of measurement, but not for those of higher levels; for instance, income can be represented by the mode, but the arithmetic mean cannot represent the distribution of party affiliation.

MEASURES OF DISPERSION

Measures of central tendency identify the most representative value of the distribution. However, a complete description of the distribution requires that we measure the extent of dispersion* about this central value. The actual observations are distributed among many values, and the extent of their spread varies from one distribution to another. For example, two classes may have the same average grade; however, one class may include some excellent students as well as some very poor ones, whereas all the students in the other may be of average ability. Similarly, income distributions with an identical mean may present different patterns of dispersion. In some distributions, most incomes are clustered around the mean; in others, the incomes are widely dispersed. The description of the extent of dispersions about the central value is obtained by several measures designated as measures of dispersion. In this section, we shall discuss the measure of qualitative variation, the range, the mean deviation, the variance, the standard deviation, and the coefficient of variation.

The Measure of Qualitative Variation

The extent of dispersion in nominal distributions can be assessed by means of an index of heterogeneity designated as the measure of qualita-

---

* In the following discussion, the terms "dispersion," "scatter," and "variation" are used interchangeably.

tive variation.* This index reflects the number of differences among the categories of the distribution and is based on the number of categories and their respective frequencies. In general, the larger the number of categories and the greater the overall differences among them, the greater will be the degree of variation. Likewise, the smaller the number of categories and their differences, the smaller will be the variation within the distribution. As an illustration, consider the racial composition of several communities. In an all-white community, there are no racial differences, but in racially mixed communities there will be smaller or larger degrees of variation. The amount of variation will depend on the composition of the community. When most belong to a single racial group, the number of racial differences among the members of the community will be relatively small. Conversely, when most members are divided among several racial groups, the number of differences will be large.

The measure of qualitative variation is based on the ratio of the total number of differences in the distribution to the maximum number of possible differences within the same distribution. In order to find the total number of differences in the distribution, the differences between each category and every other category are counted and summed. For instance, in a group of fifty whites and fifty blacks, each of the whites will differ in race from each of the blacks, thereby making a total of 2,500 racial differences. In a group of seventy whites and thirty blacks, there are 2,100 differences. In a group of one hundred whites and no blacks, there are no racial differences.

The procedure for calculating the total number of differences can be expressed in the following equation:

$$\text{Total Observed Differences} = \sum f_i f_j, \ i \neq j \qquad (9.7)$$

where f_i = frequency of category i

f_j = frequency of category j

For example, in a group of twenty Catholics, thirty Jews, and ten Muslims, there would be $(20 \times 30) + (20 \times 10) + (30 \times 10) = 1{,}100$ religious differences.

The total of observed differences is meaningful only in relation to the maximum possible number of differences, since each distribution has a different number of categories and of frequencies. Relating the observed differences to the maximum possible differences has the effect of controlling for these factors. The maximum number of differences occurs when each category in the distribution has an identical fre-

---

* The discussion of this measure is based on Nachmias and Rosenbloom (1973) and Mueller, Schuessler, and Costner (1970).

quency. Thus, the maximum number of frequencies is computed by finding the number of differences that would be observed if all frequencies were equal. Symbolically:

$$\text{Maximum Possible Differences} = \frac{n(n-1)}{2}\left(\frac{F}{n}\right)^2 \qquad (9.8)$$

where n = the number of categories in the distribution
F = total frequency

In the previous example of twenty Catholics, thirty Jews, and ten Muslims, the maximum possible differences are

$$\left(\frac{3 \times 2}{2}\right)\left(\frac{60}{3}\right)^2 = 1{,}200$$

The measure of qualitative variation is the ratio between the total observed differences and the maximum possible differences. In other words,

$$\text{Measure of Qualitative Variation} = \frac{\text{Total Observed Differences}}{\text{Maximum Possible Differences}}$$

Symbolically, the measure is expressed in the following equation:

$$\text{Measure of Qualitative Variation} = \frac{\sum f_i f_j}{\frac{n(n-1)}{2}\left(\frac{F}{n}\right)^2} \qquad (9.9)$$

The measure of variation for the last example is:

$$\text{Measure of Qualitative Variation} = \frac{1{,}100}{1{,}200} = .92$$

The measure of qualitative variation varies between zero and one. Zero indicates the absence of any variation, whereas one reflects maximum variation. The measure will be zero whenever the total observed differences are zero. It will take the value of one when the number of observed differences is equal to the maximum possible differences.

The Range and the Interquartile Range

The range measures the distance between the highest and lowest values of the distribution. For example, in the following set of observations

$$4, 6, 8, 9, 17$$

the range is the difference between 17 and 4; that is, 13 ($17 - 4 = 13$). This measure requires that observations be ranked according to size; thus, it can be applied in cases where the distribution is at least on an ordinal level of measurement. The range has a special significance when a dearth of information produces a distorted picture of reality. For instance, two factories with annual average wages of $15,000 have different pay ranges; one has a range of $2,000 to $32,000, and the other has a range of $9,000 to $21,000. Without the additional information supplied by the range, one would get the impression that the wage scales in both factories were identical. The range is a useful device for gaining a quick impression of the data. However, it is a crude measure of dispersion because it takes into account only the distribution's two extreme values. Thus, it is sensitive to changes in one single score.

An alternative to the range is the interquartile range, which is the difference between the first and third quartiles (Q_1 and Q_3). It measures the spread in the middle half of the distribution, and is less affected by extreme observations. The first and third quartiles will vary less from distribution to distribution than will the most extreme observations; thus, the interquartile range is a more stable measure of dispersion than is the range (Blalock, 1972). To illustrate the interquartile range, consider the data in Table 9.6. The first quartile (Q_1) for these data* is 27.76, and the third quartile (Q_3) is 58.75. The interquartile range is thus $58.75 - 27.76 = 30.99$. This figure indicates that the range of the middle half of this age distribution is 30.99. The principle of the interquartile range can be applied to any part of the distribution. For example, one can calculate the range between the ninth and first deciles (C_9 and C_1) to measure the dispersion of the middle 80 percent of the observations.

The various measures of dispersion discussed above have a major drawback in that, being based on two values alone, they reflect only the dispersion in some defined section of the distribution. Some measure must be devised that will reflect the aggregate dispersion in the distribution. However, to measure aggregate dispersion it is necessary to establish the deviation of all the values in the distribution from some criterion. In other words, some norm is to be decided upon that will permit one to determine which value is higher, or lower, than expected. For example, the evaluation of income as "high" or "low" is meaningful only in relation to some fixed criterion. Income evaluated as "high" in India would be considered "low" in the United States.

Any of the measures of central tendency analyzed so far can be chosen as a norm. It is possible to measure deviations from the mode, the median, or the arithmetic mean; however, the latter is used as a basis for calculation of measures of dispersion that are employed more extensively.

The simplest way to obtain a measure of deviation is to calculate the average deviation from the arithmetic mean:

---

* These values were calculated according to Equations (9.2) and (9.3).

$$\text{Average deviation} = \frac{\sum_{i=1}^{N}(X_i - \overline{X})}{N}$$

where X_i = each individual observation
$\overline{X}$ = arithmetic mean
N = total number of observations

However, the sum of the deviations from the mean is always equal to zero; thus, the average deviation will be zero, since its numerator will always be zero. This property of the mean can be by-passed in two ways: by ignoring the signs and taking the deviations' absolute values or by squaring the deviations. The mean deviation is obtained with the first method; the standard deviation, with the second.

The Mean Deviation

The mean deviation makes use of every observation in the distribution. It is computed by taking the difference between each observation and the mean, summing the absolute value of these deviations, and dividing the sum by the total number of observations. Symbolically, the measure is expressed in Equation (9.10):

$$\text{Mean deviation} = \frac{\sum_{i=1}^{N}|X_i - \overline{X}|}{N} \qquad (9.10)$$

where X_i = each individual observation
$\overline{X}$ = arithmetic mean
N = total number of observations
$|\ |$ = the absolute difference

For example, to compute the mean deviation of the scores

$$2, 4, 6, 8, 10$$

we subtract the mean

$$\overline{X} = \frac{2 + 4 + 6 + 8 + 10}{5} = \frac{30}{5} = 6$$

from each score and obtain the following deviations:

$$-4, -2, 0, +2, +4$$

These deviations are summed by ignoring the signs and dividing by the number of scores:

$$\text{Mean deviation} = \frac{4 + 2 + 0 + 2 + 4}{5} = \frac{12}{5} = 2.4$$

178 DATA PROCESSING AND ANALYSIS

This figure indicates that the mean difference between each score and the arithmetic mean is 2.4.

The advantage of the mean deviation is that it takes into account all the observations in the distribution. However, absolute values are not amenable to arithmetic manipulations; thus, the mean deviation, which is based on such values, cannot be applied when further mathematical calculations are required.

The Variance and the Standard Deviation

The computation of the variance and standard deviation is similar to the mean deviation, except that, instead of taking the deviation's absolute values, they are squared and then summed and divided by the total number of observations. The definitional formula for the variance is:

$$s^2 = \frac{\sum_{i=1}^{N}(X_i - \overline{X})^2}{N} \tag{9.11}$$

where s^2 = variance.

In other words, the arithmetic mean is subtracted from each score; the differences are then squared, summed, and divided by the total number of observations. The numerical example of Table 9.9 illustrates the various steps involved in the computation of the variance. In a simpler computational formula of the variance, the squared mean is subtracted from the squared sum of all scores divided by the number of observations; that is,

$$s^2 = \frac{\sum_{i=1}^{N} X_i^2}{N} - \overline{X}^2 \tag{9.12}$$

TABLE 9.9. Computation of the Variance

X_i	$X_i - \overline{X}$	$(X_i - \overline{X})^2$	X_i^2
3	−6	36	9
4	−5	25	16
6	−3	9	36
12	3	9	144
20	11	121	400
Total		200	605

$\overline{X} = 9 \quad s^2 = \dfrac{200}{5} = 40$

Equation (9.12) is applied to the same data of Table 9.9:

$$s^2 = \frac{605}{5} - 81 = 121 - 81 = 40$$

In reflecting squared deviations, the variance expresses the average dispersion in the distribution not in the original units of measurement but in squared units. This problem is by-passed by taking the square root of the variance, thereby transforming the variance into the standard deviation. The standard deviation is a measure expressing dispersion in the original units of measurement. Symbolically, the standard deviation is expressed in Equations (9.13) and (9.14) corresponding to Equations (9.11) and (9.12) respectively:

$$s = \sqrt{\frac{\sum_{i=1}^{N}(X_i - \bar{X})^2}{N}} \qquad (9.13)$$

$$s = \sqrt{\frac{\sum_{i=1}^{N} X_i^2}{N} - \bar{X}^2} \qquad (9.14)$$

where s = standard deviation

For the previous example, the value of the standard deviation is—using Equation (9.13)—

$$s = \sqrt{\frac{200}{5}} = \sqrt{40} = 6.3$$

The standard deviation has various advantages over other measures of dispersion. First, it is more stable from sample to sample.* Second, it has some important mathematical properties that enable the researcher to obtain the standard deviation for two or more groups combined.† Furthermore, its mathematical properties make it a useful measure in more advanced statistical work, especially in the area of statistical inferences (see Chapters 12 and 13).

The application of the standard deviation as a research device is illustrated in the following example. Table 9.10 compares differences in feelings of life satisfaction among several countries, using the mean and standard deviation of the variable "life satisfaction" in each country.

The mean scores are almost identical, implying that satisfaction with life is similar in the countries studied. However, there are differences in

---
* On sampling, see Chapter 12.
† For computational formulae, see McNemar (1962).

TABLE 9.10. Mean and Standard Deviation on an Index of Life Satisfaction in Four Western Nations (Hypothetical Data)

England (903)		Germany (950)		Italy (998)		USA (980)	
Mean	SD	Mean	SD	Mean	SD	Mean	SD
6.7	1.0	6.7	1.2	6.6	3.2	6.5	1.3

NOTE: The figures in parentheses denote the number of persons interviewed in each group.

the standard deviations of each country. The relatively low standard deviations in England, Germany, and the United States indicate that these countries are homogeneous as far as satisfaction is concerned; that is, people have a satisfaction score which is close to their group's mean score. In Italy, however, the dispersion is greater, suggesting that the degree of satisfaction reflected by the mean is not common to all the Italians in the group studied.

Standard deviations cannot be compared in absolute magnitudes in instances where the distributions compared have very different means. A standard deviation of 2, for instance, would convey a different meaning in relation to a mean of 6 than to a mean of 60. Therefore, the degree of dispersion must be calculated relative to the mean of the distribution. This principle is implemented in the coefficient of variation, which reflects relative variation. Symbolically, the coefficient of variation is defined as follows:

$$V = \frac{s}{\overline{X}} \quad (9.15)$$

where V = coefficient of variation
s = standard deviation
$\overline{X}$ = arithmetic mean.

To illustrate the application of the coefficient of variation, consider the data in Table 9.11 from di Palma's comparative investigation on political behavior. Presented are the means and standard deviations of

TABLE 9.11. Political Participation in Four Countries: Mean and Standard Deviation

England (963)		Germany (955)		Italy (995)		USA (970)	
Mean	SD	Mean	SD	Mean	SD	Mean	SD
4.75	2.7	5.4	2.9	2.8	2.8	5.64	2.7

SOURCE: Giuseppe di Palma. *Apathy and Participation*. New York: Free Press, 1970, p. 220. Copyright © 1970 by The Free Press, a division of Macmillan Publishing Co., Inc. Reprinted with permission of the publisher.
NOTE: The figures in parentheses denote the number of cases; scores ranged from 0 to 12.

the variable "political participation." In absolute magnitudes, there are no significant differences among the standard deviations in the four countries. However, there are substantial differences between the means, indicating varying degrees of participation in each country. In Italy, for example, the mean participation is much lower than in the other countries, but the degree of dispersion is almost identical. Intuitively, however, it seems that a deviation of 2.8 has a greater significance in relation to a mean of 2.8 than to a mean of 4.75 or 5.4. To correct for these discrepancies, the standard deviations were converted into coefficients of variation. The results are displayed in Table 9.12. It is noticed that, indeed, the relative deviation from the mean is higher in Italy than in other countries, reflecting the lower degree of homogeneity in political participation.

TYPES OF FREQUENCY DISTRIBUTIONS

The discussion of univariate distributions has thus far been limited to descriptive measures reflecting central tendencies and dispersion. The next step in describing a distribution is to identify its general form. Distributions may have distinctive forms with few low scores and many high scores, with many scores concentrated in the middle of the distributions, or with many low scores and few high scores.

The simplest way to describe a distribution is by a visual representation. Examples of different forms are presented in Figure 9.1.

The values of the variable are represented along the baseline, and the area under the curve represents the frequencies. For example, in distribution a, the frequency of the interval 25–35 is represented by the area under the curve in that interval. The distribution of Figure 9.1a is a symmetrical distribution; that is, the frequencies at the right and left tails of the distribution are identical, so that if the distribution is divided into two halves, each will be the mirror image of the other. This usually means that most of the observations are concentrated at the middle of the distribution, and that there are few observations with very high or very low scores. An example of a symmetrical distribution is the height of adults. Few people are very short or very tall; most are of medium

TABLE 9.12. Mean Political Participation and Coefficient of Variation in Four Countries

England (963)		*Germany* (955)		*Italy* (955)		*USA* (970)	
Mean	V	Mean	V	Mean	V	Mean	V
4.75	0.57	5.4	0.54	2.8	1.00	5.65	0.48

NOTE: The figures in parentheses denote the number of cases.

FIGURE 9.1. Types of Frequency Distributions

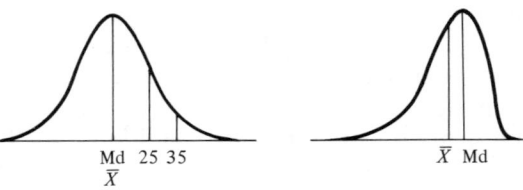
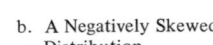
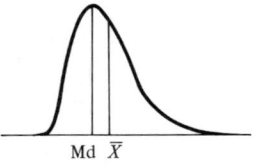

a. A Symmetrical Distribution   b. A Negatively Skewed Distribution   c. A Positively Skewed Distribution

height. Many other phenomena tend to be distributed symmetrically, and this form of distribution plays an important role in the field of statistical inference (see Chapters 12 and 13).

In nonsymmetrical distributions, there are more extreme cases in one direction of the distribution than in the other. A nonsymmetrical distribution in which there are more extremely low scores is referred to as a negatively skewed distribution (Figure 9.1b). When there are more extremely high scores, the distribution is positively skewed (Figure 9.1c). Most income distributions are negatively skewed, with few families having extremely high incomes.

Skewness can also be identified according to the positions of the measures of central tendency. With symmetrical distributions, the mean will coincide with the median and the mode; with skewed distributions, there will be discrepancies between these measures. In a negatively skewed distribution, the mean will be pulled in the direction of the lower scores; in a positively skewed distribution, it will be located closer to the high scores. This property of skewed distributions makes the choice of an average value a critical issue. Since the mean is pulled in the direction of the extreme scores, it loses its typicality, and hence its usefulness as a representative measure. In such instances, it might be useful to employ the median or the mode instead.

The Normal Curve

One type of symmetrical distribution is called the normal curve; it has great significance in the field of statistics. A normal curve is shown in Figure 9.2. Its principal properties are as follows: (1) it is symmetrical and bell-shaped; (2) the mode, the median, and the mean coincide at the center of the distribution; (3) the curve is based on an infinite number of observations; and (4) a single mathematical formula describes how frequencies are related to the values of the variable.

The fourth property of the normal curve is its most distinct characteristic. In any normal distribution, a fixed proportion of the observations lies between the mean and fixed units of standard deviations. The

FIGURE 9.2. A Normal Curve

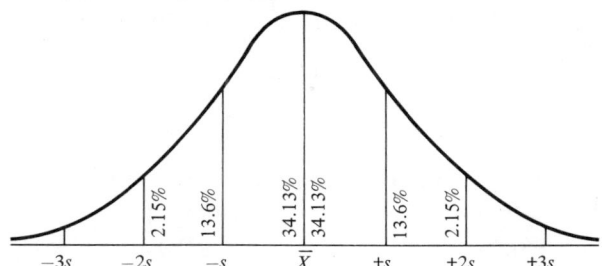

proportions can be seen in Figure 9.2. The mean of the distribution divides it exactly in half: 34.13 percent is included between the mean and one standard deviation to the right of the mean; the same proportion is included between the mean and one standard deviation to the left of the mean. The plus signs indicate standard deviations above the mean, and the minus signs, standard deviations below the mean. Thus, between $\overline{X} \pm 1s$ are included 68.26 percent of all observations in the distribution; between $\overline{X} \pm 2s$ are 95.46 percent of the observations; and between $\overline{X} \pm 3s$ are 99.76 percent of the observations.

In any univariate distribution that is normally distributed, the proportion of observations included within fixed distances of the mean can be determined. For example, in a distribution of intelligence with a mean of 110 and a standard deviation of 10, 68.26 percent of all cases have an intelligence quotient between $110 \pm 1s$—that is, between 100 and 120—and 95.46 percent have a score that is not below 90 and does not exceed 130.

To evaluate the proportion of observations included within an interval desired, observations need to be expressed in standard deviation units. For instance, to find the proportion of cases that have an IQ between 110 and 130, one has to determine how many standard deviations away from the mean the score of 130 is located. Observations are converted into standard deviation units by means of Equation (9.16):

$$Z = \frac{X_i - \overline{X}}{s} \qquad (9.16)$$

where Z = number of standard deviation units
X_i = any observation
$\overline{X}$ = arithmetic mean
s = standard deviation

Z, sometimes referred to as a standard score, expresses the distance between a specific observation (X_i) and the mean in terms of standard deviation units. A Z of 2 means that the distance between the mean of the distribution and X_i is two standard deviations. For example, in a distribution with a mean of 40 and a standard deviation of 5, the score of 50 is expressed as follows:

$$Z = \frac{50 - 40}{5} = \frac{10}{5} = 2$$

The score of 50 lies two standard deviations above the mean. Similarly, 30 is two standard deviations below the mean:

$$\frac{30 - 40}{5} = \frac{-10}{5} = -2$$

To determine the proportion of observations that lie between the mean and any observation in the distribution, special tables have been constructed for the standard form of the normal curve. The tables show proportions for various Z values. Table 2 in the Appendix is such a table. In the left-hand column are listed the first two digits of Z; the third digit is shown across the top. Thus, for example, the proportion included between the mean and a Z of 1 is .3413, or 34.13 percent; the value for a Z of 1.65 is .4505. Only one-half of the curve's proportions is given, because the curve is symmetrical. Thus, the distance between the mean and a Z of −1.0 is identical to the area between the mean and a Z of 1.0. To use the table, one first finds the appropriate Z score for any particular observation by Equation (9.16), and then consults Table 2 in the Appendix.

To illustrate the use of the standard normal table, suppose the distribution of income in a particular community is normal, its mean income is $10,000, and the standard deviation is $2,000. We want to determine what proportion of the people in this community have an income between $6,000 and $10,000. First, $6,000 is converted into standard deviation units:

$$Z = \frac{6{,}000 - 10{,}000}{2{,}000} = -2$$

Next, it is seen in Table 2 that .4773 of all observations are included between the mean and a Z of 2. In other words, 47.73 percent of all people in the community earn between $6,000 and $10,000 a year. This is shown in Figure 9.3.

What proportion of the community earns between $11,000 and $15,000? Both figures are converted into standard scores:

$$Z_1 = \frac{11{,}000 - 10{,}000}{2{,}000} = 0.5$$

$$Z_2 = \frac{15{,}000 - 10{,}000}{2{,}000} = 2.5$$

FIGURE 9.3.

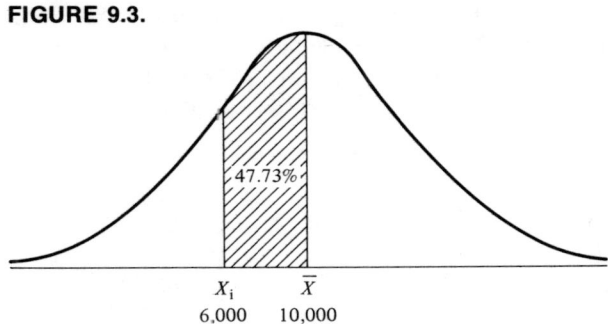

Table 2 indicates that .4938 is included between the mean and 2.5 standard deviation units, and .1915 between the mean and 0.5 units. Therefore, the area included between $11,000 and $15,000 is .4938 − .1915 = .3023 (30.23 percent). This is shown in Figure 9.4.

FIGURE 9.4.

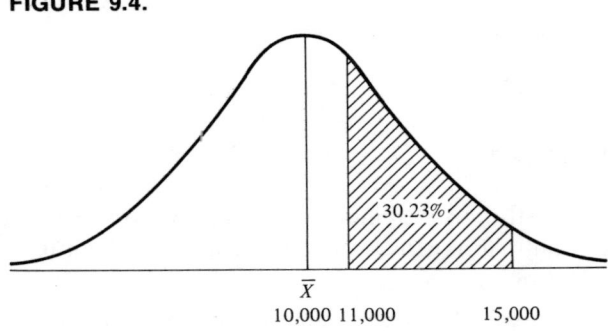

SUMMARY

This chapter centered around the description of the single variable. Four principal stages were pointed out: description of a univariate frequency distribution; measures of central tendency; measures of dispersion; and types of distributions. The univariate distribution consists of the categories of the variable and their frequencies. The distribution can be expressed in absolute frequencies, in proportions, or in percentages. It can also be represented by measures of central tendency: the mode, which is the value with the highest frequency; the median, which is the value bisecting the distribution; and the arithmetic mean, which is based on all the observations.

Measures of dispersion assess the variation within the distribution: the range measures the distance between the most extreme values of the distribution. The interquartile range assesses the variation with the first and third quartiles. The coefficient of variation measures the degree of heterogeneity within nominal distributions. The variance and the standard deviation reflect the aggregate dispersion in the distribution. In the last section, various types of distributions, symmetrical and skewed, were described.

REFERENCES

Blalock, Hubert M. *Social Statistics*. 2d ed. New York: McGraw-Hill, 1972.

McNemar, Quinn. *Psychological Statistics*. New York: Wiley, 1962.

Mueller, John H., Schuessler, Karl F., and Costner, Herbert L. *Statistical Reasoning in Sociology*. Boston: Houghton Mifflin, 1970.

Nachmias, David, and Rosenbloom, David H. "Measuring Bureaucratic Representation and Integration." *Public Administration Review* 33 (1973):590–597.

STUDY SUGGESTIONS

1. Table 9.13 describes the employment status of women in two communities. What conclusions can be drawn from the absolute numnumbers? From the percentages?

   TABLE 9.13. Employment Status of Women in Two Communities

	Community A		Community B	
In labor force				
Professional	10,000	2%	10,000	5%
Skilled	30,000	6	16,000	8
Semiskilled	50,000	10	20,000	10
Unskilled	150,000	30	20,000	10
Not in labor force	260,000	52	134,000	67
Total	500,000	100%	200,000	100%

2. Give two examples of problems in which (a) the mean is the best measure of central tendency; (b) the mode is the best measure of central tendency; (c) the median is the best measure of central tendency.

3. Give the mean, median, and mode of the following distribution:

   22, 41, 43, 56, 33, 22, 20, 37.

4. The following is the income distribution of a group of workers:

Income	Frequency
$ 5,000	6
6,010	3
6,500	3
7,000	2
24,000	1
	N = 15

   a. Which measure of central tendency would you use to represent the income of this group?
   b. Compute this measure.
5. On the curve shown below, what would be the approximate position of the mean? the median? and the mode? Define the curve with respect to skewness.

6. Suppose you obtain a set of scores of attitudes toward legal abortion from a group of respondents and that the standard deviation of this set of scores is zero. What does this imply about the group?
7. In one community, 40 percent of the people are black; in another, 63 percent. Compare the degree of heterogeneity of the two communities by using the measure of qualitative variation.
8. Attitudes toward authority often can be treated as an interval variable. Suppose this variable is normally distributed with a mean score of 60 and a standard deviation of 10.
   a. What proportion of cases has a score between 60 and 63?
   b. What proportion has a score less than 48?
   c. What proportion is between 72 and 83? 52 and 55?

CHAPTER 10
The Bivariate Distribution

Once single variables have been summarized and their pattern of distribution described, the researcher confronts the next task in the analysis of data: examining the pattern of relationship between the variables under investigation. This chapter examines different methods for measuring bivariate relationships between variables. The first section discusses the concept of relationship; the second section describes nominal measures of relationship; the third section deals with ordinal measures of relationship; and the last section presents interval measures of relationship.

THE CONCEPT OF RELATIONSHIP

Each of us, whether scientist or layperson, is aware of what relationships are. We know that, in the world around us, things go together. It is observed that as children grow, their weight increases; that cities tend to be more polluted than rural areas; and that the crime rate is higher in slums than in suburbs. Each of these observations is a statement of a relationship: between age and weight, between degree of urbanization and pollution, and between living conditions and crime.

To say that people who live in slums are usually unskilled is to describe a relationship between living conditions and achievement. This statement can be made only if it is known that people who have better living conditions are also better educated and trained for skilled work. In other words, to state a relationship between X and Y is to say that certain categories of the variable "X" go with certain categories of the variable "Y." This—the principle of covariation—is basic to the notion of association and relation, and it refers to the idea that observations can be placed in several categories simultaneously. For example, lower-class people are also often Democrats, and highly educated individuals have higher incomes.

The principle of covariation is demonstrated in Tables 10.1, 10.2, and 10.3 (Mueller, Schuessler, and Costner, 1970). These tables summarize information on two variables: religious affiliation and social class. Table 10.1 illustrates a pattern of perfect covariation of the variables. It is observed that all the Catholics are classified into the low social-class category, that all Jews belong to the middle class, and that the Protestants occupy the high social-class category. The two variables covary, since specific categories of the variable "religious affiliation" go with specific categories of the variable "social class."

The same pattern recurs in Table 10.2, but to a lesser extent, since

TABLE 10.1. Social Class by Religious Affiliation (Perfect Covariation)

| Social Class | Religious Affiliation | | | |
	Catholic	Jewish	Protestant	Total
Upper	0	0	8	8
Middle	0	8	0	8
Low	8	0	0	8
Total	8	8	8	24

TABLE 10.2. Social Class by Religious Affiliation (Moderate Covariation)

| Social Class | Religious Affiliation | | | |
	Catholic	Jewish	Protestant	Total
Upper	0	2	6	8
Middle	1	6	1	8
Low	7	0	1	8
Total	8	8	8	24

TABLE 10.3. Social Class by Religious Affiliation (Near Zero Covariation)

| Social Class | Religious Affiliation | | | |
	Catholic	Jewish	Protestant	Total
Upper	2	3	3	8
Middle	3	2	3	8
Low	3	3	2	8
Total	8	8	8	24

not all members of a given religious affiliation belong to the same class. Yet it can still be said that most members of a particular religion belong to a particular social stratum.

When variables are not related, it is said that they are independent of each other, that is, that they do not "go together." Table 10.3 illustrates this point. There is no clear pattern for any of the religious groups in the table. Catholics can be upper, middle, or lower class, since they are more or less equally distributed among the three classes; the same goes for the Jews and the Protestants. One cannot say anything about a person's socioeconomic status on the basis of his or her religion.

Tables 10.1, 10.2, and 10.3 are examples of bivariate distributions arranged in tabular form. The bivariate distribution consists of the categories of two variables and their joint frequencies. Its components are displayed in the bivariate tables of our example. Each table has two dimensions, one per variable. The variables are divided into a number of categories; for example, the variable "social class" has been divided into the categories "upper," "middle," and "low," and the variable "religious affiliation" into "Catholic," "Jewish," and "Protestant." The cells of the table constitute an intersection between two categories, each of one variable. The frequencies in each cell are of those observations that have two traits in common. For example, Table 10.3 shows 2 Catholics from the upper class, 3 from the middle class, and 3 from the lower class. The Jews have 3 members of the upper class, 2 members in the middle class, and 3 in the lower class; finally, there are 3 Protestants in the upper class, 3 in the middle class, and 2 in the lower class.

The bivariate table can also be visualized as a series of univariate distributions (Anderson and Zelditch, 1968). By splitting each table down its columns, and taking each column separately, we will have divided each bivariate distribution into three univariate distributions, representing the class affiliations of Protestants, Catholics, and Jews. In a comparison of the three univariate distributions derived from, say, Table 10.2, it is seen that each distribution differs from the others in its pattern of dispersion. In the Protestant distribution, most of the respondents tend to cluster at the upper extremity of the distribution; the Jews incline to the center; and the Catholics tend toward the lower section. This is even more pronounced in Table 10.1, where the tendency becomes absolute (i.e., all Protestants are upper class, etc.). In Table 10.3, on the other hand, there is practically no difference among the three distributions, the dispersion being identical in each. Thus, the amount of covariation in a bivariate table can be determined by a comparison of the univariate distributions that constitute the table. The larger the difference, the higher the degree of covariation of the two variables.

Percentaging Bivariate Tables

A generally useful way of summarizing a bivariate table and comparing its univariate distributions to assess covariation is by expressing its frequencies as percentages. Percentaging tables is appropriate whenever the variables are nominal, but the use of percentages is predominant even when the variables being analyzed are ordinal or interval. In Table 10.4, the observations of students' social class and track assignment have been cross-tabulated to examine the hypothesis that social class, measured by father's occupation, determines the assignment of secondary school students to different tracks. The table has been set up in the conventional way: father's occupation (the independent variable) is at the top of the table, and track assignment (the dependent variable) is on the left-hand side.

Each occupational group can be visualized as a univariate distribution, and its frequencies transformed into percentages using the total number of cases in each distribution as a base for percentaging (i.e., 518 blue-collar students and 583 white-collar students each represent 100 percent). The standardized frequencies are presented in Table 10.5. The next step is a comparison of the univariate distributions to determine the extent of covariation between father's occupation and track assignment. Whereas the computation of percentages goes down the columns, the comparison cuts across the rows. The proportion of blue-collar

TABLE 10.4. Distribution Between Tracks by Father's Occupation

	Father's Occupation	
	Blue Collar	*White Collar*
College prep	249	484
Non–college prep	269	99
Total	518	583

SOURCE: Walter E. Schafer and Carol Olexa. *Tracking and Opportunity.* New York: Chandler, 1971.

TABLE 10.5. Distribution Between Tracks by Father's Occupation

	Father's Occupation	
	Blue Collar	*White Collar*
College prep	48%	83%
Non–college prep	52	17
Total	100 (518)	100 (583)

students assigned to the college-prep tracks is compared with the proportion of white-collar students so assigned (48 percent and 83 percent). The percentages of blue-collar and white-collar students assigned to the non–college-prep track can also be compared.

Table 10.5 displays a clear pattern of covariation: a blue-collar occupation is associated with a non–college-prep track, and a white-collar occupation with a college-prep track. The two univariate distributions differ in their pattern of distribution between tracks; most students from white-collar backgrounds are in the college-prep tracks, whereas the blue-collar students are more or less equally divided, with a slight tendency toward the non–college-prep tracks.

Whenever one variable can be considered the cause and the other the effect, the percentages should be computed in the direction of the causal factor.* If track assignments were considered an independent variable and father's occupation the dependent variable (which seems unlikely in this example), then percentages would be computed across the rows, instead of along the columns. In instances when neither variable is assumed to influence the other, or when each is dependent on the other, one of the variables can be selected arbitrarily as the independent variable, whereupon the procedure is continued in the manner discussed.

The Median and the Mean as Measures of Covariation

When the variables of a bivariate distribution are ordinal, the medians of the various univariate distributions can be used as measures of covariation. The hypothetical data of Table 10.6 will illustrate this point. One hundred and twenty-two individuals were classified according to their race and attitude toward education. The dependent variable "attitude toward education" is on the left-hand side, and each racial group is assumed to be a univariate distribution. The variable "attitude toward education" is ranked from 1, expressing a positive attitude, to 4, a negative attitude. The appropriate summary measure for ordinal data is the median, which can be utilized to summarize each of the three distributions: the Mexican-American, the blacks, and the whites. Among whites, the middle case is 19; among blacks, 18; and among the Mexican-Americans it lies between the twenty-fifth and twenty-sixth cases. Their scores on the attitude toward education scale are thus 1, 2, and 3, respectively. The whites show the most positive attitude toward education; blacks' attitudes are intermediate; and Mexican-Americans display the most negative attitude. The fact that the pattern in each distribution is different indicates a covariation of races and attitudes toward education.

* Provided the sample is representative in that direction (Zeisel, 1968).

TABLE 10.6. Attitude Toward Education by Race

Attitude Toward Education	Race			
	Mexican-American	Black	White	Total
1	5	15	20	40
2	10	10	10	30
3	15	4	5	24
4	20	6	2	28
Total	50	35	37	122

With interval variables, the arithmetic mean can be used as a comparative measure. Table 10.7 is a bivariate distribution of intelligence test scores by age. Each age group can be visualized as a distribution and summarized by the arithmetic mean. Table 10.8 presents the arithmetic means of the distribution. Each pair of means can be compared. It is noted that average grades rise with age, a fact that permits one to deduce that the variables "age" and "intelligence" covary.

THE MEASUREMENT OF RELATIONSHIP

So far, the extent of covariation of two variables has been assessed by comparing the univariate distributions that constitute the bivariate table. However, there are various statistical techniques that allow the researcher to assess the extent to which two variables are associated by a single summarizing measure. Such measures of relationship, often referred to as correlation coefficients, reflect the strength and the direction of association between the variables and the degree to which one variable can be predicted from the other.

The notion of prediction is inherent in the concept of covariation. When two variables covary, it is possible to use one to predict the other; when they do not, information about one will not enable the prediction of the other. As an illustration, consider Tables 10.1, 10.2, and 10.3 again;

TABLE 10.7. Intelligence Test Scores by Age (Hypothetical Data)

IQ Test Scores	Age				
	6–10	11–15	16–20	21–25	Total
0–4	10	6	4	1	21
5–9	8	10	3	2	23
10–14	6	7	8	8	29
15–19	4	3	3	10	20
Total	28	26	18	21	93

TABLE 10.8. Mean of IQ Test Scores in Four Age Groups

Age Group	Mean
6–10	7.7
11–15	8.3
16–20	9.8
21–25	13.4

assume that no information is available about the religious affiliation of the 24 subjects, and that the social status of each one is to be guessed. Generally, the best guess will be the most frequent category. However, since in all three tables the frequencies of all the categories are identical, any category can be arbitrarily selected. Suppose the middle class is chosen as the best guess. Since only 8 cases in each table do in fact belong to the middle class, there will be 16 errors out of 24 guesses in each of the three tables.

Religious affiliation can be used to predict social class only if it is likely to reduce the number of errors in prediction. Suppose it is predicted that all Protestants are upper class, all Jews are middle class, and all Catholics are lower class. In Table 10.1, this prediction is accurate in each of the 24 cases; in Table 10.2, there are 5 errors; in Table 10.3, there are 16 errors.

The advantage of employing religious affiliation to predict social class can be calculated by subtracting the new number of errors from the previous total. In Table 10.1, the advantage is absolute since the reduction in the number of errors is the greatest ($16 - 0 = 16$). In Table 10.2, a considerable advantage is gained, the number of errors being reduced by 11 ($16 - 5 = 11$). In Table 10.3, there is no change in the number of errors, despite the employment of religious affiliation ($16 - 16 = 0$).

The strength of the association between social class and religious affiliation can be assessed by calculating the proportional reduction in prediction error when using one variable to predict another. The proportional reduction of error is defined as follows (Mueller, Schuessler, and Costner, 1970):

$$\frac{b-a}{b} \qquad (10.1)$$

where b = original number of errors (before employing the independent variable as a predictor)

a = new number of errors (after employing the independent variable as a predictor)

Using Equation (10.1), the proportional reduction in errors of prediction can be calculated from Tables 10.1, 10.2, and 10.3.

For Table 10.1: $\dfrac{16-0}{16} = \dfrac{16}{16} = 1$

For Table 10.2: $\dfrac{16-5}{16} = \dfrac{11}{16} = .69$

For Table 10.3: $\dfrac{16-16}{16} = \dfrac{0}{16} = 0$

The proportional reduction of error is absolute in Table 10.1, as reflected in the magnitude of the coefficient 1, expressing a perfect relationship between the variables "religious affiliation" and "social status." The number of errors in Table 10.2 has been reduced by almost 70 percent, following the employment of religious affiliation as a predictor. This is expressed by the coefficient .69. In Table 10.3, there is no advantage in using religious affiliation: the coefficient (0) expresses the absence of any association between the two variables.

Any measure of association can be developed along similar lines, provided it is based on two kinds of rules (Costner, 1965): (a) rules that allow the prediction of the dependent variable on the basis of an independent variable; and (b) rules that allow the prediction of the dependent variable independently of an independent variable. On this basis, any measure of association can be defined as in Equation (10.2):

$$\text{Measure of Association} = \frac{\text{Error by Rule (b)} - \text{Error by Rule (a)}}{\text{Error by Rule (b)}} \qquad (10.2)$$

Most of the measures of relationship introduced in this chapter will be analyzed according to this definition. In the following sections we discuss lambda and Goodman and Kruskal's tau, which measure the relation between nominal variables. Next, we introduce gamma and Kendall's tau-b and tau-c as ordinal coefficients. In the last section, Pearson's r as an interval measure of relation is discussed.

NOMINAL MEASURES OF RELATIONSHIP
Guttman Coefficient of Predictability (lambda—λ)

The correlation lambda (λ), also known as the Guttman coefficient of predictability (Guttman, 1941), is suitable for calculating relationships between nominal variables. To illustrate its calculation, suppose one is interested in predicting the party identification of non-Southern whites during the 1960s. One possibility is to use the distribution of party identification during 1960, thereby making use of prediction rule (b).

The univariate distribution of party identification is presented in Table 10.9.

The most effective way of guessing the party identification of each of these 900 voters, on the basis of the above distribution, is to use a measure of central tendency that will yield the smallest number of errors in prediction. Since party identification is a nominal variable, the mode is the most appropriate. As Democrats are the most frequent category ($f = 378$), the best guess is that each voter identified with the Democratic party, for the number of errors will not exceed 522 (234 Independents and 288 Republicans). Any other guess would magnify the number of errors. When guessing voters' party identification on the basis of the dependent variable alone, the most frequent category is chosen. According to this rule (b), the number of errors is 522 out of 900 guesses, that is, 58 percent.

The percentage of error might be reduced if another variable, "party identification prior to the 1956 election," is used as a predictor. Information is available on each of the 900 voters regarding their party identification in 1956. On this basis, it is possible to construct a bivariate table (Table 10.10) where all voters are classified according to two variables: their identification in 1956 and in 1960. With this additional information, one can predict the party identification of non-Southern whites prior to the elections of 1960 on the basis of their 1956 party identification. First, take those who declared themselves Democratic in 1956; there were 324 respondents, 279 of whom gave the same identification in 1960. As this is the most frequent category, it is assumed that anyone who identified with the Democratic party in 1956 did so again in 1960. With this assumption, 45 errors of predictions are made, since 45 of the 324 identified themselves otherwise in 1960.

Two hundred and seventy voters identified themselves as Inde-

TABLE 10.9. 1960 Party Identification among Non-Southern Whites*

Non-Southern Whites	f
Democrat	378
Independent	234
Republican	288
Total	900

SOURCE: Angus C. Campbell et al. *Elections and the Political Order.* New York: Wiley, 1966, p. 232.

* The original data appear in percentages. Due to differences in rounding in the original table, the total frequencies are not identical.

TABLE 10.10. 1956 and 1960 Party Identification among Non-Southern Whites

Party Identification, 1960	Party Identification, 1956			1960 Overall
	Democrat	Independent	Republican	
Democrat	279	81	18	378
Independent	45	144	45	234
Republican	*	45	243	288
1956 overall	324	270	306	900

SOURCE: Angus C. Campbell et al. *Elections and the Political Order*. New York: Wiley, 1966, p. 225.

* Less than half of 1 percent.

pendents in 1956; 144 of them did so again in 1960. It can therefore be assumed again that whoever identified themselves as Independents in 1956 did so in 1960 as well. With this assumption, the number of errors is 81 + 45 = 126, the number who did not identify themselves as Independents. Finally, for those 306 who identified with the Republicans in 1956, it is assumed that the preference patterns did not change; as a result, 45 + 18 = 63 errors are made.

The total number of errors made by using the new rule (a) is

$$45 + 126 + 63 = 234$$

Two hundred and thirty-four errors out of 900 predictions is a percentage of 26 percent. Using an independent variable as a predictor leads to a decrease in the error of prediction, as expressed in the magnitude of the correlation, which can now be calculated:

$$\text{error stemming from rule (b)} = 522$$
$$\text{error stemming from rule (a)} = 234$$
$$\text{lambda } (\lambda) = \frac{522 - 234}{522} = .55$$

Thus, 55 percent of the errors of prediction concerning party affiliation in 1960 were eliminated by utilizing the identification pattern preceding the 1956 elections.

Lambda is an asymmetrical coefficient, as it reflects relationships between variables in one direction only. In practice, it is often represented as λ_a, "a" indicating that it is asymmetrical. The coefficient .55 expresses the relationship between party affiliations in 1956 and 1960, with that of 1956 serving as an independent variable. The correlation coefficient can also be calculated in the opposite direction, with 1960 serving as the independent variable. The method of calculation is identical: we compute the number of errors made when estimating 1956 identification patterns without reference to 1960 data, and then calculate the advantage obtained by gauging the 1956 data from those of 1960.

Lambda can also be computed by a slightly simpler procedure using Formula (10.3) (Freeman, 1965):

$$\lambda_a = \frac{\sum f_i - F_d}{N - F_d} \tag{10.3}$$

where f_i = the modal frequency within each category of the independent variable

F_d = the modal frequency in the marginal totals of the dependent variable.

N = the total number of cases

We can now repeat our calculation of the correlation between the data from 1956 and from 1960, with 1956 identification serving as the independent variable.

$$\sum f_i = 279 + 144 + 243 = 666$$
$$F_d = 378$$
$$N = 900$$
$$\lambda_a = \frac{666 - 378}{900 - 378} = \frac{288}{522} = .55$$

To summarize, the magnitude of lambda expresses the proportional reduction in error of estimate when switching from rule (b) to rule (a). The strength of the association between the two variables reflects the improvement in prediction attainable with the aid of a second variable. Lambda may range from 0 to 1.0; zero indicates that there is nothing to be gained by shifting from one prediction rule to another, whereas 1.0 reflects the fact that the use of an independent variable permits the dependent variable to be predicted without any error at all.

Lambda has a limitation in situations when the modal frequencies of the independent variable are all concentrated in one category of the dependent variable. In such a case, lambda will always be zero even in instances where the two variables are in fact related. For example, in the bivariate distribution presented in Table 10.11, it can be seen that place of residence is associated with self-esteem. More residents of rural areas (75 percent) have high self-esteem than do residents of cities (66 percent). However, since the sum of all modal frequencies of the variable place of residence ($\sum f_i = 300 + 200$) is equal to the modal frequency of the marginal totals of the variable self-esteem ($F_d = 500$), lambda will take on the value of zero. Such a pattern of distribution is likely to occur when the marginal totals of the dependent variable are extremely uneven. Lambda would then be inappropriate and a different

TABLE 10.11. Place of Residence and Self-Esteem

Self-Esteem	Place of Residence		Total
	Rural Areas	Cities	
High	300	200	500
Low	100	100	200
Total	400	300	700

measure of association such as Goodman and Kruskal's tau is to be preferred.

Goodman and Kruskal's Tau (τ_b)

Goodman and Kruskal's tau (τ_b) measures association between nominal variables and can be applied in situations when lambda is inappropriate. Like lambda, tau is an asymmetrical coefficient and is based on the same principle of minimizing error of prediction by introducing a predictor— the independent variable. Tau ranges from 0 to 1.0 with 0 implying no reduction in error and 1.0 indicating prediction with no error. The main difference between lambda and tau is in the method of computing error, which is more restrictive in the case of tau.

In order to illustrate the computation of tau, let us go back to Table 10.10. Party identification in 1960 is to be guessed from its marginal distribution, while maintaining the observed distribution. Following this rule, 378 cases would be assigned to the category "Democrat," 234 to "Independent," and 288 to "Republican." Although the predicted marginal distribution is identical to the observed one, the cases assigned by this rule to the respective categories would not necessarily be the same cases that actually belong to these categories. Thus, it is expected that in the long run, some cases will be misclassified. The error in misclassification is computed as follows: for the category "Democrat" there are 378 cases who may belong to this category but 522 who would be wrongly assigned. The error in prediction is then:

$$\frac{522}{900} \times 378 = 219.24$$

Similarly, for the category "Independent," there are

$$\frac{666}{900} \times 234 = 173.16 \text{ errors}$$

and for the "Republican" category,

$$\frac{612}{900} \times 288 = 195.84 \text{ errors}$$

The total number of errors obtained when predicting party identification in 1960 with no prior knowledge is then:

$$219.24 + 173.16 + 195.84 = 588.24$$

Next, we calculate the number of errors when prediction is made with knowledge of the independent variable—1956 party identification. Cases are assigned to cells on the basis of the observed frequencies. Thus, of the 324 cases who voted Democratic in 1956, 279 will be assigned to the category "Democrat" and 45 to the category "Independent." For this column the number of errors would be:

$$\left(\frac{45}{324} \times 279\right) + \left(\frac{279}{324} \times 45\right) = 77.5$$

For the category "Independent," the total number of errors is:

$$\left(\frac{189}{270} \times 81\right) + \left(\frac{126}{270} \times 144\right) + \left(\frac{225}{270} \times 45\right) = 56.7 + 67.2 + 37.5 = 161.4$$

Similarly, for the category "Republican," there are:

$$\left(\frac{288}{306} \times 18\right) + \left(\frac{261}{306} \times 45\right) + \left(\frac{63}{306} \times 243\right)$$
$$= 16.94 + 38.38 + 50.03 = 105.35 \text{ errors}$$

The total sum of errors obtained when the 1956 party identification is used to predict identification is:

$$77.5 + 161.4 + 105.35 = 344.25$$

Tau is defined as follows:

$$\tau_b = \frac{S_1 - S_2}{S_1} \qquad (10.4)$$

where S_1 = Total sum of errors obtained when no predictor is used
S_2 = Total sum of errors obtained when a predictor is used

Accordingly,

$$\tau_b = \frac{588.24 - 344.25}{588.24} = .41$$

Note that tau has a smaller numerical value than lambda; this is a function of its more restrictive method for computing error.

ORDINAL MEASURES OF RELATIONSHIP

When both variables of a bivariate distribution are ordinal, the construction of a measure of relationship is based on the principal property of the ordinal scale, by which observations can be ranked in relation to the variables being measured. With a single variable, one is generally interested in evaluating the relative position of the observations on the variable. For example, professions can be ranked according to the amount of prestige they command, and students, according to their relative degree of political tolerance. The same principle can be applied with two variables. Here, the interest is in examining whether the ranking of observations on each of the variables is identical, similar, or different. Every two observations are compared, and it is noted whether one that is ranked high on one variable is as high with regard to the other. For instance, one can examine whether the ranking of professions by their prestige in the 1950s resembles their ranking in the 1970s, or whether persons with a conservative orientation on foreign affairs show a similar tendency on internal issues.

When observations display the same order on both variables, the relationship is said to be positive; when the order is inverse, so that the observation ranking highest on one variable is the lowest on the second variable, the relationship is negative. When there is no clear pattern in the relative position of the observations on both variables, then the variables are said to be independent of each other. Consider the following example: if all military personnel with high rank are also more liberal on political issues than the lower-ranking officers, then one may say that military rank and political liberalism are positively related. If, however, the high-ranking officers are less liberal, the association is negative. When some high officers are liberal and others are not, then rank and liberalism are independent of each other.

Most ordinal measures of relationship are based on the pair as a unit of analysis and its relative ranking on both variables. For example, we can compare every pair of officers in terms of their rank and liberalism. The number of pairs that can be formed out of N cases is obtained by Formula (10.5):

$$\binom{N}{2} = \frac{N(N-1)}{2} \qquad (10.5)$$

Suppose six officers are classified according to their rank and degree of liberalism. The observations are presented in Table 10.12. According to Formula (10.5), 15 pairs can be formed out of 6 observations:

$$\binom{6}{2} = \frac{6(5)}{2} = 15$$

Table 10.13 lists the 15 pairs according to cell number and rank on each of the variables. The first column designates the pair's number, the second column the cell number (with "a" designating the first member of the pair, and "b" the second member), and the third and fourth

TABLE 10.12. Liberalism by Rank (Hypothetical Data)*

Liberalism (Y)	Rank (X)		Total
	Low	High	
Low	$2(_{11})$	$1(_{12})$	3
High	$1(_{21})$	$2(_{22})$	3
Total	3	3	6

* The numbers in parentheses designate the cell numbers.

columns their rank and liberalism. The last column describes the relative position of the pair on the two variables.

For instance, the first pair, designated as tied on X and Y, consists of two officers, both classified in cell 11. These officers have the same rank and share the same political views. Pairs tied on Y are officers of different ranks and sharing the same political views; pairs tied on X are officers of the same rank but of different political views; pairs designated as "same" are officers who have the same relative position on both variables, so that if one has the highest rank that officer would be the most liberal as well. Pairs designated as "inverse" have a different relative position on both variables, so that if one has the highest rank that officer would be the least liberal of the pair.

From the total number of pairs that can be constructed from N observations, the following groups can be distinguished:

1. Pairs that display the same order on both X and Y; they will be denoted as Ns.
2. Pairs that display an inverse order on X and Y; they will be denoted as Nd.
3. Pairs tied on X, denoted as Tx.
4. Pairs tied on Y, denoted as Ty.
5. Pairs tied on X and on Y, denoted Txy.

1. To find Ns in the general bivariate table, the frequency in every cell is multiplied by the total of all the frequencies in the cells below it and to its right, and the products are added up. In Table 10.11, the number of pairs displaying the same ranking on both variables is $2 \times 2 = 4$.

2. To calculate Nd in the general bivariate table, the frequency in each cell is multiplied by the total of all the frequencies in the cells below it and to its left, and the products are added up. In Table 10.12, the number of pairs displaying different rankings on the two variables is $1 \times 1 = 1$.

3. To find the number of pairs tied on X (Tx), the frequency in every

TABLE 10.13. Relative Position of Officers in Rank and Liberalism

Pair	From Cell	Rank of Officer (X)	Degree of Liberalism (Y)	Order
1	a 11	L	L	Tie on X and Y
	b 11	L	L	
2	a 11	L	L	Tie on Y
	b 12	H	L	
3	a 11	L	L	Tie on Y
	b 12	H	L	
4	a 11	L	L	Tie on X
	b 21	L	H	
5	a 11	L	L	Tie on X
	b 21	L	H	
6	a 11	L	L	Same
	b 22	H	H	
7	a 11	L	L	Same
	b 22	H	H	
8	a 11	L	L	Same
	b 22	H	H	
9	a 11	L	L	Same
	b 22	H	H	
10	a 12	H	L	Inverse
	b 21	L	H	
11	a 12	H	L	Tie on X
	b 22	H	H	
12	a 12	H	L	Tie on X
	b 22	H	H	
13	a 21	L	H	Tie on Y
	b 22	H	H	
14	a 21	L	H	Tie on Y
	b 22	H	H	
15	a 22	H	H	Tie on X and Y
	b 22	H	H	

cell is multiplied by the total of all the frequencies in the cells in that column, and the products are added up. The number of pairs tied on X is $(2 \times 1) + (1 \times 2) = 4$.

4. To find the number of pairs tied on Y (T_y), the frequency in each cell is multiplied by the sum of the frequencies in the cells in that row, and the products are added up. The number of pairs tied on Y in Table 10.12 is $(2 \times 1) + (1 \times 2) = 4$.

5. To work out the number of pairs that are tied on X and Y (Txy), all the pairs that can be created from every cell, by means of the formula $\binom{N}{2}$, are added up. In Table 10.11, the ties on X and Y are:

$$\text{Cell 11: } \frac{2(1)}{2} = 1$$

$$\text{Cell 12: } \frac{1(0)}{1} = 0$$

$$\text{Cell 21: } \frac{1(0)}{1} = 0$$

$$\text{Cell 22: } \frac{2(1)}{2} = 1$$

The total number of pairs of all kinds that can be constructed out of N observations is:

$$\binom{N}{2} = Ns + Nd + Tx + Ty + Txy$$

In our example:

$$\binom{6}{2} = 4 + 1 + 4 + 4 + 2 = 15$$

Gamma (γ or G)

Gamma, a coefficient used for measuring the association between ordinal variables, was developed by Goodman and Kruskal (1954). It is a symmetrical statistic, based on the number of same-order pairs (Ns) and the number of different-order pairs (Nd). Tied pairs play no part in the definition of gamma.

The coefficient is defined by Formula (10.6) (Mueller, Schuessler, and Costner, 1970):

$$\gamma = \frac{0.5(Ns + Nd) - Min\ (Ns, Nd)}{0.5(Ns + Nd)} \qquad (10.6)$$

To illustrate the calculation of gamma, consider the data presented in Table 10.14 on class standing and political tolerance of students. If these two variables are associated, it will be possible to predict students' political tolerance on the basis of their class standing with a minimum of error.

First, the number of pairs that can be constructed from 1,032 observations is counted. With tied pairs excluded, the overall number of pairs that can be constructed from a bivariate table is $Ns + Nd$. Ns and Nd are calculated according to the definitions presented previously.

THE BIVARIATE DISTRIBUTION

TABLE 10.14. Political Tolerance of College Students by Class Standing

	Class Standing						
	Fresh-man	Sopho-more	Junior	Senior	Graduate Student (Full time)	Graduate Student (Part time)	Total
Less tolerant	30	30	34	33	40	15	182
Somewhat tolerant	66	75	79	79	120	45	464
More tolerant	28	51	59	63	151	34	386
Total	124	156	172	175	311	94	1,032

$Ns = 30(75 + 51 + 79 + 59 + 79 + 63 + 120 + 151 + 45 + 34)$
$\quad + 66(51 + 59 + 63 + 151 + 34)$
$\quad + 30(79 + 59 + 79 + 63 + 120 + 151 + 45 + 34)$
$\quad + 75(59 + 63 + 151 + 34) + 34(79 + 63 + 120 + 151 + 45 + 34)$
$\quad + 79(63 + 151 + 34) + 33(120 + 151 + 45 + 34)$
$\quad + 79(151 + 34) + 40(45 + 34) + 120(34)$
$\quad = 157{,}958$

$Nd = 15(120 + 151 + 79 + 63 + 79 + 59 + 75 + 51 + 66 + 28)$
$\quad + 45(151 + 63 + 59 + 51 + 28)$
$\quad + 40(79 + 63 + 79 + 59 + 75 + 51 + 66 + 28)$
$\quad + 120(63 + 59 + 51 + 28) + 33(79 + 59 + 75 + 51 + 66 + 28)$
$\quad + 79(59 + 51 + 28) + 34(75 + 51 + 66 + 28) + 79(51 + 28)$
$\quad + 30(66 + 28) + 75(28)$
$\quad = 112{,}882$

The total number of pairs (tied pairs excluded) is $Ns + Nd = 157{,}958 + 112{,}882 = 270{,}840$.

Next, the relative political tolerance of the students is determined on the basis of the dependent variable alone—rule (b). To find the relative position of each of the 270,840 pairs, some random system can be used.* For example, members of each pair can be labeled as heads or tails, and by flipping a coin it is decided which member is more tolerant.

---
* Since the univariate distribution of the variable "political tolerance" does not provide information about the relative political tolerance of the students, it cannot be used as a basis of prediction.

When this process is repeated for each pair, it can be expected that in the long run 50 percent of the guesses about the relative position of the students will be accurate, whereas the other 50 percent will be erroneous. Hence, prediction rule (b) will produce $Ns + Nd/2 = 135{,}420$ errors.

Prediction rule (a) states that if there are more pairs displaying the same order (Ns), an identical ranking for all the pairs will be predicted. In that case, the number of errors will be Nd, that is, the number of pairs whose ranking is different on the two variables. In the same way, should the number of inverted pairs (Nd) be greater, pairs will be given a different ranking, whereupon the number of errors will equal Ns, that is, the number of pairs with identical ranking.

The calculations based on the information in Table 10.14 indicate that the number of pairs with the same ranking is greater than the number of those whose ranking is inverted ($Ns > Nd$). Hence, the relative position of political tolerance for each pair will be predicted on the basis of its member's class standing, so that the student with the greater seniority exhibits greater tolerance. If Mary is a sophomore and John is a freshman, Mary will be more tolerant than John. As not all pairs display the same order, the number of errors made by such a prediction rule is $Nd = 112{,}882$.

The relationship between class standing and political tolerance can now be asserted, using the general formula for measures of association:

$$\frac{b - a}{b}$$

where $b = 0.5(Ns + Nd)$
$a = Min\ (Ns, Nd)$

Accordingly,

$$\gamma = \frac{0.5(Ns + Nd) - Nd}{0.5(Ns + Nd)} = \frac{135{,}420 - 112{,}882}{135{,}420} = \frac{22{,}538}{135{,}420} = .17$$

A value of .17 for γ reflects the advantage gained by using the variable "class standing" in predicting political tolerance. By using this variable, 17 percent of the total number of errors were eliminated.

Gamma can also be calculated by using Formula (10.7)

$$\gamma = \frac{Ns - Nd}{Ns + Nd} \qquad (10.7)$$

This formula reflects the relative predominance of same-order or different-order pairs. When same-order pairs predominate, the coefficient is positive; when different-order pairs predominate, it is negative. When the ranking on both variables is identical, the number of same-order pairs (Ns) will equal the total number of pairs, since Nd will be zero. Gamma will then equal 1.0.

$$\gamma = \frac{Ns - 0}{Ns + 0} = \frac{Ns}{Ns} = 1.0$$

A coefficient of 1.0 indicates that the dependent variable can be predicted on the basis of the independent variable without any error. When $Ns = 0$, the coefficient will be negative, but prediction is still accurate:

$$\gamma = \frac{0 - Nd}{0 + Nd} = \frac{-Nd}{Nd} = -1.0$$

When the number of different-order pairs is equal to the number of same-order pairs, gamma is zero:

$$\gamma = \frac{Ns - Nd}{Ns + Nd} = \frac{0}{Ns + Nd} = 0$$

A gamma of zero reflects that there is nothing to be gained by using the independent variable to predict the dependent variable.

The main weakness of gamma as a measure of ordinal association is the exclusion of ties from its computation. Hence, it will reach a value of ± 1 even under conditions of less than perfect association. For example, a perfect relationship was described early in the chapter as in the following table:

50	0
0	50

$\gamma = 1$

However, since gamma is based on untied pairs only, it becomes 1 under the following conditions as well:

50	50
0	50

$\gamma = 1$

In general, in marginal distributions that are uneven, with a concentration of many observations in few categories, there will be many tied pairs, and gamma will be based on a smaller proportion of pairs. This is especially acute in 2×2 tables, where the proportion of untied pairs will be small, even when all marginal frequencies are equal. Although there is no simple solution to the problem of ties, it is advisable to have as many categories as possible of the two variables, thereby to minimize the number of tied pairs and maximize the number of pairs on which gamma is based.

With many ties, a different measure that handles the problem of ties can be used. It is Kendall's tau-b defined as follows:

$$\tau_b = \frac{Ns - Nd}{\sqrt{(Ns + Nd + Ty)(Ns + Nd + Tx)}} \quad (10.8)$$

Tau-b varies from -1 to $+1$ and is a symmetrical coefficient. It has the same numerator as gamma, but has a correction factor for ties, in its denominator (Ty and Tx). For example, for the following bivariate distribution we get:

$$Ns = 600 \qquad Ty = 2700$$
$$Nd = 2100 \qquad Tx = 2300$$

	x		
y	30	70	100
	30	20	50
	60	90	150

Therefore,

$$\tau_b = \frac{600 - 2100}{\sqrt{(600 + 2100 + 2700)(600 + 2100 + 2300)}} = \frac{-1500}{5196} = -.29$$

Note that under the same conditions, gamma gives a considerably higher figure than tau-b:

$$\gamma = \frac{600 - 2100}{600 + 2100} = \frac{-1500}{2700} = -.56$$

Gamma will always exceed tau-b when there are tied pairs. With no ties, its value will be identical with tau-b.

Tau-b reaches a maximum of ± 1 when the number of rows (r) and columns (c) are equal. For rectangular tables, tau-c, a variant of tau-b can be substituted. Tau-c is defined below:

$$\tau_c = \frac{Ns - Nd}{\frac{1}{2}N^2(m-1)/m} \quad (10.9)$$

$$m = \text{Min } (r, c)$$

Both tau-b and tau-c are difficult to interpret as measures which designate a proportional reduction of error in prediction. In this respect, they are less satisfactory than gamma.

INTERVAL MEASURES OF RELATIONSHIP

At lower levels of measurement, the ability to make predictions is restricted even when the variables considered are associated. At most, one can point out an interdependence of certain categories or properties, such as the fact that Catholics tend to vote Democratic; or, one can expect the same relative position of observations on two variables, for instance, that military rank is associated with liberalism. However, predictions of this type are imprecise, and there is frequently a need for more accurate predictive statements, as for example, when one wishes to predict individuals' future income on the basis of their level of education, or a city's crime rate from its racial composition.

When the variables being analyzed are at least interval, one can be more precise in describing the nature and the form of the relationship. Precise prediction rules are quite frequently made in the natural sciences in the form of prediction functions. For instance, there are functions that express the relationship between acceleration distance and time in the form $K = PV/T$; or between voltage resistance and current in the form $C = V/R$.

In the social sciences, however, prediction functions are expressed in much simpler terms. Most relationships can in fact be formulated in terms of a linear function rule. A function is said to be linear when pairs of X,Y values fall exactly into a function that can be plotted as a straight line. All such functions have rules of the form $Y = a + bX$, where a and b are constant numbers.

For example, there is a perfect linear relationship between the distance and the time that a car travels at a fixed speed (Table 10.15). If its speed is sixty miles per hour, it will go sixty miles in one hour, or X miles in Y time. The linear function expresses the relationship between the time and the distance that the car travels. Such a function takes the form of $Y = 1X$, reflecting the fact that a change of one unit of distance (miles) will bring about a change of one unit of time (minutes). The constant 1 preceding X in the formula is called b, or the slope, expressing the number of units of change in Y accompanying one unit of change in X.

This method of specifying the nature of a relationship between two variables is referred to as regression analysis. The task of regression is to find some algebraic expression by which to represent the functional relationship between the variables. The equation $Y = a + bX$ is a linear regression equation, meaning that the function describing the relation between X and Y is that of a straight line. Ordinarily, the observations of X and Y, and the regression line connecting them, are displayed in the form of a graph. X and Y are represented by two intersecting axes. Each observation is entered as a dot at the point where the X and Y scores intersect. In Figure 10.1, we have entered the observations from Table 10.15 to illustrate the graphical presentation of bivariate observations and the functional form describing their interrelationship. X, the independent variable, is placed on the horizontal axis; Y, the dependent variable, on the vertical axis; and each observation is plotted at the inter-

TABLE 10.15. Distance by Time

X (Miles)	Y (Time in Minutes)
1	1
3	3
5	5
10	10
15	15

section of the two axes. For example, the last observation of Table 10.15 is plotted at the intersection of the two axes on the score 15, to represent its score of 15 on the two variables.

The regression line does not always pass through the intersection of the X and Y axes. When a straight line intersects the Y axis, there is a need for another constant to be introduced into the linear regression equation. This constant is symbolized by the letter "a" and is called the Y intercept. "a" reflects the value of Y when X is zero. Each of the three regression lines in Figure 10.2 has different values for a and b. The three different values of a (6, 1, 2) are reflected in the three different intersections of the lines. The different values of b (−3, 0.5, 3) reflect the steepness of the slopes. The higher the value of b, the steeper the slope. Finally, the sign of b expresses the direction of the relationship between X and Y: when b is positive, an increase in X is accompanied by an increase in Y; when b is negative, Y decreases as X increases (Figure 10.2, I).

Most relationships in the social sciences can be fairly well expressed by the linear function. Thus, for example, the equation $Y = 2{,}000 + 1{,}000X$ expresses the relation between income and education; a is the

FIGURE 10.1 Regression of Y on X

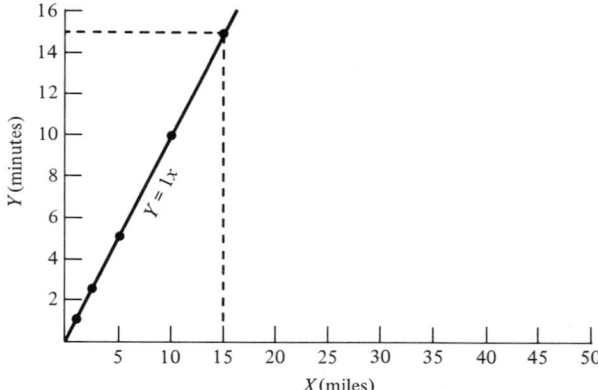

FIGURE 10.2.

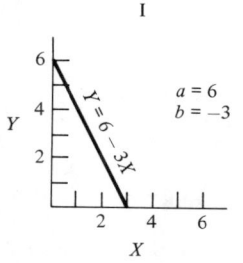
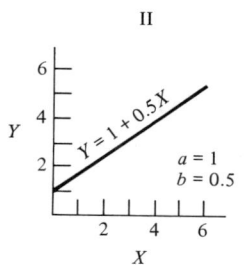
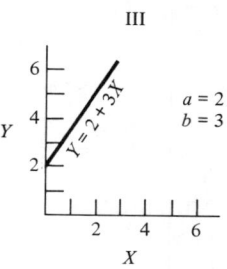

initial yearly salary ($2,000) for individuals who had no education at all, and b (1,000) stands for an increment of $1,000 for each additional year of education. Using this prediction rule, we could expect individuals having ten years of schooling to make $12,000 a year.

The regression equation, however, is only a prediction rule; thus, there are discrepancies between actual observations and the ones predicted. The goal is to construct such an equation that the deviations, or error of prediction, will be at a minimum. If a specific criterion is adopted in determining a and b of the linear equation, it is possible to create a function that will minimize the variance around the regression line. This is the criterion of least squares, which minimizes the sum of the squared differences between the observed Y's and the Y's predicted with the regression equation. According to this criterion, a and b can be calculated by the following formulas:

$$b = \frac{\sum_{i=1}^{N}(X_i - \overline{X})(Y_i - \overline{Y})}{\sum_{i=1}^{N}(X_i - \overline{X})^2} \qquad (10.10)$$

$$a = \frac{\sum_{i=1}^{N} Y_i - b \sum_{i=1}^{N} X_i}{N} = \overline{Y} - b\overline{X} \qquad (10.11)$$

A more convenient formula for computing b is as follows:

$$b = \frac{N \sum XY - (\sum X)(\sum Y)}{N \sum X^2 - (\sum X)^2} \qquad (10.12)$$

To illustrate the construction of a precise prediction rule for interval variables, consider the series of observations in Table 10.16 on per capita GNP and the percentage of the urban population living in cities with a population of over 20,000. These observations were assembled from

TABLE 10.16. GNP per Capita and Percentage of the Urban Population in Cities of Over 20,000

Country	Percent-age of Urban (x)	Per Capita GNP (y)	xy	x^2	y^2
Nepal	4.4	45	198.0	19.36	2,025
Afghanistan	7.5	50	375.0	56.25	2,500
Laos	4.0	50	200.0	16.00	2,500
Burma	10.0	57	570.0	100.00	3,249
Libya	18.4	60	1,104.0	338.56	3,600
Pakistan	11.8	70	826.0	139.24	4,900
Bolivia	19.4	99	1,920.6	376.36	9,801
Iran	21.0	108	2,268.0	441.00	11,664
Jordan	25.5	129	3,289.5	650.25	16,641
Egypt	29.1	142	4,132.2	846.81	20,164
Iraq	23.6	156	3,681.6	556.96	24,336
Syria	38.8	173	6,712.4	1,505.44	29,929
Turkey	18.2	220	4,004.0	331.24	48,400
Spain	39.8	293	11,661.4	1,584.04	85,849
Japan	43.1	306	13,188.6	1,857.61	93,636
Chile	46.3	379	17,547.7	2,143.69	143,641
Total	360.9	2,337	71,679.0	10,962.81	502,835

SOURCE: Adapted from Bruce M. Russet et al. *World Handbook of Political and Social Indicators*. New Haven: Yale University Press, 1964, pp. 294–298.

sixteen countries, with the aim of exploring the relationship between the degree of urbanization (as an indicator of modernization) and per capita GNP. The variable to be predicted (the dependent variable) is "per capita GNP," and the independent variable is the "percentage of urban population."

To predict the per capita GNP of any country, without any additional information, a value that will produce the smallest possible number of errors is chosen as an estimate for each country in the distribution. The arithmetic mean is the best guess for every interval distribution, since the mean of its squared deviations is lower than for any other value. The average per capita GNP, according to the data, is

$$\overline{Y} = \frac{\sum_{i=1}^{N} Y_i}{N} = 146$$

To assess the prediction error, each observation is subtracted from the mean (to calculate the deviations), and the deviations are squared. The sum of the squared deviations, referred to as total variation about $\overline{Y}$, is selected as an estimate of error of prediction—rule (b)—since it produces the minimum of errors. The total variation about $\overline{Y}$ is defined as in Equation (10.13):

$$\text{Total variation} = \sum_{i=1}^{N}(Y_i - \overline{Y})^2 \qquad (10.13)$$

The next step is to reduce the errors of prediction of per capita GNP by employing a second variable, "percentage of urban," as a predictor. This can be accomplished by constructing a prediction rule in the form of a regression equation that will best describe the relationship between these two variables and that will allow us to predict per capita GNP on the basis of percentage of urban population with a minimum of error.

The observations of Table 10.16 can be displayed in a scatter diagram, which is a graphic device providing a first approximation of the relationship between the two variables (Figure 10.3). Each dot represents an observation that has a fixed X and Y characteristic. For example, the dot designated as A represents Chile, with a per capita GNP of $379 and 46.3 percent of its urban population in cities of over 20,000. Next, a line that best approximates the trend the dots display is drawn. Obvi-

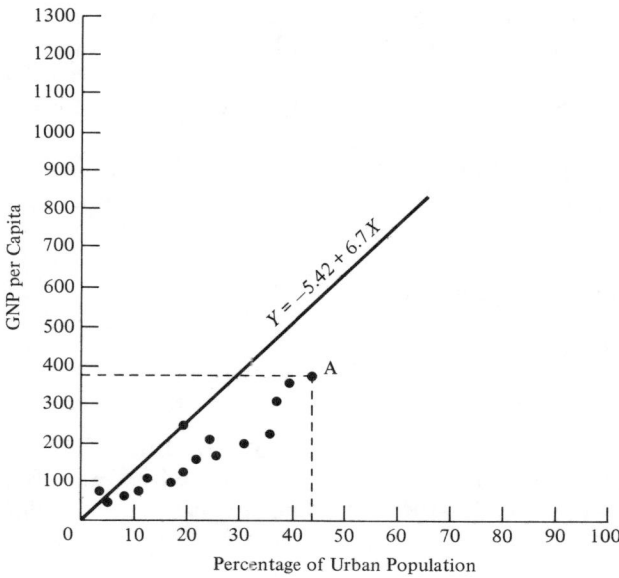

FIGURE 10.3. GNP per Capita and Percentage of Urban Population

ously, several such lines can be drawn between the dots, but only one, the line of least squares, comes as close as possible to all the individual observations. Before drawing this line, the constants a and b are calculated:

$$b = \frac{16(71,679) - (360.9)(2,337)}{16(10,962.81) - 130,248.81} = 6.7$$

$$a = 146 - 6.7(22.6) = -5.42$$

The resulting linear equation is therefore:

$$Y = -5.42 + 6.7X$$

The estimated regression line can now be drawn and applied to predict per capita GNP for every level of urban population. For example, if a country had only 10 percent of its urban population in cities of over 20,000 inhabitants, its per capita GNP is expected to be $Y = -5.42 + 6.7(10) = 61.58$.

One can see from Figure 10.3 that most of the actual observations are spread around the regression line. The deviations of the actual observations from the predicted ones represent the errors produced when using the prediction rule specified above in guessing per capita GNP on the basis of the percentage of urban population.

The error involved in predicting per capita GNP from percentage of urban population can be estimated by measuring the deviations of the actual observations from the regression line. The predicted per capita GNP for each country is subtracted from the actual observations recorded in Table 10.16. For example, for Nepal, the predicted per capita GNP according to the prediction rule $Y = -5.42 + 6.7X$ is $-5.42 + 6.7(4.4) = -5.42 + 29.48 = 24.06$. The actual per capita GNP of Nepal is 45; the error of prediction is thus $45 - 24.06 = 20.94$.

The sum of the squared errors of prediction is the variation unexplained by the independent variable. It is defined in Formula (10.14):

$$\text{Unexplained variation} = \sum_{i=1}^{N}(Y_i - Y_p)^2 \qquad (10.14)$$

where Y_i = actual observations

Y_p = predicted observations

It is noted that there are two measures of variability for Y. The first, the total variation about $\overline{Y}$, is the error obtained when one predicts Y with no prior knowledge of X—rule (b).* The second, the unexplained

---

* Rule (b) is the total variation about $\overline{Y}$.

variation, is the error obtained when using linear regression as the prediction rule—rule (a). For the data in Table 10.16, the figures are:

$$\text{Total variation} = 161{,}487$$

$$\text{Unexplained variation} = 34{,}088$$

These two estimates of error enable the construction of an interval measure of association that reflects a proportional reduction in error when one shifts from the first prediction rule—(b), the mean—to the second—(a), the linear regression equation—to evaluate Y. This measure, r^2, is defined in Equation (10.15):

$$r^2 = \frac{\text{Total Variation} - \text{Unexplained Variation}}{\text{Total Variation}} \qquad (10.15)$$

In our example,

$$r^2 = \frac{161{,}487 - 34{,}088}{161{,}487} = .789$$

The unexplained variation is subtracted from the original error of prediction to evaluate the proportional reduction in error. r^2 reflects the proportional reduction in error when X is used to predict Y. When the percentage of urban population is used to predict per capita income, the proportional reduction in error is 78.9 percent. Unexplained variation of zero means that the regression equation eliminated all errors in predicting Y, and r^2 then equals 1, meaning that any variation in Y can be explained by X. On the other hand, when the unexplained variation is identical to the total variation, r^2 is zero, indicating complete independence between X and Y.

Conventionally, it is the square root of r^2, r, designated as Pearson's r, rather than r^2, that is used as a coefficient of correlation. Pearson's r ranges from -1 to $+1$, where a negative coefficient indicates inverse relations between the variables. A simple formula for computing r is:

$$r = \frac{N \sum XY - (\sum X)(\sum Y)}{\sqrt{[N \sum X^2 - (\sum X)^2][N \sum Y^2 - (\sum Y)^2]}} \qquad (10.16)$$

The size of r^2 or r is determined by the spread of the actual observations around the regression line. Thus, if all the observations are on the line, r will be 1; if they are randomly scattered, r will approximate zero. Figure 10.4 illustrates the possibilities of a strong positive relationship, a weak positive relationship, and no relationship. When r or r^2 approximates or equals zero, one should not rush to the conclusion that there is no correlation between the variables. The relationship may be curvilinear—that is, it cannot be described by a straight line—so that a coefficient based on the linear model would not give a correct picture

FIGURE 10.4.

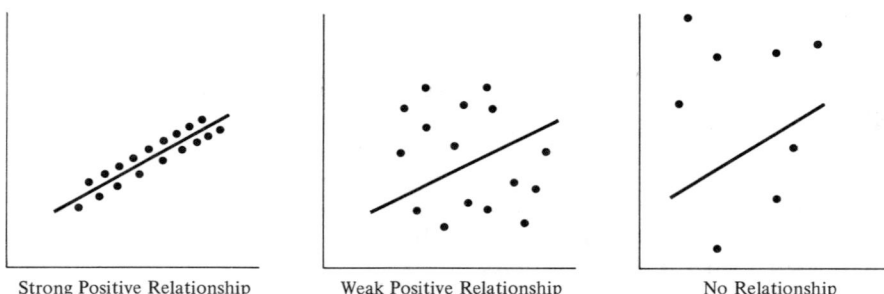

Strong Positive Relationship   Weak Positive Relationship   No Relationship

of the statistical relationship. In general, a careful scrutiny of the scatter diagram will give an indication as to what extent the observations display a linear or a curvilinear trend, or whether they are just scattered at random. When the data are clearly nonlinear, the eta coefficient can be employed instead of Pearson's r. The linear model corresponds to many research situations in the social sciences; therefore, we will not discuss the subject of curvilinear regressions.*

SUMMARY

This chapter focused on the nature of relationships between two variables and on the construction of measures of relationship. It was demonstrated that when variables are related, they vary together so that specific categories of one variable "go together" with specific categories of the second, or that there is some correspondence in the relative position of the two variables. Sometimes, when interval variables are related, it is possible to describe the relationship by employing specific functions enabling exact predictions.

A relationship between two variables can be assessed by comparing the univariate distributions constituting the bivariate table, using summary measures such as the median or the mean. Alternatively, associations can be described by special measures of relationships that reflect the relative utility of using one variable to predict another.

Measures of relationship usually correspond to the variables' level of measurement. Nominal relations are assessed by lambda, or by Goodman and Kruskal's tau. Either gamma or Kendall's tau is used to calculate relations between ordinal variables. Finally, Pearson's r is an interval measure of relationship that reflects the proportional reduction of

* The interested student will find relevant material in Hubert M. Blalock, *Social Statistics*, 2d ed. (New York: McGraw-Hill, 1972), pp. 408–413; and Mueller, Schuessler, and Costner (1970:325–333).

error when one shifts from the mean as a prediction rule to the linear regression equation.

REFERENCES

Anderson, Theodore R., and Zelditch, Morris, Jr. *A Basic Course in Statistics*. New York: Holt, Rinehart & Winston, 1968.

Costner, Herbert L. "Criteria for Measures of Association." *American Sociological Review* 30 (1965):341–353.

Freeman, Linton C. *Elementary Applied Statistics*. New York: Wiley, 1965.

Goodman, Leo A., and Kruskal, William H. "Measure of Association for Cross Classifications." *Journal of the American Statistical Association* 49 (1954): 732–764.

Guttman, Louis. "An Outline of the Statistical Theory of Prediction." In Paul Horst (ed.), *The Prediction of Personal Adjustment*. New York: Social Science Research Council, Bulletin 48, 1941.

Mueller, John H., Schuessler, Karl F., and Costner, Herbert L. *Statistical Reasoning in Sociology*. Boston: Houghton Mifflin, 1970.

Zeisel, Hans. *Say It with Figures*. New York: Harper & Row, 1968.

STUDY SUGGESTIONS

1. Discuss the concept of relationship between variables in terms of the proportional reduction of error.
2. Give an example of a bivariate nominal distribution for which lambda is not suitable as a measure of relationship. What measure would you use instead?
3. Table 10.17 is a bivariate distribution of alienation by social status. By making a percentage comparison, and by using a suitable measure of relationship, assess the following hypothesis: As status increases, the degree of alienation decreases. What other measures of relationship can be used to test this hypothesis?

TABLE 10.17. Alienation by Social Status

| *Alienation* | *Social Status* | | | *Total* |
	Low	*Medium*	*High*	
High	93	41	10	144
Medium	77	78	46	201
Low	68	128	140	336
Total	238	247	196	681

4. Construct a 2 × 2 table based on two hundred respondents in which 69 percent are Democrats and 58 percent are for legalizing marijuana. Of the Democrats, 56 percent are for legalizing marijuana. With attitudes toward the legalization of marijuana as the dependent variable, compute lambda. Discuss the relationship between the two variables.
5. Suppose that the correlation $r = .28$ exists between social class and college intentions. Analyze the meaning of this correlation.
6. Social scientists have been attempting to identify social variables that may be associated with economic variables. The following data can be used to investigate the relationship between unemployment rates and other variables. Which of the independent variables is most closely related to unemployment? Base your assessment on the following measures: bXY, r, r^2.

Country	Unemployment Rate	Political Stability	Level of Economic Development	Rate of Urbanization
United States	3.2	8.0	2.34	1.8
New Zealand	3.0	8.6	1.71	0.8
Norway	2.1	8.6	1.41	1.2
Finland	2.6	8.1	.83	0.7
Uruguay	5.2	3.2	.46	0.9
Israel	3.8	8.1	.40	0.9
Taiwan	4.8	7.2	.80	0.6
Ghana	7.1	5.0	.02	0.2
England	7.2	2.6	1.46	1.11
Greece	7.8	2.1	.09	0.9

CHAPTER 11
Multivariate Analysis

The examination of a bivariate relationship is but the first step in data analysis. Next, the substantive implications of the findings are evaluated, and causal inferences may be drawn. The bivariate measure of a relation is limited to the establishment of covariation and its direction. To interpret the findings and to assess the causal priorities of the investigated variables, other variables are introduced into the analysis. Suppose one finds a relationship between parents' age and child-rearing practices; that is, older parents tend to be more restrictive with their children than younger parents. What interpretation can be given to this finding? One may claim that the variables are causally related and that increasing age of parents is associated with a shift from permissive toward restrictive attitudes. However, alternatively, it is a possibility that a difference in child-rearing practices is due, not to a difference in age, but rather, to a difference in orientation: Older parents were exposed to an orientation stressing restriction, whereas younger parents behave according to a more liberal orientation advocating more permissive practices. In other words, the relationship between parents' age and child-rearing practices is due to the fact that the variables "age" and "child-rearing practices" are both associated with a third variable, "orientation."

An observed correlation between two or more variables does not, of itself, permit the investigator to make causal interpretations. A bivariate relationship may be the product of chance, or it may exist because the variables are related to a third, unrevealed variable. Furthermore, the phenomenon under investigation can often be explained by more than a single independent variable. In either case, the introduction of additional variables serves the purpose of clarifying and elaborating the original relationship.

Multivariate analysis focuses on the analysis of more than two variables. It serves three major functions in empirical research: control, interpretation, and prediction. The first function substitutes for the mechanism of experimental control when such is lacking. The second clarifies bivariate relationships by introducing intervening or conditional variables. The third is served by analyzing two or more independent variables to account for the variation in the dependent variable. This chapter discusses ways in which a third variable may enter into empirical research. In the first three sections, we consider the strategy of controlling for a third variable and interpreting relationships. The fourth section deals with multivariate counterparts to the bivariate measures of relations. In the last section, some techniques of causal modeling are examined.

THE CONCEPT OF CONTROL

An association between two variables is not a sufficient basis for an inference that the two are causally related. Other variables need to be ruled out as alternative explanations of the relation. For example, a relationship between height and income can probably be accounted for by the variable "age." Age is related to both income and height, and this joint relationship produces a statistical relationship that has no causal significance. The original relation between height and income is said to be spurious. Spuriousness is a concept that applies to situations where an extraneous variable produces a "fake" relation between the independent and dependent variables. It is essential that an investigation uncover the extraneous factors contaminating the data in this way. Thus, in validating bivariate associations, an important step is to rule out the largest possible number of variables that might conceivably explain the original association. This is achieved by a process denoted as control, a basic principle in all research designs. With experimental designs, control is accomplished by dividing subjects into experimental and control groups, the allocation being made by a process of randomization. The logic of controlled experimentation assures the researcher that all extraneous variables have been controlled, and that the two groups differ only with regard to their exposure to the stimuli. However, social scientists find it difficult to manipulate social groups and to apply experimental treatment prior to observations. Consequently, they lack control over numerous factors that throw doubt on any association between independent and dependent variables employed in the investigation.

In quasi-experimental designs, statistical techniques substitute for the experimental method of control. These techniques are employed during data analysis rather than at the data-collection stage. There are two major methods of statistical control. The first entails subgroup comparisons and is accompanied by the technique of cross tabulation. The second technique, partial correlation, employs mathematical procedures to readjust the value of a bivariate correlation coefficient.

METHODS OF CONTROL

Cross Tabulation

The cross-tabulation method of control can be compared to the mechanism of matching, which is employed in experiments. In both techniques, the investigator attempts to equate the groups examined with respect to variables that may interfere with the results. With matching, the subjects are equated prior to their exposure to the independent variable. This is done by a physical allocation to the experimental and control groups, resulting in pairs that are identical with respect to the controlled factors. With cross tabulation, the respondents are allocated to the respective groups only during the analysis stage. Thus, whereas matching is a physical control mechanism, cross tabulation is a statistical operation.

Cross tabulation involves the division of the sample into subgroups according to the categories of the controlled variable. The original bivariate relation is then reassessed within each subgroup. The division into subgroups removes the biasing inequality by computing a measure of relationship for groups that are internally homogeneous with respect to the biasing factor.

Generally, only variables that are associated with both the independent variable and the dependent variable will bias the results. Thus, only variables that show an association with the independent and dependent variables under investigation are selected as control variables.

The following example illustrates the steps involved in controlling for a third variable through cross tabulation. Suppose a sample of 900 respondents is selected to test the hypothesis that people from urban areas are politically more liberal than rural dwellers. The data obtained are presented in Table 11.1. It is observed that 50 percent of urban residents are liberal, compared with only 28 percent of the respondents from rural areas. Thus, it may be concluded that political liberalism is associated with place of residence. Next, the problem is whether such a result suffices for acceptance of the suggested hypothesis. The question is whether the association obtained is real (in which case the hypothesis is supported) or is based on an accidental relation with a third variable (in which case the relationship is spurious). One such additional variable might be education, which is associated with both place of residence and political liberalism, as reflected in the hypothetical bivariate distributions of Tables 11.2 and 11.3.

TABLE 11.1. Political Liberalism by Residential Area

Political Liberalism	Urban Area	Rural Area
High	50%	28%
	(200)	(140)
Low	50	72
	(200)	(360)
Total	100	100
	(400)	(500)

TABLE 11.2. Residential Area by Education

Residential Area	Education	
	High	Low
Urban area	75%	20%
	(300)	(100)
Rural area	25	80
	(100)	(400)
Total	100	100
	(400)	(500)

TABLE 11.3. Political Liberalism by Education

Political Liberalism	Education	
	High	Low
High	60%	20%
	(240)	(100)
Low	40	80
	(160)	(400)
Total	100	100
	(400)	(500)

To control for education, the 900 subjects are divided into two groups according to their level of education (high, low). Within each group, urban-rural location is cross-tabulated with political liberalism. The original bivariate association is then estimated in each of the subgroups. The controlled data are summarized in Table 11.4.

The resulting two bivariate tables of Table 11.4 are referred to as

TABLE 11.4. Political Liberalism by Urban-Rural Location, Controlling for Education (Spurious Relationship)

Political Liberalism	High Education		Low Education	
	Urban Area	Rural Area	Urban Area	Rural Area
High	60%	60%	20%	20%
	(180)	(60)	(20)	(80)
Low	40	40	80	80
	(120)	(40)	(80)	(320)
Total	100	100	100	100
	(300)	(100)	(100)	(400)

partial tables, since each one reflects only part of the total association. Each pair of parallel cells in the two partial tables adds up to the corresponding cell in the original table (Table 11.1). For example, the 180 highly educated respondents who come from urban areas and are liberals, plus the 20 respondents who are urban liberals with a low level of education, together constitute the 200 respondents in the original bivariate table who are liberal and from urban areas.

To assess the partial association, a measure of relationship is computed for each of the control groups and is compared with the original result. Appropriate measures are selected in the same way as for regular bivariate distributions. Difference of percentages, gamma, or Pearson's r can be used, depending on the scale of measurement. With the computation of the measure, the value of the partial association can be found to be identical (or *almost* identical) to the original one; it can vanish; or, it can change. When an attempt is being made to uncover spurious relationships, only the first two possibilities apply. In the first case, the control variable does not account for the original relation; in the second, it may be concluded that the third extraneous variable produced the association, which is accordingly considered spurious.*

In the hypothetical example of Table 11.4, education completely accounts for the relation between residence and liberalism, for there is no difference between rural and urban residents in their degree of liberalism within either of the two educational groups. Sixty percent of the highly educated rural residents, like 60 percent of the highly educated urban residents, are politically liberal. Within the low-education group, 20 percent are liberal wherever they reside. The overall association

---

* A third variable may intervene between the dependent and the independent variables, in which case the partial association will also vanish (or approximate zero). An example will be considered in the next section.

between the independent and dependent variables is completely accounted for by the association of each with education. This pattern can be presented graphically, as in Figure 11.1.

Education determines both political liberalism and place of residence. That is, people who are educated tend to live in cities and are generally politically liberal. There is no inherent link between political liberalism and place of residence, and the association between them is spurious.

The control of a third variable may lead to entirely different results. In the hypothetical example of Table 11.5, the original bivariate association remains unchanged by the educational level. In the total sample, as well as in each educational group, 50 percent of urban residents are liberal, compared with 28 percent of rural residents. This result indicates that the overall relationship between the two original variables is not accounted for by the control variable. The investigator can be confident that education is an irrelevant factor with respect to this particular association.

In practice, the results are not as clear-cut as they were presented here. It is very rare for associations either to vanish or to remain identical with the original results. Often, the partial tables show a clear decrease in the size of the original relationship; at times, the reduction is slight. This is because of the numerous factors that can account for a bivariate association. In the above example, other variables such as income, party identification, or religious affiliation might conceivably explain the relationship between place of residence and political liberalism. This characteristic of variables has been referred to as "block-booking" (Rosenberg, 1968). It refers to the multidimensionality of human beings and of their social interaction. When a comparison is made between people in terms of social class, only one dimension is tackled. People may differ thoroughly from each other in a great many things, and all these other factors may enter into the phenomenon to be explained. The block-booked factors become our control variables; but when we control for only one or some of them, the rest may still explain the remaining residual in the dependent variable.

The procedure, then, is to hold constant all other factors that may be relevant to the subject of investigation. The selection of these vari-

FIGURE 11.1.

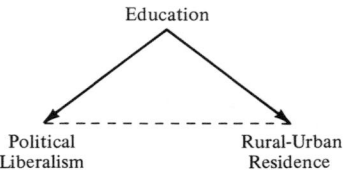

TABLE 11.5 Political Liberalism by Urban-Rural Location, Controlling for Education (Nonspurious Relationship)

Political Liberalism	High Education		Low Education	
	Urban Area	Rural Area	Urban Area	Rural Area
High	50%	28%	50%	28%
	(50)	(35)	(150)	(105)
Low	50	72	50	72
	(50)	(90)	(150)	(270)
Total	100	100	100	100
	(100)	(125)	(300)	(375)

ables is a logical and theoretical operation, the only statistical guideline being the requirement that the potential control factor be related to both the independent and dependent variables. Of course, one can never be completely sure that all relevant variables have been introduced into the analysis. However, the more relevant factors controlled for, the greater the confidence that the relationship is not spurious.

Partial Correlation

The cross-tabulation control operation is quite popular in empirical research, and it is applied to all levels of measurement. However, it has a drawback that limits its use when the number of cases is relatively small. The cross-tabulation method of control entails a subdivision of the sample into progressively smaller subgroups, according to the number of categories of the controlled factor. This reduces the number of cases serving as a basis for computing the coefficient, thus rendering its validity and reliability questionable. This is particularly acute when there are several variables controlled simultaneously.

A second method of control, not limited by the number of cases, is the partial correlation. This is a mathematical adjustment of the bivariate correlation, designed to cancel out the effect of the control variable on the independent and dependent variables. The logic underlying the calculation of this measure of association is similar to that of cross tabulation. The original association between the independent and dependent variables is reassessed so that it reflects a direct association, unmarred by the variables' association to a third extraneous factor.

Suppose a correlation is found of $r = .60$ between self-esteem and educational expectation. To test the nature of this association, it is reasonable to introduce an additional variable, "social class," which is related to both self-esteem ($r = .30$) and educational expectation ($r = .40$).

Partial correlation can be used to obtain a measure of association with the effect of social class removed. The formula for calculation of the partial correlation coefficient is given in Equation (11.1):

$$r_{12.3} = \frac{r_{12} - (r_{13})(r_{32})}{\sqrt{1 - r_{13}^2} \sqrt{1 - r_{32}^2}} \quad (11.1)$$

where X_1 = independent variable
X_2 = dependent variable
X_3 = control variable

The symbol on the right-hand side of the dot indicates the variable to be controlled. Thus, $r_{12.3}$ is the correlation between variables 1 and 2 controlling for variable 3. Similarly, a partial coefficient between variables 1 and 3 controlling for 2 would be denoted as $r_{13.2}$. A partial with one control is referred to as a first-order partial to distinguish it from a bivariate correlation, often denoted as a zero-order correlation. A partial with two controls is referred to as second-order partial, and so on. When more than one variable is controlled for simultaneously, their numbers are added to the right of the dot. Thus, controlling for variables 3 and 4 would be expressed as $r_{12.34}$.

The partial correlation for self-esteem and educational expectation can now be calculated:

$$r_{12.3} = \frac{.60 - (.30)(.40)}{\sqrt{1 - (.30)^2} \sqrt{1 - (.40)^2}} = \frac{.48}{\sqrt{.7644}} = \frac{.48}{.87} = .55$$

where X_1 = self-esteem
X_2 = educational expectation
X_3 = social class

Notice that the total correlation between the original variables appears first in the numerator of the formula. The effect of the correlation between the control variable and each of the original ones is then subtracted from it. The result is standardized by two correction factors in the denominator, which reflect the variation explained in the independent and dependent variables by the control variable (Blalock, 1972).

The squared partial correlation reflects the proportion of variation left unexplained by the control variable and explained by the independent variable. Thus, 30 percent ($.55^2 \times 100$) of the variation in educational expectation was explained by self-esteem after removing the effect of social class.

In contrast to the cross-tabulation method of control, the partial correlation yields a single summarizing measure that reflects the degree of correlation between two variables controlling for a third. Thus, when the partial associations vary according to different categories of the controlled variable, this is not expressed by the partial correlation since it averages out the different partials. This property of the measure is its main disadvantage, as it might obscure otherwise essential information. In cases where the investigator suspects that there are significant differences between the partials of the various subgroups, it is advisable to use the cross-tabulation technique instead.

A partial correlation may be employed to control for more than one variable. The formulas for higher-order coefficients have a similar logic, where the lower-order partial replaces the zero-order correlation in the original first-order formula. Following are the formulas for second-order and third-order partial correlation coefficients:

Second-order partial correlation:
$$r_{12.34} = \frac{r_{12.3} - (r_{14.3})(r_{24.3})}{\sqrt{1 - r_{14.3}^2} \sqrt{1 - r_{24.3}^2}} \quad (11.2)$$

Third-order partial correlation:
$$r_{12.345} = \frac{r_{12.34} - (r_{15.34})(r_{25.34})}{\sqrt{1 - r_{15.34}^2} \sqrt{1 - r_{25.34}^2}} \quad (11.3)$$

INTERPRETATION

The mechanism of control discussed in the preceding section is designed to uncover factors that might invalidate the original bivariate association. When such a mechanism is applied, there are two alternative outcomes: the partial association is zero, or close to it, in which case it can be concluded that the original relationship is spurious; or the partial association is almost identical to the original one, in which case the investigators may be satisfied that the bivariate association has a substantive significance. In the first instance, the investigators are likely to turn to other factors that can be employed as independent variables and repeat the process of validating the relationship, if a relationship is observed. On the other hand, if they are convinced that the relationship observed is nonspurious, they can proceed to a more advanced stage of analysis and interpret the bivariate association. Interpretation usually involves the introduction of other variables to determine the links between the independent and dependent variables or the specification of the conditions under which the association takes place.

Let us illustrate the meaning of interpretation with some concrete examples. For a long time it has been argued that social class determines the mobility orientations of adolescents. Various investigators have attempted to provide an explanation for this association. Some have maintained that the difference between social classes is reflected in different cultural backgrounds, and that it is this difference that largely accounts for the variation in mobility orientations (Hyman, 1953). Others indicated that lower and middle classes adopt different child-rearing practices that influence the motivation to achieve (Douvan, 1966).

What is the meaning of the different interpretations suggested? The association between class and mobility orientations is explained by cultural background or by child-rearing practices. In the first interpretation, cultural background is determined by social class, whereas mobility orientations are dependent upon cultural background. In the second interpretation, child-rearing practices determine mobility orientations and are themselves determined by social class. These relationships may be represented schematically as follows:

Social Class → Cultural Background → Mobility Orientations
Social Class → Child-rearing Practices → Mobility Orientations

In the two alternative interpretations, the third variable (cultural background or child-rearing practices) provides a link between social class and mobility orientations. The third variable is said to intervene between the two original variables.

In another set of studies, it was demonstrated that women are less likely to vote than men (Lazarsfeld, Berelson, and Gaudet, 1948). It was suspected that the amount of interest in politics might account for the difference in involvement. Women, it was believed, are less interested in politics and thus less likely to vote in elections. However, when interest was controlled for it was found that this interpretation was only partially true. Indeed, among women, noninterest is accompanied by nonvoting. But this does not hold among men. Men tend to vote even if their interest is rather limited. In this example, the original bivariate association is pronounced only under certain conditions, that is, among noninterested citizens. The control variable is thus said to be a conditional variable.

These two types of interpretations, which are among the most common ones, provide a refinement to the bivariate relationship. In the first case, the interpretations answer the question, "*Why* are the independent and dependent variables related?" In the second case, the interpretation specifies under what conditions the relationship will hold.

Interpretation, like control, involves holding a third variable constant and reexamining the original association. This can be accomplished by using either cross tabulation or partial correlation coefficients.

Intervening Variables

Let us start with the first case, in which the controlled variable is said to intervene between the independent and dependent variables. The data summarized in Table 11.6 examine the relationship between social class and participation in elections. The findings in Table 11.6 demonstrate

TABLE 11.6. Social Class and Intention to Vote

Willingness to Vote	Social Class	
	Upper	Lower
Will not vote	6%	15%
Will vote	94	85
Total	100	100
	(1,600)	(2,000)

that these two variables are associated: persons from the upper class are more likely to vote in an election than are those in lower classes. The investigators hypothesized that this association could be explained with the variable "political interest." That is, it was claimed that social class affects voting indirectly through political interest. Upper-class people tend to be more interested in politics and consequently are more likely to vote during an election.

To test this hypothesis, political interest was held constant, and the original relationship was reexamined. If, as suggested, social class has only an indirect influence on voting, then when the intermediate link is controlled for, the association between social class and voting should disappear. The results in Table 11.7 confirm the hypothesis: among groups with identical interest, social class does not seem to influence the propensity to vote. The original relationship diminishes considerably when political interest is controlled for. The order of the variables, which can be inferred from the data, is displayed diagramatically below:

Social Class → Political Interest → Voting

The conditions for the interpretation given above require that the control variable be associated with both the independent and dependent variables; and that when controlled for, the original relationship should

TABLE 11.7. Social Class and Intention to Vote by Political Interest

Willingness to Vote	Political Interest					
	Great		Medium		Low	
	Upper Class	Lower Class	Upper Class	Lower Class	Upper Class	Lower Class
Will not vote	2%	2%	6%	9%	35%	35%
Will vote	98	98	94	94	65	65
Total	100	100	100	100	100	100
	(480)	(500)	(960)	(1,120)	(160)	(380)

disappear (or diminish considerably) in all categories of the control variable. To the reader who exclaims that these were the identical conditions required for declaring the relationship spurious, we can only confirm that this is indeed the case. The statistical tests in both cases are identical, but the interpretation is significantly different. With a spurious interpretation, the statistical results invalidate an hypothesis about the relationship between the independent and dependent variable; an intervening interpretation, on the other hand, clarifies and explains such a relationship. How, then, can a distinction be made between the two?

Rosenberg (1968) maintains that the difference is a theoretical issue rather than a statistical one, and that it lies in the assumed causal relationship among the variables. With a spurious interpretation, it is assumed that there is no causal relation between the independent and dependent variables; in the intervening case, the two are indirectly related through an intermediate link, the control variable. The difference between the two interpretations is presented graphically in Figure 11.2.

In the first case (a), the control variable precedes both independent and dependent variables; in the second (b), the independent variable is first in the time sequence. Only factors that precede the independent variable in time can be invalidating factors. That is, only when a factor precedes the independent variable can one say that it determines both the independent variable and the dependent variable. In the last example, political interest is not likely to precede social class; thus, we are satisfied with the intervening interpretation. However, the time sequence cannot always be determined accurately. For instance, one's self-esteem can determine one's popularity, which in turn influences one's occupational achievement. But self-esteem may also intervene between popularity and achievement. In both cases, the statistical test will yield the same result. In such a situation, both interpretations are feasible, and the investigator might have to introduce other factors that will help to reject one of these two possibilities.

FIGURE 11.2. Spurious and Intervening Interpretations

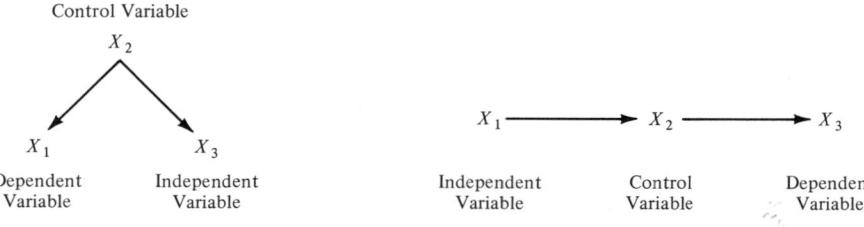

Conditional Interpretation

The second type of interpretation involves a specification of conditions or contingencies necessary for the occurrence of the relationship. We will illustrate the meaning of conditional interpretation using the example on voting behavior. Lazarsfeld, Berelson, and Gaudet found that nonvoting is associated with sex; their findings are reported in Table 11.8.

The data reflect a clear pattern of association. The greatest proportion of nonvoters is found among women: 18 percent of all women abstained from voting, compared with 2 percent of all men. To gain further insight, the investigator controlled for the variable "interest in politics." The results are presented in Table 11.9.

It is observed that among the categories of the control variable, "level of interest," the association differs considerably. Whereas it has virtually disappeared in the high-interest category, it is pronounced in the low-interest group. In other words, "the less a group is interested in the election, the greater will be the amount of deliberate non-voting among women as compared with men" (Lazarsfeld, Berelson, and Gaudet, 1955:158). The difference, it is maintained, is due to difference

TABLE 11.8. Voting and Sex

Voting	Men	Women
Voted	98%	82%
Did not vote	2	18
Total	100	100
	(1,294)	(1,418)

SOURCE: Paul F. Lazarsfeld, Bernard Berelson, and Hazel Gaudet. *The People's Choice.* New York: Columbia University Press, 1968, p. 48.

TABLE 11.9. Voting and Sex by Level of Interest

	Level of Interest					
	Great		Medium		None	
Voting	Men	Women	Men	Women	Men	Women
Voted	99%	98%	98%	87%	83%	44%
Did not vote	1	2	2	13	17	56
Total	100	100	100	100	100	100
	(449)	(328)	(789)	(852)	(56)	(238)

SOURCE: Paul F. Lazarsfeld, Bernard Berelson, and Hazel Gaudet. *The People's Choice.* New York: Columbia University Press, 1968, p. 48.

in socialization patterns that put more social pressure on men to go to the polls, even if they are not interested in the events of the campaign and the election results. In this example, the control variable, "level of interest," is a conditional factor that specifies a condition facilitating a relationship between sex and voting behavior. Conditional relationships such as this one are quite common in social science research and can be inferred whenever the relative size or direction of the original bivariate relationship is more pronounced in one category of the control variable than in another. The presence of such differences between subgroups reflects the nature of social reality, where each variable can be broken down into various components. Indeed, many conditional factors are associated with almost any two-variable relationships. This makes the analysis of conditional relationships one of the most important aspects of multivariate analysis.

Hyman (1955) analyzed the various factors that are generally considered conditions for most bivariate associations and classified them into three major groups. The first class involves variables that specify relationship in terms of interest and concern. In many situations, interest and concern specify the conditions under which the effectiveness of a stimulus is more or less pronounced. For instance, consider the finding that self-esteem is associated with intensity of political discussion (Rosenberg, 1962). Adolescents with low self-esteem, who are more self-conscious, tend to avoid expressing their political views. Taking into account the level of political interest, it is observed that the relationship holds only among those who are interested in politics. Those who are not interested in politics also do not discuss politics, even though they might have a high degree of self-esteem. Thus, the utilization of the conditional factor helps to clarify and purify the original findings. People tend to differ in their interests, which, in turn, affects their attitudes and behavior patterns. Thus, social stimuli are likely to have differential effects on them, and the identification of these differing patterns may prove to be essential to the social scientist.

The second class of factors specifies associations in terms of time and place. A relationship between two variables can vary according to the time and place at which it is studied. Almond and Verba (1963), for example, in their five-nation study, found a positive relationship between social class and the belief that one would receive equal treatment before the law. Lower-class people were less likely to expect equal treatment than were upper-class people. However, when this association was examined in several countries, it was found that this was not equally true in all of them. In the English-speaking countries (the United States and Britain), there is hardly any difference between the classes. In Germany, the difference is greater; in Italy and Mexico, the differences are substantial. These findings specify that the nature of the stratification system, and its effect on attitudes and beliefs, are different in the various countries.

Specification by time is meaningful, especially when the dynamic aspect of a relationship is considered. Often, a relationship that holds at one time will be diminished or changed at another. An example is the general process of development and socialization. The family is known to affect various behavioral patterns in children. This effect is pronounced, especially at the early stages, when the child is more exposed and more vulnerable to his or her family. At later stages, however, other aspects of socialization play an important role, and the family's influence diminishes. Thus, a relationship between family characteristics and behavioral orientations would not stay constant if examined at different times.

The last class of factors is special qualifications and characteristics of the units of analysis. Often, associations are likely to differ for persons or groups that do not share the same characteristics. Thus, the relation between class position and voting behavior is different for men and for women, and the effect of teachers' encouragement on self-esteem is not identical for black and white children. These distinctions are perhaps the most common among the types of specifications employed in the social sciences. In fact, some researchers employ such control variables as "social class," "level of education," "sex," and "age" almost automatically, reexamining all relationships obtained.

MULTIPLE RELATIONSHIPS

Up to this point, consideration has been given only to situations in which one independent variable is said to determine the phenomena being studied. However, in real situations, it is seldom that only one variable is relevant to what is to be explained. Often, various variables are directly associated with the dependent variable. Population change, for example, is explained by four variables: "birth rate," "death rate," "immigration rate," and "emigration rate." Similarly, a well-known theory of delinquency employs the variables "barrier to legitimate opportunities" and "degree of exposure to illegitimate opportunities" to account for rates of delinquency (Cloward and Ohlin, 1960). Thus, there are often several variables, each of which may contribute to the prediction of the dependent variable.

The simultaneous effect of several independent variables on the dependent variable can be assessed by constructing a multiple regression equation, which describes the amount of linear relationship between the dependent and independent variables. The equation is presented in Formula (11.4)

$$Y_1 = a_{1.23} + b_{12.3}X_2 + b_{13.2}X_3 \qquad (11.4)$$

where Y_1 represents the dependent variable and X_2 and X_3 the independent variables. $b_{12.3}$ and $b_{13.2}$, designated as partial regression coefficients, are the slopes of the regression line for each independent variable, controlling for the other. Thus, $b_{12.3}$ reflects the amount of change in Y_1 associated with a given change in X_2, holding X_3 constant. $a_{1.23}$ designates the intercept point on the Y_1 axis for both X_2 and X_3.

Just as in the two-variable situation, the constants of the multiple linear regression equation are estimated so as to minimize the average square error in prediction. This is accomplished by using the least-square criterion to obtain the best fit to the data. The computing formulas for $b_{12.3}$, $b_{13.2}$, and $a_{1.23}$ are presented in Equations (11.5), (11.6), and (11.7):

$$b_{12.3} = \frac{b_{12} - (b_{13})(b_{32})}{1 - b_{23}b_{32}} \qquad (11.5)$$

$$b_{13.2} = \frac{b_{13} - (b_{12})(b_{23})}{1 - b_{32}b_{23}} \qquad (11.6)$$

$$a_{1.23} = \overline{Y}_1 - b_{12.3}\overline{X}_2 - b_{13.2}\overline{X}_3 \qquad (11.7)$$

Note that b_{32} is not the same as b_{23}. The regression coefficient is asymmetrical, so the subscripts are not interchangeable.

To illustrate the computation of the multiple-regression constants using Equations (11.5), (11.6), and (11.7), we shall attempt to estimate the simultaneous effect of education and self-esteem on the extent of political liberalism.

Designating liberalism as Y_1, education as X_2, and self-esteem as X_3, the following are the b coefficients for the simple bivariate effect of these variables upon each other:

$b_{12} = 0.7 \rightarrow$ effect of education on liberalism

$b_{13} = 1.3 \rightarrow$ effect of self-esteem on liberalism

$b_{32} = 0.5 \rightarrow$ effect of education on self-esteem

$b_{23} = 1.8 \rightarrow$ effect of self-esteem on education

These coefficients are substituted into Equations (11.5) and (11.6):

$$b_{12.3} = \frac{0.7 - (1.3)(0.5)}{1 - (1.8)(0.5)} = .50$$

$$b_{13.2} = \frac{1.3 - (0.7)(1.8)}{1 - (0.5)(1.8)} = .40$$

To compute the constant a, the mean values of the three variables are obtained:

$$\text{Mean score of self-esteem } (\overline{X}_3) = 5.8$$
$$\text{Mean score of liberalism } (\overline{Y}_1) = 6.5$$
$$\text{Mean score of education } (\overline{X}_2) = 8.9$$

According to Equation (11.7):

$$a_{1.23} = 6.5 - (0.5)(8.9) - (0.4)(5.8) = -.27$$

With the obtained values of $b_{12.3}$, $b_{13.2}$ and $a_{1.23}$, the complete multiple regression equation for predicting liberalism on the basis of education and self-esteem would therefore be:

$$Y_1 = -0.27 + 0.5X_2 + 0.4X_3$$

It indicates the extent of political liberalism that would be expected, on the average, with a given level of education and a given level of self-esteem. For example, for a person with 10 years of schooling and a self-esteem score of 8, the expected level of liberalism would be:

$$Y_1 = -0.27 + (0.5)(10) + (0.4)(8) = 7.93$$

Since the b coefficients reflect the net effect of each variable, they can be compared so as to denote the relative importance of the independent variables. However, since each variable is measured on a different scale in different units, b must be standardized to be comparable. The standardized equivalent of the b coefficient is called the beta weight, or the beta coefficient; it is symbolized as β. The beta weights are obtained by multiplying b by the ratio of the standard deviation of the independent variable to the standard deviation of the dependent variable. Thus, $\beta_{12.3}$ would be expressed as:

$$\beta_{13.2} = b_{13.2} \frac{s_3}{s_1} \qquad (11.8)$$

For the previous example, the standard deviations are:

$$s_1 \text{ (liberalism)} = 3$$
$$s_2 \text{ (education)} = 4.1$$
$$s_3 \text{ (self-esteem)} = 2.2$$

Accordingly:

$$Y_1 = -0.27 + 0.5\left(\frac{4.1}{3}\right)X_2 + 0.4\left(\frac{2.2}{3}\right)X_3$$

Therefore, the multiple regression equation, expressed in beta coefficients is:

$$X_1 = -0.27 + 0.68 X_2 + 0.29 X_3$$

This would indicate that for every increase of one standard deviation in education, liberalism increases by 0.68 standard deviation; and with an increase of one standard deviation in self-esteem, liberalism increases by 0.29 standard deviation. When the relative importance of the two factors is compared, it is evident that education contributes more (0.68) to liberalism than does self-esteem (0.29).

Just as with simple regression, one needs to estimate how well the multiple-regression rule fits the actual data. In simple regression, the fit (or the relative reduction of error) was measured using r^2, which is defined as the ratio of the variation explained to the total variation in the dependent variable. Similarly, when the prediction is based on several variables, an estimate of the relative reduction of error is based on the ratio of the variation explained with various variables simultaneously to the total variation. This measure, R^2, is termed the coefficient of multiple determination and designates the percentage of the variation explained by all the independent variables in the multiple-regression equation. The square root of R^2 indicates the correlation between all independent variables taken together with the dependent variable; it is thus denoted as the coefficient of multiple correlation.

For the three-variable case, the formula for R^2 is presented in Equation (11.9):

$$R_{1.23}^2 = \frac{r_{12}^2 + r_{13}^2 - 2 r_{12} r_{13} r_{23}}{1 - r_{23}^2} \tag{11.9}$$

In the multiple correlation coefficient, note that the symbol for the dependent variable is to the left of the dot, whereas all the independent variables are placed to the right. For instance, the multiple correlation coefficient between the dependent variable Y_1 and X_2, X_3, X_4 would be designated as $R_{1.234}$.

As an example, let us calculate the percentage of variation explained in modernization (Y_1), using education (X_2) and urbanization (X_3) as predictors. The zero-order correlations are: $r_{12} = .60$; $r_{13} = .50$; $r_{23} = .20$. $R_{1.23}^2$ is then

$$R_{1.23}^2 = \frac{.60^2 + .50^2 - 2(.60)(.50)(.20)}{1 - .20^2} = \frac{.49}{.96} = .51$$

This means that 50 percent of the variation in modernization is accounted for by the combined effect of education and urbanization. Note the $R_{1.23}$ ($\sqrt{R_{1.23}^2}$), which is .714, is larger than either r_{12} or r_{23}. R always reaches maximum value relative to the zero-order coefficients when the independent variables employed are not correlated. When the correlation between the independent variables is zero, R^2 is simply the sum of the squared zero-order correlations. For example, when r_{23} is zero, we get:

$$R_{1.23}^2 = r_{12}^2 + r_{13}^2$$

When the intercorrelation between the independent variables is high, the obtained multiple coefficient would not ordinarily be much larger than the largest zero-order correlation. In such a case, using the other independent variables would not improve the prediction, and the investigator would be better off omitting the variable from the prediction equation. In other words, to improve the prediction, one should introduce the greatest possible number of relevant independent variables that are independent of each other.

CAUSAL MODELS

The discussion has focused on methods of control that provide an interpretation of the relation between two variables. It was indicated that a "real" relationship is one that does not prove to be spurious. This is determined by the time sequence of the variables and the relative size of the partial associations.

These two elements—the size of the partials relative to the original bivariate associations and the assumed time order between the variables—have been suggested by Lazarsfeld as the kind of evidence required for inferring causation: "We can suggest a clear-cut definition of the causal relation between two attributes. If we have a relationship between X and Y, and if for any antecedent test factor c the partial relationship between X and Y does not disappear, then the original relationship should be called a causal one" (1959:146). Although one can never directly demonstrate causality from correlational data, it is possible to make causal inferences concerning the adequacy of specific causal models. Simon (1957) and Blalock (1964) suggested a method that enables such inferences. This method involves a finite set of explicitly defined variables, assumptions about how these variables are interrelated causally, and assumptions about the effect of outside variables on the variables included in the model.

The Simon-Blalock method can be applied to situations involving three or more variables. To simplify matters, however, our discussion will be limited to the three-variable case. Later on, we shall illustrate the analysis of models involving four variables.

Theoretically, there could be six causal connections between three variables X_1, X_2, and X_3. These possibilities are diagrammed in Figure

FIGURE 11.3. Causal Connections Among Three Variables

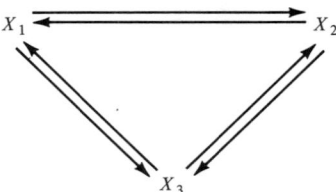

11.3.* A simplifying assumption rules out two-way causation, either directly in the form $X_1 \rightleftarrows X_2$ or indirectly in the form

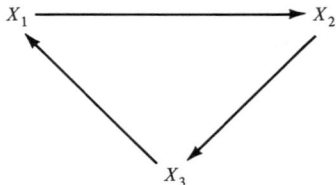

This assumption limits the number of causal connections between three variables to three. Furthermore, under this assumption a dependent variable cannot determine any of the variables preceding it in the causal sequence. Thus, in a causal system having three variables X_1, X_2, and X_3—where X_1 is the independent variable, X_2 the intervening variable, and X_3 the dependent variable—X_2 cannot determine X_1, and X_3 cannot determine X_2 or X_1.

The problem of adequately representing a system that rules out two-way causation can be handled by a recursive system of equations. This system allows variables to be hierarchically arranged in terms of their causal priorities. Thus, the previously described causal system having three variables X_1, X_2 and X_3 could be described as follows:

$$X_1 = e_1$$
$$X_2 = b_{21} X_1 + e_2$$
$$X_3 = b_{31.2} X_1 + b_{32.1} X_2 + e_3$$

This set of equations indicates that X_1 depends only on outside variables represented by e_1; that X_2 depends on X_1 and other outside factors; and that X_3 depends on X_1 and X_2, as well as on outside factors. The e_i's designate the outside factors and are commonly referred to as error terms. The particular causal ordering represented by these equations is diagramatically presented in Figure 11.4.

* The direction of causality is indicated by an arrowhead.

FIGURE 11.4.

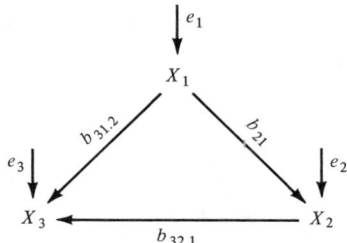

It is noted that the equations are simple linear regression equations* indicating the relation of each variable to another. We have used the conventional notation for regression coefficients,† where b_{21}, for instance, measures the effect of X_1 on X_2; and $b_{31.2}$ measures the effect of X_1 on X_3 when X_2 is held constant. Any slope involves controls only for variables that have explicitly appeared in the equation; thus, b_{21} does not involve any controls for the remaining variables, whereas $b_{31.2}$ and $b_{32.1}$ each control for the other variable.

In addition to the a priori assumption of no reciprocal causation, another assumption involves the error terms (e_i) included in each of the equations. It is assumed that the errors are uncorrelated; that is, that "all other" factors influencing the dependent variable are unrelated to the other independent variables in the system (Simon, 1954).

Having satisfied these two assumptions, and if one can also assume that the model diagramed in Figure 11.4 is theoretically correct, it is possible to study each equation separately, and to use ordinary least-square procedures to estimate the three coefficients b_{21}, $b_{31.2}$, and $b_{32.1}$. However, one can rarely assume that a given model is correct. Rather, one proceeds by making causal inferences concerning the adequacy of models by eliminating those that make predictions inconsistent with the data. In our recursive system, however, the number of unknowns is the same as the number of equations,‡ so that each of the coefficients can be estimated uniquely, regardless of the data. To test the adequacy of a model, the number of unknowns is reduced by setting one or more of the b's equal to zero. This imposes conditions that the data must satisfy for the equations to be mutually consistent. A coefficient equal to zero is equivalent to saying that there is no direct link between the two variables concerned. Thus, going back to the original diagram (Figure 11.4),

---

* We assume linearity and additive effects of the independent variables.

† The constant "a" has been omitted from each of the equations. This can be done whenever each variable is measured in standardized form.

‡ Due to lack of space we cannot demonstrate this algebraically. The reader is urged to refer to Simon (1957:41–42) for a more extensive discussion.

if we set $b_{21} = 0$, we are saying that there is no direct causal link between X_1 and X_2; $b_{31.2} = 0$ implies that X_1 and X_3 are not directly related; similarly, $b_{32.1} = 0$ means that X_3 and X_2 have no direct link. These three alternatives are presented in Figure 11.5. Each of these three alternative models imposes a specific condition that the equations must satisfy. In Model I, $b_{21} = 0$; in Model II, $b_{31.2} = 0$; and in Model III, $b_{32.1} = 0$. The appropriate arrows have been eliminated in each of the three diagrams.

The conditions imposed on each of the specific models are the predictions that should hold true if a model is correct. These predictions can be expressed in terms of correlation coefficients; that is, the vanishing of a b is equivalent to the vanishing of the comparable correlation coefficient. Thus, $b_{21} = 0$ implies that $r_{21} = 0$; $b_{32.1} = 0$, that $r_{32.1} = 0$; and $b_{31.2} = 0$, that $r_{31.2}$ should be zero as well.

The predictions derived from the models to be tested are always in terms of vanishing partials or zero-order coefficients that are set to zero. Predictions are always in terms of coefficients that reflect the uniqueness of the model under study. In other words, models are tested not in terms of their causal links, but rather by a test of the relationship between all pairs of unconnected variables. This means that the number of predictions for each causal model is a function of the number of variables in the system and the number of coefficients that were set to zero. The number of predictions that can be derived can be determined by Formula (11.10):

$$P = \frac{n(n-1)}{2} - K \qquad (11.10)$$

where P = number of predictions
n = number of variables
K = number of nonzero coefficients (or the number of causal arrows)

In our example, $n = 3$ and $K = 2$ in each of the models; thus,

$$P = \frac{3(2)}{2} - 2 = 1$$

FIGURE 11.5. Three Causal Models

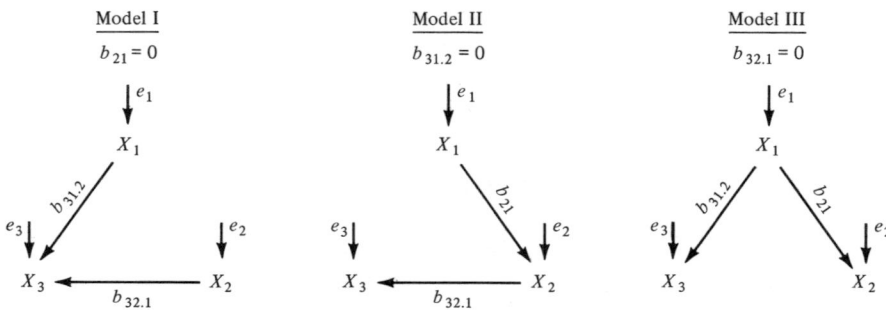

This method for drawing causal inferences is demonstrated in the following example on political behavior and its determinants.* It is hypothesized that the sociological characteristics of an individual's father (X_1) and the father's party identification (X_2) are the causal determinants of the individual's partisan attitudes (X_3). The alternative causal priorities of the variables are expressed in three alternative models.

The first causal model suggests that the sociological characteristics of the father directly influence both his own party identification as well as his child's partisan attitudes. This causal ordering is displayed in Figure 11.6. This model implies that there is no causal link between one's partisan attitudes and one's father's party identification, and that the statistical association between them is due to a third factor—the father's sociological characteristics, which determine them both. Thus, the correlation between them is expected to vanish when the third factor is held constant.

In Model II (Figure 11.7), the party identification of the father intervenes between his own sociological characteristics and his child's partisan attitudes. In this model, there is a direct link between the party identification of the parent and the partisan attitudes of the respondent, and no direct link between the father's sociological characteristics and the partisan attitudes. The prediction of this model is therefore $r_{31.2} = 0$.

Finally, a hypothetical alternative is one in which the parent's sociological characteristics and his party identification are assumed to be independent causes of a person's partisan attitudes. In such a case, we would expect the zero-order relation between the two independent variables to approach zero. The last model is presented in Figure 11.8.

FIGURE 11.6.

Model I: Partisan Attitudes and Party Identification
Determined by Sociological Characteristics

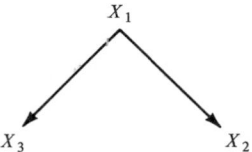

X_1 = Father's Sociological Characteristics
X_2 = Father's Party Identification
X_3 = Respondent's Partisan Attitudes

Prediction
$r_{32.1} = 0$

---

* This example is based on Goldberg's study (1966). Because we were limited to a three-variable case, several adaptations were made.

FIGURE 11.7.

Model II: Father's Party Identification Intervening Between Sociological Characteristics and Respondent's Partisan Attitudes

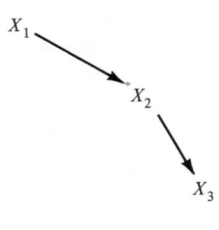

X_1 = Father's Sociological Characteristics
X_2 = Father's Party Identification
X_3 = Respondent's Partisan Attitudes

Prediction
$r_{31.2} = 0$

Making use of the intercorrelations between the variables supplied by Goldberg (1966), the three alternative models can be tested. The matrix of correlations is given in Table 11.10. The predictions and the empirical results are summarized in Table 11.11.

The correlation between the father's sociological characteristics and his party identification is numerically larger than would be expected if the variables were not causally related. Model III is thus eliminated as unplausible. Model I provides a better fit to the data, but the discrepancy between the prediction and the empirical results is still substantial. The prediction for Model II, however, fits the actual results fairly well and thus receives our support. It is noted that one can proceed only by the elimination of unplausible models rather than by establishing directly the validity of any particular model. The criterion of rejection and ac-

FIGURE 11.8.

Model III: Father's Sociological Characteristics and his Party Identification as Independent Causes of Respondent's Partisan Attitudes

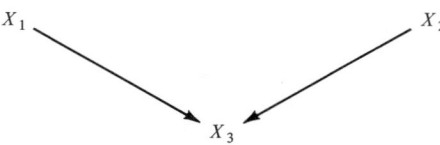

X_1 = Father's Sociological Characteristics
X_2 = Father's Party Identification
X_3 = Respondent's Partisan Attitudes

Prediction
$r_{21} = 0$

TABLE 11.10. Intercorrelations Between Father's Sociological Characteristics, Father's Party Identification, and Respondent's Partisan Attitudes

	X_2	X_3
X_1	.454	.318
X_2		.453

X_1 = Father's sociological characteristics
X_2 = Father's party identification
X_3 = Respondent's partisan attitudes

TABLE 11.11. Predictions and Empirical Results for Models I, II, and III

	Prediction	Empirical Results
Model I	$r_{32.1} = 0$	.366
Model II	$r_{31.2} = 0$	.141
Model III	$r_{21} = 0$	.454

ceptance is empirical, and the models that provide the best predictions are supported.

The extension of the technique discussed above to a four-variable model is quite straightforward. Using the underlying logic, the prediction equations for any particular four-variable model can be worked out.* With four variables, there are six pairs of relationships and 2^6 (64) alternative models. Some of these models are trivial; still, the number of significant ones is quite large. Thus, it is virtually impossible to compare a set of data against all possible models; the researcher can proceed only by selecting models that are theoretically plausible and then testing them against the data. For more than four variables, the derivation of prediction equations would involve rather tedious computations, and an alternative computing routine would have to be used.

A Four-Variable Model

Before concluding, we shall discuss briefly a four-variable model to illustrate how the method can be applied in more complex cases. In a study on adolescent achievement variables (Rehberg, Shafer, and Sinclair, 1970), data from 1,455 male high-school freshmen were used to evaluate the tenability of the causal ordering of adolescent achievement variables: "socioeconomic status," "mobility attitudes," "measured

---

* An extensive discussion of four-variable causal models can be found in Blalock (1962).

FIGURE 11.9. Two Temporal Sequences of Adolescent Achievement Variables

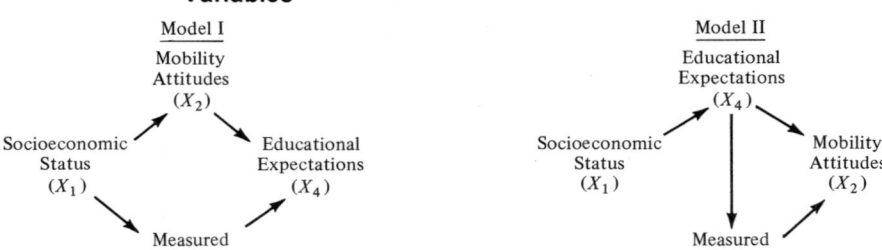

intelligence," and "educational expectations." In Model I, which is consistent with a traditional perspective of sociology, adolescents' educational expectations are linked with socioeconomic status via mobility attitudes and measured intelligence. In Model II,* mobility attitudes and measured intelligence are linked with socioeconomic status via educational expectation. These two perspectives are depicted in Figure 11.9.

As is evident from the diagrams depicting the two models, some of the arrows connecting the variables have been eliminated, which is equivalent to setting the parallel coefficients to zero. In Model I, mobility attitudes and measured intelligence are not directly connected; thus, the coefficient indicating the path from X_2 to $X_3 \rightarrow r_{32.1}$ is set to zero. Similarly, X_4 is not directly influenced by X_1, which is equivalent to saying that $r_{41.23} = 0$. In Model II, the arrow connecting socioeconomic status and mobility attitudes is missing. Therefore, $r_{21.34} = 0$. Similarly, socioeconomic status and measured intelligence are not directly related; thus, $r_{31.4} = 0$.

We can now write the predictions and the empirical values obtained in Rehberg, Shafer, and Sinclair's data. In Table 11.12, the original zero-order associations are summarized; in Table 11.13, the predictions and the empirical tests are presented.

As is evident from the empirical results, there is little support for Model I. The correlations between mobility attitudes and intelligence, and between socioeconomic status and educational expectations, remain substantial after removing the effect of the control variables. On the other hand, the data support the two predictions of Model II. Partialling out the influence of intelligence and educational expectations virtually eliminates the relationship between the variables (X_1 to X_2, and X_1 to X_3). The empirical test thus renders Model II more tenable than Model I.

---

* Model II has been slightly modified for illustrative purposes.

TABLE 11.12. Zero-Order Correlations

	X_2	X_3	X_4
X_1	.120	.210	.390
X_2		.210	.390
X_3			.420

X_1 = Socioeconomic status
X_2 = Mobility attitudes
X_3 = Measured intelligence
X_4 = Educational expectations

TABLE 11.13. Predictions and Empirical Results

	Prediction	*Empirical Values*
Model I	$r_{32.1} = 0$	.191
	$r_{41.23} = 0$	.341
Model II	$r_{21.34} = 0$	.029
	$r_{31.4} = 0$	.050

Concluding the discussion on causal inference, it is noted that the technique has both advantages and limitations. Its value lies in providing a framework that enables the researcher to evaluate causal relations between several variables simultaneously and to eliminate models that are not supported by the data. The great limitation of the technique is that it depends on several a priori assumptions that may well be untenable. Because the validity of the model being tested hinges on the validity of the required assumptions, the technique cannot be applied to situations where the reasonableness of the assumptions cannot be ascertained.

SUMMARY

Multivariate analysis has three basic functions: control, interpretation, and prediction. Statistical control is a substitute for experimental control and is accomplished through cross tabulation or partial correlation. With cross tabulation, an attempt is made to equate groups exposed to the independent variable with those not exposed, in all relevant matters. The selection of relevant control variables is based on substantive as well as statistical considerations. It is required that the variable be associated with both independent and dependent variables. The partial correlation is a method of statistically adjusting the zero-order correlation to cancel out the effect of the test variable on the independent and dependent variables.

When the mechanism of control is applied to a bivariate association, it can either cancel out the original relationship or have no effect on it. In the first case, the association is either spurious or mediated by the control variable; in the second case, the association is considered real and is subject to further analysis. Whereas a spurious interpretation invalidates a bivariate association, an intervening interpretation clarifies it and explains how the independent and dependent variables are related. A second class of interpretation specifies the conditions under which the association holds. Specification can be made according to interest and concern, time and place, and specific qualifications or characteristics.

Multiple regression and correlation is a technique for assessing the simultaneous effect of several independent variables on the phenomenon under study. In multiple regression, a prediction rule is estimated that evaluates the extent of change produced in the dependent variables by an independent variable, holding other relevant independent variables constant. The multiple correlation estimates the degree of fit of the prediction equation with the empirical data. R^2, the multiple correlation coefficient, measures the amount of variance in the dependent variable explained by the independent variables employed.

To make causal inferences, a method can be employed that uses correlational techniques. This, the Simon-Blalock method, assumes that the causal system is recursive and that the variables outside of the system are uncorrelated with the determinants of the dependent variable. Predictions are based on links between variables that are assumed to be zero. Assuming that some of the links in the system are unrelated imposes conditions that the data must satisfy for the prediction equations to be mutually consistent. Causal models are not tested directly; rather, inadequate models are eliminated.

REFERENCES

Almond, Gabriel A., and Verba, Sidney. *The Civic Culture*. Princeton, N.J.: Princeton University Press, 1963.

Blalock, Hubert M. "Four-Variable Causal Models and Partial Correlation." *American Journal of Sociology* 68 (1962): 182–194.

Blalock, Hubert M. *Causal Inference in Nonexperimental Research*. Chapel Hill: University of North Carolina Press, 1964.

Blalock, Hubert M. *Social Statistics*. 2d ed. New York: McGraw-Hill, 1972.

Cloward, Richard, and Ohlin, Lloyd E. *Delinquency and Opportunity*. New York: Free Press, 1960.

Douvan, Elizabeth, and Adelson, Joseph. *The Adolescent Experience*. New York: Wiley, 1966.

Goldberg, Arthur S. "Discerning a Causal Pattern among Data on Voting Behavior." *American Political Science Review* 60 (1966):913–922.

Hyman, Herbert H. "The Value System of Different Classes: A Social Psychological Contribution to the Analysis of Stratification." In Richard Bendix and Seymour M. Lipset (eds.), *Class, Status and Power*. Glencoe, Ill.: Free Press, 1953.

Hyman, Herbert H. *Survey Design and Analysis*. New York: Free Press, 1955.

Lazarsfeld, Paul F. "The Algebra of Dichotomous Systems." In Herbert Solomon (ed.), *Studies in Items Analysis and Prediction*. Stanford, Calif.: Stanford University Press, 1959.

Lazarsfeld, Paul F., Berelson, Bernard, and Gaudet, Hazel. *The People's Choice*. New York: Columbia University Press, 1968.

Lazarsfeld, Paul F., Berelson, Bernard, and Gaudet, Hazel. "Political Interest and Voting Behavior." In Paul F. Lazarsfeld and Morris Rosenberg (eds.), *The Language of Social Research*. New York: Free Press, 1955.

Rehberg, Richard A., Schafer, Walter E., and Sinclair, Judie. "Toward a Temporal Sequence of Adolescent Achievement Variables." *American Sociological Review* 35 (1970):34–48.

Rosenberg, Morris. "Self-Esteem and Concern with Public Affairs." *Public Opinion Quarterly* 26 (1962):201–211.

Rosenberg, Morris. *The Logic of Survey Analysis*. New York: Basic Books, 1968.

Simon, Herbert A. "Spurious Correlation: A Causal Interpretation." *Journal of the American Statistical Association* 49 (1954):467–479.

Simon, Herbert A. *Models of Man: Social and Rational*. New York: Wiley, 1957.

STUDY SUGGESTIONS

1. Table 11.14 shows the relationship between religion and life satisfaction. Table 11.15 shows the relationship between religion and life satisfaction when a third variable is held constant.
   a. Examine the relationship between the independent and dependent variables in the two tables by making a percentage comparison.
   b. Define the control variable. How does it affect the original relationship?

   TABLE 11.14. Life Satisfaction by Religion

	Religion	
	Protestant	*Catholic*
Satisfied	256	126
Not Satisfied	258	139
Total	514	265

TABLE 11.15. Life Satisfaction by Religion Controlling for a Third Variable

	Education					
	High		Medium		Low	
	Protestant	Catholic	Protestant	Catholic	Protestant	Catholic
Satisfied	89	13	116	35	51	78
Not Satisfied	104	20	124	59	30	60
Total	193	33	240	94	81	138

2. Table 11.16 shows the relationship between vote and social class, controlling for sex.
   a. Examine and describe (by making a percentage comparison) the relationship between the independent and dependent variables in the partial tables.
   b. Reconstruct the bivariate table showing the relationship between sex and social class.
   c. Reconstruct the bivariate table showing the relationship between sex and vote.
   d. Reconstruct the bivariate table showing the relationship between vote and social class.

TABLE 11.16. Vote by Social Class Controlling for Sex

	Male			Female		
	Upper Class	Lower Class	Total	Upper Class	Lower Class	Total
Democratic	55	45	100	115	285	400
Republican	545	355	900	285	615	900
Total	600	400	1,000	400	900	1,300

3. Using the data of Question 6, Chapter 10:
   a. Obtain the partial correlation between unemployment and political stability controlling for economic development.
   b. Obtain the partial correlation between unemployment and economic development controlling for political stability.
   c. Obtain the multiple regression equation for these data taking unemployment as the dependent variable. Evaluate the relative effect of each independent variable on unemployment by comparing the beta weights. How does this compare with your previous evaluation of Question 6, Chapter 10?
   d. What percentage of the variance in unemployment is explained by the three independent variables taken together?

PART 4
Inferential Methods

CHAPTER 12
Sampling and Sample Designs

Up to this point, we have been concerned with the collection, processing, and analysis of data. What is the central tendency of the data? How much variation is there? Do the variables correlate? Usually, however, data are collected in order to predict or make inferences about situations that have not been measured in full. For example, what can the government expect the level of political discontent to be during the coming year? Questions of this kind require predictions of future states to be made on the basis of current knowledge. Inferential statistics is concerned with making predictions from one set of data either to a future state or to some larger body of data. One example of the use of inferential statistics can be found in the polls used to predict the outcome of elections. Pollsters attempt to achieve two things: (1) to predict from a small sample how the population of voters would vote if the election were held at the time the poll was taken, and (2) to predict how the electorate will vote when the actual election is held. Both of these predictions involve employing a subset of the total electorate (a sample) and predicting the behavior of the entire set (the electorate or population).

The purpose of this chapter is to explain in general terms the principles underlying sampling theory. We do not attempt to present the theory itself in rigorous terms; rather, we attempt to acquaint the reader with some basic principles and the commonly used sampling designs.

AIMS OF SAMPLING

The drawing of conclusions from data generally requires researchers to rest their case on partial information. In a survey, it is impractical to interview all possible respondents; in a controlled experiment, it is impossible to test the hypothesis on all potential subjects. However, inferences based on a subset of the whole aggregate may be fairly accurate. Well-selected subsets may reflect precisely the characteristics of the aggregate. With a few thousand survey votes, one can predict the voting intentions of millions of voters. When the data are partial and used to characterize the whole, the subset is called a sample and the whole is called a population. A specified value of the population, such as the variance, is named a parameter; its counterpart in the sample is termed a statistic. The chief aim of sampling is to make an inference about a parameter that is unknown from a sample statistic that can be measured.

A second aim of sampling is to test a statistical hypothesis about a population, for example, the hypothesis that at least 60 percent of the families in a town own cars. A sample of families is selected, and the proportion owning cars calculated. Suppose the researcher observes that 56 percent own cars. The question now is whether the sample result is such as to accept or reject the statistical hypothesis. Chapter 13 is devoted to testing statistical hypotheses; in the present chapter our concern is with estimation, that is, inferences about parameters from sample statistics.

In order to arrive at unbiased estimates of parameters, the researcher should deal effectively with the following three problems: (1) the definition of population, (2) the size of the sample, and (3) the representativeness of the sample, or the sample design.

THE POPULATION

A population is the aggregate of all cases that conform to some designated set of specifications (Chein, 1959). For example, by the specifications "people" and "residing in Britain," we define a population consisting of all people who reside in Britain. Similarly, by the specifications "students" and "enrolled in state universities in the United States," we define a population consisting of all students enrolled in state universities in the United States. One may similarly define populations consisting of all households in a given community, all the registered voters in a particular precinct, all the case records in a file. A population may be a group of people, houses, records, legislators, and so on. The specific nature of the population depends on the purpose of investigation. If one is studying voting behavior in a presidential election, the population is all those who are eligible to vote. On the other hand, if one is investigating consumer behavior in a particular city, the population might be all the households in that city.

A single member of a population (a voter or a household) is referred to as a sampling unit. Usually, sampling units have numerous traits, one or more of which may interest the researcher in particular. For example, if the population is defined as all third-graders in a town attending public school on a particular day, the sampling units are all third-graders. Third-graders, however, have many traits, including grades, habits, opinions, and expectations. A researcher may attempt to describe the distribution of a single trait (the distribution of arithmetic grades) or the joint distribution of two or more traits (arithmetic grades and IQ scores).

A population may be finite or infinite, depending upon whether the sampling units are finite or infinite. By definition, a finite population contains a countable number of sampling units, for example, all registered voters in a particular city in a given year. On the other hand, an infinite population consists of an endless number of sampling units, such as an unlimited number of coin tosses. Sampling designed to produce information about some trait of a finite population is usually termed survey sampling.

One of the first problems facing a researcher who wishes to estimate a population value from a sample value is the determination of the population involved. If one is interested in voting behavior in Britain and wishes to draw a sample so as to predict how the election will turn out, one must not include anyone under eighteen in the sample. The population of voters in Britain is not the same as the population of Britain. Even "all British citizens eighteen years of age or older" is not an adequate definition of the population of voters, since the individual is required to meet certain standards set by the law before the election is held. Individuals who do not meet these standards are not eligible to vote; hence, they are not part of the population of voters. The population, then, has to be defined in terms of (1) content, (2) extent, and (3) time. One may wish to specify: (1) all persons over eighteen years of age living in private dwelling units, (2) in England, (3) on May 28, 1975.

SAMPLE SIZE

A sample is any subset of sampling units from a population. A subset is any combination of sampling units that does not include the entire set of sampling units that has been defined as the population. A sample may be one sampling unit, all but one sampling unit, or any number in between.

There are various common misconceptions about the necessary size of a sample. One is that the sample should be a regular proportion (often put at 5 percent) of the population; another is that the sample should total about 2,000; still another is that any increase in the sample size will increase the precision of the sample results. No such rule-of-thumb method is adequate. The size of the sample is properly estimated by deciding what level of accuracy is required and, hence, how large a standard error is acceptable. The notion of "standard error"* is central to sampling theory and to the understanding of how to determine a sample size. The basic idea of standard error can be clarified by considering a small hypothetical population and confining the discussion to what is termed simple random sampling. This is a method for selecting sampling units whereby each possible sample of n units from a population of N units has an equal chance of being selected.

Suppose that the population consists of 5 individuals earning $500, $650, $400, $700 and $600 per month, so that the population's mean monthly income (denoted by μ) is $570. A sample of 2 is drawn ($n = 2$) with the purpose of estimating μ. Suppose also that the draw results in the selection of the two individuals earning $500 and $400. The sample mean (denoted by $\bar{x}$) is therefore $450; this is taken as an estimate of μ, the population mean. Since in this example it is already known that μ is $570, one can see that the estimate of $450 is inaccurate. Had the selection fallen upon the two members earning $650 and $700, the estimate of μ would have been $675, which is also inaccurate. The accuracy of a sample estimate refers to its closeness to the correct population value; but since the latter is usually unknown, the actual accuracy of the sample estimate cannot be assessed. Nevertheless, its probable accuracy can be estimated.

Consider all the samples of size $n = 2$ that could have been selected from this population. It is assumed that sampling is without replacement; that is, having selected the first individual, one selects the second individual from the remaining four; after selecting the second individual, one selects a third individual from the remaining three, and so on. Table 12.1 presents the ten possible samples and the estimate of μ derived from each. If this process continued indefinitely, each of the samples given in Table 12.1 would be drawn over and over again. The distribution resulting from the value of $\bar{x}$ derived from this infinite number of samples is called the sampling distribution of the mean. Since each of the ten samples has an equal chance of being selected, and therefore in the long run occurs an equal number of times, the average of the estimates derived from all the possible samples is $5,700/10 = 570$, which is equal to the population mean, μ.

The average of the estimates of a population parameter obtained from an infinite number of samples is called the expected value of the estimator. The estimator is the method of estimating the population parameter from the sample statistic (which, in our example, is the sample mean). An estimate, on the other hand, is the value obtained by using the method of estimation for a specific sample. If the expected value of the estimator is equal to the population parameter, the estimator is unbiased; if not, it is biased. The difference between the expected value

---

* Some statisticians use the term "sampling error" for "standard error."

TABLE 12.1. Estimates of the Population's Mean

Possible Samples of n = 2 (Incomes of Individuals Selected)	$\bar{x}$ (Estimate of μ)
500 and 650	575
500 and 400	450
500 and 700	600
500 and 600	550
650 and 400	525
650 and 700	675
650 and 600	625
400 and 700	550
400 and 600	500
700 and 600	650
Total	5,700

and the true population value $(E\bar{x} - \mu)$ is termed the bias. Although in the above example the sampling was random and the sample mean was unbiased, the estimates all differ somewhat from each other and from μ. This is so because each estimate rests on one sample, and each sample consists of different observations. In practice, the estimate of a population parameter is based on only one sample, and one can estimate from any random sample how big the differences (sampling fluctuations) are likely to be on average. This estimate is based on a measure indicating the spread of the sampling distribution. The most common measure of the spread of any distribution is the standard deviation or its square, the variance (see Chapter 9). The standard deviation of the sampling distribution in our example is

$$[(575 - 570)^2 + (450 - 570)^2 + (600 - 570)^2 + (550 - 570)^2$$
$$+ (525 - 570)^2 - (675 - 570)^2 + (625 - 570)^2 + (550 - 570)^2$$
$$+ (500 - 570)^2 + (650 - 570)^2]/10 = \sqrt{4,350} = 65.95$$

The standard deviation of the sampling distribution of means is called the standard error of the mean [denoted $S.E.(\bar{x})$], and serves as a criterion for evaluating the probable accuracy of one's estimate. $S.E.(\bar{x})$ can be estimated from a single sample and can be represented by the following formula:

$$S.E.(\bar{x}) = \sqrt{\frac{\sigma^2}{n} \cdot \frac{N-n}{N-1}}$$

where σ = the standard deviation in the population
N = the number of units in the population
n = the number of units in the sample

One can use a modified definition of the population standard deviation, S, rather than σ (Moser and Kalton, 1971). The modified standard deviation is defined as

$$S = \sqrt{\frac{\sum_{i=1}^{N}(x_i - \mu)^2}{N - 1}}$$

With this definition,

$$S.E.(\bar{x}) = \sqrt{\frac{S^2}{n} \cdot \frac{N - n}{N}} = \sqrt{\frac{S^2}{n}\left(1 - \frac{n}{N}\right)} \tag{12.1}$$

If the population is very large relative to the sample, the factor $1 - n/N$, which is called the finite population correction, approximates unity and can be omitted.* In the present example, it obviously cannot be omitted, and we calculate the standard error from Equation (12.1), with $N = 5$, $n = 2$ and

$$S^2 = \frac{(500 - 570)^2 + (650 - 570)^2 + (400 - 570)^2 + (700 - 570)^2 + (600 - 570)^2}{4}$$

$$= \frac{58{,}000}{4} = 14{,}500$$

Therefore,

$$S.E.(\bar{x}) = \sqrt{\frac{14{,}500}{2} \cdot \frac{5 - 2}{5}} = \sqrt{4{,}350} = 65.95$$

which agrees with the previous result.

The formula for the standard error of the mean is based on two factors: the value of n (i.e., sample size) and the value of S or σ (i.e., the variability in the population). In practice, however, the value of S is almost never known, and one has to substitute for S the standard deviation of incomes calculated from the sample (to be denoted s) and then estimate the standard error from Formula (12.1). Thus,

$$s = \sqrt{\frac{1}{n - 1}\sum_{i=1}^{n}(x_i - \bar{x})^2}$$

is an unbiased estimate for S, and its value can be calculated from the sample. The term "unbiased estimate" refers to the fact that as one draws more and more samples from the same population and finds the mean of

* In this case, the formula becomes $S.E.(\bar{x}) = S/\sqrt{n}$.

all these unbiased estimates, the mean of these unbiased estimates approaches the population value. Sample means, then, are unbiased estimates of the population mean.

One more concept needs to be introduced before discussing the method by which a sample size is determined. This concept is "confidence interval," and it was first proposed by Neyman (1937). In the preceding discussion, the point was made that the population mean is equal to the mean of all the sample means that can be drawn from a population, and that one can estimate the standard deviation of these sample means. If the distribution of sample means is normal or approximates normality, we can use the properties of the normal curve to estimate the location of the population mean. If one knew the mean of all sample means (the population mean) and the standard deviation of these sample means (standard error of the mean), one could compute Z scores and determine the range within which any percentage of the sample means can be found. Between $-1Z$ and $+1Z$, one would expect to find 68 percent of all sample means; between $-1.96Z$ and $+1.96Z$, one would expect to find 95 percent of all sample means; and between $-2.58Z$ and $+2.58Z$, one would expect to find 99 percent of all sample means (see Chapter 9). However, it is this mean of the population that is unknown and that one wishes to estimate on the basis of a single sample.

The normal curve can be used for this purpose. A sample mean that was $+1.96Z$ scores (or standard errors of the mean) above the population mean has a .025 probability of occurrence; 97.5 percent of all sample means will be smaller than $+1.96$ standard errors of the mean. If it is a rare event for a sample mean to be 1.96 or more standard errors of the mean above the population mean, it is just as rare for the population mean to be 1.96 standard errors of the mean below a given sample mean. But one does not know whether the sample mean is larger or smaller than the true mean of the population. Nevertheless, if we were to construct an interval of -1.96 to $+1.96$ about the sample mean, we could have great confidence that the population mean is located somewhere in that interval. We do not expect that the sample mean will in fact be as far as ± 1.96 standard errors of the mean away from the population mean, and we are confident that the population mean is no further than this from the sample mean. If we construct an interval of ± 1.96 standard errors of the mean about the sample mean, we expect the population mean to be within this interval with 95 percent confidence. There is a 5 percent chance that we are wrong; that is, that the population mean is not within the interval (see Figure 12.1). If one does not wish to run a 5 percent risk of being incorrect, one can use a different confidence interval. The chances that the population mean will be within $+2.58$ and -2.58 standard errors of the mean if the sample mean is 99 out of 100, and this is the 99 percent confidence interval. The width of

FIGURE 12.1. Normal Curve: Percent Areas Form the Mean to Specified Standard Error Distances

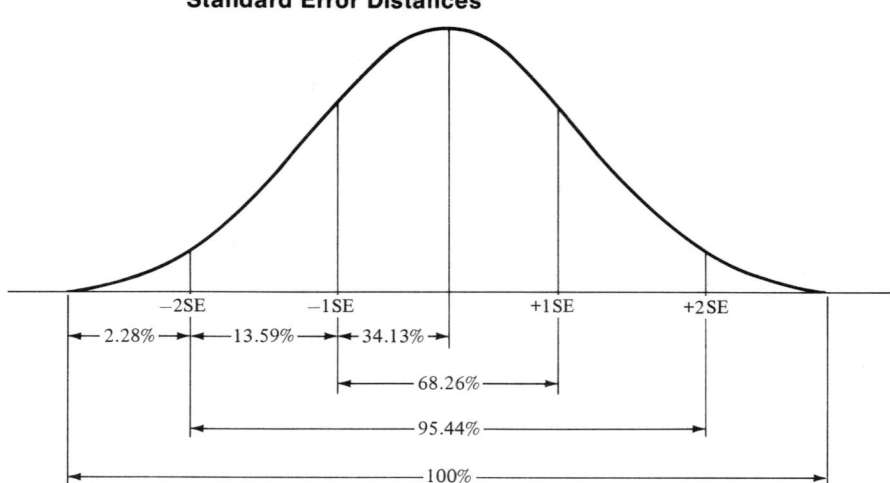

the confidence interval around the sample mean is decided by the researcher. The confidence interval can be made extremely narrow if the researcher is willing to run a large risk of being wrong. The researcher could use an interval of ±.68 standard errors of the mean and have only a 50 percent chance of being correct in assuming that the population mean is within the interval.

To sum up: if a given sampling distribution is known to be approximately normal, one is able to infer that about 68 percent of the sample estimates of which it is comprised will lie between its mean and one standard error, about 95 percent between its mean and twice the standard error, and so on. This knowledge is put to use by phrasing statements about population estimates in forms such as the following: given that the sample mean, $\bar{x}$, is an unbiased estimator of the population mean, μ, one can be 68 percent confident that the range $\bar{x} \pm S/\sqrt{n}$ includes the population mean, and one's confidence would be approximately 95 percent that the range $\bar{x} \pm 2(S/\sqrt{n})$ includes μ, and so on.

We are now in a position to deal with the size of samples. If cost and other practical limitations do not enter into the decision about the sample size, there is no difficulty in determining the desired size. Recall Formula (12.1) for the standard error of the mean:

$$S.E.(\bar{x}) = \sqrt{\frac{S^2}{n}\left(1 - \frac{n}{N}\right)}$$

Ignoring the finite population correction, we get

$$S.E.(\bar{x}) = \frac{S}{\sqrt{n}} \qquad (12.2)$$

where S is the standard deviation of the trait under study in the population. Inverting, we then have

$$n = \frac{S^2}{[S.E.(\bar{x})]^2} \qquad (12.3)$$

In order to calculate the sample size, n, the researcher has to have some idea of the standard deviation in the population and must also decide how big a standard error can be tolerated. If, for example, a random sample is to be drawn from a population consisting of 10,000 sampling units, and $S^2 = .20$, and the desired $S.E.(\bar{x}) = .016$, the estimated sample size is

$$n = \frac{.20}{.00026} = 769$$

If the sample size represents a sizeable proportion of the population, the finite population correction has to be included. In such cases, the final sample size is calculated by

$$n' = \frac{n}{1 + \left(\frac{n}{N}\right)} \qquad (12.4)$$

where N is the population size. In our example, if $N = 10,000$, then

$$n' = \frac{769}{1 + \frac{769}{10,000}} \cong 714$$

Formulae (12.3) and (12.4) illustrate the principle involved in estimating the size of a sample. In practice, decisions concerning the sample size are more complicated. The first difficulty relates to the precision required. Researchers must decide how precise they want their sample results to be; that is, how large a standard error they can tolerate. Second, the decision on a sample size is also governed by the way the results are to be analyzed. Third, if more than one trait is to be studied, a sample that is adequate for one trait may be unsatisfactory for another. Fourth, in order to use Formula (12.3) one needs an estimate of S, which, by definition, leads only to a rough estimate of the required sample size. It is beyond the scope of the present chapter to deal with these complications. The reader is urged to consult Kish (1965), Yamane (1967), and Moser and Kalton (1971).

SAMPLE DESIGNS

In the last two sections, we discussed sampling problems in relation to the definition of the population and the size of the sample. The third sampling problem arises in connection with the method of securing a representative sample. The essential requirement of any sample is that it be as representative as possible of the population from which it is drawn. A sample is said to be representative if the analyses made on its sampling units produce results equivalent to those that would be obtained had the entire population been analyzed.

In modern sampling theory, a basic distinction is made between probability and nonprobability sampling. The distinguishing characteristic of probability sampling is that one can specify for each sampling unit of the population the probability that it will be included in the sample. In the simplest case, each of the units has the same probability of being included in the sample. In nonprobability sampling, there is no way of specifying the probability that each unit has of being included in the sample, and there is no assurance that every unit has some chance of being included. If a set of units has no chance of being included in the sample, a restriction on the definition of the population is implied; that is, if the traits of this set of units are unknown, then the precise nature of the population also remains unknown (Chein, 1959). Accordingly, only probability sampling makes possible representative sampling designs.

A properly executed sample design can guarantee that, if a researcher were to repeat the study on a number of different samples drawn from a given population, his or her findings would not differ from the true population figures by more than a specified amount. A probability sample design makes it possible for the researcher to estimate the extent to which the findings based on one sample are likely to differ from what he or she would have found by studying the entire population. With a probability sample design, it is possible to attach estimates of standard errors to the sample results.

In spite of the great advantage of probability samples, social scientists do sometimes employ nonprobability samples. The major advantages of nonprobability samples are convenience and economy, which, under certain circumstances, may outweigh the risks involved in not using probability sampling. Also, when a population cannot be defined because of factors such as a nonavailable list of the population, the researcher may be forced to use a nonprobability sample (Moser and Kalton, 1971).

Three major designs of nonprobability samples have been used by social scientists: convenience samples, purposive samples, and quota samples. A convenience sample is obtained when the researcher selects whatever sampling units are conveniently available. Thus, a college professor may select students in his class; a researcher may take the first 200 people she or he meets on the street who are willing to be interviewed. There is no way of estimating the representativeness of convenience samples, and one cannot attach estimates of standard errors to the sample results.

With purposive samples, occasionally referred to as judgment samples, the sampling units are selected subjectively by the researcher, who attempts to obtain a sample that appears to him or her to be representative of the population. The chance that a particular sampling unit will be selected for the sample depends upon the subjective judgment of the researcher. Since it is impossible to determine precisely why each different researcher judges each sampling unit he or she selects to contribute to the representativeness of the sample, it is impossible to determine the probability of any specific sampling unit being included in the sample. Purposive samples have been used with some success in attempts to forecast election turnouts. In the United States, for example, a number of small election districts in each state are selected, their election returns in previous years having approximated the overall state returns. All the eligible voters in the selected districts are interviewed on their voting intentions, and the forecast is based on these reports. The underlying (and indeed risky) assumption is that the selected districts are still representative of their respective states.

The chief aim of quota samples is the selection of a sample that is as closely as possible a replica of the population. For example, if it is known that the population has equal numbers of Catholics and Protestants, the researcher selects an equal number of Protestants and Catholics in the sample. If it is known that 15 percent of the population is black, 15 percent of the total sample is black. In quota sampling, interviewers are given an assignment of quota groups specified by traits such as sex, age, social class, and ethnicity. Disproportions between the sample and the population are likely to occur in traits that have not been included as part of the specifications for the interviewers' quotas.

In addition to the major shortcoming of quota samples (the impossibility of estimating sampling errors), two other limitations are significant: (1) within the quota groups, interviewers may fail to secure a representative sample of interviewees; (2) the method makes strict control of field work difficult (Moser and Kalton, 1971).

Earlier, it was pointed out that in contrast to nonprobability sampling, probability sample designs permit one to specify for each sampling unit the probability that it will be included in the sample, and accordingly to attach estimates of standard errors to the sample results. In the following pages, we consider four major designs of probability samples: simple random sampling, systematic sampling, stratified sampling, and cluster sampling.

Simple Random Samples

Simple random sampling is the basic probability sampling design, and it is incorporated into all the more elaborate probability sampling designs. Simple random sampling is a sampling procedure that gives each of the

N sampling units of the population an equal nonzero probability of being selected. To ensure this requirement, one of the following two basic procedures is used: (1) The "lottery method." Each member of the population is represented by a disc; the discs are placed in an urn and mixed well; and a sample of the desired size is drawn. (2) The use of a table of random digits, such as that reproduced in Table 1 in the Appendix. The operational procedure is quite simple. Each sampling unit of the population is listed and given a number, from 0 to N. The table of random digits is entered at some random starting point. Each digit that appears in the table is read in order (up, down, or sideways; the direction does not matter, so long as it is consistent). Whenever a digit that appears in the table of random digits corresponds to the number of a sampling unit in the list, that sampling unit is selected for the sample. This process is continued until the desired sample size is reached. The selection of any given sampling unit places no limits on which other sampling units can be selected.

Either of these two procedures ensures that every sampling unit of the population has an equal nonzero probability of being included in the sample; this probability is n/N, where n stands for the size of the sample and N for the size of the population.* For example, if the population consists of 50,389 eligible voters in a town, and a simple random sample of 1,800 is to be drawn, the probability of each sampling unit of the population being included in the sample is 1,800/50,389.

Systematic Samples

Systematic sampling consists of selecting every Kth sampling unit of the population after the first sampling unit is selected at random from the first K sampling units. Thus, if one desires to select a sample of 100 persons from a population of 10,000, one takes every hundredth individual ($K = N/n = 10,000/100 = 100$). The first selection must be determined by some random process, such as the use of a table of random digits. Suppose the fourteenth person were selected; the sample would then consist of individuals numbered 14, 114, 214, 314, 414, and so on.

Systematic sampling is much simpler than simple random sampling. When interviewers who are untrained in sampling are to execute the sampling in the field, it is much simpler to instruct them to select every Kth person from a list than to have them use a table of random digits. Also, whenever a population is too large or a large sample is to be drawn, the use of systematic sampling is more convenient.

With systematic sampling, each sampling unit in the population has a $1/K$ probability of being included in the sample; hence, the sample

---

* For the mathematical proof, see Kish (1965:39–40).

mean is an unbiased estimate of the population mean. However, the variance of the sample may not be a good estimate of the population variance, since one is, in effect, dividing the sample units into strata, each of K size. There may be a systematic pattern in the data occurring at every Kth unit, and this will bias the sample. For example, if dwelling units on blocks are selected, and the first chosen is a corner house, every Kth element may also be a corner house. In cases where the population exhibits a systematic pattern, if the list can be thoroughly shuffled first, problems may be alleviated; the subsequent selection can then be treated as a simple random sample.*

Stratified Samples

Stratified sampling is used primarily to ensure that different groups of a population are adequately represented in the sample, so that the level of accuracy in estimating parameters is increased. Furthermore, all other things being equal, stratified sampling reduces the cost of execution considerably. The underlying idea in stratified sampling is that already existing knowledge of the population is used "to divide it into groups such that the elements within each group are more alike than are the elements in the population as a whole" (Hansen, Hurwitz, and Madow, 1953:40). If a series of homogeneous groups can be sampled in such a way that, when the samples are combined, they constitute a sample of a more heterogeneous population, then increased accuracy will result. For example, suppose that it is known that there are 700 whites, 200 blacks, and 100 Mexican-Americans in a given population. If a random sample of 100 persons were drawn, one would probably not get exactly 70 whites, 20 blacks, and 10 Mexican-Americans; the proportion of Mexican-Americans, especially, might be relatively either too large or too small. On the other hand, a stratified sample of 70 whites, 20 blacks, and 10 Mexican-Americans would assure better representation of these groups. It should be emphasized that stratification does not imply any departure from the principle of randomness, since a probability sample is subsequently drawn within each stratum.

The necessary condition for division into homogeneous strata is that the criteria for division be correlated with the variable being studied. A second condition is that the criteria used do not require so many subsamples as to increase the size of the sample over that required by a simple random sample (Goode and Hatt, 1952). Suppose a researcher who wants to estimate the average family income in a small town knows the traits of all the families in the population. Since it has already been established that income correlates with occupation, education, race, age,

---

* For some other procedures for avoiding problems caused by systematic patterns in populations, see William Cochran, *Sampling Techniques*, 2nd ed. (New York: Wiley, 1963).

and sex, these would become logical bases for stratification. However, if all these bases were used, the value of stratified sampling would diminish, for the number of subsamples would become enormous. Consider what would happen if there were 4 categories of occupation, 3 of education, 3 of race, 3 of age, and 2 of sex. The number of subsamples would then equal $4 \times 3 \times 3 \times 3 \times 2$, or 216. Since a statistically satisfactory frequency in the smallest cell could not possibly be less than 10 cases, this would require a minimum of 2,160, assuming that the frequencies in all cells were equal. No one could consider such a number as a sample of a small town. To solve this problem, it is assumed that many such stratification bases occur as associated factors. Thus, if social status is chosen to stand for occupation, education, and race, the number of subsamples can be reduced to 4 (social-status groups) × 3 (age groups) × 2 (sex groups) = 24 subsamples. This is a more usable sample design, and the researcher would obtain a more representative sample than the one obtainable with a simple random sample.

Sampling from the different strata can be either proportional or disproportional. If one draws into the sample the same number of sampling units from each stratum, or a uniform sampling fraction (n/N), the sample is known as a proportionate stratified sample. The sample size from each stratum is proportional to the population size of the stratum. On the other hand, if there are variable sampling fractions (i.e., the total number in each stratum is different), the sample is a disproportionate stratified sample. Most often, researchers will use a disproportionate stratified sample when they wish either to assess the differences between two or more particular strata or to analyze one stratum intensively. When a disproportionate stratified sample is used, a mean computed for the population based on the means of all the strata would have to be weighted in accordance with the number in each stratum. In this case, the population mean can be defined as

$$\bar{X} = W_1 \bar{X}_1 + W_2 \bar{X}_2 + \cdots + W_n \bar{X}_n = \sum_{i=1}^{n} W_i \bar{X}_i$$

where $\bar{X}$ is the estimated mean based on strata; W_n is the weight of each stratum (computed as $W_i = N_i/N$, where N_i is the number of elements in the ith stratum and N is the total number in the population); and $\bar{X}_n$ is the mean for each stratum.

Cluster Samples

Large-scale survey studies rarely make use of simple, systematic, or stratified random samples, because of the enormous expense associated with them; instead, they make use of cluster sampling. A researcher arrives at the set of sampling units to be included in the sample by first sampling larger groupings, called clusters. The clusters are selected by a simple or stratified sample. If not all the sampling units in these clusters are to be included in the sample, the final selection from within the clusters is also carried out by a simple or stratified sampling procedure.

Suppose that the research objective is to study the political attitudes of adults in the various election districts of a city; that there is no single list available containing all the names; and that it is too expensive to compile a list. However, a list or a map of the election districts is readily available. A researcher can randomly select election districts from the list (first-stage cluster sampling). Within each of the districts, the researcher may then select blocks at random (second-stage cluster sampling) and interview all the persons in these blocks. The researcher may also use a simple random sample within each block selected, in which case a three-stage cluster sample will be obtained.* Similarly, a survey of urban households may take a sample of cities; within each city that is selected, a sample of districts; and within each selected district, a sample of households.

Moser and Kalton (1971) suggest three general points about clustering. First, the decision to call a particular aggregate of units a cluster depends on the enquiry unit. Thus, an area can be called a cluster since it contains a number of households, the household being the unit of enquiry. On the other hand, if the area is the unit of enquiry, it cannot be called a cluster. Second, clusters need not necessarily be natural aggregates such as districts, schools, or classes. Clustering does take advantage of existing groupings of the population, but artificial clusters can also be made, such as when researchers impose grids onto maps. Third, in any one sample design, several levels of clusters may be used. In the last example, cities, districts, and households were used.

These four designs of probability sampling do not exhaust the range of probability sampling procedures, and the reader is advised to consult Ackoff (1953) and Kish (1965) for other designs. However, these are the basic designs most commonly used by social investigators. By way of a summary, a brief description of the four designs is given in Table 12.2.

NONSAMPLING ERROR

Sampling theory is essentially concerned with the error introduced by the sampling procedure. In a perfect design, this error is minimized for an individual sample. The error in estimates refers to what is expected

---

* This sampling method is also called area probability sampling or just area sampling.

TABLE 12.2. Description of Four Probability Samples

Type of Sampling	Description
Simple random	Assign to each population element a unique number; select sample units by use of a table of random digits.
Systematic	Determine the sampling interval (N/n); select the first sample unit randomly; select remaining units according to interval.
Stratified	
Proportionate	Determine strata; select from each stratum a random sample proportionate to the size of the strata in the population.
Disproportionate	Determine strata; select from each stratum a random sample of the size dictated by analytical considerations.
Cluster	Determine the number of levels of clusters; from each level of clusters select randomly; ultimate units are groups.

in the long run, if a particular set of procedures is followed. However, even if the sampling error is minimized, there are other sources of error, for example, measurement error (see Chapter 4). In survey research, the most pervasive error is the nonresponse error. Nonresponse is defined as those observations that are not carried out because of refusal to answer, not-at-homes, lost forms, and so on. Nonresponse can introduce a substantial bias into the findings. The amount and kind of bias is related to the following conditions:

1. The greater the nonresponse proportion, the greater will be the biasing effects. The response proportion can be computed with Formula (12.5):

$$R = 1 - \frac{(n-r)}{n} \qquad (12.5)$$

For example, if the original sample size is 1,200, and 1,000 responses are actually obtained, the response rate is $1 - (1,200 - 1,000)/1,200 = 0.84$, and the nonresponse rate is .16, or 16 percent.

2. The seriousness of the nonresponse bias depends on the extent to which the population mean of the nonresponse stratum differs from that of the response stratum (Moser and Kalton, 1971). In symbols,

$$\mu_1 - \mu = \mu_1 - (R_1\mu_1 + R_2\mu_2)$$
$$= \mu_1(1 - R_1) - R_2\mu_2$$
$$= R_2(\mu_1 - \mu_2)$$

where N_1 is a "response stratum," N_2 a "nonresponse stratum," $N_1/N = R_1$, and $N_2/N = R_2$.

3. Each of the following nonresponse types affects the sample results in a different way:*

a. Uninterviewables: every selected sample is likely to include some people who are ill, illiterate, or have language barriers.
b. Not found: this includes people who have moved and those who are inaccessible, for instance, who cannot make an appointment.
c. Not-at-homes: some people are out when the interviewer calls, but could be reached by re-calling.
d. Refusals: some people refuse to cooperate and will not answer survey questions. Refusals may also vary with the type of question being asked.

The proportion of nonrespondents varies in relation to factors such as the nature of the population, the type of data-collection method being used, the kinds of questions being asked, the skill of the interviewers, and the number of call-backs that can be made. A poorly designed and administered interview schedule might yield a very low response rate. To estimate the effect of nonresponse, information about the nonrespondents should be collected on call-backs. Based on such knowledge, imputations can be made. Suppose, for example, that voters are surveyed to estimate the proportions that identify with one party or another, and that the survey has a 10 percent nonrespondent rate. This can be corrected with information about the education or income of the nonrespondents (Palumbo, 1969). Suppose that 10 percent amounts to 300 voters and that, of these, 70 percent have incomes of about \$12,000 a year. If one knew that, in general, 90 percent of the people in this income level are Democrats, one might estimate that $.70 \times 300 \times .90 = 189$ are Democrats. However, there is no way of computing the possible error of this estimate. Imputation can be used to correct for nonresponse only if the response rate is relatively low.

SUMMARY

Inferential statistics is concerned with making predictions from one set of data either to a future state or to some larger body of data. In this

---

* These types apply to entire schedules, as well as to parts of an interview or questionnaire or to single questions.

chapter, the focus was on drawing population estimates from sample statistics. In order to arrive at accurate estimates of parameters, the researcher has to deal effectively with three problems: (1) definition of the population, (2) determination of the sample size, and (3) selection of a representative sample.

A population has to be defined in terms of (1) content, (2) extent, and (3) time. A sample is any subset of sampling units from the population. A sample may be one sampling unit, all but one sampling unit, or any number in between. The determination of a sample size is essentially dependent on the value of the standard error and on the width of the confidence interval that is set by the researcher. The confidence interval can be made extremely narrow if the researcher is willing to run a large risk of being wrong or extremely wide if the researcher opts to run a negligible risk.

Upon the definition of a population and the determination of the size of the sample, a representative sampling design has to be selected. A sample is representative if the analyses made on its units produce results equivalent to those which would be obtained had the entire population been analyzed. Most often, researchers use probability sampling designs because they can specify for each unit of the population the probability of its being included in the sample, thus assuring representativeness. Four basic probability samples were considered—simple random sample, systematic sample, stratified sample, and cluster sample —the characteristics of which were summarized in Table 12.2.

In survey research, in addition to sampling error, nonresponse error is most pervasive. Nonresponse is defined as those measurements which are not carried out because of refusal to answer, not-at-homes, lost forms, and so on. Nonresponse can introduce a substantial bias into the findings, and some of the methods for estimating bias were briefly discussed.

REFERENCES

Ackoff, Russell. *The Design of Social Research*. Chicago: University of Chicago Press, 1953.

Chein, Isidor. "An Introduction to Sampling." In Claire Selltiz et al., *Research Methods in Social Relations*. New York: Holt, Rinehart & Winston, 1959.

Goode, William J., and Hatt, Paul K. *Methods in Social Research*. New York: McGraw-Hill, 1952.

Hansen, Morris H., Hurwitz, William N., and Madow, William G. *Sampling Survey Methods and Theory*. New York: Wiley, 1953.

Kish, Leslie. *Survey Sampling*. New York: Wiley, 1965.

Moser, C. A., and Kalton, G. *Survey Methods in Social Investigation*. London: Heinemann Educational Books, 1971.

Neyman, Jerzy. *Outline of a Theory of Statistical Estimation Based on the Classical Theory of Probability*. Philosophical Transactions of the Royal Society, series A, vol. 236, 1937.

Palumbo, Dennis J. *Statistics in Political and Behavioral Science*. New York: Appleton-Century-Crofts, 1969.

Yamane, Taro. *Elementary Sampling Theory*. Englewood Cliffs, N.J.: Prentice-Hall, 1967.

STUDY SUGGESTIONS

1. Suppose a random sample, $N = 1,016$, is drawn, and the researcher finds that $\bar{x} = 55$, while $s = 9$. Find the 95 percent and 99 percent confidence intervals for these data.
2. Estimate the sample size for a random sample to be drawn from a population consisting of 25,000 sampling units, and $s^2 = 0.30$ and the desired $S.E.(\bar{x}) = 0.016$.
3. To investigate voting intentions of various ethnic groups in a small town, what sample design could yield: (1) most accurate results? (2) adequate representation?
4. What are some of the reasons for nonresponse? How can one attempt to maximize the response rate?

CHAPTER 13
Hypothesis-Testing

In the previous chapter, we introduced the general idea of inferential statistics, which deals with the problem of evaluating population characteristics when only the sample evidence is given. It was demonstrated that sample statistics may give good estimates of particular population parameters, but that virtually any estimate will deviate from the true value due to sampling fluctuations. The process of statistical inference enables investigators to evaluate the accuracy of their estimates.

A second use of inferential statistics is the assessment of the probability of specific sample results under assumed population conditions. This type of inferential statistics is called hypothesis-testing and will occupy us throughout this chapter. With estimation, a sample is selected to evaluate the population parameter; with the testing of hypotheses, on the other hand, assumptions about the population parameter are made in advance, and the sample then provides the test of these assumptions. With estimation, the sample provides information about single population parameters such as the mean income or the variance of education; with hypothesis-testing, an inference is usually being made about relationships among variables—as, for example, the relationship between education and income or between occupation and particular political attitudes.

This chapter describes the strategy of hypothesis-testing by focusing on concepts such as the sampling distribution, type I and type II errors, and the level of significance. We then consider several methods of testing hypotheses about the relationship between two variables: difference between means, Pearson's r, the Mann-Whitney runs test, and the Chi-square test.

THE STRATEGY OF TESTING HYPOTHESES

The first step in testing a hypothesis is to formulate the hypothesis in statistical terms. We have already discussed how to draw a hypothesis from a theory or how to formulate a research problem as a hypothesis. However, in order to test the hypothesis, it needs to be formulated in terms that can be analyzed with statistical tools. For example, if the purpose of the investigation is to establish that educated individuals have higher incomes than do noneducated individuals, the statistical hypothesis might be that there is a positive correlation between education and income, or that the mean income of a highly educated group will be larger than the mean income of a group with a lower level of education. In both cases, the statistical hypothesis is formulated in terms of descriptive statistics (such as a correlation or a mean) as well as a set of specifying conditions about these statistics (such as a positive correlation or a difference between the means).

The statistical hypothesis always applies to the population of interest. In the above example, no inferences would be necessary if the population could be directly tested; then, any difference between the means (or a positive correlation of any size) would support the hypothesis. However, sample results are subject to sampling fluctuations, which would account for the difference between the means or for the positive coefficient. Thus, a result in line with the hypothesis may imply either that the hypothesis is true or that it is false, with the results being due to chance factors. On the other hand, a deviation between the sample results and the expected population value could mean either that the hypothesis is false or that it is true, with the difference between the expected and obtained values being due to chance. Table 13.1 illustrates these four possibilities.

Whether a sample result is according to expectation or deviates from expectation, either case can imply that the hypothesis is either *true* or *false*. Therefore, sample results cannot be interpreted directly; a decision rule is needed to enable the researcher to reject or retain a

TABLE 13.1. Alternative Interpretations of Sample Results

Hypothesis Is	Sample Results	
	According to Expectation	*Deviation from Expectation*
True	Results validate hypothesis	Results due to sampling fluctuation
False	Results due to sampling fluctuation	Results validate hypothesis

hypothesis about the population on the basis of sample results. The procedure of statistical inference enables the researcher to determine whether a particular sample result falls within a range that can occur by chance or could not possibly be a result of chance. This procedure involves the steps listed below, which are discussed in some detail:

1. Formulate a null hypothesis and a research hypothesis.
2. Choose a sampling distribution and a statistical test according to the null hypothesis.
3. Specify a significance level (α) and define the region of rejection.
4. Compute the statistical test and reject or retain the null hypothesis accordingly.

The Null and the Research Hypotheses

There are two statistical hypotheses involved in the process of testing hypotheses. The first is the research hypothesis, which is usually symbolized by H_1. The second, symbolized by H_0, is the null hypothesis; it is set up artificially for logical purposes.

Suppose the research hypothesis states that Catholics have larger families than do Protestants. With the mean score for the size of family in the Catholic population designated as μ_1, and in the Protestant population as μ_2, the research hypothesis would be:

$$H_1: \mu_1 > \mu_2$$

The null hypothesis would be:

$$H_0: \mu_1 = \mu_2$$

The null hypothesis can be expressed in several different ways. However, it is usually an expression of no difference or no relationship between the variables. Both the null hypothesis and the research hypothesis are expressed in terms of the population parameters, not in terms of the sample statistics. The null hypothesis is the one that is tested directly; the research hypothesis is supported when the null hypothesis is rejected as being unlikely.

The need for two hypotheses arises out of a logical necessity: the null hypothesis is based on negative inference in order to avoid the fallacy of affirming the consequent. That is, one must eliminate false hypotheses rather than accept true ones. For instance, suppose theory A implies empirical observation B. When B is false, one knows that A must also be false. But when B is true, A cannot be accepted as true, since B can be an empirical implication of several other theories that are not necessarily A. Acceptance of A as true would be the fallacy of affirming the consequent.

Durkheim's theory on suicide may serve as an illustration. One of the implications of this theory is that bachelors have a higher suicide rate than do married persons (B). This implication derives from one of the propositions of the theory: that people in individualistic situations are more likely to commit suicide (A). If B proves to be false (if there is no difference in the suicide rates of married and single persons), then theory A is false. But what if B is true? A cannot be accepted as true; there are many other explanations for B that are not necessarily A. For instance, the higher suicide rate of bachelors might be explained not by individualism, but rather by their excessive drinking, which may lead to depression and to suicide. Thus, observation B might imply that A_1, another theory, is true.

Usually, many alternative theories might explain the same observations; the scientist has to select the most credible one. Thus, the credibility of a theory can be established only by the elimination of all alternative theories: "For any given observation which is an implication of A, say B_1, there will be *some of* the possible alternative theories which will imply not —B_1. If we then demonstrate B_1, these alternative theories are falsified. This leaves us with *fewer alternative possible theories* to our own" (Stinchcombe, 1968:20).

THE SAMPLING DISTRIBUTION

Having chosen a specific null hypothesis, the investigator proceeds to test it against the sample results. For instance, if the hypothesis states that there is no difference between the means of two populations ($\mu_1 = \mu_2$), the procedure would be to draw a random sample from each population, compare the two sample means ($\overline{X}_1$ and $\overline{X}_2$), and make an inference from the samples to the populations. However, the sample result is subject to sampling error; therefore, it does not always reflect the true population value. If samples of the same size are drawn from the population, each sample will usually produce a different result.

In order to determine the accuracy of the sample statistic, it has to be compared to a statistical model that gives the probability of observing such a result. Such a statistical model is called a sampling distribution. A sampling distribution of a statistic is obtained by drawing a large number of random samples of the same size from the defined population, computing the statistic for each sample, and plotting the frequency distribution of the statistic. We have seen in Chapter 12 an example of such a distribution: the sampling distribution of the mean. It is possible to construct a sampling distribution of any other statistic, for example, of the variance (s^2), of the standard deviation (s), of the difference between means ($\overline{X}_1 - \overline{X}_2$), or of proportions ($p$).

As an illustration, let us go back to Durkheim's theory on suicide. The hypothesis to be tested is that bachelors have a relatively higher suicide rate than does the general population. One way of evaluating the relative frequency of suicide among bachelors is by comparing the number of suicides in this group to the average rate in the population at large. Suppose the records of health centers indicate that the national suicide rate in the adult population is 2 out of every 100, or .02. The research hypothesis implies that the rate of suicide among bachelors is higher than .02. Thus, H_1: the proportion of suicides among bachelors > .02. The null hypothesis states that the suicide rate of bachelors is identical to the national rate. Therefore, H_0: the proportion of suicides among bachelors = .02.

Suppose that a sample of 100 is drawn from the records on bachelors' suicides, and that the rate of suicide is .30. Is this result sufficiently larger than .02 to justify the rejection of the null hypothesis? To assess the likelihood of obtaining a rate of .30 under the assumption of the null hypothesis, it is compared to a distribution of suicide rates of the adult population. Let us assume that 1,000 random samples of 100 each are drawn from the records on suicide, and the suicide rate is computed for each sample. The obtained hypothetical sampling distribution* is presented in Table 13.2. This sampling distribution may serve as a statistical model for assessing the likelihood of observing a suicide rate of .30 among bachelors if their rate were equivalent to that of the adult population. The probability of observing any particular result can be determined by dividing its frequency in the distribution by the total number of samples. The obtained probabilities are displayed in the third column of Table 13.2. For example, the suicide rate of .38–.39 occurred 5 times; therefore, the probability that any sample of size $n = 100$ will have this suicide rate is 5/1,000 or .005; that is, we would expect to obtain such a result in approximately 0.5 percent of the samples of 100 drawn from the population. Similarly, the probability of obtaining a rate of .30–.31 is .015, or 1.5 percent. The probability of obtaining a rate of .30 or more is equal to the sum of the probabilities of .30–.31, .32–.33, .34–.35, .36–.37, .38–.39, and .40 or more; that is, .015 + .010 + .010 + .010 + .005 + .000 = .050. Thus, we would expect 5 percent of all samples of 100 drawn from this population to have a suicide rate of .30 or more.

Level of Significance and the Region of Rejection

Following the construction of the sampling distribution, the likelihood of the result of .30 (given the assumption of the null hypothesis) can now be evaluated. The decision as to what result is sufficiently unlikely to

---

* Such a distribution is often denoted as an experimental sampling distribution, since it is obtained from observed data.

TABLE 13.2. Hypothetical Sampling Distribution of Suicide Rates for 1,000 Random Samples (Sample: $n = 100$)

Suicide Rate	Number of Samples (f)	Proportion of Samples ($p = f/n$)
.40 or more	0	.000
.38–.39	5	.005
.36–.37	10	.010
.34–.35	10	.010
.32–.33	10	.010
.30–.31	15	.015
.28–.29	50	.050
.26–.27	50	.050
.24–.25	50	.050
.22–.23	150	.150
.20–.21	200	.200
.18–.19	150	.150
.16–.17	100	.100
.14–.15	100	.100
.12–.13	50	.050
.10–.11	15	.015
.08–.09	10	.010
.06–.07	10	.010
.04–.05	10	.010
.02–.03	5	.005
.01 or less	0	.000
Total	1,000	1.000

justify the rejection of the null hypothesis is quite arbitrary. Any set of extreme results can be selected as a basis for rejection of the null hypothesis. The range of these results is designated as the region of rejection. The sum of the probabilities of the results included in the region of rejection is denoted as the level of significance, or α. It is customary to set the level of significance at .05 or .01, which means that the null hypothesis is to be rejected if the sample outcome is among the results that would have occurred 5 percent or 1 percent of the time.

Figure 13.1 graphically represents the sampling distribution of Table 13.2 and the region of rejection with $\alpha = .05$. The region of rejection includes all the suicide rates of .30 and above. The sum of the probabilities of these results is equal to the level of significance, .05.

The obtained sample result of .30 falls within the region of rejection; thus, the null hypothesis can be rejected at the .05 level of significance. The rejection of the null hypothesis supports the research hypoth-

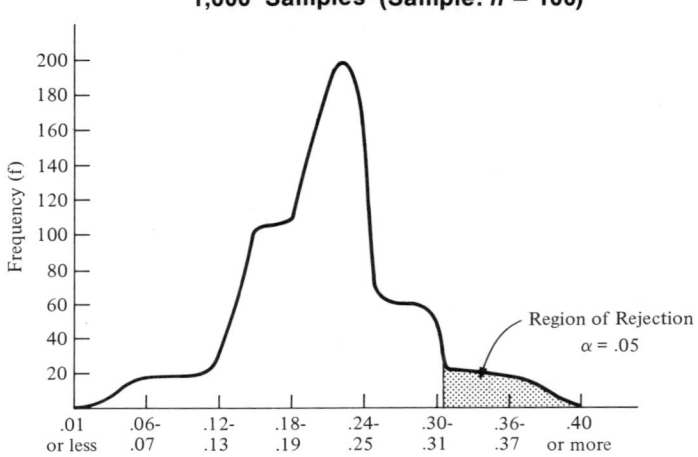

FIGURE 13.1. Sampling Distribution of Suicide Rates for 1,000 Samples (Sample: $n = 100$)

esis that the suicide rate of bachelors is higher than the rate in the general adult population.

One-Tailed and Two-Tailed Tests

In the above example, the set of extreme results was selected from the right tail of the sampling distribution. However, extreme sample outcomes are also located at the left-hand tail. In Table 13.2, the probability of a suicide rate of .10 and below is equal to the probability of obtaining a rate of .30 and above; in both cases, it is .05.

A statistical test may be one-tailed or two-tailed. In a two-tailed test, the region of rejection is located at both left and right tails. In a one-tailed test, extreme results leading to the rejection of the null hypothesis can be located at either tail.

The decision to locate the region of rejection in one or two tails will depend on whether H_1 implies a specific direction to the predicted results, and whether it specifies large or small values. When H_1 predicts large values, the region of rejection will be located at the right tail of the sampling distribution (as in the example on suicide). When H_1 implies lower values, the left tail is selected as a region of rejection. For instance, suppose the research hypothesis had implied that bachelors have a lower suicide rate than does the general adult population; that is, H_1: proportion of suicide in bachelor population $< .02$. The results considered unlikely under this hypothesis are at the left tail of the distribution. At the .05 level of significance, the critical region will consist of the following rates: .10–.11, .08–.09, .06–.07, .04–.05, .02–.03, .01 or less.

The sum of the probabilities of these results is $.015 + .010 + .010 + .010 + .005 + .000 = .050$. Figure 13.2 presents the right-tail and left-tail alternatives.

There are occasions when the direction of the research hypothesis cannot be predicted accurately. For example, we may have suspected that bachelors have a different suicide rate but were unable to specify the direction of the difference. The research hypothesis would have been expressed as H_1: proportion of bachelors' suicide $\neq .02$. When H_1 cannot be accurately specified, H_0 is rejected whenever extreme values in either direction are obtained. In such a case, the statistical test is designated as a two-tailed test, and the level of significance is divided in two. Thus, a .05 level of significance would mean that H_0 will be rejected if the sample outcome falls among the lowest 2.5 percent or the highest 2.5 percent of the sampling distribution. This alternative is diagramed in Figure 13.3.

Let us select the .05 level of significance and make use of a two-tailed test in the suicide example. The critical region will consist of the alternatives .34–.35, .36–.37, .38–.39, .40 or more $(.010 + .010 + .005 = .025)$ and .06–.07, .04–.05, .02–.03, .01 or less $(.010 + .010 + .005 = .025)$. With a two-tailed test, a sample result of .30 is not included in the region of rejection; thus, the null hypothesis would not have been rejected in this case. With a one-tailed test, the null hypothesis is more likely to be rejected, since there is a greater probability that the sample result will fall within the critical region.

Type I and Type II Errors

In statistical hypothesis-testing, the entire population is not measured directly, so the statistical test can never prove if the null hypothesis is true or false. The only evidence it provides is whether the sample result is sufficiently likely or unlikely to justify the decision to retain or to reject the null hypothesis.

The null hypothesis can be either true or false, and in both cases

FIGURE 13.2. Right-Tail and Left-Tail Tests

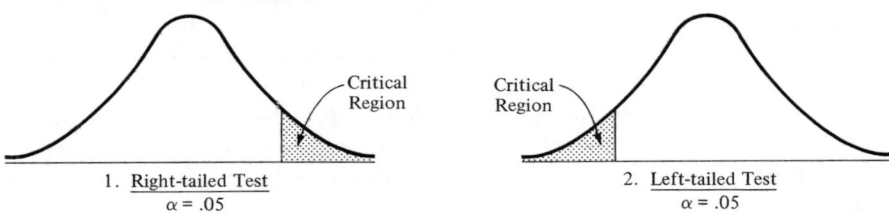

1. Right-tailed Test
$\alpha = .05$

2. Left-tailed Test
$\alpha = .05$

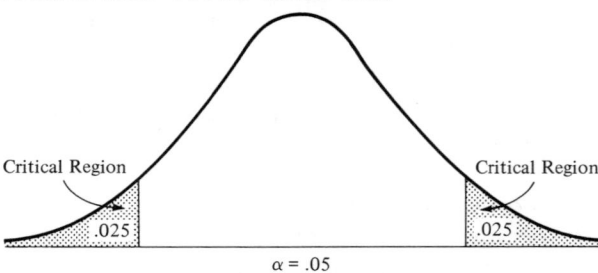

FIGURE 13.3. A Two-Tailed Test

it can be rejected or retained. If it is true and is rejected nonetheless, the decision is in error. The error is the rejection of a true hypothesis—a type I error. If the null hypothesis is false but is retained, the error committed is the acceptance of a false hypothesis; this error is designated as a type II error. The four alternatives are presented schematically in Table 13.3.

The probability of rejecting a true hypothesis—a type I error—is equivalent to the level of significance. Thus, in the long run, an investigator employing the .05 level of significance will falsely reject 5 percent of the true hypotheses he or she tests. Naturally, one would be interested in minimizing the error of rejecting a true hypothesis by making the level of significance as low as possible. However, type I errors and type II errors are inversely related. Thus, a decrease in the error of rejecting a true hypothesis leads to an increase in the probability of retaining a false one. Under these conditions, the selection of α is determined by (1) the type of problem one is investigating, and (2) the consequences of rejecting a true hypothesis or retaining a false one. If, for example, the subject of investigation is the effect of an experimental teaching method on the achievement of disadvantaged children, where the results of the study will determine the employment of the method throughout the school system, the researcher should carefully consider the consequences of making a mistake. Suppose the null hypothesis states that the new teaching method has negative effects. If it were to be rejected when it is actually true, the consequences could be very severe; hundreds of thousands of disadvantaged children would be harmed. If, on the other hand, it is not rejected when it is actually false, the employment of the new method will be postponed until further evidence is available. Therefore, in this case it would be preferable to minimize α, since the implications of rejecting a true hypothesis are more severe than those of retaining a false one.

When a study does not have practical implications, the selection of α will be arbitrary, but the choice will usually be governed by accepted conventions. The significance levels commonly used in the social sciences are .001, .01, and .05.

PARAMETRIC AND NONPARAMETRIC TESTS

In the following sections, we shall discuss several specific tests that are most common in social science research. The tests are divided into two major groups: parametric tests and nonparametric tests. The employment of parametric tests is based on two major assumptions: (1) the population is normally distributed, and (2) the variables are measured on an interval scale. When normality cannot be assumed or when an interval scale cannot be used, the second group of tests is ordinarily applied. Such tests are referred to as nonparametric tests, since they do not require assumptions about the parameters of the population from which the sample is drawn.

In practice, one need not go through the laborious procedure of constructing a sampling distribution. In many instances, sampling distributions have been constructed by previous researchers and are known in advance. Moreover, there are distributions that can be used as approximations of certain sampling distributions. For example, the sampling distribution of the mean closely approximates the normal curve distribution, which can therefore be used in testing hypotheses about means.

In the discussion of specific tests that follows, reference will be made to existing sampling distributions that have been constructed in advance or that approximate the desired distribution. The sampling distributions that are employed in this section are provided in the Appendix, in Tables 2 through 6.

Parametric Tests

Difference between means. Many hypotheses in empirical research involve a comparison between populations. For example, to assess the relationship between social class and voting, one could compare different social classes with respect to voting patterns. Similarly, in comparing Jews and Mexican-Americans with respect to achievement, one is relating ethnic affiliation to achievement.

When the dependent variable being investigated is measured on an interval scale, a comparison of means can be used to reflect the amount of relationship between two variables (see Chapter 10). To assess the significance of a difference between means, the difference-between-means test is used.

TABLE 13.3. Alternative Decisions in Hypothesis-Testing

Decision	Hypothesis Is True	Hypothesis Is False
Reject hypothesis	Type I error	No error
Accept hypothesis	No error	Type II error

TABLE 13.4. Mean Scores of Mental Health Scale of Receiving Ward Patients and College Students

	Receiving Ward Patients	College Students
n	101.00	126.00
$\overline{X}$	6.10	3.60
s	4.52	3.04

SOURCE: Jerome G. Manis et al. "Validating a Mental Health Scale." *American Sociological Review* 28 (1963):108–116.

To illustrate the testing of hypotheses about the difference between means, let us center around a concrete problem for which data are presented in Table 13.4, showing the mental health test scores of two samples. One is of hospitalized mental patients, and the other is of supposedly mentally healthy college students. The investigation was designed to evaluate the validity of a mental health scale. The assumption that the scale accurately measures mental health would lead to the research hypothesis that on a mental health scale, mental patients have a higher score* than do college students; that is, $H_1: \mu_1 > \mu_2$, where μ_1 is the mean score of the population of mental patients and μ_2 the mean of college students. The null hypothesis could state that there is no difference in the mean score of the two populations; that is, $H_0: \mu_1 - \mu_2 = 0$.

Inspection of the data reveals a difference between the two sample means of 2.50 (6.10–3.60). Although this difference is in the expected direction, its probability of occurrence under the assumption of the null hypothesis has to be determined. If such a difference is unlikely to occur, assuming that the population means are identical, we shall reject the null hypothesis.

The selection of the appropriate sampling distribution for testing the difference between means depends on the sample size. When each sample is larger than 30 ($n > 30$), the sampling distribution of the difference between means approaches normality, and, thus, the normal curve (Appendix, Table 2) can be used as the statistical model. The procedure is similar to the one employed in estimating population means (see Chapter 12). One can translate the difference between the means to standard Z scores and then determine its probability of occurrence according to the normal curve distribution. For a two-tailed test, using the .05 level of significance, the critical region expressed in Z scores includes all the positive scores of 1.96 and above or all the negative scores of −1.96 and below, whose likelihood of occurrence is .025. For a one-tailed test, the critical region contains all scores of 1.65 and above

---
* A high score on the scale reflects mental illness.

or -1.65 and below. Similarly, for the .01 level of significance, Z is ± 2.58 and ± 2.33, respectively.

To test the null hypothesis on the mental health test scores, we can select a right-tail test because H_1 is a directional hypothesis implying large values. The level of significance selected will be .01; any value larger than 2.33 will lead to the rejection of the null hypothesis.

To determine the significance of the difference between the means using the normal curve, the difference is converted to standard scores. This can be accomplished using a test statistic denoted as t, which is defined in Formula (13.1):

$$t = \frac{(\overline{X}_1 - \overline{X}_2) - (\mu_1 - \mu_2)}{\hat{\sigma}\bar{x}_1 - \bar{x}_2} \qquad (13.1)$$

where $\overline{X}_1 - \overline{X}_2$ = difference between the sample means

$\mu_1 - \mu_2$ = the mean of the sampling distribution of the difference between means

$\hat{\sigma}\bar{x}_1 - \bar{x}_2$ = an estimate of the standard error* of the sampling distribution of the difference between means

t, like Z, measures deviations from the mean in terms of standard deviation units; $\overline{X}_1 - \overline{X}_2$ replaces X, $\mu_1 - \mu_2$ replaces $\overline{X}$, and $\hat{\sigma}\bar{x}_1 - \bar{x}_2$ replaces s. Z, however, cannot be calculated when the variances of the two populations (σ_1^2 and σ_2^2) are unknown. That is, t substitutes for Z whenever sample variances (s_1^2 and s_2^2) are used as estimates of the populations' parameters. Because the populations' variances are almost never available, for all practical purposes, the t statistic is used to transform mean differences to standard scores. t is normally distributed when $n > 30$; thus, the normal distribution can be employed whenever each sample size is >30. However, when $n \leq 30$, the normal approximation is not appropriate and the sampling distribution of t has to be used.

The estimate of the standard error ($\hat{\sigma}\bar{x}_1 - \bar{x}_2$) can be obtained by two methods. The first assumes that the two population variances are equal—for instance, $\sigma_1^2 = \sigma_2^2$—and, thus, the variances of the two samples are combined into a single estimate of σ_1^2 or σ_2^2. The standard error under these conditions is as follows:

$$\hat{\sigma}\bar{x}_1 - \bar{x}_2 = \sqrt{\frac{n_1 s_1^2 + n_2 s_2^2}{n_1 + n_2 - 2}} \sqrt{\frac{n_1 + n_2}{n_1 n_2}} \qquad (13.2)$$

where n_1 and n_2 are sample sizes of sample 1 and sample 2, respectively, and s_1^2 and s_2^2 are variances of sample 1 and sample 2.

---

* The standard error is the standard deviation of the sampling distribution; see Chapter 12 for an extensive representation of this concept.

When there is no basis for assuming that the population variances are identical, it is not possible to pool the sample variance. In this instance, the estimation for the two variances is separate, and the obtained formula for the standard error is

$$\hat{\sigma}\bar{x}_1 - \bar{x}_2 = \sqrt{\frac{s_1^2}{n_1 - 1} + \frac{s_2^2}{n_2 - 1}} \tag{13.3}$$

To calculate t for the data summarized in Table 13.4, we assume that $\sigma_1^2 = \sigma_2^2$ and estimate the pooled estimate of the standard error:

$$\hat{\sigma}\bar{x}_1 - \bar{x}_2 = \sqrt{\frac{(101)(4.52)^2 + 126(3.04)^2}{101 + 126 - 2}} \sqrt{\frac{101 + 126}{(101)(126)}} = .50$$

Since under the null hypothesis it has been assumed that $\mu_1 = \mu_2$, the definition of t reduces to

$$t = \frac{\overline{X}_1 - \overline{X}_2}{\hat{\sigma}\bar{x}_1 - \bar{x}_2} \tag{13.4}$$

We obtain the following result for our example:

$$t = \frac{6.1 - 3.6}{.50} = \frac{2.5}{.50} = 5$$

Referring to the normal curve table (Appendix, Table 2), we observe that the value of t is in fact greater than the value needed for rejection (2.33) at the .01 level of significance. In other words, the difference between the sample mean of mental patients and that of college students is not likely to be due to sampling error. Accordingly, we reject H_0 and conclude that the difference between the samples reflects different degrees of mental health, and that the measuring scale is therefore valid.

When either or both of the sample sizes are less than 30, the normal curve does not approximate the sampling distribution of the difference between means. As a result, using the normal curve to determine the probability of H_0 will yield inaccurate results, and the sampling distribution of t has to be utilized instead. t is actually a family of curves, each determined by the sample size. Thus, for a sample size of 7, t has a different distribution than for a sample size of 10. The sampling distribution of t is reproduced in the Appendix, Table 3. The values in this table are given in terms of the significance level (one tail and two tails) and the degrees of freedom (df).

The concept of degrees of freedom is a basic one and will be used in other statistical tests. It refers to the number of free choices one can make in repeated random samples that constitute sampling distributions. If, for example, one is allowed to pick two numbers freely, there are two degrees of freedom. If, on the other hand, the two numbers must sum to 20, there is only one free choice or one degree of freedom, since after the first number has been freely chosen, the second number is determined by the sum total. The number of degrees of freedom of the t distribution is limited by the fact that for each sample, the population variance has to be estimated, and there are only $n - 1$ quantities that are free to vary. The number of degrees of freedom is then equal to $n - 1$ for each sample. Thus, to test a hypothesis about difference between two samples, df is equivalent to $(n_1 - 1) + (n_2 - 1) = n_1 + n_2 - 2$.

To illustrate the use of the t table, we shall test the hypothesis that achievement is associated with assignment to tracks in a secondary school. The data are summarized in Table 13.5. The investigators hypothesized that achievement and track assignment were related so that a type A program (college preparatory) had more students that were high achievers than did a type B program (noncollege). The null hypothesis to be tested is that the mean achievements of the two populations are identical, whereas the research hypothesis states that the mean achievement of type A is larger than that of type B.

$$H_0: \mu_A = \mu_B$$
$$H_1: \mu_A > \mu_B$$

We can proceed with the same procedure in calculating the standard error and the t ratio, using Equations (13.2) and (13.4):

$$\hat{\sigma}\bar{x}_1 - \bar{x}_2 = \sqrt{\frac{13(23.6)^2 + 6(12.2)^2}{13 + 6 - 2}} \sqrt{\frac{13 + 6}{(13)(6)}} = 10.8$$

$$t = \frac{48.3 - 20.5}{10.8} = \frac{27.8}{10.8} = 2.574$$

The obtained t can now be compared with the appropriate value in the sampling distribution of t. The number of degrees of freedom for sample sizes of 13 and 6 is 17 $(13 + 6 - 2)$. At the .01 level of significance with a one-tailed test (right tail), the t for which H_0 will be rejected is 2.567. A t larger than 2.567 is unlikely to occur if H_0 is true. Since 2.574 is larger than 2.567, the null hypothesis is rejected, and the investigator can conclude that the difference in achievement between the two tracks is statistically significant.

TABLE 13.5. Tracking and Achievement

	Type A	Type B
n	13.0	6.0
$\bar{X}$	48.3	20.5
s	23.6	12.2

A Significance test for Pearson's r. The correlation coefficient Pearson's r—like $\overline{X}$, Md, or b—is a statistic obtained from sample data; as such, it is just an estimate of a population parameter. Pearson's r corresponds to the population correlation denoted as ρ or rho. As a sample statistic, r is subject to sampling fluctuations; the test of its statistical significance is an assessment of the likelihood that the obtained correlation is due to sampling error. For example, a researcher may test the hypothesis that liberalism is correlated with income and draw a random sample of 24, obtaining an r of .30. It is probable that in the population these two variables are not correlated at all, and that the obtained coefficient is a result of chance factors. In other words, is an r of .30 large enough to make the hypothesis of no relation unlikely?

The strategy of testing such a hypothesis is similar to that used in the difference-of-means test; the null hypothesis states that the correlation in the population is zero, and the research hypothesis that it is different from zero:

$$H_0: \rho = 0$$
$$H_1: \rho \neq 0$$

When ρ is assumed to be zero under the null hypothesis, the statistical significance of r can be tested using the normal curve of the t distribution. When n is larger than 50, the sampling distribution of r is approximated by the normal curve, with a mean of zero and a standard error defined as:

$$\sigma_r = \frac{1}{\sqrt{n-1}} \tag{13.5}$$

The standard score Z is obtained by subtracting from r the mean of the sampling distribution (0) and dividing by the standard error. The definition of Z is given by Equation (13.6):

$$Z = r \Big/ \frac{1}{\sqrt{n-1}} = r\sqrt{n-1} \tag{13.6}$$

As an example, suppose that a sample of 101 observations produced a correlation of $r = .50$ between social class and delinquency. To reject the null hypothesis at the .05 level of significance, Z must be smaller than -1.96 or larger than 1.96 ($-1.96 > Z > 1.96$). Since

$$Z = .50\sqrt{101 - 1} = 5$$

the null hypothesis of no correlation is rejected, and the relationship between social class and delinquency is said to be significant. If n is less than 50, the significance of r can be tested using the t distribution with $n - 2$ degrees of freedom,* where t is defined as:

$$t = \frac{r\sqrt{n-2}}{\sqrt{1-r^2}} \qquad (13.7)$$

To illustrate the use of t in testing the significance of Pearson's r, let us suppose that a correlation of .30 between income and political participation is obtained from a sample of $n = 24$ ($df = 2$). t is equal to:

$$t = \frac{.30\sqrt{22}}{\sqrt{1-.30^2}} = 1.475$$

From the distribution of t in Table 3 (Appendix), we see that at the .05 level of significance for a two-tailed test and with 22 df, the value of t required to reject the null hypothesis is 2.074. Since the obtained t is smaller than this value, the null hypothesis cannot be rejected, and the relationship between income and political participation is said to be not significant.

When ρ is different from zero, the sampling distribution of r is skewed, and the normal curve or t approximations cannot be used. In that case, a different procedure is employed; it is applicable to high and low r's and can be used with large or small samples. With this procedure (developed by R. A. Fisher), r is transformed into another statistic, Fisher's z,† having a distribution that is approximately normal for all sample sizes and all values of ρ. z is related to r by the following formula:

$$z = 1.151 \log_{10} \frac{1+r}{1-r} \qquad (13.8)$$

The standard error of Fisher's z is equal to:

$$\sigma_z = \frac{1}{\sqrt{n-3}} \qquad (13.9)$$

The transformation of r to Fisher's z or vice versa can be made by reference to Table 4 (Appendix). The table is entered with values of r and their corresponding z's. For example, if $r = .85$, $z = 1.256$; for $z = 2.185$, $r = .975$. The transformed r's can now be used to construct a standard Z score by the following expression:

$$\frac{z_r - z_\rho}{\sigma_z} \qquad (13.10)$$

---

* The significance of r is also a test of the significance of the regression coefficient, which is zero when r is zero. The regression involves two constants, a and b; therefore, 2 degrees of freedom are lost in determining the line.

† Fisher's z has no connection with the standard score Z used with the normal curve.

where z_r = Fisher's z for r

z_ρ = Fisher's z for ρ

σ_z = standard error of Fisher's z

As an example, let us test the null hypothesis that the correlation between occupational aspiration and occupational attainment is $\rho = .70$, against the alternative research hypothesis that $\rho > .70$. A sample of 252 cases drawn at random gives a correlation of $r = .81$. The hypothesis is tested with the .05 level of significance and is right-tailed. From Table 4 (Appendix), we find that for $r = .81$, $z = 1.127$. Similarly, ρ of .70 is equivalent to a z of .867. The standard error of z is:

$$\sigma_z = \frac{1}{\sqrt{249}} = .063$$

The standard Z score is then:

$$\frac{1.127 - .867}{.063} = \frac{.260}{.063} = 4.127$$

To reject the null hypothesis at the .05 level with a one-tailed test, a standard score of at least 1.65 is required. Since the obtained standard Z score is larger than this value, the null hypothesis is rejected.

Nonparametric Tests

The Mann-Whitney runs test. The Mann-Whitney runs test is applicable whenever we wish to test the null hypothesis that two samples have been drawn from the same population against the alternative research hypothesis that the populations differ from each other (Siegel, 1956). The only assumptions required in making the runs test are that the two samples are independently and randomly drawn, and that the level of measurement of the variables under investigation is at least ordinal.

Suppose we have sampled 13 blacks ($n_1 = 13$) and 14 whites ($n_2 = 14$) and have given each one a score reflecting their level of alienation:

Black sample: 5, 7, 10, 13, 19, 24, 25, 28, 30, 32, 33, 36, 37

White sample: 1, 3, 4, 6, 9, 12, 14, 15, 17, 18, 20, 21, 22, 23

Assuming that the population of whites is identical to the population of blacks with respect to level of alienation, it is expected that the values in the two samples will be similar. If the values have similar magnitudes, blacks will have larger alienation scores in approximately one-half of the black-white pairs; in the rest of the pairs, the whites' scores will exceed the blacks'. We can count the number of pairs in which the scores of blacks exceed the scores of whites, and designate it as U; the number of pairs for which the opposite is true is designated U'. If the null hypothesis of identical populations were true, we would expect U and U' to be approximately equal (Mueller, Schuessler, and Costner, 1970).

To determine U, we can use the following equation:

$$U = n_1 n_2 + \frac{n_2(n_2 + 1)}{2} - R_2 \qquad (13.11)$$

where n_1 = sample size of sample 1

n_2 = sample size of sample 2

R_2 = the sum of ranks for sample 2

The ranks are obtained by arranging all the scores in order of magnitude. For instance, the first three whites (1, 3, 4) head the scale, with number 4 being the first black (score 5). Thus, the ranks for blacks are 4, 6, 8, 10, 15, 20, 21, 22, 23, 24, 25, 26, 27, and the ranks for whites are 1, 2, 3, 5, 7, 9, 11, 12, 13, 14, 16, 17, 18, 19. To determine U', we subtract U from the total number of pairs

$$U' = n_1 n_2 - U \qquad (13.12)$$

For our data,

$$U = (13)(14) + \frac{14(14 + 1)}{2} - 147 = 140$$

$$U' = (13)(14) - 140 = 182 - 140 = 42$$

To evaluate the significance of H_0, we compare the smaller of the two values U or U' with the significant values of the sampling distribution of U in Table 5 in the Appendix.* At the .05 level, we need a U of 50 or smaller when direction is not predicted, or 56 or smaller when direction is predicted. In either case, the obtained value (42) is smaller and enables us to reject the null hypothesis.

The sampling distribution of U approaches normality when the samples' size increases. When either of the samples is larger than 20, we can compute standard scores and use the normal distribution. The mean of the sampling distribution would then be:

$$\mu_U = \frac{n_1 n_2}{2}$$

and the standard error would be:

$$\sigma_U = \frac{\sqrt{n_1 n_2 (n_1 + n_2 + 1)}}{12}$$

* For situations in which one of the samples is smaller than 9, another table of probabilities is used.

Z is obtained using the following formula:

$$Z = \frac{U - n_1 n_2/2}{\sqrt{n_1 n_2 (n_1 + n_2 + 1)/12}} \qquad (13.13)$$

The Chi-square test (χ^2). This section discusses a general test designed to evaluate whether the difference between observed frequencies and expected frequencies under the null hypothesis can be attributed to sampling fluctuations or to nonchance factors. The statistic used for this purpose is Chi square (χ^2), defined by:

$$\chi^2 = \sum \frac{(f_o - f_e)^2}{f_e} \qquad (13.14)$$

where f_o = observed frequency

f_e = expected frequency

The Chi-square test is frequently applied to problems in which two nominal variables are cross-classified. In Chapter 10, it was seen that in analyzing bivariate tables, the most common question asked by the investigator is whether there are differences between the univariate distributions. The Chi-square test evaluates whether these differences are large enough to warrant the conclusion that the null hypothesis is false and can be rejected in favor of an alternative stating that there *is* a relationship between the two variables. The data summarized in Table 13.6 are an example of a research problem to which the Chi-square test is applicable.

The variables cross-tabulated are religious affiliations of both husband and wife. The data were designed to study the effects of religious rules on an individual's marital choice. When the frequencies are converted to percentages (in parentheses), it is observed that whereas 93 percent of the Catholic wives married Catholic husbands, only 24 percent of the Protestant wives, and none of the Jewish wives, had a Catholic husband. We want to examine whether such differences can be

TABLE 13.6. Religious Affiliation of Husband and Wife

	Wife			
Husband	*Catholic*	*Protestant*	*Jewish*	*Total*
Catholic	(93%) 271	(24%) 20	0	291
Protestant	(6%) 17	(74%) 61	0	78
Jewish	1	(2%) 1	(100%) 66	68
Total	289	82	66	437

SOURCE: August B. Hollingshead. "Cultural Factors in the Selection of Marriage Mates." *American Sociological Review* 15(1950):619–627.

explained by chance factors or whether religious affiliation does influence the selection of marriage mates, as the research hypothesis suggests.

The null hypothesis implies that there is no difference among the three groups of wives in their pattern of mate selection. That is, we would expect Catholic, Protestant, or Jewish wives to have the same proportion of Catholic, Protestant, or Jewish husbands. We can compute the expected frequencies and then compare them with the observed ones. If the differences are small, χ^2 will be small. The greater the differences between the observed frequencies and those expected under the null hypothesis, the larger will be the value of χ^2. If the differences are so large as to occur only rarely (5 percent or 1 percent of the time) were the null hypothesis true, the null hypothesis is rejected.

To compute the expected frequencies for any cell, the following formula is used:

$$f_e = \frac{(\text{row total})(\text{column total})}{n} \qquad (13.15)$$

For Table 13.6, the expected frequency for the Catholic-Catholic pair is equal to

$$\frac{(289)(291)}{437} = 192$$

Table 13.7 is the reconstructed table containing frequencies we would expect if religious affiliation had no effect on mate selection.

To compute χ^2, the expected frequencies of each cell are subtracted from the observed frequencies, squared, divided by the expected frequency of the cell, and then summed for all cells. The calculations for Table 13.6 are summarized in Table 13.8. Note that χ^2 would have been zero if the observed frequencies were identical with the expected frequencies. That is, the larger the difference between what is observed and what would be expected were the hypothesis of no relations true, the larger will be the value of χ^2.

TABLE 13.7. Religious Affiliation of Husband and Wife: Expected Frequencies

| Husband | Wife | | | |
	Catholic	Protestant	Jewish	Total
Catholic	192	55	44	291
Protestant	52	14	12	78
Jewish	45	13	10	68
Total	289	82	66	437

TABLE 13.8. Calculation of χ^2 for Data of Table 13.6

f_o	f_e	$f_o - f_e$	$(f_o - f_e)^2$	$\dfrac{(f_o - f_e)^2}{f_e}$
271	192	79	6241	32.5
17	52	−35	1225	23.5
1	45	−44	1936	43.0
20	55	−35	1225	22.3
61	14	47	2209	157.8
1	13	−12	144	11.1
0	44	−44	1936	44.0
0	12	−12	144	12.0
66	10	56	3136	313.6
				$\chi^2 = 659.8$

To evaluate the χ^2 statistic obtained, we need to compare it to the sampling distribution of χ^2, and to observe whether the value of 659.8 is large enough and thus unlikely if the null hypothesis is true. The sampling distribution of χ^2 is reproduced in Table 6 in the Appendix. There are two factors that determine the distribution: (1) the level of significance (α), and (2) the number of degrees of freedom. Thus, χ^2 is really a family of curves, each determined by different parameters. We shall select for this problem a level of significance of .01, which means that only if we obtain a χ^2 larger than what we would expect to find in no more than 1 out of 100 of our samples will the null hypothesis be rejected.

The number of degrees of freedom of the χ^2 sampling distribution is set by the number of cells for which expected frequencies can be selected freely. For any bivariate table, the cells that can be determined arbitrarily are limited by the marginal total of both variables. Thus, in a table of 2 × 2, for instance, there is only one cell that is free to vary, the three others being predetermined by the marginal total. Generally, we can compute the number of degrees of freedom using the following formula:

$$df = (r - 1)(c - 1) \tag{13.16}$$

where r = number of rows

c = number of columns

Thus,

in a 2 × 2 table, $df = (2 - 1)(2 - 1) = 1$
in a 3 × 3 table, $df = (3 - 1)(3 - 1) = 4$
in a 4 × 3 table, $df = (4 - 1)(3 - 1) = 6$

The probabilities under H_0 are given at the top of each column in Table 6 (Appendix), and the row entries indicate the number of degrees of freedom. The probabilities are the appropriate ones for a right-tailed test; even though the research hypothesis did not imply a specific direction, we are usually interested in the upper tail of the distribution, since, regardless of the direction, a relationship means that we would obtain a Chi-square value larger than would be expected by chance.

For our example, with 4 df and .01 level of significance, the entry is 13.277, indicating that a value of 13.277 will occur in only 1 percent of the samples. Our obtained sample result of 659.8 is much larger than that and is obviously very unlikely under the null hypothesis. In fact, even higher levels of significance—of .001, for example ($\chi^2 = 18.465$)—will enable the rejection of the null hypothesis with no difficulties at all.

THE TEST OF SIGNIFICANCE CONTROVERSY

In the last decade, social scientists have engaged in a debate over the uses and misuses of statistical tests of significance. The controversy has centered around several specific issues. In this section, we briefly outline three major ones: the problem of sampling, the confusion between substantive and statistical significance, and the criteria for selecting a level of significance.*

The first issue raises two fundamental questions: First, can significance tests be applied to nonprobability samples? Second, is there any meaning to these tests when the unit of analysis is a universe (population) rather than a sample? It is recalled that statistical tests of significance enable the researcher to infer about population characteristics on the basis of evidence obtained from a sample. The sample statistic is compared with a theoretical model—a sampling distribution—to evaluate its likelihood of occurrence under specified conditions. The controversy regarding sampling has evolved around the legitimacy of applying tests of significance to nonprobability samples. Those who oppose the application of the tests under these conditions maintain that only when probability samples are drawn from a specified population can a sample statistic be compared with a sampling distribution to assess its likelihood of occurrence under the conditions specified by the null hypothesis. Since the assumption of random sampling is not often met in social research, it is argued that in most cases, tests of significance are inappropriately used (Camilleri, 1962; McGinnis, 1958; Morrison and Henkel, 1969). Advocates of statistical tests, on the other hand, argue that even when samples cannot be assumed to be random, the tests are a

---

* For a comprehensive documentation of these and other aspects of the controversy, see Denton E. Morrison and Ramon E. Henkel, eds., *The Significance Test Controversy* (Chicago: Aldine, 1970).

useful device given that any set of data is subject to measurement error and this error can be assumed to be random. Furthermore, it can be assumed that nonrandom samples have been drawn from a hypothetical population that includes all possible samples that could have been drawn under equivalent circumstances. Finally, even when tests of significance are not being used as a device enabling generalizations to a population, they are useful in providing a screen for results that are worth further exploration (Gold, 1969).

A related question is the applicability of tests of significance in studies employing the whole universe. A typical case is the selection of one unit, for example, a precinct or a school, and including in the study all the cases in that unit. Obviously, the attempt to generalize to the population by using statistical tests is inappropriate since the whole population is already included. However, it is often claimed that the unit can be conceived of as a subuniverse (Galtung, 1967). That is, an attempt is being made to generalize the findings to other units of the same kind, for example, other precincts or other schools. The main criticism lodged at such an approach is that unless other units to which inferences are being made can be assumed to be homogeneous with the researched universe, generalizations on the basis of statistical significance are inappropriate.

The issue of statistical versus substantive significance derives from a confusion between two independent concepts: statistical significance and theoretical significance. Findings may show statistical significance without confirming substantive hypotheses, or they may have a substantive meaning without being statistically significant. Although substantive and statistical significance may coincide, a problem of interpretation arises when they do not. The error of confusing the two is committed when a relatively weak relationship between a number of variables is given a theoretical interpretation because it is statistically significant, or when relationships of considerable magnitude and of theoretical importance are rejected for lack of statistical significance (Selvin, 1957). Since statistical significance can be a function of sample size as well as of random fluctuations, this approach may lead to the rejection of what is theoretically interesting and to the elaboration of the trivial (Galtung, 1967). Investigators who use statistical tests to test substantive hypotheses too often have accepted weak associations just because they were found to be statistically significant. Consequently, complex interpretations and theorizing were based on rather small, but statistically significant differences.

The view that statistical tests of significance can be utilized to assess substantive significance holds that statistical tests provide a method by which investigators can screen substantive findings. Gold (1969:43) maintains:

A meaningful and useful interpretation can be given to a test of significance applied to any set of data. . . . A test of significance can be viewed as an attempt to fit observed data to a model. The model is that of a random process which, for a given set of data, can generate a sampling distribution of a statistic whose characteristics are known. A decision about the substantive significance or importance, not statistical significance, of an observed relationship can be made on the basis of the degree to which the model provides a good fit. In the absence of other explicit criteria, the degree of fit can be taken as an explicit minimum criterion which any relationship taken to be important must meet and which is superior to subjective variable judgments of importance.

Gold and others who have taken the same stance (Davis, 1958; Blalock, 1960) claim that tests of significance can be used as a necessary (but not sufficient) condition for substantive significance. In other words, relationships that are too weak to be statistically significant should not be considered worthy of further investigation. This view has been criticized as fostering an atheoretical view of the social sciences. That is, it promotes a false notion of what should be considered a sufficient basis for substantive significance by putting variables in a quantitative competition rather than in a competition based on theory (Morrison and Henkel, 1969).

Adherence to a statistical rather than a theoretical criterion in evaluating empirical results leads to another problem that is the third issue in the significance-test controversy. This is the issue of selecting a level of significance. As was pointed out in previous sections, most researchers select the .05, .01, or .001 levels of significance in assessing their research results. These levels are conventionally selected usually regardless of the type of problem under investigation (Skipper, Guenther, and Nass, 1967). Employing a conventional level of significance does have certain advantages of avoiding ambiguity and of providing a consistent criterion for evaluating research findings. That is, findings can be easily compared with regard to their statistical significance. However, the disadvantages of arbitrarily adhering to a given level of significance might outweigh the advantages. By indiscriminately selecting significance levels as cutting points between either rejecting the null hypothesis or failing to reject it, one enforces a dichotomy on a probabilistic continuum, thereby losing important nuances and often rejecting results that one supported either by the theory or by previous findings just because they fail to attain significance by a small fraction (Galtung, 1967; Morrison and Henkel, 1969).

Alternative procedures for setting and reporting levels of significance have been suggested by Galtung (1967), Skipper, Guenther, and Nass (1967), and Labovitz (1968). It is argued that the choice of a level of significance can be decided upon rationally only when the cost of the decision can be evaluated in advance. Since in the social sciences the cardinal decision has to do with whether to publish the findings, researchers should report the obtained level of significance rather than choosing an arbitrary level (Skipper, Guenther, and Nass, 1967). Labovitz (1968) has suggested several criteria to consider when choosing a significance level. First, the selection should be dictated either by the practical consequences of rejection or relative to a body of knowledge and to theory. For example, when the practical consequences of committing a type I error are serious, it is advisable to select a small level of significance. Similarly, findings that have no theoretical or empirical support would be assessed on the basis of a small level of rejection, so as to avoid a hasty rejection of the null hypothesis.

The sample size is another criterion in selecting a level of significance. With large samples, variables that are only slightly correlated will be statistically significant. For example, in a sample of 1,000 cases or more, a correlation of .10 is significant at the .01 level. However, such a relationship is of little substantive meaning. Therefore, it is generally advisable to select a small level of significance with large samples but not with small samples where large differences may not be statistically significant.

The controversy over tests of significance demonstrates more than anything else that the application of the tests in empirical research cannot be a matter of routine. Problems arise both with regard to the method of application and in the interpretation given to the findings. There are many situations in which samples are not random or include all members of the population. Moreover, in survey research, random samples are often accompanied by a high refusal rate leading to various sources of error. Under these circumstances, the application of significance tests can be misleading. Caution should be taken also in the interpretation of relationships that prove to be statistically significant. Tests of significance are relatively insensitive to the strength of association between variables, especially in large samples. Thus, substantive interpretations should be given in terms of the size of association, and interpretations regarding generalizations are to be expressed in terms of levels of significance.

SUMMARY

Statistical inference refers to a procedure that allows the investigator to decide between two hypotheses about a population parameter on the basis of a sample result. The hypothesis to be tested is referred to as the null hypothesis and usually states that two or more populations are identical or that variables are not related. Its alternative, the research hypothesis, is generally derived from a theory and expresses, in statistical terms, a substantive hypothesis. It may be nonspecific, in which case the hypothesis to be tested is nondirectional and two-tailed; or it may express a direction, resulting in a one-tailed test. The test of significance is actually a comparison between the sample statistic and the population parameter defined by the null hypothesis. The null hypothesis also specifies the sampling distribution, which permits an estimate of the probability of obtaining the sample result if H_0 were true. This probability is the level of significance or the probability of rejecting a true hypothesis (type I error). When the likelihood of obtaining the sample result is very small, under the assumptions of the null hypothesis, H_0 is rejected and the rejection adds to our confidence in the research hypothesis.

Hypotheses can be tested on nominal, ordinal, or interval variables. The Chi-square test was suggested as an applicable test for nominal variables. It evaluates the difference between observed frequencies and expected ones. The Mann-Whitney runs test was suggested for ordinal data. Finally, difference between means employing the normal and t distributions and the significance of Pearson's r are appropriate for interval variables.

REFERENCES

Blalock, Hubert M. *Social Statistics*. New York: McGraw-Hill, 1960.

Camilleri, Santo F. "Theory, Probability and Induction in Social Research." *American Sociological Review* 27 (1962):170–178.

Davis, James. "Review of Robert K. Merton et al., *The Student Physician*." *American Journal of Sociology* 63 (1958):445–446.

Galtung, Johan. *Theory and Methods of Social Research*. New York: Columbia University Press, 1967.

Gold, David. "Statistical Tests and Substantive Significance." *American Sociologist* 4 (1969):42–46.

Labovitz, Sanford. "Criteria for Selecting a Significance Level: A Note on the Sacredness of .05." *American Sociologist* 3 (1968):200–222.

McGinnis, Robert. "Randomization and Inference in Sociological Research." *American Sociological Review* 23 (1958):408–414.

Morrison, Denton E., and Henkel, Ramon E. "Significance Tests Reconsidered." *American Sociologist* 4 (1969):131–140.

Mueller, John H., Schuessler, Karl F., and Costner, Herbert L. *Statistical Reasoning in Sociclogy*. Boston: Houghton Mifflin, 1970.

Selvin, Hanan C. "A Critique of Tests of Significance in Survey Research." *American Sociological Review* 22 (1957):519–527.

Siegel, Sidney. *Nonparametric Statistics for the Behavioral Sciences.* New York: McGraw-Hill, 1956.

Skipper, James K., Jr., Guenther, Anthony L., and Nass, Gilbert. "The Sacredness of .05: A Note Concerning the Uses of Statistical Levels of Significance in Social Science." *American Sociologist* 2 (1967): 16–18.

Stinchcombe, Arthur L. *Constructing Social Theories.* New York: Harcourt, Brace & World, 1968.

STUDY SUGGESTIONS

1. Select three studies of your choice that were published in major journals in your field, in which hypotheses are statistically tested.
   a. Define the research and null hypotheses that were used in the study.
   b. Indicate the sampling distribution and statistical tests that were used.
   c. Specify the significance level of the results and indicate whether the test was a one- or two-tailed test.
2. An investigator is testing the following two hypotheses: (a) the brakes on my car are safe; (b) the brakes on my car are too old to be safe. Regarding the decision on each of these hypotheses, which error (type I or type II) would have the most dangerous implications?
3. An investigator is studying the common belief that academic women have generally lower incomes than academic men, even in equivalent positions. A random sample of men is drawn with $n = 200$, a mean of \$14,000 with a standard deviation of \$1,000. For women, $n = 130$, the mean is \$10,000 and the standard deviation is \$600. Can you say that the difference between the two groups is due to factors other than chance?
4. A sample of size 40 has a mean of 12.2 and a standard deviation of 3.6. A second sample is of size 60 with a mean of 13 and a standard deviation of 3.
   a. With a two-tailed test at the .01 level of significance, test the hypothesis that the means of the two populations are equal, assuming that their variances are equal.
   b. Test the same hypothesis for samples of size 24 and 35. Compare the results.
5. Suppose an investigator examines the hypothesis that there is no difference in the degree of political participation between men and women. To test the hypothesis respondents are ranked on their degree of political participation (with 1 designating the lowest degree of participation) and later classified according to sex. The data obtained are:

Men: 1, 3, 6, 7, 8, 11, 14, 16, 17
Women: 1, 2, 4, 6, 9, 11, 12, 13, 16

Test the hypothesis at the .05 level of significance.

6. With the data of Question 1, Chapter 11, using the χ^2 test, test whether the percentage differences you observed (in both Tables 11.14 and 11.15) can be accounted for by chance.

Appendix

TABLE 1. Random numbers

10 09 73 25 33	76 52 01 35 86	34 67 35 48 76	80 95 90 91 17	39 29 27 49 45
37 54 20 48 05	64 89 47 42 96	24 80 52 40 37	20 63 61 04 02	00 82 29 16 65
08 42 26 89 53	19 64 50 93 03	23 20 90 25 60	15 95 33 47 64	35 08 03 36 06
99 01 90 25 29	09 37 67 07 15	38 31 13 11 65	88 67 67 43 97	04 43 62 76 59
12 80 79 99 70	80 15 73 61 47	64 03 26 66 53	98 95 11 68 77	12 17 17 68 33
66 06 57 47 17	34 07 27 68 50	36 69 73 61 70	65 81 33 98 85	11 19 92 91 70
31 06 01 08 05	45 57 18 24 06	35 30 34 26 14	86 79 90 74 39	23 40 30 97 32
85 26 97 76 02	02 05 16 56 92	68 66 57 48 18	73 05 38 52 47	18 62 38 85 79
63 57 33 21 35	05 32 54 70 48	90 55 35 75 48	28 46 82 87 09	83 49 12 56 24
73 79 64 57 53	03 52 96 47 78	35 80 83 42 82	60 93 52 03 44	35 27 38 84 35
98 52 01 77 67	14 90 56 86 07	22 10 94 05 58	60 97 09 34 33	50 50 07 39 98
11 80 50 54 31	39 80 82 77 32	50 72 56 82 48	29 40 52 42 01	52 77 56 78 51
83 45 29 96 34	06 28 89 80 83	13 74 67 00 78	18 47 54 06 10	68 71 17 78 17
88 68 54 02 00	86 50 75 84 01	36 76 66 79 51	90 36 47 64 93	29 60 91 10 62
99 59 46 73 48	87 51 76 49 69	91 82 60 89 28	93 78 56 13 68	23 47 83 41 13
65 48 11 76 74	17 46 85 09 50	58 04 77 69 74	73 03 95 71 86	40 21 81 65 44
80 12 43 56 35	17 72 70 80 15	45 31 82 23 74	21 11 57 82 53	14 38 55 37 63
74 35 09 98 17	77 40 27 72 14	43 23 60 02 10	45 52 16 42 37	96 28 60 26 55
69 91 62 68 03	66 25 22 91 48	36 93 68 72 03	76 62 11 39 90	94 40 05 64 18
09 89 32 05 05	14 22 56 85 14	46 42 75 67 88	96 29 77 88 22	54 38 21 45 98
91 49 91 45 23	68 47 92 76 86	46 16 28 35 54	94 75 08 99 23	37 08 92 00 48
80 33 69 45 98	26 94 03 68 58	70 29 73 41 35	53 14 03 33 40	42 05 08 23 41
44 10 48 19 49	85 15 74 79 54	32 97 92 65 75	57 60 04 08 81	22 22 20 64 13
12 55 07 37 42	11 10 00 20 40	12 86 07 46 97	96 64 48 94 39	28 70 72 58 15
63 60 64 93 29	16 50 53 44 84	40 21 95 25 63	43 65 17 70 82	07 20 73 17 90
61 19 69 04 46	26 45 74 77 74	51 92 43 37 29	65 39 45 95 93	42 58 26 05 27
15 47 44 52 66	95 27 07 99 53	59 36 78 38 48	82 39 61 01 18	33 21 15 94 66
94 55 72 85 73	67 89 75 43 87	54 62 24 44 31	91 19 04 25 92	92 92 74 59 73
42 48 11 62 13	97 34 40 87 21	16 86 84 87 67	03 07 11 20 59	25 70 14 66 70
23 52 37 83 17	73 20 88 98 37	68 93 59 14 16	26 25 22 96 63	05 52 28 25 62
04 49 35 24 94	75 24 63 38 24	45 86 25 10 25	61 96 27 93 35	65 33 71 24 72
00 54 99 76 54	64 05 18 81 59	96 11 96 38 96	54 69 28 33 91	23 28 72 95 29
35 96 31 53 07	26 89 80 93 54	33 35 13 54 62	77 97 45 00 24	90 10 33 93 33
59 80 80 83 91	45 42 72 68 42	83 60 94 97 00	13 02 12 48 92	78 56 52 01 06
46 05 88 52 36	01 39 09 22 86	77 28 14 40 77	93 91 08 36 47	70 61 74 29 41
32 17 90 05 97	87 37 92 52 41	05 56 70 70 07	86 74 31 71 57	85 39 41 18 38
69 23 46 14 06	20 11 74 52 04	15 95 66 00 00	18 74 39 24 23	97 11 89 63 38
19 56 54 14 30	01 75 87 53 79	40 41 92 15 85	66 67 43 68 06	84 96 28 52 07
45 15 51 49 38	19 47 60 72 46	43 66 79 45 43	59 04 79 00 33	20 82 66 95 41
94 86 43 19 94	36 16 81 08 51	34 88 88 15 53	01 54 03 54 56	05 01 45 11 76

SOURCE: The RAND Corporation. *A Million Random Digits with 100,000 Normal Deviates*, pp. 1–3. Reprinted with the kind permission of the publisher.

TABLE 1. Random numbers (continued)

```
98 08 62 48 26   45 24 02 84 04   44 99 90 88 96   39 09 47 34 07   35 44 13 18 80
33 18 51 62 32   41 94 15 09 49   89 43 54 85 81   88 69 54 19 94   37 54 87 30 43
80 95 10 04 06   96 38 27 07 74   20 15 12 33 87   25 01 62 52 98   94 62 46 11 71
79 75 24 91 40   71 96 12 82 96   69 86 10 25 91   74 85 22 05 39   00 38 75 95 79
18 63 33 25 37   98 14 50 65 71   31 01 02 46 74   05 45 56 14 27   00 38 75 95 79

74 02 94 39 02   77 55 73 22 70   97 79 01 71 19   52 52 75 80 21   80 81 45 17 48
54 17 84 56 11   80 99 33 71 43   05 33 51 29 69   56 12 71 92 55   36 04 09 03 24
11 66 44 98 83   52 07 98 48 27   59 38 17 15 39   09 97 33 34 40   88 46 12 33 56
48 32 47 79 28   31 24 96 47 10   02 29 53 68 70   32 30 75 75 46   15 02 00 99 94
69 07 49 41 38   87 63 79 19 76   35 58 40 44 01   10 51 82 16 15   01 84 87 69 38

09 18 82 00 97   32 82 53 95 27   04 22 08 63 04   83 38 98 73 74   64 27 85 80 44
90 04 58 54 97   51 98 15 06 54   94 93 88 19 97   91 87 07 61 50   68 47 66 46 59
73 18 95 02 07   47 67 72 52 69   62 29 06 44 64   27 12 46 70 18   41 36 18 27 60
75 76 87 64 90   20 97 18 17 49   90 42 91 22 72   95 37 50 58 71   93 82 34 31 78
54 01 64 40 56   66 28 13 10 03   00 68 22 73 98   20 71 45 32 95   07 70 61 78 13

77 51 30 38 20   78 54 24 27 85   13 66 15 88 73   04 61 89 75 53   31 22 30 84 20
19 50 23 71 74   81 33 31 05 91   40 51 00 78 93   32 60 46 04 75   94 11 90 18 40
21 81 85 93 13   81 59 41 36 28   51 21 59 02 90   28 46 66 87 95   77 76 22 07 91
51 47 46 64 99   61 61 36 22 69   50 26 39 02 12   55 78 17 65 14   83 48 34 70 55
99 55 96 83 31   00 39 75 83 91   12 60 71 76 46   48 94 97 23 06   94 54 13 74 08

77 51 30 38 20   86 83 42 99 01   68 41 48 27 74   51 90 81 39 80   72 89 35 55 07
19 50 23 71 74   69 97 92 02 88   55 21 02 97 73   74 28 77 52 51   65 34 46 74 15
21 81 85 93 13   93 27 88 17 57   05 68 67 31 56   07 08 28 50 46   31 85 33 84 52
51 47 46 64 99   68 10 72 36 21   94 04 99 13 45   42 83 60 91 91   08 00 74 54 49
99 55 96 83 31   62 53 52 41 70   69 77 71 28 30   74 81 97 81 42   43 86 07 28 34

33 71 34 80 07   93 58 47 28 69   51 92 66 47 21   58 30 32 98 22   93 17 49 39 72
85 27 48 68 93   11 30 32 92 70   28 83 43 41 37   73 51 59 04 00   71 14 84 36 43
84 13 38 96 40   44 03 55 21 66   73 85 27 00 91   61 22 26 05 61   62 32 71 84 23
56 73 21 62 34   17 39 59 61 31   10 12 39 16 22   85 49 65 75 60   81 60 41 88 80
65 13 85 68 06   87 64 88 52 61   34 31 36 58 61   45 87 52 10 69   85 64 44 72 77

38 00 10 21 76   81 71 91 17 11   71 60 29 29 37   74 21 96 40 49   65 58 44 96 98
37 40 29 63 97   01 30 47 75 86   56 27 11 00 86   47 32 46 26 05   40 03 03 74 38
97 12 54 03 48   87 08 33 14 17   21 81 53 92 50   75 23 76 20 47   15 50 12 95 78
21 82 64 11 34   47 14 33 40 72   64 63 88 59 02   49 13 90 64 41   03 85 65 45 52
73 13 54 27 42   95 71 90 90 35   85 79 47 42 96   08 78 98 81 56   64 69 11 92 02

07 63 87 79 29   03 06 11 80 72   96 20 74 41 56   23 82 19 95 38   04 71 36 69 94
60 52 88 34 41   07 95 41 98 14   59 17 52 06 95   05 53 35 21 39   61 21 20 64 55
83 59 63 56 55   06 95 89 29 83   05 12 80 97 19   77 43 35 37 83   92 30 15 04 98
10 85 06 27 46   99 59 91 05 07   13 49 90 63 19   53 07 57 18 39   06 41 01 93 62
39 82 09 89 52   43 62 26 31 47   64 42 18 08 14   43 80 00 93 51   31 02 47 31 67
```

TABLE 1. Random numbers (continued)

```
59 58 00 64 78   75 56 97 88 00   88 83 55 44 86   23 76 80 61 56   04 11 10 84 08
38 50 80 73 41   23 79 34 87 63   90 82 29 70 22   17 71 90 42 07   95 95 44 99 53
30 69 27 06 68   94 68 81 61 27   56 19 68 00 91   82 06 76 34 00   05 46 26 92 00
65 44 39 56 59   18 28 82 74 37   49 63 22 40 41   08 33 76 56 76   96 29 99 08 36
27 26 75 02 64   13 19 27 22 94   07 47 74 46 06   17 98 54 89 11   97 34 13 03 58

91 30 70 69 91   19 07 22 42 10   36 69 95 37 28   28 82 53 57 93   28 97 66 62 52
68 43 49 46 88   84 47 31 36 22   62 12 69 84 08   12 84 38 25 90   09 81 59 31 46
48 90 81 58 77   54 74 52 45 91   35 70 00 47 54   83 82 45 26 92   54 13 05 51 60
06 91 34 51 97   42 67 27 86 01   11 88 30 95 28   63 01 19 89 01   14 97 44 03 44
10 45 51 60 19   14 21 03 37 12   91 34 23 78 21   88 32 58 08 51   43 66 77 08 83

12 88 39 73 43   65 02 76 11 84   04 28 50 13 92   17 97 41 50 77   90 71 22 67 69
21 77 83 09 76   38 80 73 69 61   31 64 94 20 96   63 28 10 20 23   08 81 64 74 49
19 52 35 95 15   65 12 25 96 59   86 28 36 82 58   69 57 21 37 98   16 43 59 15 29
67 24 55 26 70   35 58 31 65 63   45 13 42 65 29   26 76 08 36 37   41 32 64 43 44

53 85 34 13 77   36 06 69 48 50   58 83 87 38 59   49 36 47 33 31   96 24 04 36 42
24 63 73 87 36   74 38 48 93 42   52 62 30 79 92   12 36 91 86 01   03 74 28 38 73
83 08 01 24 51   38 99 22 28 15   07 75 95 17 77   97 37 72 75 85   51 97 23 78 67
16 44 42 43 34   36 15 19 90 73   27 49 37 09 39   85 13 03 25 52   54 84 65 47 59
60 79 01 81 57   57 17 86 57 62   11 16 17 85 76   45 81 95 29 79   65 13 00 48 60

03 99 11 04 61   93 71 61 68 94   66 08 32 46 53   84 60 95 82 32   88 61 81 91 61
38 55 59 55 54   32 88 65 97 80   08 35 56 08 60   29 73 54 77 62   71 29 92 38 53
17 54 67 37 04   92 05 24 62 15   55 12 12 92 81   59 07 60 79 36   27 95 45 89 09
32 64 35 28 61   95 81 90 68 31   00 91 19 89 31   76 35 59 37 79   80 86 30 05 14
69 57 26 87 77   39 51 03 59 05   14 06 04 06 19   29 54 96 96 16   33 56 46 07 80

24 12 26 65 91   27 69 90 64 94   14 84 54 66 72   61 95 87 71 00   90 89 97 57 54
61 19 63 02 31   92 96 26 17 73   41 83 95 53 82   17 26 77 09 43   78 03 87 02 67
30 53 22 17 04   10 27 41 22 02   39 68 52 33 09   10 06 16 88 29   55 98 66 64 85
03 78 89 75 99   75 86 72 07 17   74 41 65 31 66   35 20 83 33 74   87 53 90 88 23
48 22 86 33 79   85 78 34 76 19   53 15 26 74 33   35 66 35 29 72   16 81 86 03 11

60 36 59 46 53   35 07 53 39 49   42 61 42 92 97   01 91 82 83 16   98 95 37 32 31
83 79 94 24 02   56 62 33 44 42   34 99 44 13 74   70 07 11 47 36   09 95 81 80 65
32 96 00 74 05   36 40 98 32 32   99 38 54 16 00   11 13 30 75 86   15 91 70 62 53
19 32 25 38 45   57 62 05 26 06   66 49 76 86 46   78 13 86 65 59   19 64 09 94 13
11 22 09 47 47   07 39 93 74 08   48 50 92 39 29   27 48 24 54 76   85 24 43 51 59

31 75 15 72 60   68 98 00 53 39   15 47 04 83 55   88 65 12 25 96   03 15 21 92 21
88 49 29 93 82   14 45 40 45 04   20 09 49 89 77   74 84 39 34 13   22 10 97 85 08
30 93 44 77 44   07 48 18 38 28   73 78 80 65 33   28 59 72 04 05   94 20 52 03 80
22 88 84 88 93   27 49 99 87 48   60 53 04 51 28   74 02 28 46 17   82 03 71 02 68
78 21 21 69 93   35 90 29 13 86   44 37 21 54 86   65 74 11 40 14   87 48 13 72 20
```

TABLE 1. Random numbers (*continued*)

```
41 84 98 45 47   46 85 05 23 26   34 67 75 83 00   74 91 06 43 45   19 32 58 15 49
46 35 23 30 49   69 24 90 34 60   45 30 50 75 21   61 31 83 18 55   14 41 37 09 51
11 08 79 62 94   14 01 33 17 92   59 74 76 72 77   76 50 33 45 13   39 66 37 75 44
52 70 10 83 37   56 50 38 73 15   16 52 06 96 76   11 65 49 98 93   02 18 16 81 61
57 27 53 68 98   81 30 44 85 85   68 65 22 73 76   92 85 25 58 66   88 44 80 35 84

20 85 77 31 56   70 28 42 43 26   79 37 59 52 20   01 15 96 32 67   10 62 24 83 91
15 63 38 49 24   90 41 59 36 14   33 52 12 66 65   55 82 34 76 41   86 22 53 17 04
92 69 44 82 97   39 90 40 21 15   59 58 94 90 67   66 82 14 15 75   49 76 70 40 37
77 61 31 90 19   88 15 20 00 80   20 55 49 14 09   96 27 74 82 57   50 81 69 76 16
38 68 83 24 86   45 13 46 35 45   59 40 47 20 59   43 94 75 16 80   43 85 25 96 93

25 16 30 18 89   70 01 41 50 21   41 29 06 73 12   71 85 71 59 57   68 97 11 14 03
65 25 10 76 29   37 23 93 32 95   05 87 00 11 19   92 78 42 63 40   18 47 76 56 22
36 81 54 36 25   18 63 73 75 09   82 44 49 90 05   04 92 17 37 01   14 70 79 39 97
64 39 71 16 92   05 32 78 21 62   20 24 78 17 59   45 19 72 53 32   83 74 52 25 67
04 51 52 56 24   95 09 66 79 46   48 46 08 55 58   15 19 11 87 82   16 93 03 33 61

83 76 16 08 73   43 25 38 41 45   60 83 32 59 83   01 29 14 13 49   20 36 80 71 26
14 38 70 63 45   80 85 40 92 79   43 52 90 63 18   38 38 47 47 61   41 19 63 74 80
51 32 19 22 46   80 08 87 70 74   88 72 25 67 36   66 16 44 94 31   66 91 93 16 78
72 47 20 00 08   80 89 01 80 02   94 81 33 19 00   54 15 58 34 36   35 35 25 41 31
05 46 65 53 06   93 12 81 84 64   74 45 79 05 61   72 84 81 18 34   79 98 26 84 16

39 52 87 24 84   82 47 42 55 93   48 54 53 52 47   18 61 91 36 74   18 61 11 92 41
81 61 61 87 11   53 34 24 42 76   75 12 21 17 24   74 62 77 37 07   58 31 91 59 97
07 58 61 61 20   82 64 12 28 20   92 90 41 31 41   32 39 21 97 63   61 19 96 79 40
90 76 70 42 35   13 57 41 72 00   69 90 26 37 42   78 46 42 25 01   18 62 79 08 72
40 18 82 81 93   29 59 38 86 27   94 97 21 15 98   62 09 53 67 87   00 44 15 89 97

34 41 48 21 57   86 88 75 50 87   19 15 20 00 23   12 30 28 07 83   32 62 46 86 91
63 43 97 53 63   44 98 91 68 22   36 02 40 09 67   76 37 84 16 05   65 96 17 34 88
67 04 90 90 70   93 39 94 55 47   94 45 87 42 84   05 04 14 98 07   20 28 83 40 60
79 49 50 41 46   52 16 29 02 86   54 15 83 42 43   46 97 83 54 82   59 36 29 59 38
91 70 43 05 52   04 73 72 10 31   75 05 19 30 29   47 66 56 43 82   99 78 29 34 78
```

TABLE 2. Areas under the normal curve

Fractional parts of the total area (10,000) under the normal curve, corresponding to distances between the mean and ordinates which are Z standard-deviation units from the mean.

Z	.00	.01	.02	.03	.04	.05	.06	.07	.08	.09
0.0	0000	0040	0080	0120	0159	0199	0239	0279	0319	0359
0.1	0398	0438	0478	0517	0557	0596	0636	0675	0714	0753
0.2	0793	0832	0871	0910	0948	0987	1026	1064	1103	1141
0.3	1179	1217	1255	1293	1331	1368	1406	1443	1480	1517
0.4	1554	1591	1628	1664	1700	1736	1772	1808	1844	1879
0.5	1915	1950	1985	2019	2054	2088	2123	2157	2190	2224
0.6	2257	2291	2324	2357	2389	2422	2454	2486	2518	2549
0.7	2580	2612	2642	2673	2704	2734	2764	2794	2823	2852
0.8	2881	2910	2939	2967	2995	3023	3051	3078	3106	3133
0.9	3159	3186	3212	3238	3264	3289	3315	3340	3365	3389
1.0	3413	3438	3461	3485	3508	3531	3554	3577	3599	3621
1.1	3643	3665	3686	3718	3729	3749	3770	3790	3810	3830
1.2	3849	3869	3888	3907	3925	3944	3962	3980	3997	4015
1.3	4032	4049	4066	4083	4099	4115	4131	4147	4162	4177
1.4	4192	4207	4222	4236	4251	4265	4279	4292	4306	4319
1.5	4332	4345	4357	4370	4382	4394	4406	4418	4430	4441
1.6	4452	4463	4474	4485	4495	4505	4515	4525	4535	4545
1.7	4554	4564	4573	4582	4591	4599	4608	4616	4625	4633
1.8	4641	4649	4656	4664	4671	4678	4686	4693	4699	4706
1.9	4713	4719	4726	4732	4738	4744	4750	4758	4762	4767
2.0	4773	4778	4783	4788	4793	4798	4803	4808	4812	4817
2.1	4821	4826	4830	4834	4838	4842	4846	4850	4854	4857
2.2	4861	4865	4868	4871	4875	4878	4881	4884	4887	4890
2.3	4893	4896	4898	4901	4904	4906	4909	4911	4913	4916
2.4	4918	4920	4922	4925	4927	4929	4931	4932	4934	4936
2.5	4938	4940	4941	4943	4945	4946	4948	4949	4951	4952
2.6	4953	4955	4956	4957	4959	4960	4961	4962	4963	4964
2.7	4965	4966	4967	4968	4969	4970	4971	4972	4973	4974
2.8	4974	4975	4976	4977	4977	4978	4979	4980	4980	4981
2.9	4981	4982	4983	4984	4984	4984	4985	4985	4986	4986
3.0	4986.5	4987	4987	4988	4988	4988	4989	4989	4989	4990
3.1	4990.0	4991	4991	4991	4992	4992	4992	4992	4993	4994
3.2	4993.129									
3.3	4995.166									
3.4	4996.631									
3.5	4997.674									

SOURCE: Harold O. Rugg, *Statistical Methods Applied to Education* (Boston: Houghton Mifflin, 1917), appendix table III, pp. 389–390. Reprinted with the kind permission of the publisher.

TABLE 2. Areas under the normal curve (*continued*)

Z	.00	.01	.02	.03	.04	.05	.06	.07	.08	.09
3.6	4998.409									
3.7	4998.922									
3.8	4999.277									
3.9	4999.519									
4.0	4999.683									
4.5	499.966									
5.0	4999.997133									

TABLE 3. Distribution of t

df	Level of significance for one-tailed test					
	.10	.05	.025	.01	.005	.0005
	Level of significance for two-tailed test					
	.20	.10	.05	.02	.01	.001
1	3.078	6.314	12.706	31.821	63.657	636.619
2	1.886	2.920	4.303	6.965	9.925	31.598
3	1.638	2.353	3.182	4.541	5.841	12.941
4	1.533	2.132	2.776	3.747	4.604	8.610
5	1.476	2.015	2.571	3.365	4.032	6.859
6	1.440	1.943	2.447	3.143	3.707	5.959
7	1.415	1.895	2.365	2.998	3.499	5.405
8	1.397	1.860	2.306	2.896	3.355	5.041
9	1.383	1.833	2.262	2.821	3.250	4.781
10	1.372	1.812	2.228	2.764	3.169	4.587
11	1.363	1.796	2.201	2.718	3.106	4.437
12	1.356	1.782	2.179	2.681	3.055	4.318
13	1.350	1.771	2.160	2.650	3.012	4.221
14	1.345	1.761	2.145	2.624	2.977	4.140
15	1.341	1.753	2.131	2.602	2.947	4.073
16	1.337	1.746	2.120	2.583	2.921	4.015
17	1.333	1.740	2.110	2.567	2.898	3.965
18	1.330	1.734	2.101	2.552	2.878	3.922
19	1.328	1.729	2.093	2.539	2.861	3.883
20	1.325	1.725	2.086	2.528	2.845	3.850
21	1.323	1.721	2.080	2.518	2.831	3.819
22	1.321	1.717	2.074	2.508	2.819	3.792
23	1.319	1.714	2.069	2.500	2.807	3.767
24	1.318	1.711	2.064	2.492	2.797	3.745
25	1.316	1.708	2.060	2.485	2.787	3.725
26	1.315	1.706	2.056	2.479	2.779	3.707
27	1.314	1.703	2.052	2.473	2.771	3.690
28	1.313	1.701	2.048	2.467	2.763	3.674
29	1.311	1.699	2.045	2.462	2.756	3.659
30	1.310	1.697	2.042	2.457	2.750	3.646
40	1.303	1.684	2.021	2.423	2.704	3.551
60	1.296	1.671	2.000	2.390	2.660	3.460
120	1.289	1.658	1.980	2.358	2.617	3.373
∞	1.282	1.645	1.960	2.326	2.576	3.291

TABLE 4. Values of z for given values of r

r	.000	.001	.002	.003	.004	.005	.006	.007	.008	.009
.000	.0000	.0010	.0020	.0030	.0040	.0050	.0060	.0070	.0080	.0090
.010	.0100	.0110	.0120	.0130	.0140	.0150	.0160	.0170	.0180	.0190
.020	.0200	.0210	.0220	.0230	.0240	.0250	.0260	.0270	.0280	.0290
.030	.0300	.0310	.0320	.0330	.0340	.0350	.0360	.0370	.0380	.0390
.040	.0400	.0410	.0420	.0430	.0440	.0450	.0460	.0470	.0480	.0490
.050	.0501	.0511	.0521	.0531	.0541	.0551	.0561	.0571	.0581	.0591
.060	.0601	.0611	.0621	.0631	.0641	.0651	.0661	.0671	.0681	.0691
.070	.0701	.0711	.0721	.0731	.0741	.0751	.0761	.0771	.0782	.0792
.080	.0802	.0812	.0822	.0832	.0842	.0852	.0862	.0872	.0882	.0892
.090	.0902	.0912	.0922	.0933	.0943	.0953	.0963	.0973	.0983	.0993
.100	.1003	.1013	.1024	.1034	.1044	.1054	.1064	.1074	.1084	.1094
.110	.1105	.1115	.1125	.1135	.1145	.1155	.1165	.1175	.1185	.1195
.120	.1206	.1216	.1226	.1236	.1246	.1257	.1267	.1277	.1287	.1297
.130	.1308	.1318	.1328	.1338	.1348	.1358	.1368	.1379	.1389	.1399
.140	.1409	.1419	.1430	.1440	.1450	.1460	.1470	.1481	.1491	.1501
.150	.1511	.1522	.1532	.1542	.1552	.1563	.1573	.1583	.1593	.1604
.160	.1614	.1624	.1634	.1644	.1655	.1665	.1676	.1686	.1696	.1706
.170	.1717	.1727	.1737	.1748	.1758	.1768	.1779	.1789	.1799	.1810
.180	.1820	.1830	.1841	.1851	.1861	.1872	.1882	.1892	.1903	.1913
.190	.1923	.1934	.1944	.1954	.1965	.1975	.1986	.1996	.2007	.2017
.200	.2027	.2038	.2048	.2059	.2069	.2079	.2090	.2100	.2111	.2121
.210	.2132	.2142	.2153	.2163	.2174	.2184	.2194	.2205	.2215	.2226
.220	.2237	.2247	.2258	.2268	.2279	.2289	.2300	.2310	.2321	.2331
.230	.2342	.2353	.2363	.2374	.2384	.2395	.2405	.2416	.2427	.2437
.240	.2448	.2458	.2469	.2480	.2490	.2501	.2511	.2522	.2533	.2543
.250	.2554	.2565	.2575	.2586	.2597	.2608	.2618	.2629	.2640	.2650
.260	.2661	.2672	.2682	.2693	.2704	.2715	.2726	.2736	.2747	.2758
.270	.2769	.2779	.2790	.2801	.2812	.2823	.2833	.2844	.2855	.2866
.280	.2877	.2888	.2898	.2909	.2920	.2931	.2942	.2953	.2964	.2975
.290	.2986	.2997	.3008	.3019	.3029	.3040	.3051	.3062	.3073	.3084
.300	.3095	.3106	.3117	.3128	.3139	.3150	.3161	.3172	.3183	.3195
.310	.3206	.3217	.3228	.3239	.3250	.3261	.3272	.3283	.3294	.3305
.320	.3317	.3328	.3339	.3350	.3361	.3372	.3384	.3395	.3406	.3417
.330	.3428	.3439	.3451	.3462	.3473	.3484	.3496	.3507	.3518	.3530
.340	.3541	.3552	.3564	.3575	.3586	.3597	.3609	.3620	.3632	.3643
.350	.3654	.3666	.3677	.3689	.3700	.3712	.3723	.3734	.3746	.3757
.360	.3769	.3780	.3792	.3803	.3815	.3826	.3838	.3850	.3861	.3873
.370	.3884	.3896	.3907	.3919	.3931	.3942	.3954	.3966	.3977	.3989
.380	.4001	.4012	.4024	.4036	.4047	.4059	.4071	.4083	.4094	.4106
.390	.4118	.4130	.4142	.4153	.4165	.4177	.4189	.4201	.4213	.4225

SOURCE: From *Statistical Tables and Problems* by Albert E. Waugh, table A11, pp. 40–41. Copyright 1952 by McGraw-Hill Book Company. Used with permission of McGraw-Hill Book Company.

TABLE 4. Values of z for given values of r (continued)

r	.000	.001	.002	.003	.004	.005	.006	.007	.008	.009
.400	.4236	.4248	.4260	.4272	.4284	.4296	.4308	.4320	.4332	.4344
.410	.4356	.4368	.4380	.4392	.4404	.4416	.4429	.4441	.4453	.4465
.420	.4477	.4489	.4501	.4513	.4526	.4538	.4550	.4562	.4574	.4587
.430	.4599	.4611	.4623	.4636	.4648	.4660	.4673	.4685	.4697	.4710
.440	.4722	.4735	.4747	.4760	.4772	.4784	.4797	.4809	.4822	.4835
.450	.4847	.4860	.4872	.4885	.4897	.4910	.4923	.4935	.4948	.4961
.460	.4973	.4986	.4999	.5011	.5024	.5037	.5049	.5062	.5075	.5088
.470	.5101	.5114	.5126	.5139	.5152	.5165	.5178	.5191	.5204	.5217
.480	.5230	.5243	.5256	.5279	.5282	.5295	.5308	.5321	.5334	.5347
.490	.5361	.5374	.5387	.5400	.5413	.5427	.5440	.5453	.5466	.5480
.500	.5493	.5506	.5520	.5533	.5547	.5560	.5573	.5587	.5600	.5614
.510	.5627	.5641	.5654	.5668	.5681	.5695	.5709	.5722	.5736	.5750
.520	.5763	.5777	.5791	.5805	.5818	.5832	.5846	.5860	.5874	.5888
.530	.5901	.5915	.5929	.5943	.5957	.5971	.5985	.5999	.6013	.6027
.540	.6042	.6056	.6070	.6084	.6098	.6112	.6127	.6141	.6155	.6170
.550	.6184	.6198	.6213	.6227	.6241	.6256	.6270	.6285	.6299	.6314
.560	.6328	.6343	.6358	.6372	.6387	.6401	.6416	.6431	.6446	.6460
.570	.6475	.6490	.6505	.6520	.6535	.6550	.6565	.6579	.6594	.6610
.580	.6625	.6640	.6655	.6670	.6685	.6700	.6715	.6731	.6746	.6761
.590	.6777	.6792	.6807	.6823	.6838	.6854	.6869	.6885	.6900	.6916
.600	.6931	.6947	.6963	.6978	.6994	.7010	.7026	.7042	.7057	.7073
.610	.7089	.7105	.7121	.7137	.7153	.7169	.7185	.7201	.7218	.7234
.620	.7250	.7266	.7283	.7299	.7315	.7332	.7348	.7364	.7381	.7398
.630	.7414	.7431	.7447	.7464	.7481	.7497	.7514	.7531	.7548	.7565
.640	.7582	.7599	.7616	.7633	.7650	.7667	.7684	.7701	.7718	.7736
.650	.7753	.7770	.7788	.7805	.7823	.7840	.7858	.7875	.7893	.7910
.660	.7928	.7946	.7964	.7981	.7999	.8017	.8035	.8053	.8071	.8089
.670	.8107	.8126	.8144	.8162	.8180	.8199	.8217	.8236	.8254	.8273
.680	.8291	.8310	.8328	.8347	.8366	.8385	.8404	.8423	.8442	.8461
.690	.8480	.8499	.8518	.8537	.8556	.8576	.8595	.8614	.8634	.8653
.700	.8673	.8693	.8712	.8732	.8752	.8772	.8792	.8812	.8832	.8852
.710	.8872	.8892	.8912	.8933	.8953	.8973	.8994	.9014	.9035	.9056
.720	.9076	.9097	.9118	.9139	.9160	.9181	.9202	.9223	.9245	.9266
.730	.9287	.9309	.9330	.9352	.9373	.9395	.9417	.9439	.9461	.9483
.740	.9505	.9527	.9549	.9571	.9594	.9616	.9639	.9661	.9684	.9707
.750	.9730	.9752	.9775	.9799	.9822	.9845	.9868	.9892	.9915	.9939
.760	.9962	.9986	1.0010	1.0034	1.0058	1.0082	1.0106	1.0130	1.0154	1.0179
.770	1.0203	1.0228	1.0253	1.0277	1.0302	1.0327	1.0352	1.0378	1.0403	1.0428
.780	1.0454	1.0479	1.0505	1.0531	1.0557	1.0583	1.0609	1.0635	1.0661	1.0688
.790	1.0714	1.0741	1.0768	1.0795	1.0822	1.0849	1.0876	1.0903	1.0931	1.0958

TABLE 4. Values of z for given values of r *(continued)*

r	.000	.001	.002	.003	.004	.005	.006	.007	.008	.009
.800	1.986	1.1014	1.1041	1.1070	1.1098	1.1127	1.1155	1.1184	1.1212	1.1241
.810	1.1270	1.1299	1.1329	1.1358	1.1388	1.1417	1.1447	1.1477	1.1507	1.1538
.820	1.1568	1.1599	1.1630	1.1660	1.1692	1.1723	1.1754	1.1786	1.1817	1.1849
.830	1.1870	1.1913	1.1946	1.1979	1.2011	1.2044	1.2077	1.2111	1.2144	1.2178
.840	1.2212	1.2246	1.2280	1.2315	1.2349	1.2384	1.2419	1.2454	1.2490	1.2526
.850	1.2561	1.2598	1.2634	1.2670	1.2708	1.2744	1.2782	1.2819	1.2857	1.2895
.860	1.2934	1.2972	1.3011	1.3050	1.3089	1.3129	1.3168	1.3209	1.3249	1.3290
.870	1.3331	1.3372	1.3414	1.3456	1.3498	1.3540	1.3583	1.3626	1.3670	1.3714
.880	1.3758	1.3802	1.3847	1.3892	1.3938	1.3984	1.4030	1.4077	1.4124	1.4171
.890	1.4219	1.4268	1.4316	1.4366	1.4415	1.4465	1.4516	1.4566	1.4618	1.4670
.900	1.4722	1.4775	1.4828	1.4883	1.4937	1.4992	1.5047	1.5103	1.5160	1.5217
.910	1.5275	1.5334	1.5393	1.5453	1.5513	1.5574	1.5636	1.5698	1.5762	1.5825
.920	1.5890	1.5956	1.6022	1.6089	1.6157	1.6226	1.6296	1.6366	1.6438	1.6510
.930	1.6584	1.6659	1.6734	1.6811	1.6888	1.6967	1.7047	1.7129	1.7211	1.7295
.940	1.7380	1.7467	1.7555	1.7645	1.7736	1.7828	1.7923	1.8019	1.8117	1.8216
.950	1.8318	1.8421	1.8527	1.8635	1.8745	1.8857	1.8972	1.9090	1.9210	1.9333
.960	1.9459	1.9588	1.9721	1.9857	1.9996	2.0140	2.0287	2.0439	2.0595	2.0756
.970	2.0923	2.1095	2.1273	2.1457	2.1649	2.1847	2.2054	2.2269	2.2494	2.2729
.980	2.2976	2.3223	2.3507	2.3796	2.4101	2.4426	2.4774	2.5147	2.5550	2.5988
.990	2.6467	2.6996	2.7587	2.8257	2.9031	2.9945	3.1063	3.2504	3.4534	3.8002

r	z
.9999	4.95172
.99999	6.10303

TABLE 5. Table of critical values of *U* in the Mann-Whitney test

Critical values of U at $\alpha = .001$ with direction predicted or at $\alpha = .002$ with direction not predicted

N_1 \ N_2	9	10	11	12	13	14	15	16	17	18	19	20
1												
2												
3										0	0	0	0
4		0	0	0	1	1	1	2	2	3	3	3
5	1	1	2	2	3	3	4	5	5	6	7	7
6	2	3	4	4	5	6	7	8	9	10	11	12
7	3	5	6	7	8	9	10	11	13	14	15	16
8	5	6	8	9	11	12	14	15	17	18	20	21
9	7	8	10	12	14	15	17	19	21	23	25	26
10	8	10	12	14	17	19	21	23	25	27	29	32
11	10	12	15	17	20	22	24	27	29	32	34	37
12	12	14	17	20	23	25	28	31	34	37	40	42
13	14	17	20	23	26	29	32	35	38	42	45	48
14	15	19	22	25	29	32	36	39	43	46	50	54
15	17	21	24	28	32	36	40	43	47	51	55	59
16	19	23	27	31	35	39	43	48	52	56	60	65
17	21	25	29	34	38	43	47	52	57	61	66	70
18	23	27	32	37	42	46	51	56	61	66	71	76
19	25	29	34	40	45	50	55	60	66	71	77	82
20	26	32	37	42	48	54	59	65	70	76	82	88

SOURCE: D. Auble, "Extended Tables for the Mann-Whitney Statistic," *Bulletin of the Institute of Educational Research at Indiana University*, vol. 1, no. 2, Tables 1, 3, 5 and 7, 1953, with the kind permission of the publisher; as adapted in S. Siegel, *Non-parametric Statistics*, New York: McGraw-Hill, 1956, table K.

TABLE 5. Table of critical values of U in the Mann-Whitney test (continued)

Critical values of U at $\alpha = .01$ with direction predicted or at $\alpha = .02$ with direction not predicted

N_1 \ N_2	9	10	11	12	13	14	15	16	17	18	19	20
1												
2						0	0	0	0	0	1	1
3	1	1	1	2	2	2	3	3	4	4	4	5
4	3	3	4	5	5	6	7	7	8	9	9	10
5	5	6	7	8	9	10	11	12	13	14	15	16
6	7	8	9	11	12	13	15	16	18	19	20	22
7	9	11	12	14	16	17	19	21	23	24	26	28
8	11	13	15	17	20	22	24	26	28	30	32	34
9	14	16	18	21	23	26	28	31	33	36	38	40
10	16	19	22	24	27	30	33	36	38	41	44	47
11	18	22	25	28	31	34	37	41	44	47	50	53
12	21	24	28	31	35	38	42	46	49	53	56	60
13	23	27	31	35	39	43	47	51	55	59	63	67
14	26	30	34	38	43	47	51	56	60	65	69	73
15	28	33	37	42	47	51	56	61	66	71	76	82
16	31	36	41	46	51	56	61	66	71	76	82	87
17	33	38	44	49	55	60	66	71	77	82	88	93
18	36	41	47	53	59	65	70	76	82	88	94	100
19	38	44	50	56	63	69	75	82	88	94	101	107
20	40	47	53	60	67	73	80	87	93	100	107	114

Critical values of U at $\alpha = .025$ with direction predicted or at $\alpha = .05$ with direction not predicted

N_1 \ N_2	9	10	11	12	13	14	15	16	17	18	19	20
1												
2	0	0	0	1	1	1	1	1	2	2	2	2
3	2	3	3	4	4	5	5	6	6	7	7	8
4	4	5	6	7	8	9	10	11	11	12	13	13
5	7	8	9	11	12	13	14	15	17	18	19	20
6	10	11	13	14	16	17	19	21	22	24	25	27
7	12	14	16	18	20	22	24	26	28	30	32	34
8	15	17	19	22	24	26	29	31	34	36	38	41
9	17	20	23	26	28	31	34	37	39	42	45	48
10	20	23	26	29	33	36	39	42	45	48	52	55
11	23	26	30	33	37	40	44	47	51	55	58	62
12	26	29	33	37	41	45	49	53	57	61	65	69
13	28	33	37	41	45	50	54	59	63	67	72	76
14	31	36	40	45	50	55	59	64	67	74	78	83
15	34	39	44	49	54	59	64	70	75	80	85	90
16	37	42	47	53	59	64	70	75	81	86	92	98
17	39	45	51	57	63	67	75	81	87	93	99	105
18	42	48	55	61	67	74	80	86	93	99	106	112
19	45	52	58	65	72	78	85	92	99	106	113	119
20	48	55	62	69	76	83	90	90	105	112	119	127

TABLE 5. Table of critical values of *U* in the Mann-Whitney test (*continued*)

Critical values of U at $\alpha = .05$ with direction predicted or at $\alpha = .10$ with direction not predicted

N_1 \ N_2	9	10	11	12	13	14	15	16	17	18	19	20
1											0	0
2	1	1	1	2	2	2	3	3	3	4	4	4
3	3	4	5	5	6	7	7	8	9	9	10	11
4	6	7	8	9	10	11	12	14	15	16	17	18
5	9	11	12	13	15	16	18	19	20	22	23	25
6	12	14	16	17	19	21	23	25	26	28	30	32
7	15	17	19	21	24	26	28	30	33	35	37	39
8	18	20	23	26	28	31	33	36	39	41	44	47
9	21	24	27	30	33	36	39	42	45	48	51	54
10	24	27	31	34	37	41	44	48	51	55	58	62
11	27	31	34	38	42	46	50	54	57	61	65	69
12	30	34	38	42	47	51	55	60	64	68	72	77
13	33	37	42	47	51	56	61	65	70	75	80	84
14	36	41	46	51	56	61	66	71	77	82	87	92
15	39	44	50	55	61	66	72	77	83	88	94	100
16	42	48	54	60	65	71	77	83	89	95	101	107
17	45	51	57	64	70	77	83	89	96	102	109	115
18	48	55	61	68	75	82	88	95	102	109	116	123
19	51	58	65	72	80	87	94	101	109	116	123	130
20	54	62	69	77	84	92	100	107	115	123	130	138

314 APPENDIX

TABLE 6. Distribution of χ^2

df	.99	.98	.95	.90	.80	.70	.50	.30	.20	.10	.05	.02	.01	.001
1	.03157	.03628	.00393	.0158	.0642	.148	.455	1.074	1.642	2.706	3.841	5.412	6.635	10.827
2	.0201	.0404	.103	.211	.446	.713	1.386	2.408	3.219	4.605	5.991	7.824	9.210	13.815
3	.115	.185	.352	.584	1.005	1.424	2.366	3.665	4.642	6.251	7.815	9.837	11.341	16.268
4	.297	.429	.711	1.964	1.649	2.195	3.357	4.878	5.989	7.779	9.488	11.668	13.277	18.465
5	.554	.752	1.145	1.610	2.343	3.000	4.351	6.064	7.289	9.236	11.070	13.388	15.086	20.517
6	.872	1.134	1.635	2.204	3.070	3.828	5.348	7.231	8.558	10.645	12.592	15.033	16.812	22.457
7	1.239	1.564	2.167	2.833	3.822	4.671	6.346	8.383	9.803	12.017	14.067	16.622	18.475	24.322
8	1.646	2.032	2.733	3.490	4.594	5.527	7.344	9.524	11.030	13.362	15.507	18.168	20.090	26.125
9	2.088	2.532	3.325	4.168	5.380	6.393	8.343	10.656	12.242	14.684	16.919	19.679	21.666	27.877
10	2.558	3.059	3.940	4.865	6.179	7.267	9.342	11.781	13.442	15.987	18.307	21.161	23.209	29.588
11	3.053	3.609	4.575	5.578	6.989	8.148	10.341	12.899	14.631	17.275	19.675	22.618	24.725	31.264
12	3.571	4.178	5.226	6.304	7.807	9.034	11.340	14.011	15.812	18.549	21.026	24.054	26.217	32.909
13	4.107	4.765	5.892	7.042	8.634	9.926	12.340	15.119	16.985	19.812	22.362	25.472	27.688	34.528
14	4.660	5.368	6.571	7.790	9.467	10.821	13.339	16.222	18.151	21.064	23.685	26.873	29.141	36.123
15	5.229	5.985	7.261	8.547	10.307	11.721	14.339	17.322	19.311	22.307	24.996	28.259	30.578	37.697

Probability

16	5.812	6.614	7.962	9.312	11.152	12.624	15.338	18.418	20.465	23.542	26.296	29.633	32.000	39.252
17	6.408	7.255	8.672	10.085	12.002	13.531	16.338	19.511	21.615	24.769	27.587	30.995	33.409	40.790
18	7.015	7.906	9.390	10.865	12.857	14.440	17.338	20.601	22.760	25.989	28.869	32.346	34.805	42.312
19	7.633	8.567	10.117	11.651	13.716	15.352	18.338	21.689	23.900	27.204	30.144	33.687	36.191	43.820
20	8.260	9.237	10.851	12.443	14.578	16.266	19.337	22.775	25.038	28.412	31.410	35.020	37.566	45.315
21	8.897	9.915	11.591	13.240	15.445	17.182	20.337	23.858	26.171	29.615	32.671	36.343	38.932	46.797
22	9.542	10.600	12.338	14.041	16.314	18.101	21.337	24.939	27.301	30.813	33.924	37.659	40.289	48.268
23	10.196	11.293	13.091	14.848	17.187	19.021	22.337	26.018	28.429	32.007	35.172	38.968	41.638	49.728
24	10.856	11.992	13.848	15.659	18.062	19.943	23.337	27.096	29.553	33.196	36.415	40.270	42.980	51.179
25	11.524	12.697	14.611	16.473	18.940	20.867	24.337	28.172	30.675	34.382	37.652	41.566	44.314	52.620
26	12.198	13.409	15.379	17.292	19.820	21.792	25.336	29.246	31.795	35.563	38.885	42.856	45.642	54.052
27	12.879	14.125	16.151	18.114	20.703	22.719	26.336	30.319	32.912	36.741	40.113	44.140	46.963	55.476
28	13.565	14.847	16.928	18.939	21.588	23.647	27.336	31.391	34.027	37.916	41.337	45.419	48.278	56.893
29	14.256	15.574	17.708	19.768	22.475	24.577	28.336	32.461	35.139	39.087	42.557	46.693	49.588	58.302
30	14.953	16.306	18.493	20.599	23.364	25.508	29.336	33.530	36.250	40.256	43.773	47.962	50.892	59.703

For larger values of df, the expression $\sqrt{2\chi^2} - \sqrt{2df - 1}$ may be used as a normal deviate with unit variance, remembering that the probability for χ^2 corresponds with that of a single tail of the normal curve.

Author Index

Abelson, Robert P., 87
Ackoff, Russell, 265
Adelson, Joseph, 228
Alger, Chadwick F., 76, 89n
Alker, Hayward R., 23
Allport, Gordon W., 129, 130
Almond, Gabriel A., 232
American Psychological Association Committee on Psychological Tests, 64n
Anderson, Theodore R., 190
Angell, Robert C., 128
Aronson, Elliot, 46, 83–84
Asch, Solomon, 80–81, 83
Auerbach, Arthur H., 75n
Azrin, Nathan H., 82

Bales, Robert F., 76, 77, 145
Barton, Allen, 143, 146, 147, 149
Becker, Howard S., 101
Beller, Emanuel K., 78
Benson, Oliver, 88–89, 155n
Bent, Dale H., 158
Berelson, Bernard, 44, 134–36, 228, 231
Blalock, Hubert M., 19, 165n, 176, 216n, 226, 237, 243n, 246, 293
Borgatta, Edgar F., 78
Braithwaite, Richard B., 4, 11–12

Bridgman, Percy W., 19
Brody, Richard A., 86
Bühler (author), 130

Camilleri, Santo F., 291
Campbell (author), 122
Campbell, Angus C., 103, 196n
Campbell, Donald T., 32, 37, 46, 63
Cannell, Charles F., 102, 105
Carlsmith, James, 46, 83–84
Chapin, Stuart F., 32, 131
Chein, Isidor, 252, 260
Claster, Daniel S., 94
Cloward, Richard, 233
Clemens, Walter C., Jr., 87
Coch, Lester, 85
Cochran, William, 263n
Cohen, Bernard C., 89n
Coleman, James S., 89, 145, 146
Coplin, William D., 96
Costner, Herbert L., 174n, 189, 194, 195, 204, 216n, 287
Cronbach, Lee J., 62, 67, 68n
Cutright, Phillips, 127

Davis, James, 293
Davis, Otto A., 128
Dempster, M. A. H., 128
Denzin, Norman K., 93, 121, 122, 129

Deutsch, Morton, 81, 82
Dexter, Lewis A., 130
Di Palma, Giuseppe, 180
Dixon, Wilfred J., 158
Dohrenwend, Barbara S., 101
Douvan, Elizabeth, 228
Draber, Thomas E., 47
Dubin, Robert, 5
Durbin, James, 150
Durkheim, Emile, 127, 274
Dye, Thomas R., 127

Ekman, Paul, 75–76
Erikson, Kai T., 92
Evan, William M., 86–87
Evans-Pritchard, Edward E., 93

Farley, Reynolds, 45
Festinger, Leon, 92
Fishbein, Martin, 109n
Fisher, Ronald Aylmer, 285
Fiske, Donald W., 63
Flanigan, William, 9
Fode, Kermit L., 84
Fogelman, Edwin, 9
Forsythe, Alexandra I., 88n
Francis, Wayne L., 46
Freeman, Linton C., 198
French, John R. P., 85–86

Gage, Nathaniel L., 125
Galtung, Johan, 292, 293
Games, Paul, 59
Gaudet, Hazel, 44, 228, 231
Geer, Blanche, 91
Gellert, Elizabeth, 74, 147
Gibbs, Jack P., 6, 20
Gleser, Goldine C., 67, 68n
Glock, Charles Y., 45
Gold, David, 292–93
Gold, Raymond L., 92
Goldberg, Arthur S., 25, 241n, 242
Goode, William J., 17, 35, 263
Goodman, Leo A., 195, 199, 204, 216
Gordon, Raymond L., 106–7
Gottschalk, Louis A., 75
Grusky, Oscar, 128
Guenther, Anthony L., 293, 294

Guetzkow, Harold, 89–90
Gulliksen, Harold, 67
Gurr, Ted R., 125n, 126, 244
Guttman, Louis, 195

Haas, Eugene J., 47
Hagedorn, Robert, 8
Hansen, Morris H., 263
Hatt, Paul K., 17, 35, 263
Haug, Marie R., 150
Heiss, Jerold, 43
Helmstadter, G. C., 62
Hempel, Carl G., 4, 19, 20
Henkel, Ramon E., 291, 293
Henslin, James J., 123
Hermalin, Albert I., 45
Hermann, Charles F., 86
Heyns, Roger W., 79
Hollingshead, August B., 288
Holsti, Ole R., 128, 132, 134, 136
Hull, C. Hadlai, 158
Hurwitz, William N., 263
Hyman, Herbert H., 44, 227, 232

Institute of Electoral Research, 125n
Isaak, Alan C., 18

Jacobson, Lenore, 30
Janda, Kenneth, 155n
Janes, Robert W., 93
Jaros, Dean, 127
John, Vera P., 76

Kahn, Robert I., 102, 105
Kalton, G., 108, 148, 156, 256, 259–61, 265–66
Kammeyer, Kenneth C. W., 150
Kauffman, Paul E., 76
Kendal, Patricia L., 101, 208, 216
Kirchner, Wayner K., 114
Kish, Leslie, 45, 46, 259, 262n, 265
Klein, David, 101
Kluckhohn, Florence, 90
Krauss, Robert M., 81, 82
Krout, Maurice H., 139
Kruskal (author), 122
Kruskal, William H., 195, 199, 204, 216

AUTHOR INDEX 321

Labovitz, Sanford, 8, 293, 294
Lasswell, Harold D., 132, 135
Lazarsfeld, Paul F., 44, 104, 143, 146–47, 149, 228, 231, 237
Leege, David C., 46
Leggett, John C., 106
Lenski, Gerhard, 106
Lewinsohn, Richard, 4
Likert, Rensis, 116
Lindesmith, Alfred R., 91
Lindgren, E. J., 94
Lindsley, Ogden R., 82
Lipset, Seymour M., 125
Lombraso (author), 127

McClelland, David C., 134
McGinnis, Robert, 291
McKean, Kathryn O., 133
McKinney, John C., 16
McLaughlin, Barry, 133
McNemar, Quinn, 179
Maccoby, Eleanor E., 102
Maccoby, Nathan, 102
MacRae, Duncan, Jr., 125
Madow, William G., 263
Maher, Brendan A., 133
Manis, Jerome G., 91, 280
Medley, Donald M., 78
Meehan, Eugene J., 5
Meehl, Paul E., 63
Meltzer, Bernard N., 91
Mendelsohn, Robert I., 127
Merrit, Richard L., 126
Merton, Robert K., 12, 101
Middleton, Russell, 124
Milbrath, Lester W., 21
Mitzel, Harold E., 78
Morrison, Denton E., 291, 293
Moser, C. A., 108, 148, 156, 256, 259, 261, 265–66
Mosteller, Frederick, 133
Mueller, John H., 174n, 189, 194, 204, 216n, 287
Murphy, Gardner, 116
Myrdal, Gunnar, 25

Nachmias, David, 174n
Nagel, Ernest, 13

Nass, Gilbert, 293, 294
Nett, Roger, 6, 7
Neuringer, Charles, 130–31
Neyman, Jerzy, 257
Nie, Norman, 158
Niemi, Donald, 125

Ohlin, Lloyd E., 233
Olexa, Carol, 191
Oppenheim, N. A., 110

Palumbo, Dennis J., 267
Patrick, Ralph C., 92–93
Peacock, Alan T., 126n
Phillips, Derek L., 106n
Phillips, R. H., 122
Pomper, Gerald M., 45
Pool, Ithiel de Sola, 87, 133
Popkin, Samuel L., 87
Popper, Karl R., 12
Psathas, George, 123

Queen, Stuart A., 92–93

Rae, Douglas W., 126
Rajaratnam, Nageswars, 67, 68n
Rehberg, Richard A., 165, 243, 244
Reynolds, Paul D., 23
Richardson, Stephen, 101
Riecken, Henry, 92
Riesman, David, 74
Riker, William H., 125
Riley, Matilda W., 32, 74
Rokeach, Milton, 63
Rokkan, Stein, 125, 126
Rosenberg, Morris, 8, 40, 224, 230
Rosenbloom, David H., 174n
Rosenthal, Robert, 30, 84
Roth, Julius A., 150
Rummel, R. J., 160
Russett, Bruce M., 127, 212

Scammon, Richard M., 125n
Schachter, Stanley, 92
Schafer, Walter E., 191, 247
Scheffler, Israel, 3
Scheflin, Albert E., 75n
Schmid, Calvin F., 112

Schneidman, Edwin S., 133–34
Schubert, Glendon, 122, 127
Schuessler, Karl F., 174n, 189, 194, 204, 216n, 287
Schulman, Mark A., 45
Schwartz, Charlotte G., 94
Schwartz, Howard, 94
Schwartz, Morris S., 94
Seashore, Stanley E., 103
Selltiz, Claire, 42, 75, 107, 129–31
Selvin, Hanan C., 292
Shafer, Walter E., 243, 244
Sherif, Muzafer, 37
Shimberg, Ben, 125
Siegel, Sidney, 53, 286
Simon, Herbert A., 237, 239, 246
Simon, Julian L., 19
Sinclair, Judie, 165, 243, 244
Sjoberg, Gideon, 6, 7
Skipper, James K., Jr., 293, 294
Snyder, Eloise C., 127
Sobol, Marion C., 45n
Soskin, William F., 76
Spiegel, Donald E., 130–31
Stanley, Julian C., 32, 37, 46
Stevens, S. S., 50
Stinchombe, Arthur L., 273
Stone, Georgy P., 121–22
Stone, Philip J., 137n
Stouffer, Samuel A., 146
Straus, Murray A., 78
Strauss, Anselm, 95
Stuart, Alan, 150
Sullivan, Mortimer A., 92–93
Sussman, Marvin B., 150

Sutherland, Edwin H., 129

Taylor, Charles L., 125
Taylor, Michael, 126
Thomas, William I., 130
Thurstone, L. L., 137

Verba, Sidney, 232

Wagner (author), 126
Wallace (author), 122
Wallace, David L., 133
Wallace, Samuel E., 121
Wallace, Walter L., 6
Warner, W. Lloyd, 124
Watson, Jeanne, 74
Wax, Rosalie H., 90
Webb, Beatrice, 73
Webb, Eugene J., 119–24, 126, 128
Webb, Sidney, 73
Weeg, Gerald P., 158
Weick, Karl E., 75, 78, 144, 148
Whyte, William F., 93–94
Wildavsky, Aaron, 128
Winston (author), 124
Wiseman, Jack, 126n
Wrigley, Charles, 158

Yamane, Taro, 259

Zander, Alvin F., 79
Zeisel, Hans, 192
Zelditch, Morris, Jr., 86–87, 190
Zetterberg, Hans L., 9
Znaniecki, Florian, 130

Subject Index

Accretion measures, 121
"Acme-Bolt trucking game," 81
Actuarial records, 124
Administrative and Budgetary Committee of the United Nations General Assembly, 76
Aggregate data, 126
Alternative decisions in hypotheses-testing (table), 279
Ambiguity, coefficient of, 113
America at the Polls: A Handbook of American Presidential Election Statistics, 1920–1964, 125
American Federation of Labor—Congress of Industrial Organizations Committee on Political Action, 126
American Soldier, The (Stouffer), 146
Americans for Constitutional Action, 126
Analysis, 10–12
  of bivariate distribution, 188–218
    concept of relationship, 188–93
    measures of relationship, 193–217
  content, 128, 132–38
    units and categories of, 135–38
  of expressive movement, 122
  item, 115
  multivariate, 43, 219–46

    causal models for, 237–45
    control in, 220–27
    interpretation in, 227–33
    multiple relationships in, 233–37
  physical-location, 122
  regression, 209
  of univariate distribution, 163–86
    measurement of central tendency of, 167–73
    measurement of dispersion of, 173–81
Analytic induction, 91
Arbitrary scales, 110–11
Archival records, 123–37
  content analysis of, 132–38
    units and categories, 135–38
  private, 129–31
    authenticity of, 131
    autobiographies, 129
    diaries, 130
    letters, 130–31
  public, 124–28
    actuarial records, 124–27
    governmental documents, 127–28
    mass media, 128
Arithmetic mean, 171–73
Arrangements, reactive, 37–38
Association, 57
  measures of, 195

Assumptions, 15, 16
Assymetrical coefficients, 197
Attitude measurement, 55
   arbitrary scales for, 110–11
   Likert scales for, 114–16
   Thurstone scales for, 111–14
Authenticity of private records, 131
Autobiographies, 129
Automatic data processing, 156–58
Average deviation, 176–77

Behavior, observation of, 75–76
Beta coefficient, 235
Beta weight, 235
Bias, 103, 106
   due to demand characteristics, 83–84
   experimenter, 84
   in sampling, 255, 263
Biasing errors, 107, 116
Bimodal distributions, 169
Biomedical Computer Programs (BMD), 158–59
Birth records, 124
Bivariate distribution, 188–217
   concept of relationship in, 188–93
   measures of relationship in, 193–216
      interval, 208–16
      nominal, 195–200
      ordinal, 200–8
Block-booking, 224
Budgets, 128

Case study, one shot, 42
Categories
   in content analysis, 135–37
   IPA code of (table), 77
Causal inferences, 8, 91
Causal models, 237–45
Causation, 80
Census Bureau, U.S., 45, 151
Central tendency
   measurement of, 163, 167–73
      arithmetic mean, 171–73
      median, 168–71
      mode, 167–68
   of ordinal numbers, 57
Chi-square test, 288–91
CIO News (periodical), 125

Classic experimental design (table), 30
Classification, 16
Cluster samples, 264–65
Code books, 151
   format for (table), 153
Coding, 143–56
   constructing schemes for, 143–51
   process of punching and, 151–56
Coding frame, 104
Coding sheets, 151
Coefficients
   of ambiguity, 113
   beta, 235
   correlation, 193
   Guttman, 195–99
   of multiple determination, 236
   validity, 61
   of variation, 173, 180–81
Collection of data
   inobtrusive measures for, 119–38
      archival records, 123–31
      content analysis, 132–37
      intent of, 119–20
      physical traces, 120–21
      simple observation, 121–23
   observational methods of, 73–96
      characteristics of, 75–79
      controlled, 79–86
      participant, 90–95
      roles of, 73–75
      simulation, 86–90
   in survey research, 100–16
      attitude measurement, 109–16
      mail questionnaires, 107–8
      personal interviews, 100–7
      telephone interviews, 108–9
Commutation, 57
Comparison, 31
Complete participation, 92
Computer simulations, 88–89
Computers, 143, 157–58
Concepts, 15–17
Conceptual definitions, 17
Conditional interpretation, 231–33
Conditioning of panel, 45
Confidence interval, 257
Confounding factors, 86
Congress, U.S., 125–26

SUBJECT INDEX 327

Congressional Quarterly Almanac, The, 125
Congressional Record, 126
Construct validity, 62–64
Content analysis, 128, 132–38
  categories and units in, 135–37
Content validity, 59–60
Control, 4, 32–36
  in multivariate analysis, 220–27
    cross-tabulation method of, 221–25
    partial correlation method of, 225–27
Control group, 29
Control variables, 20, 22–23
Controlled experiments, 251
Controlled observations, 79–86
  in field experimentation, 84–86
  in laboratory experimentation, 80–84
Convenience samples, 260
Convergent-discrimination concept of validity, 63
Correlation, 8
Correlation coefficients, 61n, 193
Correlation designs, 42–43
Counter sorter, 157
Covariation, 8, 189
  demonstration of, 29
  median and mean as measures of, 192–93
Criterion of least squares, 211
Criterion variables, *see* Dependent variables
Critical subject, 80
Cross-sectional study, 42
Cross-tabulation method of control, 221–25

Data, 7
  aggregate, 126
Data analysis
  of bivariate distribution, 188–218
    concept of relationship in, 188–93
    measurement of relationship in, 193–217
  multivariate, 219–46
    causal models, 237–45
    concept of control in, 220–21
    interpretation in, 227–33

  methods of control in, 221–27
  multiple relationships, 233–37
  of univariate distribution, 163–86
    measures of central tendency, 167–73
    measures of dispersion, 173–81
Data collection, 10, 11
  inobtrusive measures for, 119–38
    archival records, 123–31
    content analysis, 132–37
    intent of, 119–20
    physical traces, 120–21
    simple observation, 121–23
  observational methods of, 73–96
    characteristics of, 75–79
    controlled, 79–86
    participant, 90–95
    roles of, 73–75
    simulation, 86–90
  in survey research, 100–16
    attitude measurement, 109–16
    mail questionnaires, 107–8
    personal interviews, 100–7
    telephone interviews, 108–9
Data processing, 143–61
  automatic, 156–58
  coding in, 143–56
    constructing schemes for, 143–51
    process of punching and, 151–56
Death records, 125
Deception, 84
Decile, 170
Deductive approach, 78
Deductive coding, 144
Deductive explanation, 4
Definitions, 15, 17–20
Degrees of freedom, 282
Demand characteristics, 83, 119
Dependent variables, 20–22
Description, 51
Designs
  research, 10, 11, 29–48
    comparison of, 46–47
    components of, 31–38
    experimental, 38–40
    quasi-experimental, 40–46
    structure of, 29–31
  sampling, 259–65

Determination, multiple, 236
Deviation
  average, 176–77
  mean, 177–78
  standard, 178–81, 255
Diaries, 130
Discriminative power (DP), 115
Dispersion, measurement of, 112, 163, 173–81
  mean deviation in, 177–78
  qualitative variation in, 173–75
  range and interquartile range in, 175–77
  variance and standard deviation in, 178–81
Distributions
  frequency, 164–67
    types of, 181–85
  measures of central tendency of, 167–73
    arithmetic mean, 171–73
    median, 168–71
    mode, 167–68
  measures of dispersion of, 173–81
    mean deviation, 177–78
    qualitative variation, 173–75
    range and interquartile range, 175–77
    variance and standard deviation, 178–81
  sampling, 254, 273–78, 287
  See also Relationships
Documents
  governmental, 127–28
  See also Records
Dogmatism scale, 63

Electronic computers, 157–58
Empirical approach, 78
Empirical generalizations, 10–12
Empirical research
  basic elements of, 15–27
    concepts, 15–17
    definitions, 17–20
    hypotheses, 23–27
    variables, 20–23
  designs for, 29–48

  comparison of, 46–47
  components of, 31–38
  experimental, 38–40
  quasi-experimental, 40–46
  structure of, 29–31
  measurement in, 50–69
    levels of, 53–59
    nature of, 50–53
    reliability of, 64–68
    validity of, 64–68
  scientific method in, 3–13
    aims of science, 3–6
    approaches to knowledge, 6–7
    research process, 10–13
    scientific approach, 7–10
Empirical validity, 60–62
Erosion measures, 121
Errors
  biasing, 107, 116
  nonsampling, 265–67
  prediction, 195
  standard, 254, 257
  type I and type II, 277–78
  validity impaired by, 119
  variable, 64
Estimator, 255
Evaluation of survey methods (table), 109
Exhaustive coding systems, 148
Experimental group, 29
Experimental mortality, 33
Experimental realism, 83
Experimental research designs, 30, 38–40
  interviews and, 102
Experimental stimulus, 30
Experimentation, 4
  controlled, 251
  field, 84–86
  laboratory, 80–84
Explanations, 3–4
  deductive, 4
  measurement and, 51
  probabilistic, 5
  rival, 32
  simple observation and, 123
Ex-post-facto design, 44
Expressive movement, analysis of, 123

Exterior body signs, observation of, 121–22
External validity, 37
Extralinguistic behavior, 76
Extrinsic factors, 32
Extrinsic variables, control over, 79, 85

Face validity, 59, 90
Facial expressions, observation of, 122
Federal Bureau of Investigation, 128
Federalist Papers, The, 133
Field experimentation, 84–86
First-order partial correlation, 226
Fisher's z, 285
Fixed alternative questions, 103–5
Focused interviews, 101
Formal theories, 16
Freedom, degree of, 282
Frequency distributions, 163–67
　types of, 181–85
Frequency matching, 35
Funnel sequence of questions, 105

Gamma coefficient, 193, 204–8
Generalizability, 29, 67
Generalizations, 36–68
　empirical, 10–12
　universal, 4
Gestures, observation of, 122
Goodman and Kruskal's tau, 199–200
Governmental documents, 127–28
Guinea pig effect, 119
Guttman coefficient of predictability, 195–99

Hamilton, Alexander, 133
Harwood Manufacturing Corporation, 85–86
History, 33
Hughes, Howard, 131
Hypotheses, 10–11, 23–27
　in survey research, 116
　testing of, 27, 270–95
　　nonparametric tests, 286–91
　　parametric tests, 279–86
　　sampling distribution, 273–78
　　strategy of, 271–73
　　test of significance controversy, 291–94
Hypothetical concepts, 19

IBM Card Punches, 156
Impersonal survey methods, 107–9
　mail questionnaire, 107–8
　telephone interview, 108–9
Independent variables, 20–22, 190
Indicators, 53
　See also Variables
Induction, 11
　analytic, 91
Inductive coding, 144
Inferences, 79
　causal, 8, 91
Inferential methods
　hypothesis-testing as, 270–95
　　nonparametric tests, 278–86
　　parametric tests, 278–86
　　sampling distribution, 273–78
　　strategy of, 271–73
　　test of significance controversy, 291–94
　sampling as, 251–67
　　aims of, 251–52
　　designs for, 259–65
　　nonsampling error in, 265–67
　　population, 252–53
　　sample size, 253–59
Inferential statistics, 251
Instrumentation, 33–34
Interaction Process Analysis (IPA), 76, 145
Interaction Process Scores, 78
Internal validity, 32
Inter-Nation Simulation (INS), 89
Interpretation, 227–33
　conditional, 231–33
　of intervening variables, 228–30
Interquartile range, 175–77
Interval levels, 57–58
Interval measures of relationship, 208–16
Intervening variables, 228–30
Interviewer, 101
　tasks of, 107
Interviewer effects, 120

Interviews, 74, 100–7
  questions for, 102–7
    leading, 104
    open-ended vs. fixed-alternative, 103–5
    sequence of, 105–7
    wording of, 102–3
Intrinsic factors, 33–35
Intrinsic variables, control over, 79, 85
Inverted funnel sequence of questions, 105
Isomorphism, 52
Item analysis, 115

Judicial records, 124–27

Keller, Helen, 129
Kendall's tau-b and tau-c, 195, 208
Kennedy, John F., 134
Keypunch, 156
Knowledge, approaches to, 6–7
  scientific, 7–10
Known-groups technique in construct validity, 63
Khrushchev, Nikita, 134

Laboratory experimentation, 74, 80–84
Lambda, 195–99
Leading questions, 104
Least squares, criterion of, 211
Letters, 130–31
Level of significance, 274–76
Levels of measurement, 53–59
  interval, 57–58
  nominal, 54
  ordinal, 54–57
  ratio, 58–59
Likert scales, 114–16
Linear function rule, 209
Linguistic behavior, 76
  observation of, 123

Madison, James, 126, 133
Mail questionnaires, 107–8
Man-computer simulations, 89
Man simulations, 89
Manipulation, 4, 31–32, 86
Mann-Whitney runs test, 286–88

Mapping, 51, 52
Mass media, 128
Matching, 35
Maturation, 33
Mean, 192–93
  arithmetic, 163, 171–73
  sampling distribution and, 273
Mean deviation, 177–78
Means, difference between, 279–83
Measurement, 10, 11, 50–69
  attitude, 55
    arbitrary scales for, 110–11
    Likert scales for, 114–16
    Thurstone scales for, 111–14
  of central tendency, 163, 167–73
    arithmetic mean, 171–73
    median, 168–71
    mode, 167–68
  of dispersion, 112, 163, 173–81
    mean deviation, 177–78
    qualitative variation, 173–75
    range and interquartile range, 175–77
    variance and standard deviation, 178–81
  errors resulting from, 119
  levels of, 53–59
    interval, 57–58
    nominal, 54
    ordinal, 54–57
    ratio, 58–59
  nature of, 50–53
  of relationships, 208–16
    nominal, 195–200
    ordinal, 200–8
  reliability of, 64–68
    parallel-forms technique, 67
    split-half method, 67–68
    test-retest method, 66
  validity of, 59–64
    construct, 62–64
    content, 59–60
    empirical, 60–62
Media, 128
Median, 57, 112, 163, 168–71, 192–93
Michigan, University of, 45, 103, 151
Mode, 163, 167–68
Models, causal, 237–45

Mortality, experimental, 33
Moscow News, 135
Multiple determination, coefficient of, 236
Multiple relationships, 233–37
Multitrait-multimethod matrix technique of construct validation, 63–64
Multivariate analysis, 43, 219–46
　causal models for, 237–45
　control in, 220–27
　　concept of, 220–21
　　cross-tabulation method, 221–25
　　partial correlation method, 225–27
　interpretation in, 227–33
　　conditional, 231–33
　　intervening variables, 228–30
　multiple relationships in, 233–37
Mundane realism, 83
Mutually exclusive coding categories, 149

Negatively-skewed distributions, 182
New Republic (periodical), 125
Nixon, Richard M., 134
Nominal levels of measurement, 54
　of relationships, 195–200
Nondirective interviews, 101
Nonparametric tests, 279, 286–91
Nonprobability sampling, 260
Nonrespondents, 108
Nonresponse error, 266–67
Nonsymmetrical distributions, 182
Nonverbal behavior, 75
　observation of, 106–7
Nonsampling error, 265–67
Normal curve, 182–85, 257, 258

Objectivity, 8, 91
　in content analysis, 132
Objects, *see* Variables
Observation, 7, 73–95
　characteristics of, 75–79
　controlled, 79–86
　　field experimentation, 84–86
　　laboratory experimentation, 80–84
　participant, 90–95
　roles of, 73–75

　simple, 121–23
　in simulations, 86–90
　variance and, $65n$
One-shot case study, 42
One-tailed tests, 276–77
Open-ended questions, 103–5
Operating models, 86
Operational definitions, 17–19
Ordinal levels, 54–57
Ordinal measure of relationship, 200–8

Pairwise matching, 35
Panel research design, 44–45
Parallel-forms technique, 67
Parametric tests, 279–86
Partial correlation method of control, 225–27
Partial tables, 223
Participant observation, 90–95
Pearson's r, 195, 215
Percentages, 166
Percentaging of bivariate tables, 191–92
Personal interviews, 100–7
Physical-location analysis, 122
Physical signs, observation of, 121–22
Physical traces, 120–21
Political records, 124–27
Polls, 251
Population for sampling, 251–53
　restriction of, 120
Positively skewed distribution, 182
Possible relations between variables, 26
Posttest, 30
Posttest-Only Control Group design, 39–40
Precision matching, 35
Predictability, Guttman coefficient of, 195–99
Prediction, 5
　covariation and, 193–94
　measurement and, 51
　sampling and, 251
Prediction functions, 209
Predictive validity, 61
Predictor variables, *see* Independent variables,

Pretest, 30
Private records, 129–31
Probabilistic explanations, 5
Probability samples (table), 266
Probability sampling, 112, 260
Probing by interviewer, 101, 104, 108
Problems, 10
Properties of objects, *see* Variables
Property-disposition relationships, 40
Proportional reduction in prediction error, 194
Proportions, 166
Public records, 120, 124–28
Punchcards, 143, 151–56
Purposive samples, 260

Quantification, 137
Quartile, 170
Quasi-experimental research designs, 40–46, 102
   correlation, 42–43
   one-shot case study, 42
   panel, 44–45
   trend study, 45–46
Questionnaires, 107–8
Questions for interviews, 102–7
   leading, 104
   open-ended vs. fixed alternative, 103–5
   sequence of, 105–7
   wording of, 102–3
Quota samples, 260

r, Pearson's, 195, 215
Random samples, 254, 261–62
Randomization, 35–36
Range, 175–77
Rank values, 56
Ranking, 56
Ratio levels, 58–59
Reactive arrangements, 37–38
Realism, 83
Reciprocal causation, 239
Records
   private, 129–31
   public, 120, 124–28
Recursive system of equations, 238
Region of rejection, 274–76

Regression analysis, 209
Regression equation, 209
   multiple, 233
Rejection, region of, 274–76
Relations, spurious, 8–9, 29
Relationships, 23
   conditional, 232
   concept of, 188–93
      median and mean as measures of covariation, 192–93
      percentaging bivariate tables, 191–92
   measurement of, 193–216
      interval, 208–16
      nominal, 195–200
      ordinal, 200–8
   multiple, 233–37
   property-distribution, 40
   stimulus-response, 40
Reliability, 91
   coding, 150
   measurement of, 64–68
      parallel-forms technique, 67
      split-half method, 67–68
      test-retest method, 66
Replication
   in content analysis, 137
   of experiments, 86
Representative sampling, 37, 260
Research
   basic elements of, 15–27
      concepts, 15–17
      definitions, 17–20
      hypotheses, 23–27
      variables, 20–23
   measurement in, 50–69
      levels, 53–59
      nature of, 50–53
      reliability of, 64–68
      validity of, 59–64
   scientific method in, 3–13
      aims of science, 3–6
      approaches to knowledge, 6–7
      research process, 10–13
      scientific approach, 7–10
   survey, 100–16
      attitude measurement, 109–16
      mail questionnaire, 107–8

Research, survey (*continued*)
   personal interview, 100–7
   telephone interview, 108–9
Research designs, 10, 11, 29–48
   comparison of, 46–47
   components of, 46–47
      comparison, 31
      control, 32–36
      generalization, 36–38
      manipulation, 31–32
   experimental, 38–40
      Posttest-Only Control Group design, 39–40
      Solomon Four-Group design, 38–39
   quasi-experimental, 40–46, 102
      correlation designs, 42–43
      one-shot case study, 42
      panel, 44–45
      trend study, 45–46
   structure of, 29–31
   for survey, 116
Respondent, 55
Response rate to questionnaires, 107, 116
Response sets, 119
Reports, verbal, 74
Restrictions, population, 120
Review of Elections of the World, 125
Revolution and Development of Internal Relations (RADIR), 132
Rival explanations, 32
Role selection, 119–20
Roll calls, 125

Samples
   alternative interpretations of results of (table), 271
   cluster, 264–65
   representative, 37
   simple random, 254, 261–62
   size of, 253–59
   stratified, 263–64
   systematic, 262–63
Sampling
   aims of 251–52
   designs for, 252, 259–65
   nonsampling error in, 265–67

   population for, 252–53
   probability, 112
Sampling distribution, 254, 273–78, 286
Sampling unit, 252
Sampling validity, 59
Scales
   attitude, 110–16
   See also Levels of measurement
Scatter, *see* Dispersion
Scatter diagram, 213
Schedule-structured interview, 100–1
Scientific method, 3–13
   aims of, 3–6
   approaches to knowledge and, 6–7
   research process in, 10–13
Second-order partial correlation, 226, 227
Selection factors, 32
Significance
   level of, 274–76
   tests of, 291–94
Simple observation, 121–23
Simple random samples, 254, 261–62
Simulatics Corporation, 87
Simulations, 86–90
Size of sample, 253–59
Slope, 209
Solomon Four-Group designs, 38–39
Soviet Academy of Sciences, 6
Spatial behavior, 76, 122
Spearman-Brown prophecy formula, 67
Split-half method of reliability testing, 67–68, 116
Spuriousness, 8–9, 29, 220
Standard deviation, 178–81, 255
Standard errors, 254, 257
Standard score, 183
Statistical inference, 272
Statistical hypotheses, tests of, 252, 271
Statistical Package for the Social Sciences (SPSS), 159–60
Statistical significance, 291–92
Statistical tests, 272
Stimulus, experimental, 30
Stimulus-response relationship, 40
Stratified samples, 263–64
Substantive significance, 291–92

Substitution, 57
Suicide notes, 130–31
Supreme Court, U.S., 122, 127
Survey Research Center, University of Michigan, 45, 103, 151
Surveys, 100–17, 251
   attitude measurement in, 55, 109–16
      arbitrary scales for, 110–11
      Likert scales for, 114–16
      Thurstone scales for, 111–14
   mail questionnaire, 107–8
   personal interview method of, 100–7
   telephone, 108–9
Syllogisms, 7
Symmetrical distributions, 181–82
Symmetry, 57
Systematic import, 19–20
Systematic samples, 262–63

Tables, bivariate, 191–92
Tabulator, 157
Tau coefficients, 195, 208
Telephone surveys, 108–9
TEMPER simulation, 87
Test-retest method for reliability, 66
Test variables, *see* Control variables
Tests, 27, 34, 270–95
   chi-square, 288–91
   Mann-Whitney runs, 286–88
   nonparametric, 279, 286–91
   parametric, 279–86
   sampling distribution in, 273–78
   of significance, 291–94
   statistical, 252
   strategy of, 271–73
Theorizing, 8–10, 12
Theory, 9, 12
   formal, 16
Third-order partial correlation, 227
Thurstone scales, 111–14
Time order, 8, 9, 29
Time sampling, 77
Total variation, 213
Training programs, 79
Trend study, 45–46
Two-tailed tests, 276–77
Type I and type II errors, 277–78

Unbiased estimate, 256
Understanding, 5
Unexplained variation, 214
Unimodal distributions, 168
Uniqueness, 57
Unit record equipment, 143, 156
United Nations, Administrative and budgetary Committee of the General Assembly of, 76
Units in content analysis, 135–37
Univariate distribution, 165–86
   measures of central tendency of, 167–73
      arithmetic mean, 171–73
      median, 168–71
   measures of central tendency of mode, 167–68
   measures of dispersion of, 173–81
      mean deviation, 177–78
      qualitative variation, 173–75
      range and interquartile range, 175–77
      variance and standard deviation, 178–81
Universal generalization, 4
Unobtrusive measures for data collection, 119–37
   analysis of archival records as, 123–37
      content analysis, 132–38
      private, 129–31
      public, 124–28
   analysis of physical traces as, 120–21
   simple observation as, 120–23

Validity, 91
   convergent-discrimination concept of, 63
   external, 37
   face, 59, 90
   impaired by errors, 119
   internal, 32
   predictive, 61
   sampling, 59
   tests of, 59–64, 115
Validity coefficient, 61
Values, 25
   rank, 56

Variable errors, 64
Variables, 15, 20–23
  control over, 79, 85
  demonstrating covariation of, 29
  independent, 190
  intervening, 228–30
  possible relations between, 26
Variance, 65, 178–81, 255
Variation
  coefficient of, 173, 180–81
  qualitative, 173–75
  See also Dispersion
Verbal reports, 74
Verbal behavior, 76
  observation of, 123
Verstehen, 5
Voting statistics, 124

Weber, Max, 24
Wording of interview questions, 102–3
World Handbook of Political and Social Indicators (Taylor et al.), 125

Y intercept, 210

z, Fisher's, 285
Zero-order correlation, 226